Windows 95 Is Driving Me Crazy!

A Practical Guide to Windows 95 Headaches, Hassles, Bugs, Potholes, and Installation Problems

By Kay Yarborough Nelson

LightSpeed Publishing
Glen Ellen, California

Peachpit Press
Berkeley, California

Windows 95 Is Driving Me Crazy!

Kay Yarborough Nelson

Peachpit Press

2414 Sixth Street
Berkeley, CA 94710
510/548-4393
510/548-5991 (fax)

Find us on the World Wide Web at:
http://www.peachpit.com

Peachpit Press is a division of Addison Wesley Longman

Editor: Scott Calamar
Technical reviewer: Harry Henderson
Cover design: Mimi Heft
Cover illustration: Joe at Art Parts
Interior design and production: Michele Cuneo

ISBN 0-201-88626-X

9 8 7 6 5 4 3 2 1

Printed and bound in the United States of America

 Printed on recycled paper

"Divine prophecies being of the nature of their Author, with whom a thousand years are but as one day, are not therefore fulfilled punctually at once."

Sir Francis Bacon, 1561-1626

Table of Contents

Chapter 2 It Is Not Logical, Captain

Getting Around the Interface 47

Contents

Chapter 3 The Big Five Windows Pitfalls

What Windows 95 Doesn't Tell You About How You Can Get in Trouble . 91

Chapter 4 Software Purgatory

It Won't Work! 117

Chapter 5 Hardware Hell

What Won't Work with Windows 95: How to Make It Work. How to Live Without It. 151

Chapter 6 Don't Leave Home Without It!

Keeping the Good Parts of Windows 3.1 193

Chapter 7 Lost on the Internet with Windows 95?

Road Kill on the Information Highway 211

Chapter 8 It's Not Speaking to Me!

Chapter 9 Gotta Haves! Shareware, Freeware, and Other Band-Aids

And Where to Find Them on the Web 255

Chapter 10 As a Last Resort...

Introduction

Maybe you chose to use Windows 95—then again, maybe your company said you had to use it. Personally, I was just getting comfortable with Windows 3.1, and then Microsoft went and changed everything! Or most everything. Like many things in this modern world that are designed to make life "easier," Windows 95 can be quite frustrating. It's as if you're an auto mechanic who was used to working on Volkswagens, and now you're looking under the hood at an electronic emission control system. Where are the tools and controls? Features may be there for a reason, but you can't see the reason, and in the meantime, the whole situation is making you really frustrated.

Windows 95 is most likely the operating system of the future, though, if Microsoft has its way and if enough people buy it. Developers can do a lot more with Windows 95 than they ever could with Windows 3.1, and no doubt you'll be seeing some really spectacular programs coming for Windows 95. But for us just-users who are getting used to it as our operating system, Windows 95 can be a hassle. It's big. It's complicated. It takes a bit of tweaking to get it to do what you want. Sometimes it stonewalls you.

So I wrote this book. It doesn't cover every problem you can get into, of course. And it can't list every driver you may need. It's also a snapshot in time—I had to stop writing at some point, even though problems and hassles are continually being reported on the Internet, in user groups, and online services. But this book will also show you how to get the most up-to-date knowledge, bug fixes, freeware, and shareware from the Net. In fact, Chapter 10 offers the most comprehensive list of telephone and BBS numbers as well as Internet addresses that I've ever seen. You should be able to contact almost any computer-related manufacturer from the information provided in that chapter.

Think of this book not as a repository of all the answers, but as a guide to resources that can help you when you get in trouble. You're probably not interested in all the problems people can have with Windows 95: what you want is a solution to *your* Windows problems. You may find a situation that's like your own, so you can apply a similar fix. Or you may stumble upon the exact thing that's been bugging you and see a way you can work around it. At the very least, you may discover that it's not you: it's the program.

This isn't a book that will teach you how to use Windows 95 step by step. There are plenty of other books like that. It's for getting out of trouble. It's for finding more resources beyond the covers of this book. It's for those of us just-users who don't really want to know (or care) what's happening behind the scenes, as long as we can get the thing to do what we want it to do.

What's in Here?

Here's what we've got:

Chapter 1 Surviving the Installation
And Getting Windows 95 Up to Speed!

Check out this chapter if you haven't installed Windows 95 yet. Or if you're having trouble optimizing its performance (speeding it up, in other words). Or if you need to uninstall it.

Chapter 2 It Is Not Logical, Captain
Getting Around the Interface

It's not always right to do the logical thing in Windows 95. And sometimes the ways the system does things can drive you nuts. Here lie workarounds both logical and illogical.

Chapter 3 The Big Five Windows Pitfalls
What Windows 95 Doesn't Tell You About How You Can Get in Trouble

If you believe some of the stuff that's on the surface of Windows 95, you can wind up losing data as well as your mind. Watch out for the pitfalls discussed in this chapter.

Chapter 4 Software Purgatory
It Won't Work!

You've got a program that won't run right under Windows 95? Check out this chapter, where known problems and solutions are listed by manufacturer.

Chapter 5 Hardware Hell
What Won't Work with Windows 95: How to Make It Work. How to Live Without It.

Plug and Play isn't all it's cracked up to be. If you have an unruly device, check out the problems and workarounds in this chapter, listed by manufacturer.

Chapter 6 Don't Leave Home Without It!
Keeping the Good Parts of Windows 3.1

Miss the old days? There was a lot that was good about Windows 3.1. Well, this chapter shows you how to get it back. And how to make Windows 95 do what Windows 3.1 did that they say it can't.

Chapter 7 Lost on the Internet with Windows 95?
Road Kill on the Information Highway

Can't get on the Internet from Windows 95? Want to use a network other than Microsoft's? You're not alone. Check out the workarounds and resources in this chapter.

Chapter 8 It's Not Speaking to Me!
Networking Issues

Windows 95 poses unique problems for network users. Whether you're a regular user or a system administrator, the answer to what's bugging you may be in this chapter.

Chapter 9 Gotta Haves! Shareware, Freeware, and Other Band-Aids
...And Where to Find Them on the Web

Plug the holes Microsoft left by getting shareware and freeware that makes Windows 95 work the way you want. A lot of stuff is also available on

CompuServe, America Online, and other services, for people who aren't comfortable with the Web yet.

Chapter 10 As a Last Resort...
Other Resources

Even if you can't find it in this chapter, you can still find where to find it!

Using This Book

A word or two about the conventions used in this book. Commands or text that you need to type in appear in boldface. You'll find any general procedures you need to know, such as how to restore the Registry if you mess it up, at the beginning of every chapter. If you're confused by the capitalization, or lack of it, in file names, it's because Windows 95 presents most file names on the screen as initial capitals only, unlike the conventional ALL CAPITALS you may have become used to.

To further confuse you, Windows 95 supports mixed cases, but names aren't case-sensitive, so you can't have the files thisone.txt and ThisOne.Txt in the same folder. Windows 95 sees them as the same name.

The chapters aren't meant to be read in order, and some of them aren't even intended to be read completely at all! In those, like Chapter 4 and Chapter 5, just look up the item you're having trouble with and skip the rest. I'm assuming you know the basics of running Windows 95, but I'll provide general step-by-step procedures for most of the workarounds. I may not tell you to click OK every time you need to click OK; you know to do that.

You'll get the most out of this book if you have Web access, but you don't have to be on the Web to find it useful. You can find a lot of stuff on CIS, AOL, Prodigy, local user group BBSes, and the like, without going out on the Web. And in this book there are plenty of solutions and workarounds for a lot of problems as well as voice phone numbers so you can get the latest versions of software, drivers, and bug fixes from manufacturers even if you don't have a modem.

What You Need

Let's be realistic about the hardware you need to run Windows 95. You gotta have 8 Mb of RAM, as a minimum, and even then I predict you won't be happy with the speed and will want 16 Mb. Sometimes your hard disk will just sit there and grind away. If you're doing heavy-duty spreadsheets, faxing, Web browsing, and the like, you'll really need at least 16 Mb. If you're planning to use programs designed for Windows 95, they'll usually need 25 to 50 percent more memory than your old programs.

You'll want a minimum 66 Mhz 486 machine, too. Maybe you can get by with a 33 Mhz, but you'll *want* more speed. You'll want a SVGA video card and as big a monitor as you can afford. Also a 16-bit sound card. And a hard disk with plenty of disk space. Windows 95 takes up at least 50 Mb of hard disk space. If you want room for your programs, too, consider at least a 300–400 Mb hard disk.

You'll need at least a double-speed CD-ROM drive. Windows 95 comes on an incredible number of floppy disks or a CD-ROM. Trust me; you want to install it from CD-ROM. You get extra goodies with the CD-ROM that don't come with the floppy disk version, too (see "I've Installed Windows 95, but I Can't Find the "Good Stuff"—like QuickView and System Monitor!" in Chapter 1).

To browse the Web and get on America Online and CompuServe (and the Microsoft Network, if you want to), you'll need at least a 14.4 bps modem. Get a 28.8 if you can. With 14.4, you'll have to turn off graphics to get any speed out of it.

Where'd All This Stuff Come From?

I compiled the information in this book from a variety of sources, including online services, the World Wide Web, newsgroup postings, and the like. I also drew on my personal experiences in wrestling with Windows 95 and writing two other books about it (*The Little Windows 95 Book* for Peachpit Press and *Voodoo Windows 95* for Ventana Press), as well as a weekly column on the Web for Computer Life magazine (to check that out, go to http://www.zdnet.com/~complife/9508114/weekbuzz.html). In Chapter 10 you'll find long lists of Windows 95 FAQ sites and Windows 95 home pages on the Web, and that's where a lot of the information in the book came from. It also came from Microsoft's own Help files and information on the Resource Kit on the Windows 95 CD-ROM. And of course from magazine articles, newspaper reports, and personal e-mail.

Your best bet for up-to-the-minute information is the World Wide Web. The Web is busy, and Web addresses change all the time, as you probably know. So if you're looking for a specific site and can't connect to it, try again later, or try searching the Web for a key word related to what you're looking for.

There is no way that I or anyone else could completely test and verify all the combinations of equipment and solutions reported in this book. I'm reporting information I found, as best I can. If you have a specific problem that's not covered here, or if the workarounds mentioned here don't work, contact the manufacturer by using the information in Chapter 10. I'm KayNelson@aol.com (easier to remember) or kayn@southcoast.net, but I can't give you technical support.

Windows 95 isn't a terrible operating system, but it takes a lot of getting used to. It can throw you for a loop because it does things differently from its predecessors. I have a feeling that problems will persist for a while. After all, it took Microsoft until version 3.1 of Windows to get it (more or less) right. In the meantime, Windows 95 tries to do many things for a huge audience of demanding users. Sometimes it seems too simple; sometimes it seems too hard. But we're stuck with it.

Good luck...with whatever problems you may have!

Chapter 1

Surviving the Installation

And Getting Windows 95

Up to Speed

Surviving the Installation

And Getting Windows 95

Up to Speed

"640K ought to be enough for anybody."

Bill Gates, 1981

You've taken that big first step: perforated the wrap around the Windows 95 Upgrade package or hauled home those heavy cartons with your new Windows 95 computer from Computer-O-Rama. Is using Windows 95 really going to be "the newest and easiest way to do what you want to do with your computer," as its installation program promises?

In its intense marketing campaign to promote Windows 95, Microsoft created some pretty high expectations for us users. It was quite a rollout, complete with Ferris wheels in Redmond, a show with Jay Leno, and the Rolling Stones' song "Start Me Up," leased at the rate of $12 million a month (but not playing the line "you make a grown man cry...") blasting from every AM station on your car radio. It was worldwide: On August 24, 1995, in Great Britain each copy of the *London Times* was wrapped in Windows 95 advertising. In Poland, the press got submarine rides. This new product was indeed going to outperform sliced bread!

Unfortunately, many people have found that Windows 95 isn't really going to make their lives easier, or more fun, either. One major example: You'll probably need more RAM than you've got right now to run Windows 95. It will run with 8 Mb—but I predict you'll spend more time than you like listening to your hard disk spin while nothing's happening on the screen.

And getting more RAM is a hassle. It means getting out the Yellow Pages and finding a reliable supplier, as well as an installer if you don't want to take your computer apart and install RAM chips yourself. It means spending a few hundred more dollars for the extra memory. And it usually means waiting to get your computer back as the days roll past on the calendar while your boss's deadline stays the same. Although you will get a significant increase in speed when you've got 16 or 20 Mb of RAM in the box, getting there is not half the fun that the ads promise.

This isn't your only potential problem when you first start using Windows 95. Is your Setup program hanging up? Can't you duplicate the installation disks? Didn't you get everything that Windows 95 comes with when you installed it? Is it running too slow for you? Are you getting mysterious error messages? Is not being able to start with a clean desktop driving you crazy? These are the kind of things I'll be talking about in this chapter.

Editing the Registry

Before we begin... Some of the workarounds in this book require you to edit the Registry, which is where Windows 95 keeps most of its settings. The Registry replaces the Windows 3.1 files SYSTEM.INI and WIN.INI (you'll still find these files on your hard disk for your Windows 3.1 programs to use). Every program you install on your system will add its settings to the Registry. It looks pretty scary, but actually it's approachable, if you're willing to experiment. Detailed instructions about the Registry are on the CD, in the Admin\Reskit\Helpfile, and you can find more at the Web site http://www.usa.net/~rduffy/registry.htm "Getting the Most from the Windows 95 Registry."

The Registry uses a system of keys and values. A key tells you what settings a section contains, and a value is the setting itself, such as a file name extension. The six main keys in the Registry are: HKEY_CLASSES_ROOT (information about file extentions, associations, shortcuts, icons), HKEY_CURRNET_USER (desktop and ksyboard configurations), HKEY_LOCAL_MACHINE (hardware settings), HKEY_USERS (settings for multiple users), HKEY_CURRENT_CONFIG (display and printer settings), and HKEY_DYN_DATA (Plug and Play information).

The Tools You'll Need

For Registry hacking, you'll need to:

- Understand how to restore the Registry if you screw up
- Make backups of your Registry files while Windows 95 is working
- Refresh the Registry without having to restart your computer

We'll cover all that first.

Restoring the Registry

To run Regedit, a utility that lets you edit the registry, type **regedit** in the Run box. You can safely edit the Registry *if* you make a copy of these instructions and hang them on your wall. They'll get you started again in case you do something to mess up Windows 95 to the point where you can't turn on your computer. These instructions are in the Help system, but if you can't start your computer, you can't get help. (You will find, or may have already found, that there's a lot in Windows 95 that works in this Catch-22 way.) So either print out the help topic on restoring the Registry, or copy this page and put it on your wall. Or keep the book handy.

To restore the Registry:

1. Click the Start button; then click Shut Down.
2. Click Restart The Computer In MS-DOS Mode; then click Yes.
3. Change to your Windows directory. For example, if your Windows directory is C:\Windows, you'd type
   cd c:\windows and press (ENTER).
4. Type the following commands, pressing (ENTER) after each one:
   attrib -h -r -s system.dat
   attrib -h -r -s system.da0

```
copy system.da0 system.dat
attrib -h -r -s user.dat
attrib -h -r -s user.da0
copy user.da0 user.dat
```
5. Press (CTRL)+(ALT)+(DEL) to restart your computer.

Following this procedure will restore your Registry to the state it was in when you last successfully started your computer. *Keep this procedure handy.*

If you don't follow this advice, and your registry is screwed up, you may be able to press (F8) while Windows 95 is loading and get out to a bare-bones prompt, where you can at least access your hard disk. See "I Can't Start Windows!" later in this chapter.

Copying the Registry

While you have Windows 95 working, make a copy of System.DA0 and User.DA0 on a floppy disk. That way, you can get your original settings back if you need them by copying them to the Windows 95 directory on your hard disk. These files are normally hidden, so be sure to use the Explorer's Views menu, choose Options, click the View tab, and click Show All Files before you go hunting for them.

Refreshing the Registry

By the way, if you're working in Windows 95 and have edited the Registry, you don't need to restart your computer to have your new settings take effect. Press (CTRL)+(ALT)+(DEL), then select Explorer and click End Task. When Windows asks you whether you want to shut down, say No. You'll see another dialog box. In it, click End Task, which refreshes the Registry.

Troubleshoot Before You Install

One very good way to avoid problems with Windows 95's installation is to take a few steps before you start. First, run a virus scan, using whatever antivirus program you have. These programs may not work accurately with Windows 95, so make sure you're clean before you start installation.

Next, run **ScanDisk** (or CHKDSK if you don't have DOS 6) and make sure your disk is OK. Make sure you've got at least 60 Mb of free disk space, too. If you've been using the disk for a while without defragmenting it, you may want to defrag it, too.

Next, check your Autoexec.bat and Config.sys files for anything that might cause trouble. TSRs (terminate-and-stay-resident programs), for example, can conflict with Windows 95's installation program. Go out to the DOS command line and type **edit c:\config.sys c:\autoexec.bat** and remark out any lines that boot third-party memory managers (this means QEMM, too), antivirus programs, and the like. You can deactivate these TSRs by entering REM at the beginning of each line that loads one; then save the file. Here's a sample:

REM C:\CPS\mirror c:

While you're at it, if you're running an earlier version of Windows, and I'm assuming you are, edit WIN.INI to make sure nothing is loading automatically there. Look for any load= and run= lines. To disable these, insert a semicolon at the beginning of each line; then save the file. Here's a sample:

; load=Winfile.exe

Look for old .INF and .INI files left over from hardware you no longer have, and delete them. The Setup program may pick up information about these nonexistent devices when it scans your system.

Look in your StartUp group and see if anything's there. If you find something, delete it. Finally, restart your computer so that all these changes take effect.

For belt-and-suspenders protection, before you install Windows 95, decompress your hard drive if it's been compressed. You can compress it again with Windows 95's disk compression utility after you install Windows 95. If this doesn't leave enough space to install Windows 95, free up 20-30 MB or so by backing up some documents (not programs) and installing Windows 95 over Win 3.X, minimizing the amount of extra space needed.

Setup Keeps Hanging Up on Me!

Windows 95 has several switches you can use to bypass some automatic checking when your run Setup:

- /is - Ignores the check of your system (running Scandisk)
- /id - Ignores the check for whether there's enough disk space
- /iq - Ignores the test for cross-linked files and file directory integrity
- /in - Runs setup without the Network Setup Module
- /d - Bypasses your Windows 3.1 files (useful if any of them are corrupted)

If you're getting stuck at any of these points—for example, where the system check occurs—try running Setup with the /is switch to bypass the check.

If you're using the floppy disk version of Win95 rather than the CD, and you're hanging after Install Disk 2 (there was a known problem with early releases) or if one of your installation disks gets damaged, contact Microsoft at 800-207-7766 to get a replacement disk.

Other things to check, if none of this works:

🖈 Have you run a virus checker? Viruses are more common than you think.

🖈 Do you have at least 420 K of conventional memory and 3 Mb of extended memory free? Run **MEM /c/p** to see.

🖈 Are you loading HIMEM? Look in CONFIG.SYS and make sure there's a device=himem.sys line. With DOS 5 and later, make sure these three lines are there:

device=himem.sys

device=emm386.exe noems

dos=high,umb

🖈 Are you loading anything that does disk caching? If so, take it out of your AUTOEXEC.BAT.

Now try installing again.

What Emergency Startup Disk?

Be sure your emergency startup disk works, in case you have problems installing Windows 95. This disk has lots of other uses, too. It lets you get to DOS and diagnose what's going on, or get your computer started if you need to circumvent a password.

What emergency startup disk? If you have a utility program like Norton or PC Tools, you may already have a startup disk, because those programs offer to make one for you when you install them. Or, if you made an Uninstall disk when you installed DOS 5 or 6, you can start your computer with that. You probably need to put a few more items on it, though. Here's how to make an emergency startup disk from scratch:

When you install Windows 95, you'll be asked whether you want to make a startup disk. Say Yes. But just in case you don't get to that point in the installation, make sure you have a blank high-density disk, or one with data you don't need any more handy.

If you haven't installed Windows 95 yet, put a blank floppy disk in drive A (it doesn't have to be formatted first). Then start the Windows 3.1 File Manager and choose Make System Disk from the Disk menu. It will already be set up to use drive A, so just click OK. When it's done, copy the AUTOEXEC.BAT and CONFIG.SYS files from your root directory onto the disk so that you get your system configured as usual when you use the disk to start up with.

That disk will have COMMAND.COM on it, so you'll have all of DOS's internal commands (COPY so you can copy files; DIR so you can see what's in directories; ERASE or DEL; PATH so you don't have to type the path to directories you use frequently; TYPE so you can see what's in text files; RENAME for renaming files; MD and RD for making and removing directories; and so forth). If you want access to other DOS external commands such as SCANDISK or CHKDSK (to check your hard disk); FORMAT, SYS, and FDISK (just in case you have to reformat or repartition it); EDIT (so you can edit files if you have to); MSD (to diagnose problems); MEM (to check memory usage); ATTRIB (to look at hidden files); and MSDOS.SYS and IO.SYS (which are hidden files), copy them from your DOS directory onto that emergency floppy. In addition, copy any drivers that Config.sys or Autoexec.bat load. Also, you may need to edit path references when you copy AUTOEXEC.BAT or CONFIG.SYS to the floppy, and insert the c:\ part. And if you have a CD-ROM, be sure that you include a copy of the MSCDEX.EXE, the DOS CD-ROM driver, so you can run your CD-ROM! It's hard to install Windows 95 from CD-ROM if you can't run your CD-ROM... A classic Catch-22, but one they don't tell you about up front.

And, if you want to be able to use this disk to restore files you've backed up (in case of a hard disk crash), be sure you have a copy of a DOS backup program so you can back up your files without reinstalling Windows and all its trappings all over again.

Now, before you install Windows 95, test your startup disk to *make sure it will restart your system.*

If you've already installed Windows 95, you can make a startup disk by double-clicking on Add/Remove programs in the Control Panel folder, clicking the Startup Disk tab, and clicking Create Disk.

15

Can't Find Your CD Key?

If your previous version of Windows 95 required you to enter a long sequence of numbers when you installed it (the betas did, and there are lots of them out there), you'll be asked for a CD key when you upgrade to the commercial version. Just click on the ahead arrow; then click Ignore.

Maybe I'm Not Ready for Windows 95 Yet. How Can I Sort of Set It Aside and Pretend I'm Using Win 3.X for a While?

Well, if you really, really want to get rid of Windows 95 you can. But before you nuke it, you should know there's a way to make it run like Windows 3.1. Go to your Windows folder (mine is named 95win) and double-click on Progman.exe (Figure 1-1). Now you can run Windows 95 under the old interface for a while (Figure 1-2).

You can make this interface more or less permanent (until you change it) by editing your System.ini file. Choose Run from the Start menu and enter **sysedit**. By the way, using the System Editor (Figure 1-3) is a really handy way to edit your Autoexec.bat, Config.sys, Win.ini, and other files all at once.

In the [Boot] section of System.ini, change the line

shell=Explorer.exe

to

shell=Progman.exe

Now save the file and restart Windows 95, and you'll be back in the old familiar interface.

To really, really get rid of Windows 95, you'll need to have saved your system files when you installed Windows. You were asked at some point whether you wanted to save those files, and if you clicked Yes, it'll be easy to uninstall Windows 95, because a file named C:\W95UNDO.DAT was created on your hard disk. Go to the Control Panel and double-click on Add/Remove Programs. Click the Install/Uninstall tab and choose Windows 95 as the thing you want to remove.

Sometimes, though, you won't be able to get to the Control Panel, because Windows 95 isn't running (and that's why you want to remove it). Or, you may have said No when asked if you wanted to save the system files so you could

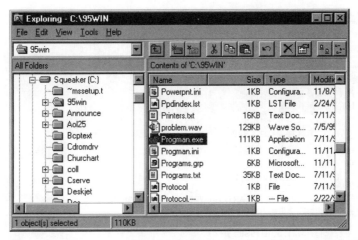

Figure 1-1. Progman.exe is the Windows 3.1 interface

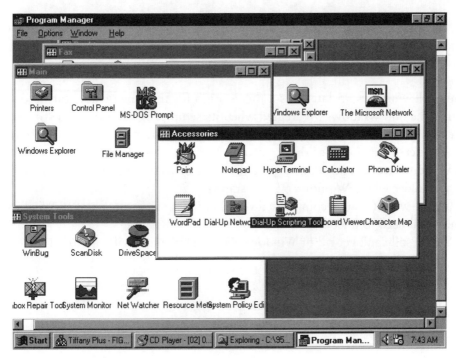

Figure 1-2. Windows 95 masquerading as a lamb

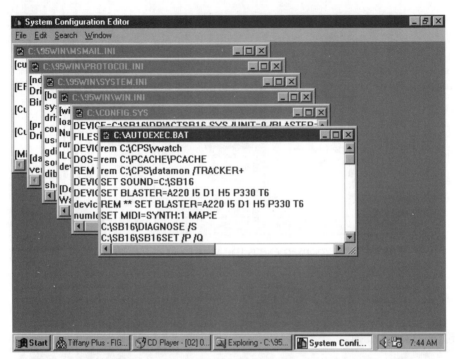

Figure 1-3. The System Editor

uninstall Windows 95 later. If so, this is a job for that emergency startup disk, either the one Windows 95 created when its setup program ran or the one you created on your own. If you use the official Windows 95 Emergency Repair disk, enter **UNINSTAL** at the A prompt. If you use the disk you created, enter **C:\windows\command\uninstal** (use the letter of your hard drive and the name of the folder where Windows 95 is installed).

By the way, if you've compressed your hard disk since you installed Windows 95, you'll need to uncompress it before you can uninstall.

If you still can't get rid of **Windows 95**, here's the manual way to uninstall:

1. Press (**F8**) on startup and choose Command Prompt Only. Then copy the Windows 95 versions of DELTREE and SCANDISK by entering:

    copy \windows\command\deltree.exe c:

    copy \windows\command\scandisk.exe c:

    Use the name of your Windows 95 folder in place of windows in this path.

2. Now use the DOS Editor to edit Scandisk.ini. Enter

   edit c:\windows\scandisk.ini

   Change these entries, if necessary, so they read:

   labelcheck=on

   spacecheck=on

   Save the file and exit the Editor.

3. Now enter **scandisk c:** at the command prompt to remove any invalid file names that Windows 95 has created.

4. When ScanDisk is done, enter **deltree windows**. Use the name of your Windows directory. Be sure before you do this that there aren't any data files you want to keep in your Windows folder or any of its subfolders!

5. Now delete the Windows 95 Config.sys, Autoexec.bat, and all the other startup files:

   deltree config.sys

   deltree autoexec.bat

   deltree winboot.*

   deltree setuplog.*

   deltree bootlog.*

   deltree detlog.*

6. If you've compressed your hard disk with Stacker (version 3.1), make a copy of the Stac Dblspace.bin file at this point. Then delete the Windows 95 compression drivers:

   deltree d??space.bin

7. Delete the Windows 95 command processor:

   deltree command.com

8. Now you're going to need a bootable floppy disk with DOS on it. Use your old DOS installation disk 1 if you don't have any others. Put it in drive A and restart your computer. Then enter

   sys c:

9. If you've compressed your hard disk, copy Dblspace.bin back to drive C.

10. Take the floppy out of drive A and press (CTRL)+(ALT)+(DEL) to restart your computer.

11. As the last steps, enter:

    REN CONFIG.DOS CONFIG.SYS

REN AUTOEXEC.DOS AUTOEXEC.BAT

This gets your original AUTOEXEC.BAT and CONFIG.SYS files back the way they were before you installed Windows 95.

But you're not done yet. Since Windows 95 removes some DOS files, you may need to reinstall DOS to get them back (see "Where Did My DOS Commands Go?" later in this chapter for the list of removed and changed files). If you installed Windows 95 for a dual boot (preserving your Windows 3.1 installation and reinstalling programs for Windows 95), you're done. However, if you installed Windows 95 over your Windows 3.1, you'll need to reinstall Windows 3.1 and your programs. What fun.

To make life easier, you can get W95INST.ZIP, which helps uninstall Windows 95. It's available in Library 13 of CompuServe's Windows New Users forum (go winnew) and in other locations as well (search for it in the software libraries of whatever service you subscribe to, or do a Lycos search for W95INST.ZIP on the Web).

What's This "Corrupt Swapfile" Message?

If you uninstall Windows 95, you'll get a "corrupt swapfile" message the next time you run Windows 3.1. Click OK to let Windows 3.1 delete the old file. Then go to the Control Panel, double-click on Enhanced, and choose None as the swap file size. Restart Windows; then go back to the Control Panel's Enhanced icon and set up a swap file.

I'm Running OS/2, and I Can't Figure out How to Install Windows 95! The Setup Program Won't Run.

OS/2 and Windows 95 are strange bedfellows, but you can install them on the same computer... Microsoft didn't make it simple, though. Read the Faq.txt file that comes with Windows 95 for the procedure, which requires you to use FDISK. Basically, this is what you do, in case you don't have access to the Faq.txt file because you haven't installed Windows 95 yet because OS/2 won't run the Setup program (this situation is chock full of Catch-22s).

Boot to DOS and run Windows 95 Setup from the DOS prompt. If you're using HPFS in OS/2, you'll need your OS/2 Disk 1, because Setup will ask for it. Then you can install Windows 95. Here's the catch: if you're using OS/2's

Boot Manager so you can pick your operating system when you start, Windows 95 will disable it. If you're *not* using Boot Manager, you'll have to reconfigure OS/2 to use it (to boot to DOS) and then let Windows 95 disable it. *And then install it again.*

To reinstall Boot Manager (I paraphrase from the Faq.txt file), choose Run from the Windows 95 Start menu. Type FDISK. Then choose Set Active Partition. Next, enter the number of the Boot Manager Partition. This is a 1 Mb non-DOS partition, usually placed at the top or bottom. Finally, quit FDISK and restart your computer. With luck, it will start, and you can choose which operating system you want to use. If you can't get OS/2 to start, at least you can read the faq.txt file for more helpful hints brought to you by Microsoft.

If you're installing both OS/2 and Windows 95 on a brand new computer, install OS/2 first; then Windows 95.

I'm Running Windows NT, and I Can't Get Windows 95 Installed!

You have to configure Windows NT so you can dual-boot between Windows and DOS. Then you can install Windows 95.

If NT isn't already configured for a dual boot, reconfigure it. Then start your computer in MS-DOS mode and type **win** to run your version of Windows. In the Program Manager, choose Run from the File menu and enter **x:\Setup.exe**, using the drive letter containing your Windows 95 Setup disk or CD-ROM instead of the x. When you're asked, specify that you want to install Windows 95 in a new directory. You can't install it into an existing Windows NT directory.

I Don't Trust This Thing, and Want to Keep My Old Version of Windows! How Do I Do That?

The easiest way to set up Windows 95 so you can boot into it or into your old DOS/Windows (by pressing F4 when you hear the startup beep) is simply to install Windows 95 into its own directory, named Windows95 or 95Windows or anything other than what you named your Windows 3.1 directory (usually "Windows"). BUT, and this is a big but, you'll have to install all the programs you want to run under Windows 95 separately. If you've got a big hard disk and lots of patience (or few apps), go ahead. If that's not practical for you, here's the workaround. It looks complicated, but it has its rewards: you get to run both Windows 3.1 and Windows 95 without reinstalling all your applications. You'll need at least 50 Mb of free space. These directions assume: 1. that you haven't installed Windows 95 yet, and 2. that you're careful to substitute the names of your real directories for the directory names used in the examples.

1. First, exit Windows 3.1. Go out to the C prompt and copy all your Windows directories:

    xcopy c:\windows*.* c:\win95*.* /s /e

    The /s switch copies all the subdirectories, and the /e switch copies any existing empty directories, such as c:\windows\temp.

2. Copy your existing DOS directory to a new location:

    xcopy c:\dos*.* c:\bakdos*.* /e

3. Still at the C prompt, edit your Config.sys and Autoexec.bat files to use the new names win95 and bakdos, or whatever you called the new directories. You'll no doubt see them in your PATH satement and maybe elsewhere, too.

    edit c:\config.sys c:\autoexec.bat

4. Edit all the .INI files in your new win95 (or whatever you've called it) directory to reflect the new directory names.

5. Edit any .INI files that you find in other directories (except in your Windows directory, 'cause it's going to get overwritten anyway) to reflect the new directory names.

6. Press (CTRL)+(ALT)+(DEL) to restart.

7. Edit the Registry to use the new directory names. In the Program Manager, choose Run from the File menu and enter **regedit /v**. Change all the references to your Windows directory to the win95 directory.

8. Install Windows 95.

9. When you've got Windows 95 running, go to the Explorer and delete the c:\dos directory. Rename c:\bakdos to c:\dos.

10. There are some old DOS commands that you shouldn't use while running Windows 95, so rename or delete these: CHKDSK, DISKCOPY, FORMAT, FDISK, RESTORE. Use their counterparts located in your Windows\Command directory, which is always on your path when you're running Windows 95. And make sure that the Windows\Command directory appears before the DOS directory, or the old ones will run when you type them.

11. Your Autoexec.bat and Config.sys files have been copied and renamed Autoexec.dos and Config.dos. These will be used when you boot back

to Windows 3.1, so edit them to change all the c:\win95 references back to c:\windows (or whatever the name of your old Windows 3.1 directory is).

12. Almost done! The more-or-less last step entails editing a file named C:\MSDOS.SYS so that you'll have the option of booting into either Windows 95 or Windows 3.1 whenever you turn on your computer. MSDOS.SYS is a hidden file, so use the Explorers Views/Options command, click the View tab, and choose "Show all files." Locate MSDOS.SYS in your root directory and double-click on it. Then choose Notepad to open it in. In the [Options] section, insert this line:

    BootMulti=1 (Figure 1-4). Then save the file.

13. Restart your computer. When you hear the computer's startup beep, press F4 to load your old DOS and then go to Windows 3.1 by typing **win** at the DOS prompt. Or press F8 for a text menu of choices. If you don't press anything, you'll boot into Windows 95.

If you want to normally boot into your old DOS instead of Windows 95, add the line **BootWin=0** to the [Options] section of MSDOS.SYS.

And, if you want to add a delay to the time Windows 95 normally gives you to make any choices when you start, add the line

BootDelay=n

where n is the number of seconds. Normally Windows 95 only waits two seconds, and if your attention wanders, you can miss this (excuse me) window.

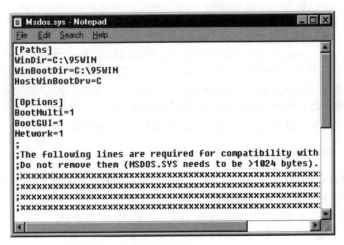

Figure 1-4. Editing MSDOS.SYS

23

I Didn't Set Up for a Dual Boot, but I Need Windows 3.1! What Do I Do Now?

If you didn't install Windows 95 for a dual boot, you can still set up a no-frills Windows 3.1 to run under Windows 95. This can come in handy if you find out later you have a few programs that refuse to run correctly under Windows 95.

1. Find your old Windows 3.1 installation disks.

2. Restart Windows 95 in MS-DOS mode (you'll see that choice when you choose Shut Down).

3. At the DOS prompt, type **a:setup**. Then follow the instructions on the screen.

4. When you're asked what kind of setup you want, type **c** for Custom setup. This is important! Otherwise you'll install all of Windows 3.1, and you probably don't want or need anything but the very basic parts.

5. When you're asked for the path to where you want Windows 3.1, specify a directory other than your Windows 95 directory. This is important, too! Otherwise you'll overwrite Windows 95. Enter **c:\win31**, for example.

6. After you enter your name and your company name, you'll see a screen asking what you want to install. Uncheck Set Up Printers (if you're not planning to print via Windows 3.1) and Set Up Applications Already on Hard Disk. You don't need any old wallpaper, screen savers, readmes, and so forth. You can leave Accessories checked if there are any of them you want, like the Calendar, Cardfile, Write, or Paintbrush (see Chapter 6 for why you might want to keep these). Click Files and choose each of the accessories you want so that you don't install all of them. If you don't want or need any of the accessories, keep that box unchecked, too.

7. Choose "Let you make the modifications later" when you're asked if Windows can change your AUTOEXEC.BAT and CONFIG.SYS.

8. When the installation is done, type **exit** to restart Windows 95.

Now you can set up a shortcut to Windows 3.1:

1. In the Explorer, find Win.com in your new Win31 folder. Drag it to the desktop to make a shortcut.

2. Click on the shortcut and press (ALT)+(ENTER) to open its property sheet.

3. Click the Program tab and check "Close on exit."

4. Click the Advanced button and check MS-DOS mode.

5. Click the Change Icon button and pick a new icon. You can find the "original" Windows 3.1 icon in c:\windows\system\shell32.dll.

6. Click OK.

Now you've set up your Windows 3.1 shortcut to run under Windows 95. When you double-click on it, you'll be told that all your other programs will shut down if you continue. That's what it's supposed to do, because Windows 3.1 is going to run in DOS mode. Click Yes to continue, and run Windows 3.1 to do whatever you need it to. When you're through with Windows 3.1, exit from it in the normal way (by closing the Program Manager), and Windows 95 will restart.

Where Did My DOS Commands Go?

Did you know that Windows 95 deletes and modifies quite a few of the old commands from DOS 6 (and earlier, depending on what version of DOS you were running when you installed Windows 95)? It deletes these:

Defrag.hlp
Mwundel.exe
Mwundel.hlp
Networks.txt
OS2.txt

And it upgrades these:

Ansi.sys	Fc.exe
Attrib.exe	Fdisk.exe
Chkdsk.exe	Find.exe
Choice.com	Format.com
Country.sys	Keyb.com
Debug.exe	Keyboard.sys
Defrag.exe	Label.exe
Deltree.exe	Mem.exe
Diskcopy.com	Mode.com
Display.sys	More.com
Doskey.com	Move.exe
Drvspace.exe	Mscdex.exe
Edit.com	Nlsfunc.exe
Ega.cpi	Ramdrive.sys
Emm386.exe	Readme.txt

Scandisk.exe	Sort.exe
Scandisk.ini	Subst.exe
Setver.exe	Sys.com
Share.exe	Xcopy.exe
Smartdrv.exe	

You may want to keep some of these. For example, if you don't set up for a dual boot, you can't reboot to your old DOS and Undelete after you've emptied the Trash. To avoid this, set up for a dual boot, so you can get your old DOS commands back. Or make a DOS floppy with your old DOS commands on it.

I've Installed Windows 95, but I Can't Find the "Good Stuff" Like QuickView and System Monitor!

That's because you probably chose a Typical installation. Windows 95's installation program doesn't tell you that this doesn't install all of Windows 95. Assuming you installed from CD-ROM (which has more goodies on it than the 3.5-inch disk version), there's lots more you can add to Windows 95. Good stuff, too, like CD Player, Quick View, Mouse Pointers, System Monitor, and the Resource Kit. And a neat helicopter game, too.

Put the Windows 95 CD-ROM in the drive and click Add/Remove Software. Click the Windows Setup tab. Anything that hasn't been completely installed has a grayed box next to it (Figure 1-5). For example, double-click on Accessories, and you'll see more accessories you can add (Figure 1-6). Check the ones you want and click OK twice to let Windows 95 install them.

What? You Can't Copy the Windows 95 Installation Disks?

That's because they're in a new format, Microsoft's proprietary Distribution Media Format (DMF). Those are 2 Mb disks (actually, they hold about 1.7 Mb), and the files on them are in a different format; they're .CAB (cabinet) files, very compressed. So basically, you can't make an archive set of installation disks.

Browse the Web and look for DiskCopy version 2.11, COPYQ121, FDFO, dskdupv5.zip, Sydex's CopyQM3.20, or the latest disk-copying utility for these big disks. That's the only way you're going to be able to copy them, because Disk Copy won't do it.

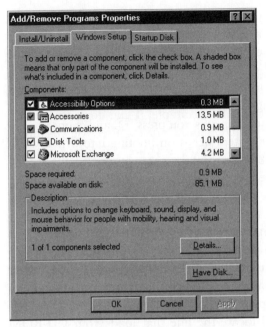

Figure 1-5. What Windows 95 has installed

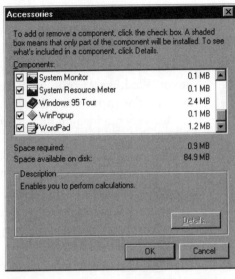

Figure 1-6. Installing more accessories

As for the .CAB files, you can extract them, but you can't COPY or XCOPY them. There's an EXTRACT command on Disk 1, or in your Windows 95 folder if you installed from CD-ROM, which you can use to extract files from the other Windows 95 installation disks or CD-ROM.

As a workaround, if you need a copy of a .CAB file or two, make a temporary directory on your hard disk. Then do this:

extract /c a:xx.cab c:\<temporary directory>

where A is the drive with the disk or CD-ROM, *xx.cab* is the file you're extracting from (the cabinet file), and c:\<*temporary directory*>is the name of the directory on drive C where you'll find the extracted file.

Be sure to get the PowerTools (see Chapter 9). It has a .CAB file viewer that lets you see what's on .CAB files and extract them by double-clicking.

I Can't Start Windows!

The first step: Press F8 when you hear the computer beep on startup and choose the Safe mode option from the screen that appears. In Safe mode,

Windows ignores startup files like the Registry, Config.sys, Autoexec.bat, and parts of System.ini. That means no access to printers, CD-ROMs, and the like. It uses a VGA display driver. You can tell when you're in Safe mode because "Safe" appears in all four corners of the screen. Once you get this stripped-down Windows 95 running, head for Help (F1), click the Troubleshooting topic, and run the various Troubleshooting Wizards.

One very maddening thing that can happen is you press (F8) and choose one of the command-line options, but your system keeps on booting into Windows. If this happens, check your Autoexec.bat file to make sure you don't have a command in it that starts Windows! When you choose Command Prompt Only, your Autoexec.bat and Config.sys files are executed, and any command that automatically starts Windows gets executed, too.

Another very maddening thing that happens is your CD-ROM drive (which you're trying to install Windows 95 from) doesn't get recognized. If you have a CD-ROM, make sure a copy of the DOS program Mscdex.exe is in your C:\DOS directory, so you can run your CD-ROM! If that file isn't there, look on your DOS installation disks and copy it there.

Look in your Config.sys file and locate the line that loads your CD-ROM driver. Write it down. Then, after you restart, type that line at the DOS prompt. Mine looks like this:

device=c:\cdromdrv\cdmke43.sys /d:MVCD001 /r /sbp:220

Then run the MS-DOS Load CD-ROM driver program Mscdex.exe and install the driver in your Windows directory. Once you can read the CD-ROM, you'll find all sorts of detailed troubleshooting information in \Admin\Reskit\Helpfile\Win95rk.hlp on the Windows 95 CD-ROM.

Another thing you can try is to copy the .CAB files for Disk 4 (Win95_04.cab) from your Windows CD-ROM to a directory on your hard disk. Then, when Windows 95 asks for the CD-ROM driver, point it to that directory.

Sometimes, if you're on a network, you can't get anywhere by pressing (F8) on startup. This is because your network administrator has restricted access to the system. You can start your machine from a floppy, if you've had the foresight to make an emergency startup disk.

I'm Getting the Message "Cannot Find HIMEM.SYS"!

It should be in your Windows\System directory. If it isn't, find it (where is it? Probably in your old DOS directory) and copy it there. Look in your Config.sys file and see what the Himem.sys line says. Write it down. At the DOS prompt, type **set** and that **Himem.sys** command line from your Config.sys file.

Mine says:

Device=c:\95win\himem.sys

Now restart your computer.

I'm Getting the Message "Cannot Load ATMSYS.DRV."

This error message usually means your default System.ini file has been changed. Run the System Editor and make sure these lines are in its [BOOT] section:

atmsys.drv=system.drv   system.drv=atmsys.drv
shell=Explorer.exe   system.drv=system.drv
mouse.drv=mouse.drv   drivers=MMSYSTEM.DLL
comm.drv=comm.drv   comm.drv=COMM.DRV
keyboard.drv=keyboard.drv

I've Got a Device That Won't Respond!

This can often happen: Windows 95's Install program says a piece of hardware isn't responding. You can get around this by rerunning the installation in Safe mode, and Windows will usually manage to complete the installation the second time, because it installs a (slower) "compatibility mode" driver. This often happens when you have a CD drive or other hardware device that doesn't have a native Windows 95 driver. The second time around, you get in.

Drastic Help for Getting Started

If you got Windows 95 started once but you can't get it started again, try this last-ditch workaround. Windows 95 creates a file named System.1st (in your root directory) the very first time you start it. After that, it ignores this file. But if you can get to the DOS prompt, you can try renaming System.1st to System.dat (first rename System.dat, which is in your Windows directory, System.old). Then put it in your Windows directory and try starting Windows 95. It should start with the same configuration settings that you originally started it with.

Hate Going to Windows 95 Every Time You Start?

You can go to DOS instead, your old DOS—that is, if you kept it by installing Windows 95 into a new directory. First, find the file named Msdos.sys. It should be in your root directory. It's a hidden system file, though, so make sure Show all files is in effect (choose Options from the View menu in Explorer and My Computer and click the View tab). Open Msdos.sys in the Notepad and add this line to the end of it:

BootMenu=1

Now you'll have the option of going to DOS every time you start Windows 95.

Hate Going to Windows 95 Every Time You Start? Part Deux.

Want to always go to DOS? Edit Msdos.sys to change the BootGUI=1 line to BootGUI=0.

Every Time I Try to Start, I Get a Windows Protection Error!

Edit Msdos.sys and remove the LoadTop= line.

Hate That Wait When You Want to Restart?

When all you want to do is restart Windows 95, you've got to wait... and wait... and wait... while it performs its shutdown routines after you click Restart Computer. To get around this problem, click the Start button, then click Shut down, then click on Restart Computer. Now hold down the (SHIFT) key and click Yes. This is much faster than a normal reboot.

It Hung Up on Me!

Press (CTRL)+(ALT)+(DEL). If that doesn't work, try pressing (CTRL)+(ESC), which might bring up the Start menu if anything's still responding, so you can reboot.

I Get Error 6102 on Bootup!

If you're getting the message "Error occurred while loading device: VNETSUP: Error 6102. The string specified by the Workgroup keyword in the Registry is too short," you need to specify a workgroup. Go to the Control Panel folder and double-click on the Network icon. Click the Identification tab. You need to put something—anything—in those boxes (Figure 1-7).

Is There Any Way to Start with a Clean Desktop?

Windows 95 is preset to start up the way you left your desktop when you shut down. But there's a way to start with all the windows closed. Press (SHIFT) when you hear the Windows startup sound, and all the windows you left open will close. Whatever's in your StartUp folder will be ignored, too.

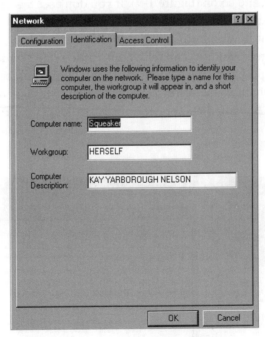

Figure 1-7. My network identification

I'm Running out of Resources, and It's Driving Me Crazy!

There's been a lot of hype about how well Windows 95 handles system resources, but the fact is there's still a problem. If you open enough folders—enough to get your system resources down to less than 50 percent—you'll see performance drop and response time slow down. To prevent this from happening, install the Resource Meter.

This handy utility comes only with the CD version of Windows 95; if you installed from floppy disks, you won't have it (visit your neighbor who installed from CD). The file's called Rsrcmtr.exe, and it's in your Windows 95 folder. Put a shortcut to it in your StartUp folder, and you'll see its icon on the far-right corner of the taskbar as you're running Windows 95. Move the pointer over it to get resource information, or double-click on it to see a chart display (Figure 1-8). If you get below 50 percent, start closing windows.

You may also want to use the System Monitor, which provides all kinds of detailed technical information about how your system is using resources, memory, its CPU, and so on (Figure 1-9). If you don't see System Monitor in your System Tools folder on the Start menu (Programs/Accessories/System Tools), go back and install it by using the Add/Remove Programs icon. I'm not going into all the things System Monitor can tell you because I don't understand them, and if you do you're probably not reading this book, which is just for us users.

One very common cause of resource overeating is use of the Microsoft Plus desktop themes. Animated cursors and fancy wallpaper eat resources, too. Just be warned.

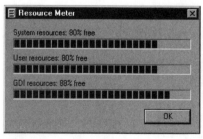

Figure 1-8. Getting resource information

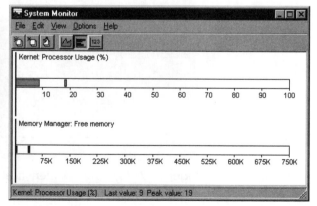

Figure 1-9. The System Monitor

I'm Getting "Specified Pathname Is Invalid" Errors!

Reinstall the programs that are giving you this message. It usually means the Registry entries for these programs were lost, not that their path names are really invalid.

How Can I Be Sure I'm Getting the Best Performance from Windows 95?

If you didn't run right out and buy all new hardware to run Windows 95 with, you may not be getting the best performance it can deliver. Fortunately, there's a way to check. Right-click on My Computer, choose Properties, and click the Performance tab. (By the way, pressing (ALT)+(ENTER) or (ALT)+double-clicking opens an icon's property sheet, too.) If you see a "system is configured for optimal performance" message, you're cool (Figure 1-10). If not, you'll see a message saying some of your devices are using MS-DOS compatibility. That means you need a new driver for that device.

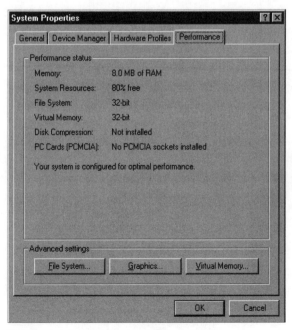

Figure 1-10. Checking performance

Go to the Control Panel and double-click on Add New Hardware. Run the wizard and see whether there's an updated Windows 95 driver. If not, go straight to Chapter 10 and find your device's vendor. Give them a call and see whether there's an updated driver available, or check out the vendor's Web site (see Chapter 10).

You'll notice at the bottom of the Performance tab that there are Advanced settings. Click File System and then click its Troubleshooting tab for some more ways you can fine-tune your system's performance (Figure 1-11). Normally, you shouldn't have to adjust these settings, but in some situations you might need to.

- If you're on a network and having problems sharing files, check the Disable new file sharing box.

- If you've had trouble with DOS programs not recognizing long file names, check the "Disable long filename preservation" box.

- If you need to install real-mode interrupt handlers to make an older program work with Windows 95, check the "Disable protect-mode hard disk interrupt handling" box.

- If your hard drive's mysteriously slowing down, check the "Disable all 32-bit protected-mode drivers" box and see if that speeds it up.

- If you're losing data over a network—for example, database records are missing, check the "Disable write-behind caching" box.

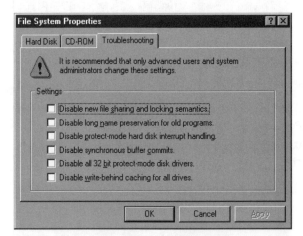

Figure 1-11. The Troubleshooting tab

Help! I'm Using a Third-Party Memory Manager, and I Can't Get Windows 95 to Start.

When Windows 95 was released, there were known problems with 386MAX, BLUEMAX 7.0, NETROOM version 3, and QEMM 7.01 -7.5 386MAX 7.0. If you have version 7.02 or later of 386MAX or BLUEMAX, you can get a free upgrade from Qualtias.

> Qualitas BBS - Dial 301-907-8030
> CompuServe - PCVENA, GO QUALITAS
> America Online - Keyword Qualitas
> Qualitas Customer Service - 301-907-7400

All of these workarounds can be found in Windows 95's supplemental files, but if you can't get your computer running, they might as well be on the moon. So here they are:

If you're using an earlier version of 386MAX or BLUEMAX and can't start, run its MAXIMIZE program. Then:

1. When your computer restarts, press **F8** when you see the "Starting Windows 95" message.
2. Choose Safe Mode Command Prompt Only.
3. At the DOS prompt, type **edit c:\config.sys**.
4. In the Editor, delete these lines from Config.sys:

    Device=\386MAX\ExtraDOS.max pro=\386MAX\ExtraDOS.pro

    Install=\386MAX\ExtraDOS.max

    Substitute BLUEMAX for 386MAX if you're running that program.
5. Save the file and open your 386max.pro or bluemax.pro file (in your 386MAX or BLUEMAX directory) and remove any lines beginning with PRGREG, HPDAREG, and STACKREG. Save the file and exit the Editor.
6. Press **CTRL**+**ALT**+**DEL** to restart your computer.
7. When you see the "Starting Windows 95" message, press **F8** and choose Command Prompt Only.

Keep pressing **F8** and choosing Command Prompt Only until MAXIMIZE is done.

There's also a known problem with NETROOM and version 1.0 of Windows 95. First look in your Autoexec.bat file and see if there's a CACHECLK line, put there by NETROOM. If there is, delete it and save the file. You can't install Windows 95 with CACHELK running.

If you can install Windows 95 but can't start it, run NETROOM's Customize program. By the time you read this, the manufacturer may have an upgrade or a patch available. See Chapter 10, "As a Last Resort," for how you can get in touch with third-party manufacturers.

There are also problems with QEMM versions 7.01-7.5. If you can't get Windows 95 to start after installing it:

1. Check Stealthing Options. Try changing ST:M to ST:F on the Qemm386.sys line in the Config.sys file and then restarting your computer. If that doesn't work, try removing the ST:M or ST:F completely from the Qemm386.sys line in the Config.sys file and then restarting your computer.

2. Run QSETUP and turn off DOS-UP, Quickboot, and Stealthing Options (see above). QSETUP will recommend running OPTIMIZE.

3. Run the OPTIMIZE program. If it still won't start, check your Config.sys file and make sure DOSDATA.SYS and DOS-UP.SYS are not there. Remove them if they are.

Is There Some Way to Automatically Get the Maximum Amount of Memory Possible When Running DOS?

This one requires editing System.ini. In the [386Enh] section, add the line

LocalLoadHigh=1

Is There Some Way to Get Rid of That Windows Startup Screen?

In Windows 3.1, you could type **win:** to get rid of the startup screen. While this may not have saved a great deal of time, it did make startup less boring. In Windows 95, you can do several things:

-   Press (ESC) and watch what's happening behind the scenes.
-   Edit Msdos.sys and add the line logo=0 to the [Options] section.
-   Create your own startup screen in Paint (or use an existing bitmap) and save it as C:\Logo.sys.

It Takes Soooo Long for All Those Cascading Menus on the Start Menu to Open!

You can fix that.

1. Open the Registry Editor and double-click on HKEY_CURRENT_USER and Control Panel.

2. Highlight desktop.

3. Right-click in the right pane.

4. Choose New; then String value. Name the new string value MenuShowDelay (Figure 1-12). (If there's already a value by that name, double-click on it.)

5. Now double-click on MenuShowDelay in the left pane.

6. Assign it a value of 10 or less. 1 is the fastest. Click OK (Figure 1-13).

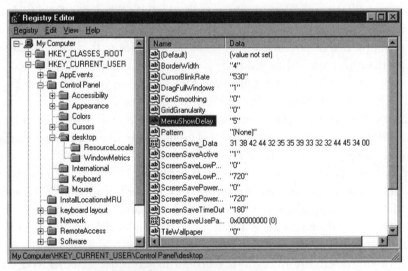

Figure 1-12. Locating MenuShowDelay

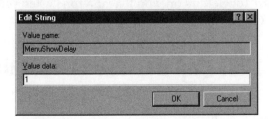

Figure 1-13. Speeding up cascading menus

37

Press (F5) to update the Registry; then close it. Now you'll have super-speedy cascading menus. The default value is 250, which is about a quarter of a second.

If the problem is the opposite and you want the menus to "stick," as they did in Windows 3.1 (where, if you opened a menu, it stayed open unless you clicked somewhere else), enter 60000, and they'll stay open about a minute.

Windows 95 Is Driving Me Crazy with All the Room It Takes Up. What Can I Get Rid of to Save Space?

Be careful getting rid of anything—but here are some guidelines for deleting with care.

In your Windows 95 directory, you can probably safely delete anything with a .Bak extension, or files with a .Log, .Old, .000, .001, or other numbered extension. In your root directory, delete anything that ends in .Old, .Log, .Dos, and .Prv. If you're really nervous about doing this, you can copy any files you're not sure about onto a floppy before you delete them. Check any files with a .Txt extension by viewing them in Notepad to see if they have something you need; if not, delete them too. Remember, you won't normally see extensions; you have to use the View menu's Options command, click the View tab, and make sure the Hide MS-DOS extensions box *isn't* checked. And also remember that if you're deleting from within Windows 95, your "deletions" are going to the Recycle Bin, so empty it!

Doing all this only frees up a relatively small amount of disk space, though. If you need to make more room, get more ruthless. Delete the games you never play. Delete the accessories you never use, like HyperTerminal and Phone Dialer (1.7 Mb) or the applets, screen savers, and the Windows 95 Tour (3.3 Mb). Getting rid of Multimedia saves about 8 Mb. Consider deleting the Accessibility programs if you don't need them. *But...*

Before you delete the Accessibility programs, consider whether you want to use ToggleKeys to prevent typing in ALL CAPS. Most folks don't know about this, but if you turn ToggleKeys on, you'll hear a tone when you press any of the "lock" keys, like Caps Lock.

My Hard Disk Is Filling up Because of That Huge Recycle Bin.

Normally the Recycle Bin is set to 10 percent of your hard disk's size. You probably don't really need that much space for it, especially if you have a huge

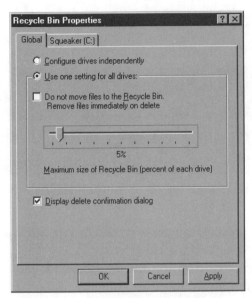

Figure 1-14. Making a smaller Recycle Bin

hard disk. If you have anything over 500 Mb, your Recycle Bin is at least 50 Mb. To fix this, right-click on the Recycle Bin, choose Properties, slide the slider down to 4 or 5 percent (Figure 1-14), and click OK.

Graphics Now Seem Slower in Windows 95. Am I Imagining This?

If you have an accelerated graphics card, you may not be getting the highest speed from it. The default setting isn't always for the highest speed. To get around this, right-click on My Computer, choose Properties, click the Performance tab, and click the Graphics button. Move the slider all the way to the right (Figure 1-15).

However (there's always a however), you can get in trouble by speeding up your graphics card too much. If you start getting "see-through" dialog boxes, or if graphics elements remain on the screen even after you've closed them, move the slider down a notch. Don't move it down to None if you're using ATM, though. If you do, and Windows 95 won't restart, press (F8) when you hear the

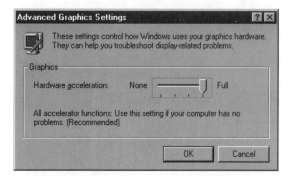

Figure 1-15. Speeding up your graphics card

startup beep. Then press ③ to start Windows in Safe Mode and change graphics acceleration from None to something else.

Pushing your graphics card too far by asking for more colors and higher screen resolutions can also slow down graphics displays. If the screen seems to be responding slowly, try changing the number of colors or reducing the display's resolution.

My Computer's Running so S-l-o-w Now That I'm Using Windows 95!

Windows 95 eats RAM. When it wipes the RAM plate clean, it goes hunting for space on your hard disk to eat. It takes a big bite of that—which is much, much slower than RAM—and swaps what's in RAM onto your hard disk to free up RAM again. When you need what's in that swap file, Windows has to access your disk, get the file, and swap everything back again. If you hear the hard disk whirring a lot and your computer's slowing down, it means you need more RAM. Forget running Windows 95 with 4 Mb. It will run with 8 Mb, but more is better. There are also programs that make your system look like it has more RAM. They seem to be a mixed bag as far as usefulness.

Seems to Me Like Windows 95 is Running Slower, Not Faster. What Is Going on?

If you have two hard drives, Windows 95 may be putting your swap file on the slower of the two. You can tell Windows 95 which drive you want the file on (pick an uncompressed drive for best performance). Right-click My Computer and choose Properties. Click the Virtual Memory button and choose "Let me specify my own virtual memory settings." Then specify which hard drive to use.

Disk fragmentation can also slow you down. Most likely you were in such a hurry to install Win 95 that you didn't defragment your hard disk first so there may be bits of files all over the place, slowing disk access time. Run the defragger (it's in the System Tools folder under Accessories). Better yet, run Norton's defragmenter, if you have it; Windows 95's can't relocate system files to the beginning of your disk, which speeds up performance.

And of course, the slowness can be caused by using too many system resources (see "I'm Running Out of Resources, and It's Driving Me Crazy!" earlier in this chapter), or by the mysterious intermittent drive access bug (see "All That Disk Activity Is Driving Me Insane!" in Chapter 2).

I've Installed Win 95, but My Screen Sure Looks Different. Am I Imagining This?

No. Windows 95 will sometimes default to VGA resolution. Right-click on the desktop, choose Properties, and click the Settings tab. Click Change Display Type and see what Windows 95 thinks you have (Figure 1-16) as an adapter type and a monitor type. If it's not right, click Change and pick the highest SuperVGA resolution your monitor is capable of.

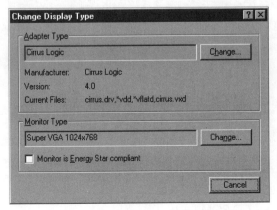

Figure 1-16. Changing the display type

My CD-ROM's Running Slower than It Did Before I Installed Windows 95.

Sometimes Windows 95 doesn't set a big enough cache for your CD-ROM. Right-click on My Computer and choose Properties. Click the Performance tab, the File System button, and the CD-ROM tab (Figure 1-17). Make sure that the cache is set to Large.

While you're at it, set the access pattern to Quad speed or higher. That can speed up even old single-speed CD-ROM drives.

Graphics Seem Slower than They Used To. Am I Crazy?

Sometimes Windows 95 doesn't get the graphics settings right, either, especially if it doesn't know what kind of monitor you have. In My Computer's Property sheet, click the Performance tab and the Graphics button. Make sure hardware acceleration is set to Full (Figure 1-18).

I'm Not Getting on CompuServe as Fast as I Used to. What's Wrong?

Windows 95 sometimes sets the maximum speed of your modem below its top speed. If you have a 14.4 Kps modem, the top speed should be 57600; for a 28.8 Kps modem, it should be 115200. Go to the Control Panel folder,

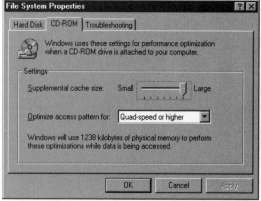

Figure 1-17. Checking your CD-ROM cache

Figure 1-18. Speeding up graphics by setting hardware acceleration to Full

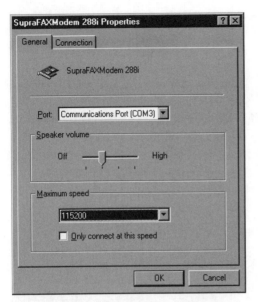

Figure 1-19. Checking your modem's speed setting

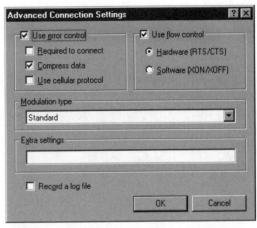

Figure 1-20. Checking error control and compression settings

double-click on the Modems icon and click the General tab. Then click Properties and check that setting (Figure 1-19).

Next, click the Connection tab and the Advanced button and make sure Use error control and Compress data (Figure 1-20) are checked (assuming you have V.32bis with V.42bis compression for 14.4 Kps modems or V.34 for 28.8 Kps modems).

Why Is Printing Taking So Long?

Because Windows 95 by default returns you to your application faster instead of printing faster. Right-click on your printer icon (in the Printers folder—or on its shortcut icon on the desktop, which you really should have made). Choose Properties, Details, and Spool Settings. For fastest printing, check Spool Print jobs and Start printing after first page is spooled (Figure 1-21). If you have a PostScript printer, click the PostScript tab (on the main property sheet) and make sure that PostScript (optimize for speed) is selected (Figure 1-22).

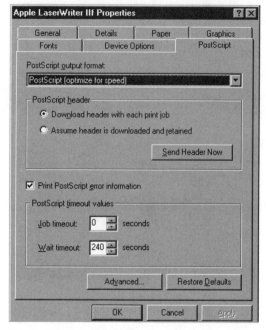

Figure 1-21. Speeding up printing

Figure 1-22. Speeding up a PostScript printer

The Sound I Get in Windows 95 Is Awful!

You're probably using your old 8-bit sound card. Get a SoundBlaster. I know Windows 95 works with a SoundBlaster. It may not always work with a "SoundBlaster compatible," though. Check the vendors in Chapter 10.

Or you may be hearing Windows 95's sounds through the PC Speaker, in which case you're guaranteed to be hearing awful sound. If you don't have a sound card, this is no doubt what's happening. To double-check, go to the Control Panel folder and double-click on Multimedia. Click the Advanced Tab, double-click on Audio Device, and see if PC Speaker is listed as an audio device (Figure 1-23). It shouldn't be if you have a sound card and external speakers.

By the way, if you're not getting any sound, check to see that you haven't accidentally muted the speaker. Click on the little speaker icon on the taskbar.

And if you don't have a sound card, here's how to hear the Windows 95 sounds (but pretty poorly) until you get one. You can download the PC Speaker driver from ftp://ftp.microsoft.com/Softlib/Mslfiles/speak.exe. (Or, if you pre-

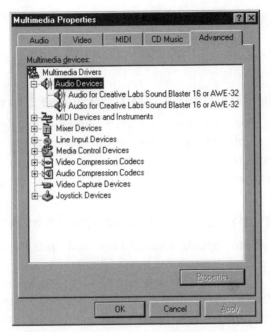

Figure 1-23. Checking to see if you're
using the PC Speaker

served your Windows 3.1 installation, you can get it from there.) Then, after
you get it:

1. Run Speak.exe to uncompress it and create the Speaker.drv file.
2. Copy Speaker.drv to your Windows 95\System folder.
3. Add these lines to System.ini:
    [speaker.drv]
    CPUSpeed=32
    Volume=1000
    Version=774
    Enhanced=1
    Maxseconds=0
4. Save System.ini and reboot.
5. Go to the Control Panel folder and double-click on the Multimedia icon.
6. Click the Advanced tab.

7. Double-click Audio Devices and click on Audio for Sound Driver for PC Speaker.

8. Click Settings, click Default, and adjust the volume if you need to.

What's That Ghost Cursor, and How Do I Get Rid of It?

From time to time, you may see a white outline of the flying Windows logo instead of your regular mouse pointer when you start. If you see it, restart. It will drive you nuts trying to point with it. The secret is to use the lower-right corner as the hot spot. But it's simpler to restart than to go blind.

I Hate Those Dumb Message Screens When I Exit!

But they're easy to replace. Launch Paint and open the files Logos.sys and Logow.sys. Check out their dimensions: Choose Attributes from the Options menu and write down the width and height. Save each one under another name if you want to keep it. Then either edit that message or create your own bitmap, or edit an existing bitmap and name *it* Logos.sys (for the "It's now safe..." message) and Logow.sys (for the "Please wait..." screen). Be sure to use the same dimensions as the originals (320 x 400 pixels).

And Next...

Now that Windows 95 is running optimally on your system *(sure)*, Chapter 2 introduces you to some of the quirks of its interface and explains how you can work around the worst of them.

Chapter 2

It Is Not Logical, Captain

Getting Around the Interface

It Is Not Logical, Captain

Getting Around the Interface

"Computers in the future may weigh no more than 1.5 tons"

Popular Mechanics, 1949

If you've been using Windows 95 for more than five or ten minutes, you've probably found the new Close box by now. They've moved it to the upper-right corner, which is where you used to click to make a window fill the screen. You no doubt found out about this the hard way—when you exited from a program by mistake instead of maximizing the window! Now you've got to find the program and start it again. Where did it go? Yep, it's over there on the Start menu, so click Start, and click Programs, and click your program folder and click your program's name. After the third or fourth time, you get used to the new Close box and you don't click in the upper-right corner of a window any more until you're ready to close it. But—trust me—it takes a while to get used to this.

There's a lot of stuff about Windows 95's interface that can drive you nuts at first because it's not consistent with the earlier version, Windows 3.1. Or it's illogical. Or just plain hard. And there's no manual: Help is buried in the online Help screens, which means you have to know a bit about Windows 95 before you can get help.

Maybe you're trying to delete an icon (like the Network Neighborhood icon), but you can't get it off the screen and into the Recycle Bin no matter how hard you try. Logically, anything you delete should go to the Recycle Bin, but some icons won't. Or say you've dragged a window off the screen and can't find a way to get it back; there's no Window menu any more, and no Task List that lets you switch between running applications. Perhaps you're tired of using the Start menu for everything when you used to double-click, or sick of seeing the same old folder every time you open the Explorer? All these new interface behaviors can drive you nuts.

None of these things will stop you dead in the water for long. They're annoyances. You'll get used to them as you get used to the system. I can't predict which will bug you the most. Some things drive some folks crazy; other things make other people tear their hair out. Any way you look at it, you'll find workarounds for many of Windows 95's many annoyances, both unintentional and intentional, in this chapter.

The Tools You'll Need

To work around the interface, you'll need these tools:

- Common sense (yours, not Microsoft's)
- Willingness to use the command line
- Willingness to do a little Registry hacking (see Chapter 1)
- Devil-may-care attitude about what others think (hey, if it works, it works)

Those #@*! Cascading Menus Won't Stay Still! And They Litter Up the Whole Screen

Those cascading menus that spring off the Start menu take a bit of getting used to, because they keep opening and closing and moving as you drag the mouse pointer across them. The target gets hard to hit.

Instead of dragging the mouse across them, click on what you want. That makes the next menu open and stay still until you make another choice by clicking on an item on it.

To clear all the cascading menus off the screen, press (ALT). To clear them off one by one, press (ESC).

Also see "It Takes Soooo Long for All Those Cascading Menus on the Start Menu to Open!" back in Chapter 1 for how to make them stick.

I Dragged a Window off the Screen, and Now There's No Way to Get It Back!

But there is, if you know the workaround for getting a stuck window unstuck. Press (ALT)+(SPACEBAR). Now type **m** for Move. Now use the arrow keys to get the window back onto the screen. As soon as you see the title bar, grab it with the mouse pointer. Now you can drag the window.

I Have So Many Windows Open That I Can't See Where I Am!

If you're opening a new window each time you open a folder in My Computer or the Explorer, you'll soon fill the screen with open windows. There's an easy way to take care of this. Choose Options from the View menu and then click the "Browse folders by using a single window..." option. Click OK and, from now on, each time you open a new folder, its contents will replace what was in the My Computer or Explorer window you were looking at.

There's a quick way to close all the folder windows you opened while looking for a particular folder. Press (SHIFT) and click in the Close box.

To *minimize* the windows all at once so that you can see the desktop, right-click on the taskbar (not over the name of an application) and choose Minimize All Windows. That won't close them, but it will get them off the screen. They're still in memory, eating system resources, though. To close them, right-click on each one's icon on the taskbar and choose Close. *One by one.* This is so tedious! Use the right mouse button to click on the icon *and* choose Close; this makes the process go a little faster.

By the way, choosing Minimize All Windows is the fast way to see the Control Panel applications and property sheets you have open. These types of windows are never represented by icons on the taskbar, and you can go nuts hunting for them if you've opened one and then clicked in another window. Such a consistent design! You can save hours of wasted time if you remember this workaround.

I'm Tired of Hunting for the Icons on the Control Panel! Is There a Way to Make a More Mac-Like Control Panel Where I Can Access the Individual Programs?

Yep. Right-click on the Start button and choose Explore. You should wind up in the Start Menu folder. Right-click the Explorer's right pane and choose New and Folder. Type this and press (ENTER):

Control Panel.{21EC2020-3AEA-1069-A2DD-08002B30309D}

Now you'll have a Control Panel entry on the top part of the Start menu. Clicking it presents a cascading menu of the individual control panels (Figure 2-1).

An even easier way to get to all the Control Panels: Just type **control** or **start control** at the DOS prompt.

If there are just a few control panels you use regularly, you can simply drag them to the Start button to put them on the Start menu.

I Can't Find a Quick Way to Get to the Desktop!

Yeah, it's easy to cover the whole desktop with windows, and then there's no easy way to click on the desktop to get back to it and open another window! For quick access to the desktop, put a shortcut to it on your Start menu (as I have in Figure 2-1). The Desktop folder is in your windows directory; just drag it to your Start menu button. The design giants at Microsoft should have done this.

Or you can put the desktop on the taskbar. Double-click on the Desktop folder icon (it's normally hidden, and you'll need to have all files showing to see

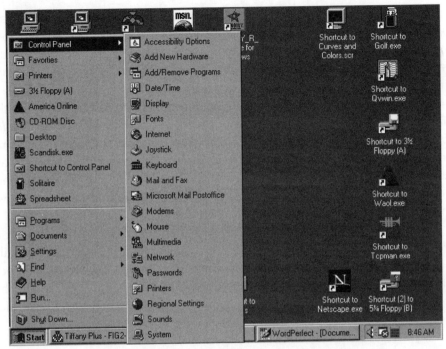

Figure 2-1. Creating a Control Panel folder on the Start menu

it). Then click its Minimize icon, and it will appear in the taskbar. Leave it there, and it will come up that way each time you start Windows 95, unless you close it. Put it in your Startup folder if you want to make sure it always appears on the taskbar.

Selecting Isn't Working the Way It Used To!

There are two different new things about selecting, and they can both drive you crazy.

The first is if you double-click on the last item that's selected in a group in an Explorer or My Computer window, you deselect it. Say that you (CTRL)-click on two documents or folders to select them. You think you can open three by double-clicking on the third one. Wrong. You'll open the first two and deselect the third one. When you go looking for that third open document, you won't find it open. (CTRL)-click on all three and keep the (CTRL) key down while you double-click on the third; that will open all three.

The *other* thing—and this one can really drive you nuts—is if you (SHIFT)-click to select items adjacent to each other in an Explorer or My Computer window, you'll select everything from the beginning of the window (the first item in the list) to the place where you (SHIFT)-click! The top item is secretly, invisibly, already selected, and it can get you into trouble.

Say that you (SHIFT)-double-click on an item. Windows 95 opens all the folders above it, starts all the programs above it—and you wind up with a *lot* of windows that you'll have to close. If you're not aware of this, and if you don't close them right away, you may run out of resources, depending on just how may windows you opened. Watch the taskbar, and if you see a tiny icon that looks like a file cabinet at the end of it, you'll know there are more windows open than the taskbar can display.

This is really one of the major design flaws of Windows 95. Why should the first item in a window be selected, with no indication that it's selected? The subsequent behavior of the system can drive beginners crazy. It can drive anybody crazy, for that matter, even if you know what's going on. To get around this problem, click once anywhere in the window so the top item isn't selected; then (SHIFT)-click as you normally would.

I Knew How to Copy and Move Files Using Keyboard Shortcuts in the Old Windows, but Now It Seems Complicated. I Can't Even Find a Copy Command on the File Menu!

It's easy, but you have to get used to thinking of Copy and Paste in a new way. You can copy, cut, and paste entire files and folders at the desktop level (either on the desktop or in My Computer and the Explorer). (CTRL)+(C) copies a file and (CTRL)+(V) pastes it; (CTRL)+(X) cuts it.

Copy is on the Edit menu now, by the way.

I Can't Get Rid of the Speaker Icon!

There's a little yellow speaker at the right end of the taskbar. It lets you adjust the speaker's volume if you click on it, or set the sound mix if you double-click on it. If you have volume knobs on your speakers, you don't need this icon. But getting rid of it isn't intuitive, as they say.

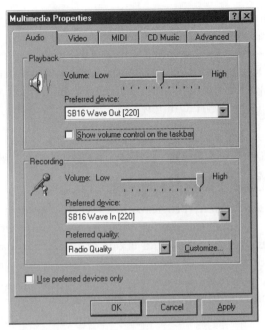

Figure 2-2. Nuking the speaker icon

1. Double-click on the Multimedia icon in the Control Panel folder.
2. Click the Audio tab .
3. Under Playback, uncheck the Show volume control on the taskbar option (Figure 2-2).

I Can't Get Rid of the Log-in Box!

If you've added a direct cable connection or dial-up networking (see Chapter 7), Windows 95 thinks you're on a network even if you aren't, and asks you to log in at startup. If you've set up your computer for more than one user, you'll also get that log-in box. In either case, all you need to do is press (ESC) to close the dialog box without filling out anything in it. But it can be annoying, so here's how to get rid of it.

If you're not using any networking capabilities, such as dial-up networking, go to the Network icon in the Control Panel folder and remove all the networking components. If you get the log-in box the next time you start up, you've probably set up your machine for multiple users. Double-click on the

Passwords icon in the Control Panel folder, click the User Profiles tab, and click the "All users of this PC use the same preferences and desktop settings" button. If you still get the log-in dialog when you restart, look in the Profiles folder in the Windows 95 folder and delete any user profiles. Also, delete any .Pwl files on your hard disk. That should stop that pesky dialog box from popping up again the next time you start Windows 95.

It Sure Looks Like I've Got Two Copies of the Same Program Open. Can This Happen?

Yep. See Figure 2-3. Many programs just switch you to their window when you open another document in the Explorer, in My Computer, or directly from an icon on the desktop, but WordPad is one of those that just goes ahead and blithely starts another copy of itself running. As a result, you can have two copies of the same program open in two (or more) windows, eating up memory. The cure? Be careful, and keep watching those taskbar icons to make sure you don't have two copies of the same program running. If you have, close one!

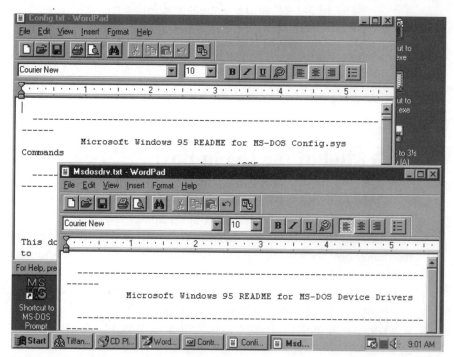

Figure 2-3. Running two copies of the same program (WordPad)

There's another cure—you can drag and drop the document into the already-running copy of the application. For example, drag a file to the program's button on the taskbar. Continue to hold the button down, and the window will open. Release the button, and the application will load the document.

My Fonts Are All Messed Up, and All I Did Was Open the Fonts Folder. How Did That Happen?

Yes, this can happen. It happens to me all the time. You see, most of the Fonts folders you see on the screen are really shortcuts. In addition, the real Fonts folder has its system attribute set, so it doesn't show up in the Explorer. To find the real Fonts folder, press (F3) and enter **fonts.** It's really in your Windows 95 folder, although you probably think it's in your Control Panels folder.

If your fonts screw up often, it's because you're naming another folder Fonts. Don't do that. If this happens to you and all your fonts go wacky, search for the Fonts folder, make sure it's still named Fonts, and make sure it has its System attribute set (right-click on it and choose Properties, Figure 2-4).

If you do go to the Fonts folder, don't delete the Marlett font, which is semi-hidden anyway. Windows 95 needs it for dialog box and window displays (it provides the symbols like the x in the Close box). And don't delete MS Sans Serif, MS Serif Times New Roman, Arial, and Courier. Too many programs depend on these fonts for displays.

I Want to See What Fonts Look Like Before I Install Them. Why Won't Windows Let Me Do That?

Again, the designers outdid themselves here. You can't see a sample of what fonts look like when you're installing them using the Install New Fonts command on the Fonts folder's File menu. But there's a back door.

1. Open the Explorer and locate the Fonts folder in your Windows 95 folder.
2. Open the folder that has the fonts you want to add.
3. Double-click on each font to see a sample (Figure 2-5). Make a note of which fonts you like and want to install.
4. Instead of using the Install New Fonts command, click on each font you want and drag it to the Fonts folder in the left pane.

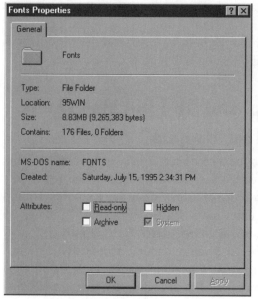

Figure 2-4. Keeping the Fonts folder's
System attribute set

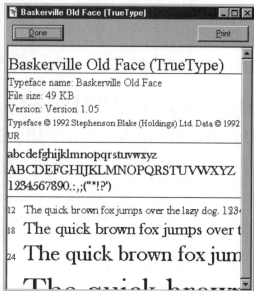

Figure 2-5. Getting a font sample

I'm Not Getting the Fonts I Asked for in My Printed Documents!

This again is by design. If you've asked for a font that Windows can't find, it substitutes another one. If you've asked for a TrueType font, you'll get a TrueType font, but it may not come close to the one you asked for, even if there's a printer font that's a closer match. Windows 95 says, in effect, "You want TrueType? You get TrueType."

Workaround: Open the Fonts folder and choose List Fonts by Similarity from the View menu (Figure 2-6). That way you'll at least have an idea of what Windows will substitute for what. As a result, you may want to install some new fonts.

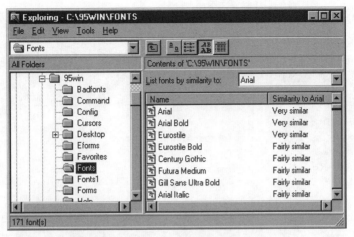

Figure 2-6. Viewing fonts by similarity

I Go Nuts Looking for My Printers. Is There an Easier Way to Access Them than via My Computer and the Printers Folder?

The easiest thing to do is put a shortcut to your printer on the desktop. Go to My Computer, open the Printers folder, and (CTRL)-drag your printer to the desktop.

If you have several printers, you can make a folder for them and put it on the Start menu. Right-click on the Start button and choose Explore. You should wind up in the Start Menu folder. Right-click the Explorer's right pane and choose New and Folder. Type this and press (ENTER):

Printers.{2227A280-3AEA-1069-A2DE-08002B30309D}

This gives you a printers folder on the Start Menu with all your installed printers in it (Figure 2-7).

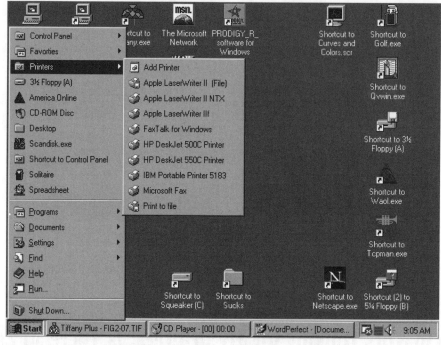

Figure 2-7. Creating a printers folder on the Start menu

Where'd the Rename Command Go?

With Windows 3.1 and DOS, you had to choose Rename or type REN to rename a file. They've changed that. There *is* a Rename command in Windows 95 (right-click on an icon, and you'll see it), but there are easier ways to rename than using a menu. Click on the name of the file you want to rename, move the mouse just a tiny bit, and you'll see a box around the name. Type the new name. Or press (F2) to get the box to appear; then type the new name.

My Start Menu Is Full. Is There a Way Around This?

You can create cascading menus off the Start menu, if you're willing to put up with their flighty behavior. Here's the fastest way.

1. Open the Start Menu folder in your Windows 95 folder. Right-clicking on the Start button and choosing Open is the fastest way.

2. Create a new folder and name it Favorites, or whatever you like.

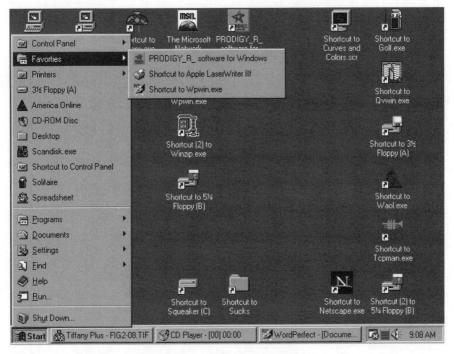

Figure 2-8. Adding a new folder to the Start menu

3. Now put whatever you want in the folder, and it will appear from the Start menu (Figure 2-8).

I'm Having a Hard Time Reading the Screen. What Can I Do?

The most obvious thing to do is open the desktop's property sheet by right-clicking on the desktop and choosing Properties. Then click the Appearance tab and pick a Large or Extra Large scheme (Figure 2-9).

But even then, the buttons on the screen may be hard to see or hit with the mouse, so there's one other thing you can try. The Minimize, Maximize, and Close buttons are sized proportionally to the font size chosen for the title bar. So select a larger title bar font (choose Active Title bar and pick a larger font) and see if that makes your buttons big enough to use.

Figure 2-9. Choosing a larger screen display

You can also double-click the Accessibility icon in the Control Panel folder, click the Display tab, and choose Settings to specify a High Contrast color scheme that can make the screen easier to read.

I Still Can't See Those Tiny Icons!

First, check to see that your desktop is set to the largest possible size.

1. Right-click on the desktop and choose Properties.
2. Click the Settings and make sure the slider is all the way over to the left (Figure 2-10).
3. Click OK.

You can make icons smaller by dragging the slider to the right. There's no direct way to make icons bigger. But there are a couple of workarounds. You can get the Microsoft Plus! Pack (see Chapter 9) and set the desktop to use large icons. And of course you might consider getting a bigger monitor!

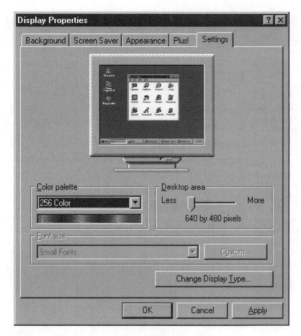

Figure 2-10. Checking desktop size

If you don't want to spend any more money, you can hack at the Registry a little. Try these steps:

1. Run Regedit and open HKEY_CURRENT_USER\Control panel\desktop\WindowMetrics.

2. Double-click on Shell Icon Size (Figure 2-11) to change the horizontal and vertical size of desktop icons in pixels.

3. Enter a new value (Figure 2-12), click OK, and exit from the registry editor.

4. Restart Windows. You'll have to experiment with different values to get the icons as large as you need.

Different Things Happen When I Drag and Drop!

Yes, indeed, they do. If you drag a file from one folder to another on the same drive, Windows moves it. If you drag it to a different drive, Windows copies it. If the file you're dragging happens to be executable (.EXE, .COM, .BAT) and you're dragging it to a destination on your hard disk, Windows makes a shortcut of it. But if you drag that same file to a floppy, Windows copies it.

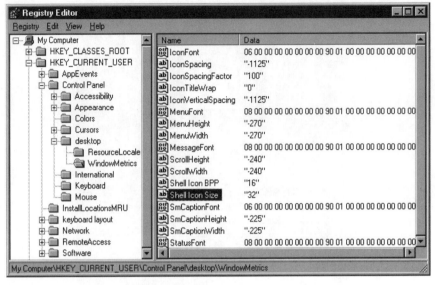

Figure 2-11. Locating Shell Icon Size

Figure 2-12. Changing icon sizes

Can you remember this? I can't. The workarounds:

(SHIFT)+drag	Moves (you see a plain icon)
(CTRL)+drag	Copies (you see a + sign)
(SHIFT)+(CTRL)+drag	Makes a shortcut (you see a curved arrow)

Or just right-click on the icon, and you'll see a menu to choose from (Figure 2-13). This may be the simplest solution.

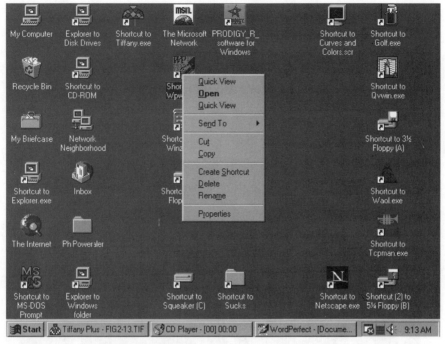

Figure 2-13. The right-click pop-up menu

Different Things Happen When I Search!

Yes, they do. *Find* searches the folder you're in, and its subfolders, unless you specifically tell it not to. This can be misleading; you may think you're searching your whole hard disk, when in fact you're just searching the current folder. To make sure you're searching your whole hard disk, clear the "Look in" box by pressing Backspace when the cursor's in it (Figure 2-14).

Don't want to search your whole hard disk, but don't want to look in just the current folder, either? You can restrict searches to specific folders by entering their names in the "Look in" box, separated by semicolons, such as 95win;wpwin\wpdocs.

For an even faster way to search, save searches you'll use again, such as documents worked on during the last month (choose Save Search from the File menu). You'll see an icon on the desktop (Figure 2-15); you may need to close the Find window to see it. Give the icon a meaningful name (keep the .fnd extension), and

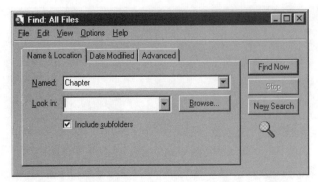

Figure 2-14. Clearing the "Look in" box to search
your whole hard disk

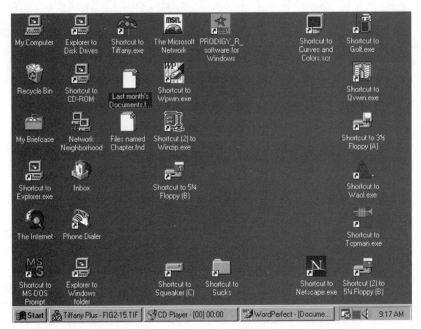

Figure 2-15. Saving a search (see "Last Month's Documents" and
"Files named chapter.fnd"

you'll never have to set that particular search up again. If you set up a lot of
searches, you might want to put your favorites in a folder rather than cluttering
up the desktop with them.

More Find Quirks!

The Find utility takes a little getting used to, particularly the way it accepts wildcards (see Chapter 6). But it is one of the things they designed correctly in Windows 95. Once you've found a file, you can copy it, move it, print it, rename it, delete it, create a shortcut for it, look in the folder it's kept in (use the Open Containing Folder command on the File menu), or even search for text within documents (use the Advanced tab).

Of course, Find has a few quirks. It can't find some things. It won't find Marlett, for example, which is the font used for symbols in dialog boxes and menus, but it will find the Fonts folder. And you should be warned that you can't move a file back to the Find window. Once you've moved it somewhere else, it's there, and there's no handy Put Away command (as there is on the other computer, the one starting with an M) that puts it back where it came from. Oh yes, and you can't copy and move from the Find utility's Browse window.

What's This "Device is Not Ready" Message?

Windows doesn't mean drive A, for example, isn't ready. It means there's just no floppy disk in the drive. You'll get this message whenever you search My Computer and your drives aren't stuffed with disks, because searching My Computer searches all your drives. Or if you try to Send something to drive A or B, and there's no floppy disk in there, you'll get this message again. When you insert the floppy disk, the icon doesn't change to let you know the drive's "ready." Even though it is. This is just another design idea that doesn't seem quite baked yet.

This Autorun Feature Is Driving Me Nuts!

When you insert a CD into your CD-ROM drive, Windows 95 uses its Autorun feature to start the thing playing. If you have a slow computer, you'll have to wait, too. There's a way to stop this behavior: Hold down the Shift key when you insert the CD. But there's a better way to turn this feature *off*:

1. Double-click on the System icon in the Control Panel folder.
2. Click Device Manager.
3. Double-click on the CD-ROM icon and then click on your CD-ROM drive.
4. Click Properties and then Settings.
5. Uncheck the Auto Insert Notification option (Figure 2-16) and click OK till you get back to the desktop.

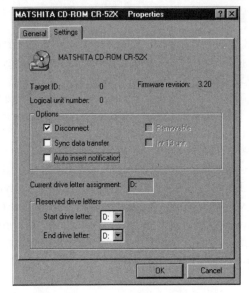

Figure 2-16. Turning off Autorun

I Hate These Zooming Windows!

Zooming windows? You know, the effect you get when you minimize or maximize windows. You can turn this behavior off with a little registry hacking:

1. Run Regedit.
2. Open HKEY_CURRENT_USER\Control Panel\desktop\WindowMetrics.
3. Choose New from the Edit menu and then choose String Value.
4. Type MinAnimate and press (ENTER).
5. Double-click on the new string value and enter a value of 0 for off (Figure 2-17). (Entering 1 turns it back on again.)

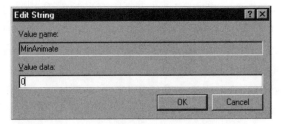

Figure 2-17. Nuking the zooming of the zooming windows

6.   Click OK, press (F5) to update the Registry, and close Regedit.
7.   Restart Windows for this change to take effect.

How on Earth Do I Get Windows 95 to Display the Date?

Move the mouse pointer over the Clock. Why do they think that's intuitive? It took me a long time to figure this out.

I Want My Screen Saver to Come Up on Demand, but Windows 95 Doesn't Provide a "Hot Spot" to Click!

Another little annoyance that, over time, becomes a PITA (that means pain in the elbow, if you didn't already know).

Most third-party screen savers let you specify a corner of the screen that you can move the pointer to and turn the screen saver on immediately—say if the boss comes in while you're playing solitaire. Windows 95's screen savers don't let you do this.

Here's the workaround. Create a shortcut on the desktop to the screen saver (.SCR file) that you're using. The ones that come with Windows 95 are in the Windows\System folder. If you need to turn the screen saver on in a hurry, just double-click on it. Be sure to use the .SCR file, not the .exe file, or you'll get the screen saver's settings when you double-click.

If you want to be able to turn the screen saver on even when you can't see the desktop, create a shortcut to it, right-click on the shortcut, choose Properties, click on the Shortcut tab, and set up a hot key combo for it (Figure 2-18).

I Can't Read the Grayed-out Text in Menus and Dialog Boxes!

Any items that can't be selected at a certain time are disabled, or grayed out. For example, you can't paste unless you've copied or cut something first. But sometimes the grayed-out color exactly matches the color of the background in dialog boxes and menus, effectively rendering those choices invisible. If you try to change screen colors by changing the desktop's properties, you'll soon find there's no setting for that disabled text.

69

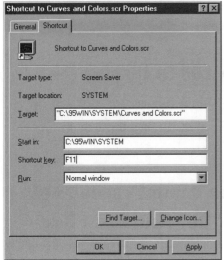

Figure 2-18. Specifying a hot key
combination for a screen saver

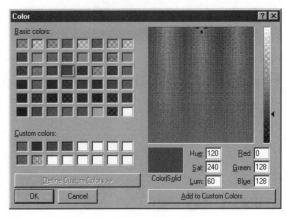

Figure 2-19. Checking color values

Here's the workaround: edit Win.ini and change the values for GrayText in the [Colors] section. Try these settings:

Menu=192 192 192
GrayText=128 128 128

If you don't like the results these values give, experiment with different values. Those numbers represent red, green, and blue, respectively. To see samples of other colors and what numbers represent them, right-click on the desktop, choose Properties, click the Appearance tab, click Color and Other (usually half-hidden by the taskbar), and look at the screen (Figure 2-19). Move the pointer in the color selector (on the right side of the screen) to see the values for the color that you're pointing to.

I'm Sharing a Computer, and I Can't Figure Out How to Set Up Windows 95 for Multiple Users.

It's not, as they say, "intuitive." To set Windows 95 up for several users, each with their own preferences and passwords, you have to go digging—in this case, in the Passwords control panel. Click User Profiles and click "Users can customize their preferences and desktop settings" (Figure 2-20). Then check the boxes that allow folks to customize their Desktop icons, Network Neighborhoods, Start Menu, and Program groups. This is also a way for one user to have several different environments, which might be handy if you do different kinds of work.

Now when you start Windows 95, it will ask who you are. If you enter a new user name and password, it will take you to a second dialog box. Click Yes, and Windows creates a profile folder for the new user, containing things like what's on the Start menu, what's in the Recent folder (what you see on the Documents menu), color scheme choices, wallpaper and sound selections, and so forth. To get on as this "user," enter the appropriate name and password.

Setting up Windows 95 for multiple users is a good idea if you have small children in the home. You can keep them out of your heavy-duty applications and restrict them to games and such. Once you're set up for multiple users, any new programs you install are accessible only to you. To make newly installed programs available to other users, put a shortcut to them in their specific user's folder, located in the Profiles folder in your Windows 95 folder (Figure 2-21).

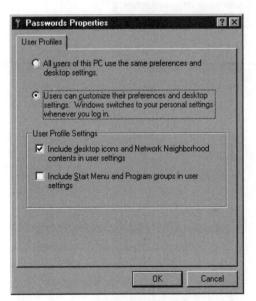

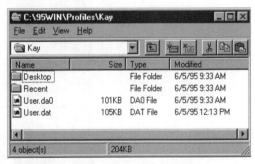

Figure 2-21. A user's profile folder

Figure 2-20. Using the Passwords control panel to set up for multiple users

Delete from the Desktop folder any shortcuts you *don't* want that user to have access to. Be warned that savvy small children can figure out how to get around this "security" (all you have to do is press ⒺⓈⒸ to close the startup dialog box). That's why I recommend it only for small children. It won't fool anybody else for long.

For a more in-depth discussion about desktop security (or, rather, the lack of it), see Chapter 3, which gives you some heavier-duty tools for protecting your work.

I Hate Looking at Only a Single Window *or* Having a New Window Open Each Time I Open a Folder. Is There Any Way to Make the Decision on the Fly?

If you're just browsing, looking for a file, it's handy to have the Explorer set up to use a single window that changes each time you open a new folder. Otherwise, your screen and taskbar get cluttered with windows and icons. But if you want to

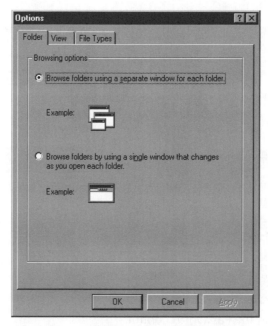

Figure 2-22. Changing the Explorer's folder browse mode

copy and move files around, it's nice to quickly open an extra window or two. If you use the Explorer's Options command (on the View menu) and click the Folder tab, you'll see that you can set it to whichever type of behavior you want (single window browse or multiple window browse, Figure 2-22).

But then you're stuck with that behavior till you change it again. Instead, pick Single window browse. Then, when you want to open multiple folder windows, (CTRL)-double click.

The Explorer Always Opens in the Start Menu Folder. Is There Any Way to Make the Explorer Open Somewhere Else?

When you choose Explore after right-clicking on the Start button, Explorer always heads to the Start menu folder. Hey, if you wanted to go there, you'd have used the Start menu! But you are *at* the Start Menu, so obviously (at least to me) you want to go somewhere else.

The workaround is to make a shortcut to the Explorer (make several of 'em while you're at it) by dragging Explorer.exe in your Windows folder to the desktop. Now right-click on the first one and choose Properties (or select it and press (ALT)+(ENTER), which takes you straight to the property sheet).

For this first one, we'll make the Explorer take you to your Windows folder. Click the Shortcut tab (Figure 2-23), and enter this in the Target box (use the name of your Windows 95 folder; mine's named 95win):

c:\windows\explorer.exe c:\95win

Now, when you double-click this shortcut, you'll go straight to your Windows folder (Figure 2-24).

Then make shortcuts that open in the other folders you usually go to. For example, to create one that opens in my WordPerfect documents folder, I'd enter **c:\95win\explorer.exe c:\wpwin\wpdocs**. Be sure to rename all these shortcuts, indicating where they go, so you can tell one from another. Keep them on your desktop, and you'll never have to go to the Start Menu folder again.

To make a shortcut that opens Explorer with all the drives shown and the folders closed (one that looks like My Computer; see Figure 2-25), enter **c:\windows\explorer.exe /e,/select,c:** in the Target box. (Use the name of your Windows 95 folder.)

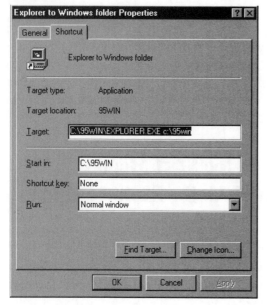

Figure 2-23. Entering a target

Figure 2-24 .Exploring c:\

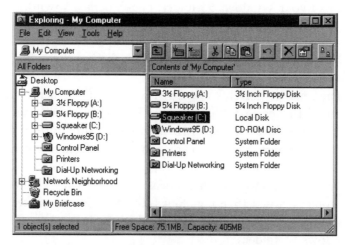

Figure 2-25. A My Computer view of Explorer

Here's how the switches work:

- /n   opens a new Explorer window

- ,/e   shows an expanded folder in tree display so you can see all subfolders

- ,/root   shows the folder as the topmost item on your system

- ,/select   displays the folder's parent

- ,folder   is the path to any folder

For example:

C:\Windows\Explorer.exe ,/select,C:\Windows\System	Highlights the System folder and displays the contents of C:\Windows (Figure 2-26)
C:\Windows\Explorer.exe /n,/e/select,C:\Windows\System	Opens a new Explorer window, displays the contents of C:\Windows\System (Figure 2-27)

There are a couple of other things you might want to do to minimize your insanity level. One is to have a shortcut to a folder automatically open to a two-pane Explorer view. To do this, put **Explorer /e,** at the beginning of the path in

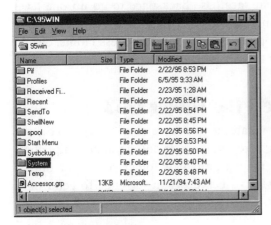

Figure 2-26. Results of C:\Windows\Explorer.exe,/select,C:\Windows \System

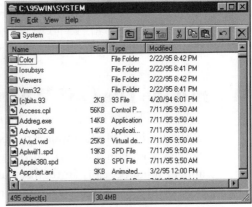

Figure 2-27. Results of C:\Windows\Explorer.exe/n,/e/select,C:\ Windows\System

the shortcut's Target box. Be sure to leave a space after the comma. Or, you can have a shortcut select a certain file when it opens. To do this, put **Explorer /Select,** (space after the comma) at the beginning of the path in the Target box and add the path to the file you want at the end.

It Makes Me Mad That Every Time I Open an Explorer Window, I Have to Tweak It to Get the View I Want and the Items Sorted the Way I Want. Are There Any Workarounds?

First, set up an Explorer window just the way you want it (Details, Status Bar, Tool Bar, and so on). Now close that window by (CTRL)-clicking on the Close box. From then on, all your Explorer windows will open that way.

Unfortunately, there's no way to sort by file extension. The Norton Navigator will let you, though, if you have it or are inclined to buy it. And there are other workarounds discussed in Chapter 6.

The Explorer Drives Me Nuts by Making Me Click, Click, Click to Go Where I Want to Go!

There are ways around the rodent race. Use Backspace to go up one level. Press (F6) to move from pane to pane. To see everything on a drive, press * on the numeric keypad. To go to the top of your drive listing, press Home. See the table of keyboard shortcuts later in this chapter for more hints.

Where'd the File Go? Where'd the Folder Go?

You probably know by now that whatever you move or copy goes to the end of the list in a My Computer or Explorer window. It doesn't appear alphabetically as you would expect. In the same way, any new folder you create doesn't appear alphabetically in the list but gets stuck down at the end. To get around this, press (F5) to refresh the screen. Or press (END) to go to the end of the list and see what's there.

Over and Over, I'm Forced to Use the Mouse Instead of the Keyboard. I Hate This.

Windows 95 relies heavily on mouse use, but there are workarounds to the endless Olympic hurdles you face to make the rodent jump. Most of them are really *not* intuitive. Here are some of the most useful ones.

Display an object's properties	(ALT)+(ENTER)
Move tab by tab in a property sheet	(CTRL)+(TAB)
Display an object's popup menu (right-click)	(SHIFT)+(F10)
Rename	(F2)
Go to menu mode	(F10) (then use the arrow and Enter keys)
Close menus	(ESC)
Move in dialog boxes	(TAB), (SHIFT)+(TAB)
Cancel a dialog box	(ESC)
Select a choice	Type the underlined letter in its name
Check a check box	(SPACEBAR)
Turn an option button on/off	(←) and (→) keys
Open a popup list	(ALT)+(↓) or (ALT)+(↑)
Choose OK	(ENTER)
Move from pane to pane in the Explorer	(F6)
Move up one level in the Explorer	(BACKSPACE)
Expand the selected folder	(→)
Collapse the selected folder	(←)
Expand folders	(+) on numeric keypad
Expand all folders	(*) on numeric keypad
Collapse folders	(-) on numeric keypad
Move up and down the panes	(CTRL)+(↑), (CTRL)+(↓)
Go to the taskbar	(CTRL)+(ESC), (ESC), (TAB), (ENTER)
Undo what you just did	(CTRL)+(Z)
Refresh the screen after a move or copy	(F5)
Run a command	(CTRL)+(ESC) (R)
Get a Mac	!!!

You can also assign keyboard shortcuts to desktop shortcuts. Just right-click on the shortcut, click the Shortcut tab, go to the Shortcut key box, and press the keys you want to use. Then once the program or document's running, you can switch back to it just by pressing that key combination instead of clicking on the taskbar.

Here are some shortcut combinations you *shouldn't* assign because Windows 95 is using them:

CTRL+C
CTRL+V
CTRL+X
CTRL+A
CTRL+ESC
ALT+TAB
ALT+PRTSC
ALT+ENTER
ALT+SPACEBAR

My Mouse Died! Now What Do I Do?

If your mouse suddenly goes out on you, it's nice to know how to manipulate Windows without it, so at least you can get to the Mouse control panel and install another mouse driver. Or start another program. Or shut Windows down while you think about it.

If the mouse goes out, press CTRL+ESC to open the Start menu. Now you can type **s** for Settings and get to the Control Panel folder. Or type **u** for shutdown. Or you can press ALT+ESC to switch between buttons on the taskbar. You get the idea.

To open the taskbar when you can't see it, once you see the Start menu, press ALT+SPACEBAR to open the control (system) menu so you can resize the taskbar. Then, to switch between buttons on the taskbar, press ALT+ESC and press ENTER when the item you want is highlighted.

To right-click on an icon sans mouse, press SHIFT+F10.

My Shortcut's Not Working. It Was Working Before. What's Happening?

Usually the cause of a non-functioning shortcut is that you deleted the original or maybe moved it. Look at the shortcut's properties (right-click it and choose Properties) and click the Shortcut tab. Click Find Target to find the shortcut.

Sometimes the problem is that you need to start the shortcut in a folder where your data files are. Right-click, choose Properties, and look at what's in the "Start in" box. Change it if you need to start in another folder.

Can I Nuke the Word "Shortcut" in Shortcuts?

Yes. You'll have more room for longer icon names, and your desktop won't look as cluttered. Just create a few shortcuts on the desktop, one right after another. After a while, Windows will quit adding "Shortcut to" to them. You can delete the extra ones, and Windows will forget about using the words "Shortcut to." You can tell a shortcut icon by the little arrow on it anyway.

All Those Little Arrows...Can I Get Rid of Them?

The little arrows on icons are there to indicate they're shortcuts, not the real thing. But you can get rid of them. Some folks like a really clean desktop.

1. Open the Registry Editor (regedit.exe) and search for these keys:

   HKEY_CLASSES_ROOT\lnkfile

   HKEY_CLASSES_ROOT\piffile

2. Right-click on the strings named IsShortcut, choose Rename, and rename them as something else, like IsNotShortcut (Figure 2-28 shows one of them).

3. Press (F5) to refresh the Registry; then close it.

Now the shortcuts you create won't have any arrows on them. To get the arrows back, go back into Regedit and rename the strings IsShortcut.

It's Driving Me Nuts That I Can't Find the Real Files (Originals)!

Windows 95 is a lot of smoke and mirrors, meaning it uses shortcuts instead of the real files much of the time.

If you want to know where the real files are, here's the list. Maybe somebody can figure out the logic behind this; I can't.

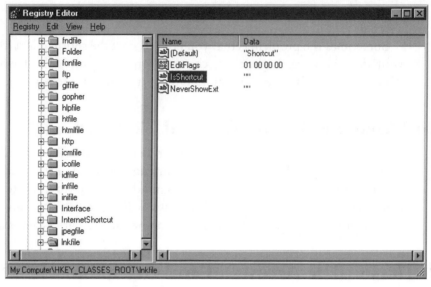

Figure 2-28. Renaming IsShortcut

It looks like there's a lot of stuff in the Start menu folder, but most of it is shortcuts. In addition, there's a Control Panels folder in your Start menu folder, but the real Control Panel (singular) folder is on My Computer, at the bottom of the list in the left-hand pane of the Explorer.

- Programs in the Programs folder are shortcuts.
- Utilities in the Control Panels folder (Add/Remove Hardware, etc.) are all shortcuts.
- The Games in the Games folder are shortcuts, too. The real games are in your Windows 95 folder.
- The Fonts folder is in your Windows 95 folder. That's a shortcut to it in the Control Panels folder.

Whatever's on your desktop is in a (usually) invisible folder named Desktop. It's really inside the Windows 95 folder, but it appears at the top of the listing in My Computer and the Explorer. To see it, use My Computer's or the Explorer's View menu, click Options and the File Types tab, then click Show all files.

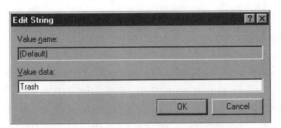

Figure 2-29. Renaming the Recycle Bin

Why Can't I Rename the Recycle Bin?

Microsoft, in its infinite wisdom, made some icons hard to rename—but not impossible. You just have to do a little registry hacking.

1. In Regedit, open HKEY_CLASSES-ROOT\CLSID.
2. Choose Find from the Edit menu (or press (CTRL)+(F)) and search for Recycle Bin.
3. Double-click (Default) and enter the new name (Figure 2-29). Of course if you rename it "Trash," a little lawyer icon from Apple will pop up.
4. Click OK, press (F5) to refresh the Registry, and close it.
5. Click on the desktop and press (F5) to refresh the screen.

I'm Tired of All Those "Are You Really, Really Sure" Messages.

If the unending delete confirmations are driving you nuts, there's a way you can shut them up. Press (SHIFT) when you press (DEL), and the items you've selected will go straight to the Recycle Bin.

You can also put a shortcut to the Recycle Bin in your Send To folder, so right-clicking on an item and choosing Send To and Recycle Bin will nuke the item without the annoying message.

I Thought I Deleted All Those Files...but They're Still There!

If you've got Norton Utilities for Windows 95 running, no matter how often you empty your Recycle Bin, the deleted files stay on your hard disk, taking up room. This can be very irritating. What's happening is that Norton's protecting you from deleting files by mistake. And there's no straightforward way to turn this feature off, like choosing "Off" from a menu.

Here's how you can do it. Find a file named Nprotect.vxd. It's normally in the Symantec directory. Rename it something else, like Nomore. Then, the next time you start Windows 95, Norton Utilities will no longer stash the files you delete.

For more about the deleting process' pitfalls, see in-depth discussion in Chapter 3 about when you're really deleting versus when you're not.

QuickView Won't Show Me Anything!

Windows 95 adds a QuickViewer that lets you peek in files before opening them (Figure 2-30). All you need to do is right-click on the file and choose QuickView in My Computer and Explorer windows.

But there are a couple of catches. The first is that you have to install QuickView yourself, because it isn't installed automatically. Use the Add/Remove Programs icon in the Control Panel folder, click Windows Setup, check Accessories, check QuickView (Figure 2-31), and click OK. You'll need your Windows 95 CD-ROM or the installation disks.

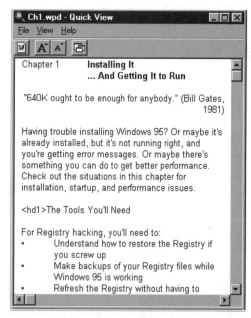

Figure 2-30. Using QuickView

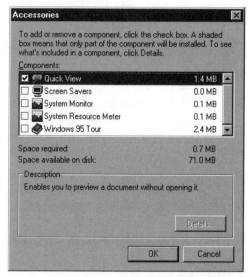

Figure 2-31. Installing QuickView

The second catch is that it only "knows" about 30 or so file extensions, and if the file you want to view doesn't have one of them, you're out of luck—unless you're willing to hack the Registry (see the next complaint). You can't cut and paste from QuickView windows to other applications, either. If you need to do this and view more file types, you can get QuickView Plus from Inso, about $45, 800-333-1395. See Chapter 9 for more band-aids.

QuickView Doesn't QuickView Everything!

But you can make it view almost anything, with a little help from the registry.

1. Run Regedit and double-click on \HKEY_CLASSES_ROOT\.
2. Look for the * key. Add it if it isn't there (choose New and Key from the Edit menu).
3. Double-click on this key and add a new key named QuickView.
4. Double-click on Default and set the value to * (Figure 2-32).
5. Press (F5) and close Regedit.

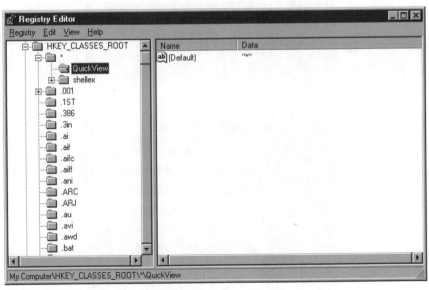

Figure 2-32. Setting the new value

It Takes Forever to See My Graphics Files!

Even on a fast machine, some graphics files may be slow to display. The workaround: Use QuickView whenever you can to get a peek of your graphic images instead of opening them in a program.

I Don't Want to Open This File in WordPad! I Hate WordPad. How Do I Open It in Another Program?

You have good reasons to hate WordPad. They're discussed in Chapter 3. But you can get around your problem. Press (SHIFT), right-click on the file's icon, and choose Open With. Then pick the program you want to use to open the file. Check the "Always use..." box if you want to permanently associate this type of file with that program. (You'll be assigning that extension to that program; see "File Types Ain't What They Used to Be" in Chapter 3 for details.)

Windows 95 does a good job of giving you control over which application opens which document, but unfortunately it doesn't take it far enough. Sometimes the right mouse pop-up menu doesn't give you the Open With choice.

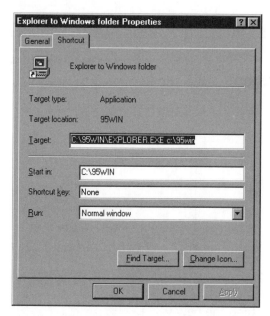

Figure 2-33. Picking the program you want to open the file

84

To get around this limitation so you can open any file with any app you like (providing that's possible, of course), just hold down the (SHIFT) key when you right-click on the file, and the Open With command will appear in the menu. Then you can choose the program you want to use (Figure 2-33).

If you don't see the program you want, click Other, find the program, and double-click on it. It will appear on the list in the Open With box from now on.

I've Installed Some Programs, but I Can't Find Them!

Look in your Program Files folder. That's where a lot of Microsoft programs put their files. This can drive you insane. Why don't they let you say where you want your program files?

By the way, the Program Files folder isn't where you'd expect, inside your Windows 95 folders. It's at the root level of your folder system.

All That Disk Activity Is Driving Me Insane!

You're not alone. There's some sort of bug/feature (you choose) in Windows 95 that makes it start spinning the hard disk like mad from time to time. You sit there and wait, watching your drive light flashing on and off. At first it was thought this was caused by low memory or large disk caches. Nope. Users with 16 Mb of RAM report the same problem. So far...there's no workaround. Enjoy your wait.

I Can't Find the Windows Easter Egg!

OK, so this is not a problem, but I had to get it in here somewhere. There are actually two Windows 95 Easter Eggs.

The first one (be sure to enter just what I've put in bold here, just as it is, exactly):

1. Right-click on the desktop and choose New and Folder.
2. Name the folder **and now, the moment you've all been waiting for**
3. Right-click on the folder and rename it **we proudly present for your viewing pleasure**
4. Right-click again and rename it **The Microsoft Windows 95 Product Team!**

Now double-click on the folder to see the Egg.

If that doesn't work, try this method: name the folder *Anything*.{986DADA0-42A0-1069-A2E7-08002B30309D}. If that doesn't work, you just can't see the Egg on your computer. Some folks report this is so.

There's another Egg, one that's lesser known and harder to see. If you want to try your hand at seeing it, you'll need to be well coordinated. When the mouse pointer first appears as Windows 95 is starting (the screen should be black at this point), press these keys in order:

Ctrl+F6+Right Shift+ Del+ Right Mouse Button

What you see, if you can get this to work, is Bill Gates' horse Nugget, in full color.

I Can't Find Backup.

Backup isn't necessarily installed when you install Windows 95. If you don't see it in your Programs\Accessories\System Tools folder on the Start menu, you can install it by double-clicking on the Add/Remove Programs icon in the Control Panel folder and clicking the Windows Setup tab. Then double-click Disk tools and check Backup (Figure 2-34). Personally, I think that if you

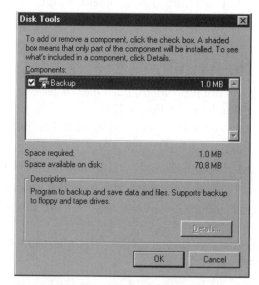

Figure 2-34. Installing Backup

haven't installed it, you might as well not. I've never run it without getting at least one error. Get Norton.

Anyway, as a workaround, if you haven't installed Backup and you have the MS-DOS 5 Backup.exe file in your path, you can use the DOS Backup program from Windows 95. Press (F1) for Help, click Contents, double-click How To..., double-click Safeguard Your Work, and click Backing Up Your Files.

Backup Won't Work with My Tape Drive!

Even Microsoft admits there are problems with Backup. It won't work with most tape drives. If you get a message that your tape drive hasn't been detected, click the Help button to see the short list of tape drives that *are* supported. See Chapter 5 for some workarounds.

These backup programs will work with Windows 95, but they don't support long file names:

Central Point Backup 2.0 (works with SCSI drives)
Norton Backup 3.0 for Windows (works with SCSI and IDE drives)
Cheyenne ARCsolo V3.02 for Windows (works with SCSI tape drives and Novell Networks)

To work around the long file name problem, use the command-line utility named LFNBACK. It's on the CD-ROM. You'll need to run it with the /b switch before the backup to save your long file names, and again with the /r switch after the backup to restore them. Read the Lfnbk.txt file that comes with it! Or, get a newer backup program that supports Windows 95's long file names.

One further word of warning: don't run LFNBACK from within Windows. Go to the DOS prompt by pressing (F8) when you hear the computer's startup beep.

For the ultimate workaround, just don't use long file names! Stick to the "8.3" convention (see the discussion in Chapter 3 that explains what 8.3 file names are and how Windows 95 has effectively reduced them to a "6.3" convention). Then you can double-click on the System icon in the Control Panels folder, click Performance, File System, and Troubleshooting, and disable long file name preservation for old programs.

One more potential problem: If you have a slow backup program (less than 1.5 Mb of data backed up per minute), whatever tape drive you use may conflict with your video card. The workaround: Start the backup operation, then open a full-screen MS-DOS window until the backup is over.

Briefcase Isn't Keeping Track of My Files!

Microsoft admits up front there also are problems with Briefcase. If you use user profiles with Briefcase, it won't always copy correctly to each profile. The workaround:

1. Go to the Control Panel folder and double-click Passwords.
2. Click the User Profiles tab and check the second option, *Users can customize their preferences and desktop settings.*
3. Delete the My Briefcase icon from your desktop.
4. Right-click on the desktop, click New, and then click Briefcase to create a new Briefcase.

Also, if you create a Briefcase and then compress your hard drive, Briefcase's association to the files will be lost. The workaround: Reassociate the files with Briefcase.

ScanDisk Is Reporting Files Are Bad When They Really Aren't.

Only worry about this one if you change code pages! Usually you do this only if you're switching from one language to another. That doesn't mean *typing in*

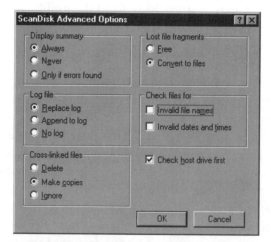

Figure 2-35. Tweaking ScanDisk's Advanced settings

your word processor in another language; it means getting a PC bought in the U.S. to work in a language other than English. If you've created files or folders with one code page in effect and then switch to another code page, ScanDisk may report errors about these files.

The workaround: Open ScanDisk's Advanced dialog box and make sure Check Files For Invalid File Names isn't checked (Figure 2-35).

And Next...

In Chapter 3, I'll discuss in a little more depth some of the general problems you can run into with Windows 95, like not having any desktop security and what those long file names can really do to you.

Chapter 3

The Big Five
Windows Pitfalls

What Windows 95 Doesn't Tell You
About How You Can Get in Trouble

The Big Five
Windows Pitfalls
What Windows 95 Doesn't Tell You
About How You Can Get in Trouble

"You ain't goin' nowhere, son."

*Advice to Elvis Presley from
Manager of Grand Ole Opry, 1954*

I n this chapter we'll look at the places where Windows 95 can get you in trouble if you believe what it says on the surface. How can this be? Well, in some respects, Windows 95 can be deceptively simple. In their quest for user friendliness, Microsoft has "dumbed down" the system too much in some places, to the point where users don't have as much control as they used to. As an analogy, say that you've been used to downshifting on hills with a manual transmission: Now you've got a car with automatic, and you can't make it accelerate like you used to.

Some of the simplicity comes at a price. Here's an example of what I mean. In DOS and Windows 3.1 you could give files names of up to eight characters, plus a three-character extension. Everybody screamed, and rightly so, because eight characters aren't enough to give a file a meaningful name. You get tired of names like REPORT54.TXT and 12AUG94R.DOC after a while, and they don't really describe what's in those files, either. So Windows 95 was designed to let you use long file names—up to 255 characters long, including spaces, they say. But practically speaking, in some situations, you've got six. That's right, six. Two less than the old DOS-style "8.3" naming convention of eight characters plus an optional three-character extension.

How can this happen? Theoretically, you can use fully descriptive filenames such as *My Letter to Uncle Sam about Bosnia* and *My Letter to Mother Teresa about India*. But behind the scenes, Windows 95 creates a file name that older programs that don't support long file names can read: It takes the first six characters and adds a tilde and a number. So *My Letter to Uncle Sam* and *My Letter to Mother Teresa* become *Mylette~1.txt* and *Mylette~2.txt*. This can confuse both you and the coworkers you swap files with! In some cases, as you'll see later in this chapter, you can actually lose data as files get overwritten.

This is just one example. There are at least four others, with their own little quirks, as you'll see as we explore the Big Five pitfalls in this chapter.

The Tools You'll Need

To do the workarounds in this chapter, you'll need:

- Courage to approach the command line
- A devil-may-care attitude about what others think (hey, if it works, it works)
- Willingness to do a little Registry hacking (see Chapter 1)
- The System Policy Editor

The first two can't be taught, but the last two can. If you're reading this book, you probably already have the first two. In this chapter you'll learn the rest.

Installing the Policy Editor

Some of the workarounds in this chapter require you to use the System Policy Editor. It lets you specify which parts of Windows 95 users can access. It's on the CD in the \Admin\Apptools\Poledit folder.

Figure 3-1. Installing the Policy Editor

1. Double-click on Add/Remove Programs in the Control Panel folder.
2. Select Windows Setup and click Have Disk.
3. Click Browse and enter **D:\Admin\Apptools\Poledit.** If your CD drive letter isn't D, substitute the correct letter.
4. Check the System Policy Editor box (Figure 3-1) and click Install.
5. When it's through installing, click OK.

I'll tell you when you need to use the System Policy Editor. You can find it in your Programs\Accessories\System Tools Folder on the Start menu, or you can just enter **poledit** in the Run box to use it.

If you have trouble using the Policy Editor, the usual cause is that the file Admin.adm hasn't been copied to your Windows\Inf folder. Go back and copy it from the Poledit folder on the CD, and the Policy Editor should work as advertised.

Pitfall #1: Falling into the Long File Name Trap

Before Windows 95, you were restricted to what's known as the 8.3 naming convention. Any file name had to consist of eight characters or fewer, followed by an (optional) period and an extension of up to three characters, which identified the file's type. Now Windows 95 comes along and tells you that you can

95

use as many as 255 characters, including spacing and capitals and lowercase, in long file names. Theoretically, you could wind up with file and folder names that are fully descriptive, such as A Letter to Aunt Mary about her Bread and Butter Pickle Recipes... but if you believe this and use long file names like that, you'll get in trouble.

Forbidden Characters

How? Several ways. In the first place, you can't use all the characters that are on your keyboard for file names. Although you can use spaces and punctuation, you can't use these characters:

\ / : ; * ? " < >|

But you can use + = [ ] and the comma, and you couldn't do that before.

Your New 6.3 Naming Convention

In the second place, behind the scenes, Windows 95 is creating equivalent 8.3-type names out of your long file names for programs that don't support long file names. So if you've followed a similar pattern when naming files, you can wind up with such meaningful names as Alette~1.txt, Alette~2.txt, and so forth, if the original files were named A Letter to Aunt Mary, A Letter to Sam, A Letter to Microsoft. Windows 95 takes the first six characters and adds a tilde and a number. Not only can this confuse you, it can really confuse programs that don't support long file names but have to deal with a lot of files, like backup programs. It can confuse coworkers using Windows 3.1 when you exchange files with them. And it effectively makes the 8.3 naming convention a 6.3 convention—*taking away* two characters instead of adding 247 more!

It's also a problem when you're on a network, running 16-bit Windows 3.1 applications that don't support long file names. Every time a user saves a document in the 16-bit application, it gets renamed back to the 8.3 convention, and the long file name is overwritten. The net result? You and your coworkers lose track of what's what. When you try to open the document's shortcut in Windows 95 under its long file name, all you'll see is the shortcut, not the document itself. And even if you're not on a network but share files with Windows 3.1 users via floppy disks, you can easily screw up all your file names when the other users edit documents and give them back to you, and vice versa.

Consider this scenario. Say that you have two files, one named Report for May.doc and another named Report for June.doc. Their truncated names are

Report~1.doc and Report~2.doc. You're ready to put them on a floppy to give to somebody who's using a Windows 3.1 or DOS machine or is on a network that doesn't recognize long file names. You copy "Report for June.doc" to drive A, and its truncated name on drive A becomes Report~1.doc. You then copy "Report for May.doc" to A: and its truncated name on drive A becomes Report~2.doc. See? The names have been exchanged.

Microsoft says that Windows 95 was intentionally designed this way. Whenever you create a file with a long file name and copy the file to a floppy (or over a network), a completely new truncated name is created, and the original truncated name is lost. Except the file still keeps its original name on your hard disk; God only knows what it will get named the next time you copy a few files over your network or onto your floppy. And think about copying it BACK to your hard disk after your coworker gets done with it! You can easily lose data when one "Report~1.doc" overwrites another. Microsoft says this is a feature. I say don't use long file names if you exchange documents with users who aren't running only new 32-bit Windows applications.

Long Names on the Screen

Even if the preceding discussion doesn't apply to you, there are other good reasons to avoid overly long file names. As a practical matter, you can't read long file names on the screen, and file names that begin similarly can wind up undistinguishable from each other (Figure 3-2). With anything over about 20 characters, you'll have to scroll to read the names in dialog boxes and Explorer and My Computer windows. Do yourself a favor and keep file names short but descriptive. Twenty characters is still more than twice the old 8-character limit.

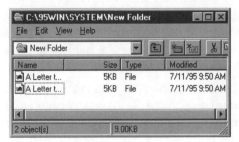

Figure 3-2. Long file names can be unreadable on the screen.

Chapter 3

Long Extensions

Microsoft tells you that extensions can be longer than three characters, too. But again, you're asking for trouble with your old programs, which can't tell a .Txt extension from a .Txty extension. Someday, perhaps, developers will use long extensions to identify file types more accurately, but until then, it's best to steer clear of assigning long extensions yourself.

Also keep in mind that if you like working from the command prompt, you'll go nuts using long file names. You have to remember to enclose them in quotes. And if you enter paths that use long file names in dialog boxes, you'll need the quotes, too. Really! See "Associating Files with Several Programs" later in this chapter for an example.

The Workarounds

- Keep file names to 20 characters or under.

- If you use a lot of "legacy" programs that don't support long file names, keep naming files with the 8.3 convention until most of your programs are updated for Windows 95.

- If you share files with coworkers, especially with coworkers who aren't using Windows 95, get together and decide how you're going to name your files. If you're going to use long file names in Windows 95, you'll no doubt want to stick to unique 6.3 names because Windows 95 truncates after the first six characters. Just when you thought you were free to be creative!

- Disable support for long file names for your older programs. To disable long file names for programs that use the 8.3 convention, go to the Control Panels, double-click the System icon, click the Performance tab, click File System, click Troubleshooting, and finally check the box that disables long file name preservation for old programs. See "I'm on a mixed network, and those long file names are causing all kinds of trouble" in Chapter 8 if you're on a network.

- If you wind up with "orphan" long file names (because you've assigned another shorter name to the file in an application that doesn't support long file names), run ScanDisk with the /autofix switch. It can locate long file names that are no longer associated with files.

Pitfall #2: File Types Ain't What They Used to Be

If you've used Windows 3.1 and DOS before, you have every reason to expect that file types are just like they were before—that the extension .Txt identifies a text file, .Exe an executable program, .Doc a Word document, and so forth. Well, that's true. Sort of. When you try to sort files by type in an Explorer window, you'll discover that file types aren't what they used to be. If you click on Type, your files won't get sorted by extension, but instead will be sorted alphabetically by "registered file type," which includes things like Application, Microsoft Word Document, and DOS file. (Choose Options from the View menu and click the File Types tab to see a list of registered file types; Figure 3-3.) It can really get confusing if you're expecting to see all your .Com files first, followed by .Exe files, followed by .Txt files, and so forth. Instead, your files are sorted by their new file types (Figures 3-4 and 3-5).

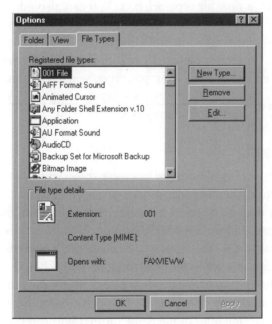

Figure 3-3. Registered file types

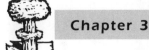

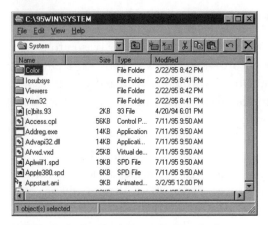

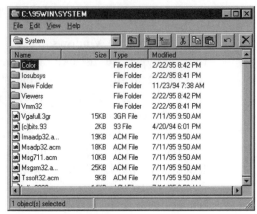

Figure 3-4 .An Explorer window before sorting

Figure 3-5. The same window after sorting

You do have some control, though. You can add new types to this list, and you can customize how a new file type behaves. You can also add a second (or third) association to a file type, which is useful, say, if you want to be able to open a bitmap (.Bmp) in Paintbrush sometimes and in Photoshop other times (I'll tell you how in a minute). In fact, sometimes you'll have to tell Windows 95 which program uses which extension—for example, when you're running an older "legacy" program whose extension Windows 95 doesn't recognize. And just when you thought you could forget about extensions!

Display Extensions!

Here's another pitfall: Windows 95 doesn't show you extensions for file types that it knows about (the "registered" ones). This can cause two different problems. The first is that it's hard to tell one type of file from another, because all you see is the name (Figure 3-6). Well, actually Windows uses different types of icons to distinguish the file types. Of course the iconography can itself be cryptic. If you want to see extensions (Figure 3-7), choose Options from My Computer's or the Explorer's View menu, click the View tab, and uncheck the Hide MS-DOS extensions box (Figure 3-8). It's a good idea to display extensions so you can tell one kind of file from another without going blind squinting at the tiny icons.

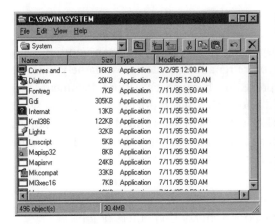

Figure 3-6. The default view is not to display extensions.

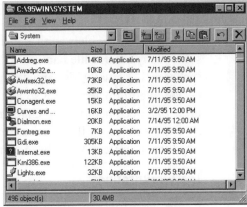

Figure 3-7. Displaying extensions

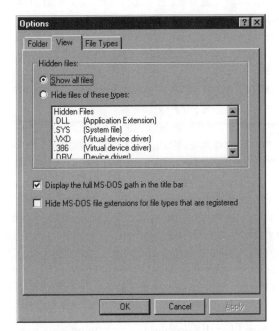

Figure 3-8. Using this dialog box to display extensions

Bizarre Extensions

The second problem with not displaying extensions is you can wind up with some really bizarre file names. Say you're renaming a file whose name you think is chapter1. Actually it's named chapter1.doc, because it's a Word document. You decide to add the extension so you'll know it's a Word document, and you wind up with a document named chapter1.doc.doc. Windows added your extension as an extra extension. If the document's really named chapter1.doc and you name it .edt to indicate that it's been edited, it winds up as chapter1.edit.doc.

The Workarounds

- Display extensions. Choose Options from My Computer's or the Explorer's View menu, click the View tab, and uncheck the Hide MS-DOS extensions box.

- If you don't like to see extensions on the screen, use this method of creating new files at the desktop: Right-click and choose New; then select the file type you want to create. That way, Windows 95 assigns the correct extension behind the scenes. Or don't create any files at the desktop, but always create files within programs; these programs will usually assign the correct extension when you save the file. (Some programs, like AOL and WordPerfect 5.1, don't always assign extensions to files, though.)

- Force the exact file name you want when renaming files by entering the file name in quotes ("chapter1.doc"), and Windows 95 won't try to append the extension you enter to the one that already exists.

- Assign new icons when Windows is using a generic icon for several different file types if you don't want to display extensions. Choose Options from the View menu in the Explorer/My Computer, click the File Types Tab, click the file type you want to change, and choose Edit. You'll see another dialog box (Figure 3-9). Click Change icon and pick a different icon for that file type (Figure 3-10). Click Browse and go hunting for more icons—look in Shell32.dll, Pifmgr.dll (neat icons; see Figure 3-11), Moricons.dll, Backup, Drvspace, and Defrag.

For a workaround for the problem of not being able to sort files by extension, use the Find utility. See "No Wildcards any More?" in Chapter 6.

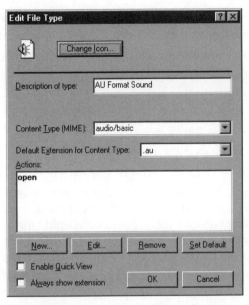

Figure 3-9. Changing a file type's icon

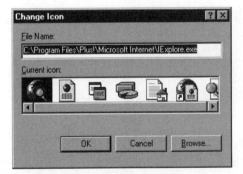

Figure 3-10. Picking a new icon

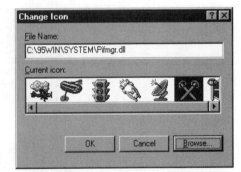

Figure 3-11. Picking a new icon from
the hidden Pifmgr.dll

Associating Files with Several Programs

Here's how to add another association to a file type (registering another extension, or associating a file with more than one program—whatever you want to call it). There's a little quirk, as usual, involved in getting Windows to recognize long file names when you do this. Say that you want to open text documents in NotePad (the default) as well as in WordPad when you right-click on them.

1. Open a folder window in the Explorer or My Computer.

2. Choose Options from the View menu.

3. Click the View tab and check "Show all files." Uncheck "Hide extensions of MS-DOS file types that are registered."

4. Click the File Types Tab.

5. Choose the file type, such as Text Document.

6. Click Edit and New (under Actions) (Figure 3-12).

7. Enter a meaningful name, such as **Open with WordPad**. If you want to be able to use the keyboard for this command put an ampersand (&) before the character you want to be able to type, such as **Open with &WordPad**, so the w is underlined on the shortcut menu on the screen (Figure 3-13).

8. Click Browse and locate the program you want to use for this action. Double-click on it. (By the way, WordPad is really over in "C:\Windows\Accessories\Wordpad.exe". (Note the quotation marks, because this path uses long file names.)

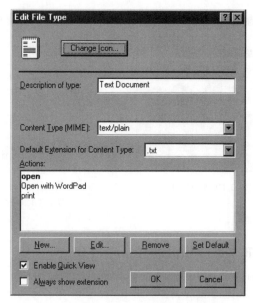

Figure 3-12. Creating a new association, part 1

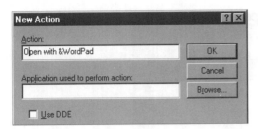

Figure 3-13. Creating a new association, part 2

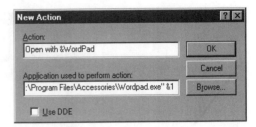

Figure 3-14. Creating a new association, part 3

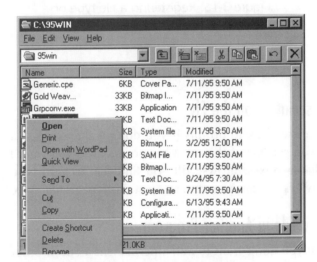

Figure 3-15. The new pop-up menu

9. Now here's the quirk. If you want to be able to use long file names with this new association, add "%1" to the end of that line (Figure 3-14).

Now close everything up and try right-clicking on a file of that type, and you'll see the new action on the menu (Figure 3-15).

Now when you double-click on the file in Explorer or My Computer, the menu will pop up and you can choose which program to use to open the file.

Figure 3-16. Registering a file type on the fly

Adding an Association on the Fly

There is an easier way to do this if you don't want to create a custom command. When you get one of those "What program do you want to use to open this with?" dialog boxes, browse till you find the program you want to use. Check the "Always use this program to open this type of file" box (Figure 3-16).

Just Opening a File in Another Program

Of course, if you don't want to add a permanent association but just want to open a file in another program on the fly, there's a much easier way. Right-Shift click on a file's name in an Explorer or My Computer window; then choose Open With (the file needs to have an extension for this to work). Now you can specify the program you want to use to open the file.

Pitfall #3: When Deleting Is—and When It Isn't

No doubt you've already been driven crazy by the dialog boxes that ask (paraphrasing) "Are you really, really sure you want to delete this?" They're there for your protection. As if it's not enough that deleted files go to the Recycle Bin and aren't really deleted anyway!

Direct to the Recycle Bin!

There are a couple of things you can do to speed up deleting files. The first is to press (SHIFT) when you press (DEL). That sends the files you've selected directly to the Recycle Bin with no irritating confirmations. After all, they stay on your hard disk until you empty the Recycle Bin, which you're not likely to do by mistake by pressing the wrong keys.

Suppressing Confirmations

The second is to suppress the confirmation dialog boxes "permanently" (until you turn them back on again). To do this, right-click on the Recycle Bin, choose Properties, and uncheck the "Display delete confirmation" dialog box (Figure 3-17) on the Global tab. Your files will still go to the Recycle Bin, but you won't be asked about it.

Sending to the Recycle Bin

Another cool way to sneak past the prompts is to put a shortcut to the Recycle Bin in your Send To folder; then you can right-click on icons and Send them To the Recycle Bin without that pesky "Do you want to..." prompt.

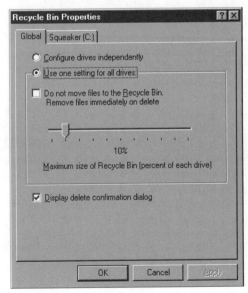

Figure 3-17. Turning off the delete confirmation dialog boxes

Bypassing the Recycle Bin

The fourth way, which *doesn't* get rid of the delete confirmation dialog box but *does* really delete the files, is to set up Windows 95 so you don't use the Recycle Bin at all. Once you delete files, they're gone. To do this, right-click on the Recycle Bin and choose Properties. Check Do Not Move Files to the Recycle Bin and click OK. (But note that the "Display delete confirmation" dialog is dimmed, which means you'll now be asked to confirm each deletion.) From now on, all the files you delete will be gone... Really gone. Because DOS 7, which is the DOS that comes with Windows 95, doesn't come with an Undelete command. If you used to rely on Undelete to restore files you deleted by mistake, forget it. If you had the foresight to move DOS into a different directory before you installed Windows 95, or if you installed Windows 95 for a dual boot (see Chapter 1), you can get deleted files back with the DOS command Undelet! (which is what Undelete has been renamed—and yes, you can rename it back to Undelete). You'll need to use the /DOS switch with Undelet! (Figure 3-18). Get help on it by entering **help undelet!** at the DOS prompt. If Undelet! can't be located, you'll need a third-party utility program like Norton Utilities to restore files after you've emptied the Recycle Bin or otherwise deleted them.

```
C:\coll>undelet! /dos

UNDELETE - A delete protection facility
Copyright (C) 1987-1993 Central Point Software, Inc.
All rights reserved.

Directory: C:\COLL
File Specifications: *.*

    Delete Sentry control file not found.

    Deletion-tracking file contains      0 deleted files.
    Of those,      0 files have all clusters available,
                   0 files have some clusters available,
                   0 files have no clusters available.

    MS-DOS directory contains     17 deleted files.
    Of those,      9 files may be recovered.

Using the MS-DOS directory method.

    ** ?IGURE1  PCX      7491 12-05-94 11:02a  ...A
Starting cluster is unavailable. This file cannot be recovered
with the UNDELETE command.  Press any key to continue.
```

Figure 3-18. Running Undelet!

The Workarounds

📌 To selectively restore files that have been sent to the Recycle Bin, open the Recycle Bin by double-clicking on it. Then select the files you want to undelete and choose Restore from the File menu.

📌 To be able to use DOS's Undelete utility, install Windows 95 for a dual boot or uncompress Undelete.Ex_ from your old (pre-DOS 7) installation disks. See Chapter 6 for how to uncompress these compressed files using the Expand command.

📌 Get a third-party undelete utility like Norton.

That's Not All You Need to Know, Either

Here are some more things you need to know about deleting and really deleting that you probably wouldn't have guessed because they aren't what you expect:

📌 What you delete from floppies doesn't go to the Recycle Bin. Those deleted files are goners if you don't have access to an Undelete utility, either a third-party utility or DOS's old one.

📌 What you Cut doesn't go to the Recycle Bin, either, only what you Delete. To get something you Cut back, press (CTRL)+(V). Of course you have to do this before you cut something else or end your Windows session.

📌 If you send something to the Recycle Bin and immediately realize you want it back, choose Undo Delete from the Edit menu in a My Computer or Explorer window.

📌 (CTRL)+(Z), Undo, doesn't work for file deletions. To get a deleted file back, use Undo Delete as described above or open the Recycle Bin and restore the file (as described above, too).

📌 Your deleted files are stored in a folder named Recycled at the root level of your folder system. It's normally hidden, but if you choose "Show all files" on the View tab after picking Options from the Explorer's or My Computer's View menu, you'll be able to see it. (You may need to press (F5) to refresh the screen.) You can get "deleted" files back from there, too, using normal copy operations.

Pitfall #4:"Type the name of a program, folder, or document, and Windows will open it for you."

It will sell you oceanfront property in Kansas, too. Yes, if you choose Run from the Start menu, you'll see this message, but don't believe it—at least, not all the time. If what you want to run is in the Windows 95 folder or specified in the PATH statement in your Autoexec.Bat, this message holds true: It will run it. (If you've Run it before, it will run it, too, because Run remembers all the things you Ran.) But if what you want to run is somewhere else, you'll get the message "Cannot find file (or one of its components). Check to ensure the path and file-name are correct and that all required libraries are available." Does this sound like DOS? It does to me, a very verbose DOS. And to get around it, you have to use a DOS-style path name, specifying exactly where the file is (folders within folders, separated by backlashes, just like always, as in c:\wp\wp51\wpdocs\book\chap3).

The Workaround

To get around this, specify a DOS-style path name or click the Browse button and locate what you want to open. You won't see all your files, just the programs. Click the down arrow next to Files and choose All Files. *Now* you can see your documents and folders, too.

Pitfall #5: There's No Such Thing as Desktop Security

If you work where others can get at your computer, you should be concerned about Windows 95's lack of desktop security. Sure, if you've chosen "Users Can Customize Their Preferences and Desktop Settings" in the Password control panel, you'll be asked for a name and password when you start Windows 95. But *all you have to do is press* (ESC) to close that dialog box, and you're in. So is anybody else. And Windows 95 gives access to all your drives, your network drives, the documents you've deleted but haven't yet emptied from the Recycle Bin, and the last 15 items you've worked with (by choosing Documents from the Start menu).

The password itself can be deleted just by deleting the .PWL file stored in your Windows folder, or in your user profile folder; then the machine won't even ask for it again. (This is a clever little file that doesn't show up in Windows; you have to go to DOS to delete it. It holds all your passwords, including those for the Microsoft Network.) And if you think using a puny screen saver that requires a password gives you some protection, guess again. Anyone who wants to get in your computer can, just by turning it off and on again.

There's not a lot you can do about this, short of buying a third-party program that provides more security, such as a BIOS access password program (though I haven't heard of one yet, but that doesn't mean one isn't available by now), or being part of a network that uses NetWare or a Windows NT Server, both of which provide a bit more security (see Chapter 8 for a discussion of some network security measures). Until you find a solution, try these workarounds. Some of them will protect you from casual access. Some of them are pretty sneaky.

The Workarounds

🖈 Set the Recycle Bin up to always "really delete".

🖈 Clear your Documents menu, either temporarily or permanently, so at least any spies won't know what you've been working on recently.

🖈 Use the Policy Editor to restrict the user's access to parts of your system.

Really Deleting

To set the Recycle Bin up to always "really delete":

1. Right-click on the Recycle Bin and choose Properties.
2. Check Do Not Move Files to the Recycle Bin and click OK.

Clearing the Documents Menu

To clear the Documents menu temporarily:

1. Right-click on an empty portion of the taskbar.
2. Select Properties.
3. Click the Start Menu Programs tab.
4. Click Clear to reset the menu.

To disable the Documents menu permanently:

1. Set the Recycle Bin up to always "really delete", following the instructions above.
2. Right-click on the Recycle Bin and choose Properties.
3. Click the Global Tab and choose "Use one setting for all drives".
4. Turn on the option labeled "Do not move files to the Recycle Bin" and click OK.
5. Open the Registry Editor (Regedit.exe) by entering **regedit** in the Run box.

111

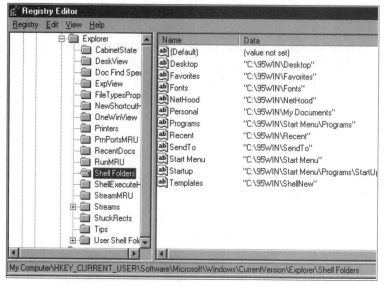

Figure 3-19. Locating the Recent folder

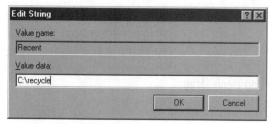

Figure 3-20. Disabling the Recent folder

6. Double-click to open HKEY_CURRENT_USER\ SOFTWARE\ Microsoft\ Windows\ CurrentVersion\ Explorer\ Shell Folders.

7. On the right side of the window (Figure 3-19), look for Recent. (If it's not there, select New from the Edit menu, select String Value, and name the new item Recent.)

8. Double-click on Recent, and under Value Data, enter **c:\recycle** (Figure 3-20).

9. Click OK and close the Registry Editor.

10. Click on the desktop and press (F5) to refresh the screen.

Now whatever shortcuts are sent to the Recent folder (that's what gets listed on the Documents menu) are sent to the Recycle Bin and really deleted.

112

Restricting Access

For even more security, you can use the System Policy Editor to restrict access to parts of the system. First, you'll need to install the Policy Editor (the instructions are at the beginning of this chapter). It's on the CD in the \Admin\Apptools\Poledit folder. You'll need an administrator account to do this if you're on a network.

1. Log on as the user you want to restrict. To restrict the default user (the guy who wanders into your office), press (ESC) at the log-in dialog box.

2. Double-click on the System Policy Editor in your Programs\Accessories\System Tools folder on the Start menu or enter **poledit** in the Run box.

3. Choose Open registry from its File menu.

4. Double-click on the Local User icon (Figure 3-21).

5. Double-click on Control Panel and then double-click on Display, Network, and Passwords.

You'll see the control panel policies you can set:

- To assign a screen saver password that a random user can't turn off easily, click Restrict Display Control Panel; then either turn off the entire utility or turn off access to the screen saver.

- If you're on a network, you can restrict the Network Control Panel's Access page to prevent unauthorized access to the machine.

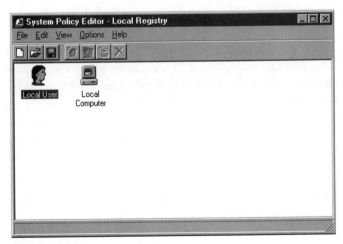

Figure 3-21. The Local User icon

🖈 Check Restrict Passwords Control Panel so that no one will have access for changing passwords.

For even more protection, click System (the other one, not the one under Control Panel) and Restrictions and check any or all of these boxes:

🖈 Disable Registry editing tools

🖈 Only run allowed Windows applications

🖈 Disable MS-DOS prompt

🖈 Disable single-mode MS-DOS applications

With all of them checked, the user can't edit the Registry or use the DOS prompt. By checking "Only run allowed Windows applications," you can specify exactly which programs the user can access (parents take note here). You'll probably want to let the user have shutdown access, unless you want the computer running all the time.

Finally, open the Notepad and edit Msdos.sys to add the line **BootGUI=1 B** so that the user always boots into Windows and can't jump-start into DOS. If the user can't get to the DOS prompt, she can't delete the .PWL file.

Pretty clever? Nah. All a user who wants access to your system needs to do is boot off a floppy and then erase the .PWL file. There ain't no such thing as desktop security with Windows 95. But at least you'll discourage casual intruders.

Keeping the Kids out of the Files

We covered this a bit in the preceding discussion, but just to be explicit, I'll be explicit. You can keep your kids, your officemates, and most other folks (except the ones who know the secret mentioned above) from using your programs. In fact, you can specify just which programs they do have access to. You'll need to set the machine up for multiple users (use the Passwords icon in the Control Panel folder); then use the System Policy Editor (see above).

Log on as the user you're restricting access for—say, your eight-year-old. When you enter a new user name and password, you'll be asked to confirm the password, and behind the scenes Windows creates a profile folder for the new user.

Now fire up the Policy Editor:

1. Enter **poledit** in the Start menu's Run box and press (ENTER).

2. Choose New File from the File menu.

3. Choose Add User from the Edit menu and enter the name of the new user.

4. Double-click on the new user's icon.

5. Double-click System and Restrictions; then click "Only run allowed Windows applications."

6. Finally, click Show and Add to add allowed applications. Then pick the applications you want that user to have access to.

7. Click OK three times, close the Policy Editor, and click Yes to save changes to the Registry.

Now when this user logs on and tries to use a program that you haven't specified, he or she will get a "This operation has been cancelled..." message when the nonlisted program tries to start.

For even more measures of security, you can restrict access to the Run and Find commands and to other drives. Click the Shell icon, then the Restrictions icon, and check what you want to restrict:

- Remove 'Run' command
- Remove folders from 'Settings' on Start Menu
- Remove Taskbar from 'Settings' on Start Menu
- Remove 'Find' Command
- Hide drives in 'My Computer'
- Hide Network Neighborhood
- No 'Entire Network' in Network Neighborhood
- No workgroup contents in Network Neighborhood
- Hide all items on Desktop
- Disable Shut Down Command
- Don't save settings at exit

By checking the "Hide all items on Desktop" box, you can prevent access to the local drive without the password, but a user with a startup floppy can still jump-start his or her way around your security.

I Forgot My Password!

This can drive you crazy unless you know the workaround. This is it: Delete the .PWL file (see the above discussion); then create a new password.

If you're on a network or maintaining profiles for several users, you can use the Password List Editor (Pwledit.exe) to delete old passwords. You can't see what the passwords actually are, but you can delete them.

This editor's in the Admin\Apptools\Pwledit folder on the CD-ROM. A couple of warnings: Make a backup of a .PWL file before you edit it, just in case anything goes wrong. You'll need to use the Password List Editor at the user's machine, because the user needs to be logged in.

And Next...

Now that we've had seen the biggest Windows 95 pitfalls, the next chapter looks at a lot of programs that are incompatible with Windows 95 and discusses how to work around those incompatibilities.

Chapter 4

Software Purgatory

It Won't Work!

Software Purgatory
It Won't Work!

*"I think there is a world market
for maybe five computers."*

Thomas Watson, chairman of IBM, 1943

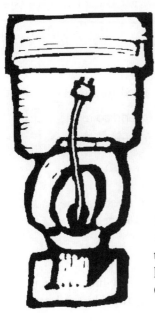

There's a bunch of stuff that won't work with Windows 95 that worked just fine in Windows 3.1. "Won't work" ranges from minor problems to completely no-go situations. Sometimes you may simply hear annoying static when you're playing a game; other times you may get the dread GPF (General Protection Fault) message, which means your program has quit on you. Fonts may disappear from font lists. Your system may stall when you try to run a program that used to run just fine under Windows 3.1. Some programs like CorelDRAW 3.0, 4.0, and Lotus Notes won't be able to print because they're stymied by Windows 95's new long printer names. Some installation programs, like ClarisWorks 1.0, can hang up. Other programs need files that Windows 3.1 provided—for example, Managing Your Money 2.0a uses the Calendar, Cardfile, and Clock programs that shipped with Windows 3.1, and they aren't there any more. What fun.

As you might expect, software manufacturers are working furiously to upgrade their products to Windows 95 capabilities, but they're not all there yet. In this chapter, you can look up (alphabetically by manufacturer) programs that won't work, as of press time, and any possible workarounds. But be aware the software manufacturer may have provided new patches or upgrades by the time you read this. Contact the software manufacturer for the most up-to-date information. You can visit their Web sites or call technical support. See Chapter 10, "As a Last Resort..."

What won't work? As a general rule, any Windows 3.1 third-party utilities that handle backup and disk compression won't work with Windows 95. Any virus checkers, alternate shells or desktops (such as Norton Desktop, PC Tools Desktop, Tabworks, Dashboard, and Direct Access Desktop 1.0), or uninstall utilities you have will need to be upgraded. Any disk repair utilities you use should definitely be upgraded, especially if you're using long file names. If you're on a network (see Chapter 8), be aware that DOS-based LANs are probably not going to work, either.

And just in case you run into problems not covered in this chapter, I've provided a section of general procedures you can use to get out of trouble (see "Getting out of Trouble").

The Tools You'll Need

To perform the workarounds in this chapter, you'll need to know:

- How to edit AUTOEXEC.BAT, CONFIG.SYS, Win.ini, and so forth
- How to find new drivers (see Chapter 10 for a list of manufacturer contacts)
- How to install new drivers
- How to run in DOS Mode (this is rather tedious, so I put it at the end of the chapter, with the game problems where you'll need it most)

Editing AUTOEXEC.BAT, CONFIG.SYS, WIN.INI, et al.

You can edit AUTOEXEC.BAT, CONFIG.SYS, and .INI files by using the System Editor (enter **sysedit** in the Run box), by using the Notepad to open c:\AUTOEXEC.BAT or c:\CONFIG.SYS or specify the path to the .ini file), or at the DOS command line (enter **edit c:\AUTOEXEC.BAT c:\CONFIG.SYS** or **edit c:\windows\win.ini,** and so forth). (Note that Windows 95's edit command lets you open more than one file at a time.) Any lines in these files that you begin with a REM and a space will be ignored when your computer starts up. Sysedit (Figure 4-1) is very useful, because it opens all your configuration files at once. No matter which editor you choose, always remember to save the file before you exit.

A word of caution: Watch out if you install older versions of "new" applications...this one can make you crazy.

When you install older DOS or Windows 3.1 programs after installing Windows 95, they may go into your AUTOEXEC.BAT file and add lines you don't want there. For example, some older database programs insist on putting Share.exe in your AUTOEXEC.BAT. And a lot of programs want to put Smartdrv.exe there. This can waste memory because Windows 95 has its own support for disk caching and file sharing. Check your AUTOEXEC.BAT after you install anything new (that is, new to you but old to Windows 95).

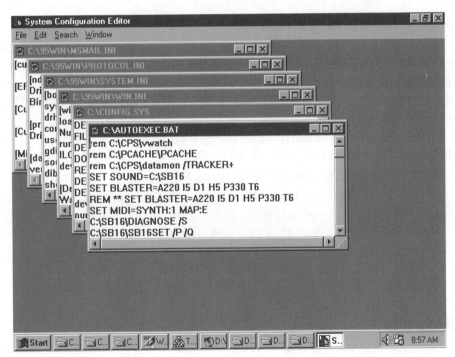

Figure 4-1. Using sysedit

Locating New Drivers

If you installed Windows 95 from CD-ROM, you can find new drivers in the Drivers directory on the CD. If you don't have the Windows 95 CD-ROM, you can get the drivers from Microsoft Product Support Services or via the Windows Drivers Library (WDL) on various on-line services, such as:

The Microsoft Network	\Categories\Computers and Software\Software\Microsoft\Windows 95
Internet File Server	ftp://ftp.microsoft.com/Products/Windows/Windows 95
World Wide Web	http://www.microsoft.com/Windows
Gopher	gopher://gopher.microsoft.com
FTP	ftp://ftp.microsoft.com
CompuServe	GO MSL
Genie	Go to Microsoft Roundtable
Microsoft Download Service (MSDL)	In the United States and Canada, call 206-936-6735

Installing and Updating Drivers

Use the Add New Hardware wizard in the Control Panel folder to install new drivers. Those that you download may be compressed; they'll have an extension of .sea or .zip. If they have an .sea extension, just double-click on them to expand them. If they're .zip files, use a utility like PKUNZIP or WINZIP to extract them.

If you're upgrading to a driver that comes with Windows 95, one that's in the Hardware Compatibility List on the CD-ROM:

1. Right-click on My Computer and choose Properties.
2. Click the Device Manager tab, and click the device type. Double-click on the device you're upgrading (Figure 4-2).
3. Click the Driver tab and the Change Driver button (Figure 4-3).
4. Click Have Disk.
5. Enter the location of the driver file and follow the instructions on the screen.

Unruly DLLs

One other problem you may encounter stems from the fact that many software manufacturers' Install programs copy their .DLL files into your Windows\System

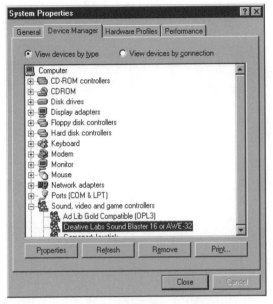

Figure 4-2. Upgrading via the Device Manager

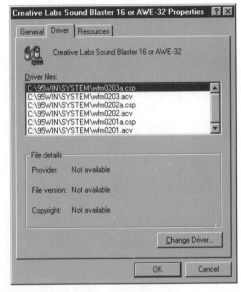

Figure 4-3. Changing a driver

folder without checking to see if the existing .DLL is newer than the one being installed. This can overwrite the newer DLLs supplied with Windows 95. If you suspect this has happened, you can expand the .DLL files from the Windows 95 CD-ROM and replace the ones that may have been overwritten.

To get a list of the .DLLs on the CD, put it in drive D (or whichever drive your CD-ROM is) and enter the following at the DOS prompt:

extract /d /a d:\win95\win05_02.cab *file*.dll.

Then use the Extract command to expand the compressed .DLL you want.

To see which .DLLs and other files a program requires, right-click on its icon (the original) and choose QuickView. You'll get an interesting screen of information about the program (Figures 4-4 and 4-5). The files this program uses will be listed under Imported-Name. Sometimes you can use this information to see whether a required file or .DLL is missing from your computer, locate it, and get your program running again. Remember, QuickView isn't automatically installed. If you don't have it, look back at Chapter 1 to see how to install it.

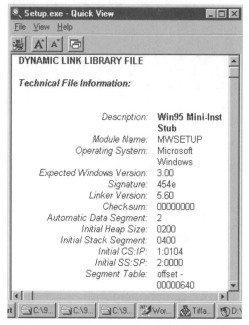

Figure 4-4. QuickViewing an executable file

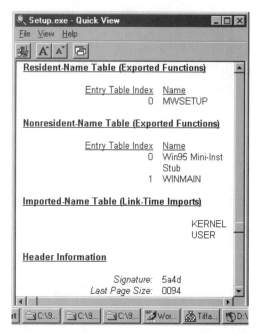

Figure 4-5. Checking to see which files a program requires

Windows 95 keeps a copy of the system files it requires in a folder in the Windows directory named Sysbckup. If you're hunting for a lost .DLL, look there.

If All Else Fails, Try Mkcompat

Windows 95 has a program called Mkcompat.exe you can use to make Win 3.x programs behave more compatibly under Windows 95. This program is in your Windows\System folder. Select Choose Program from the file menu and open the older program you're having trouble running (Figure 4-6). Try new configurations. This will be a trial-and-error process, so take notes on what you're doing. Choose Advanced Options from the File menu for many, many more settings (Figure 4-7).

Getting out of Trouble

The best way, of course, to get out of trouble, is to never get in it in the first place. But getting in trouble is inevitable. Sometimes you may even have to reinstall Windows 95 from scratch to make things work again, because problems

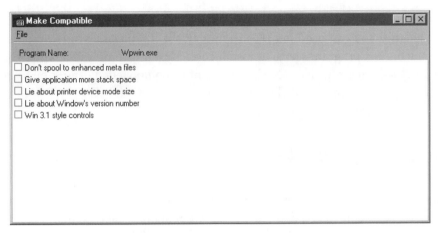

Figure 4-6. Running Mkcompat

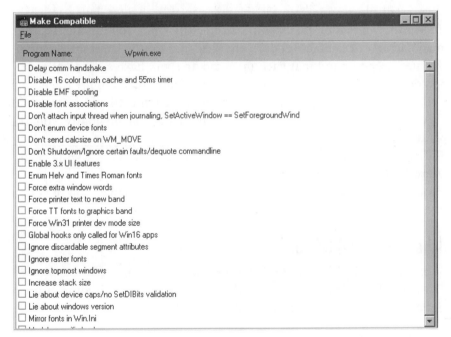

Figure 4-7. Advanced options

work both ways; the programs you run may cause problems with your operating system, and vice versa. One thing you can do, *while you've got Windows 95 running right*, is copy all your .INI files (and AUTOEXEC.BAT and

CONFIG.SYS) to a separate folder and store them there in case something goes wrong later. You can use Find (F3) to find all the .Ini files on your computer.

Sometimes a program seems to install correctly, but Windows 95 won't run it. You may see a message like "XXX (or one of its components) cannot be found." If this happens, check the PATH statement in your AUTOEXEC.BAT and make sure your program's directory is in the path.

Specific Software Problems

Following are known glitches, workarounds, and words of advice for most major business productivity applications: word processing, spreadsheets, graphics, print enhancers, databases, programming languages, e-mail programs, disk utilities, and the like. Games, too. (See Chapter 8 for known problems with networking software.)

I've listed phone numbers for upgrades in this chapter, but a much better source is the big vendor database in Chapter 10, which you can use to either call a manufacturer or contact vendors' Internet sites for the latest information and software. Keep in mind that each manufacturer will have a different policy for upgrades. Some may be free; others may cost significantly. You're the best judge of whether you need a program's most up-to-the-minute bells and whistles. If you can't get it to run at all, and you need it, then obviously you should upgrade. But maybe you can live with a few crashes rather than replacing a $300 program. You be the judge; it's your pocketbook. Check with the manufacturer to see what their policies (and prices) are.

Look up the program you're having trouble with by name. You're not meant to *read* all this stuff!

Adobe Illustrator 4.0/4.03

Can cause GPFs (General Protection Faults).

Solution: Use Windows 95's standard VGA drivers until you can upgrade. Adobe Systems Customer Service: 800-833-6687.

Adobe Persuasion 3.0

You can't install this program unless you have a CONFIG.SYS file. If you're installing it onto a new Windows 95-only machine, you may not have this file.

Workaround: Create a CONFIG.SYS file.

1. Open Notepad and create a file containing only this line
    rem config.sys
2. Save the file as C:\config.sys.

You can then install Adobe Persuasion.

Adobe Photoshop 3.01

Changing settings in dialog boxes often causes problems.
Solution: Upgrade. Adobe Systems Customer Service: 800-833-6687.

Adobe Photoshop Limited Edition

Windows Setup doesn't create a program group for Photoshop.
Solution: Run Photoshop from an Explorer window by double-clicking on Photoshp.exe.

Adobe Premiere 4.0

Some dialog boxes (Motion Settings, Preset) don't appear.
Solution: Upgrade. Adobe Systems Customer Service: 800-833-6687.

Alacrity E-Quip, Equip+

You may not be able to fax from this program.
Solution: Upgrade. Alacrity: fax 908-813-2490, BBS 908-813-2495.

Ami Pro v3.01

The tutorial doesn't run correctly under Windows 95.
Solution: Set the taskbar to Auto Hide:

1. Choose Settings from the Start menu.
2. Choose Taskbar and check the Auto Hide option.

AST Works

You may have problems using voice mail in this program.
Solution: Get new drivers from the Windows Driver Library (see the beginning of this chapter) or from AST at 800-727-1278.

Astound 2.x

You may have problems printing from this program.

Solution: Right-click on the printer's icon and choose Properties. Then turn off EMS spooling.

Asymetrix Multimedia Toolbox

You may have problems running the training demo.

Solution: Contact the manufacturer for an upgrade. Asymetrix: 206-451-1173.

ATM Fonts

In general, ATM fonts won't appear on the font list when printer drivers for the following fax programs are selected: WinFax (all versions), FaxWorks, and older Quick Link 2 versions. Windows 95 substitutes the nearest matching TrueType font.

Solution: Live with the TrueType font.

AT&T Mail Access PLUS

If you have a version earlier than version 2.7, you'll need an upgrade. AT&T: 800-242-6005; ask for Department 95.

AT&T Mail versions 2.5 and earlier will install a TSR that doesn't allow disk utilities to repair disks.

Solution: Contact AT&T to get the latest release.

Borland Pascal Pro 7.0

You may get the message "Cannot run a unit or DLL" when you're trying to run Turbo debugger.

Solution: Double-check the IDE and Debugger configurations to make sure all the paths are correct and present.

Borland C++ 4.0, 4.02

There are various problems with these versions. OLE may not work correctly. The system may stall if you view READMEs during setup. Some function keys may not work. If you try to run this program with only 4 Mb of RAM, it will be very slow.

Solution: Upgrade to version 4.5. Borland: 800-524-8420.

CA-CricketGraph 1.3.1

You need to upgrade. Computer Associates: 800-225-5224.

Central Point Anti-Virus 1.0-1.5

Will not run under Windows 95.
Solution: Upgrade. Symantec: 800-441-7234.

Central Point Backup

Some features will not work.
Solution: Upgrade. Symantec: 800-441-7234.

Central Point PC Tools 6.0-7.1

Some features will not work.
Solution: Upgrade. Symantec: 800-441-7234.

ClarisWorks for Windows 3.0 v1

Setup won't run from disk 1.
Solution: Run the Setupcw program on Disk 2.

Connectsoft Email Connection v. 2.03

Has difficulty accessing CompuServe.
Solution: Upgrade. Contact Connectsoft at 206-827-6467.

CorelDRAW 3.0, 4.0

Cannot handle long printer names. Version 3.0 is incompatible with some large hard drives (1 Gb and larger). Version 4.0 drops rotated ATM fonts when exporting graphics as bitmaps.

Solution: Use a network printer redirected to an LPT port if possible.

Network paths (also known as UNC names) in Windows 95 are often longer than their Windows 3.1 equivalent and can include spaces, so sometimes the network can't find a printer. They're in the format *server**share*. See your system administrator about changing the path so that it's shorter and doesn't contain spaces. Or assign a local name to the network resource, such as assigning one of your LPT ports to a network printer. Or assign a drive letter to a remote disk drive. (This was the way Windows 3.1 worked, and you can still do it in Windows 95.)

Corel Photo Paint

Can't handle long printer names. See above.

Corel Ventura 4.2

Slow while reading system fonts. Sometimes scrolls incorrectly.
Solution: Upgrade to version 5.00E2 or later. Corel: 800-836-7274.

DaVinci Email 2.02c, 2.50a, 3.0

To avoid problems with network printers, make sure the network path is associated with a printer port. In version 3.0, you can't add user licenses under Windows 95.
Solution: Upgrade to version 3.1.

Delrina FormFlow Versions 1.0, 1.1

GPFs occur when trying to read messages.
Solution: Upgrade. Contact Delrina at 800-268-6082.

Delrina PerFORM Pro 1.0

Problems occur when trying to print to a network printer.
Solution: Make sure the network path is associated with a printer port.

DragonDictate for Windows

Upgrade: Dragon Systems, 800-825-5897 or 617-965-5200.

Faxworks v3.0

Long printer names may prevent the Call Center from appearing.
Solution: Shorten the printer name or, if you're printing to a network printer, capture the printer port.

FaxWorks Version 3.00f.041

The Advanced AGC option (audio gain control) doesn't work with Windows 95. If you use it, you'll create a .tmp file in your \Temp directory that will fill your disk and ultimately lock up your system.

Solution: Contact Faxworks, 800-345-4329.

File Director

Macros and Find File operations may not work correctly. You may have mouse problems when running in DOS mode.

Solution: Run in full-screen mode. See the section "Running in DOS Mode" later in this chapter for help.

Finesse

The Windows 3.1 version won't display taskbar buttons correctly in Windows 95.

Solution: To switch between open programs, press (ALT)+(TAB). Contact Toshiba at 800-999-4273 for an upgrade.

FutureSoft DynaCom Elite v. 3.44, 3.501

Stalls during the QuickStart.

Solution: Use the System font for menus. Right-click on the desktop, choose Properties, click the Appearance tab. Under Item, choose Menu; under Font, choose System.

GoldDisk Astound v2.0

Has problems with OLE objects.

Solution: Contact GoldDisk at 905-602-0395 for the v.2.01 patch.

HP NewWave Desktop 4.1

The Shell may not be fully functional under Windows 95.

Solution: Contact HP at 800-752-0900.

Inset HiJaak Graphic Suite

You may have problems running Smuggler.exe with Windows 95 because it uses a lot of system resources.

Solution: Use this screen capture utility for only short periods of time. If you have to run Smuggler for a long time, restart your computer from time to time. Upgrade. Contact Inset Systems, Inc. at 800-DR-INSET; outside the United States call 203-740-2400.

Inset HiJaak Pro 2.0

Shows an error message when it can't find SmartDrive.
Solution: Choose Yes, and Setup continues normally.

Intersolv PCVS Version Manager v 5.2.00

To avoid errors on startup, change your user ID using the license configuration utility.

Landmark DataSafe 2.0

Remove this version before installing Windows 95, or your system may become unstable.
Solution: Upgrade. Contact Landmark Research International at 800-683-0854.

Landmark WinProbe 3.0.0

Not compatible with Windows 95. RAM test locks your system.
Solution: Upgrade. Contact Landmark Research International at 800-683-0854.

Lotus Ami Pro 3.01

The tutorial doesn't run correctly.
Solution: Set your taskbar to Auto Hide.

Lotus Notes

You need to map a drive letter to install Lotus Notes from a network computer.

1. Choose Programs from the Start menu.
2. Choose Windows Explorer.
3. Choose Map Network Drive from the Tools menu.

4. In the Path box, type the path to the network server and click OK.

5. Click the drive you just mapped.

6. Locate the Notes Setup program and install Lotus Notes.

Also, Lotus Notes can't handle long printer names. See the CorelDraw entry for a fix.

Lotus cc:Mail 2.0-2.2

May not be able to read X.400 or VAX messages if their headers are longer than 86 characters.

Solution: Upgrade. Contact Lotus at 800-223-1662.

In general, ccMail can't handle long printer names. Network paths (also known as UNC names) in Windows 95 are often longer than their Windows 3.1 equivalent and can include spaces, so sometimes the network can't find a printer. They're in the format \\server\share. See your system administrator about changing the path so that it's shorter and doesn't contain spaces. Or assign a local name to the network resource. See the entry for Corel Draw for an example.

Lotus 1-2-3 v. 3.0

Run this one in DOS mode. See the section "Running in DOS Mode" later in this chapter for help.

Lotus SmartSuite 3.1

There's a problem with deleting read-only files in Ami Pro's File Management System. You won't be able to save any other file under that file name.

Solution: Upgrade. Contact Lotus at 800-223-1662.

Managing Your Money v. 2.0a for Windows

This program uses the Calendar, Cardfile, and clock programs that shipped with Windows 3.x. If you didn't keep Windows 3.x, you won't be able to use the Calendar, Cardfile, or Clock. See Chapter 3 for how to get them back.

McAfee VirusScan

Upgrade to the Windows 95 version. Contact McAfee at 408-988-3832.

MaxSoft-Ocron: Business Card Reader 2.0, ColorFax, ImagePhoto, and Wordlinx 2.0

May not work correctly under Windows 95.
Solution: Upgrade. Contact MaxSoft-Ocron, Inc. at 510-252-0200.

MCS Stereo v. 1.05

If you switch between standard and enhanced environments, the mixer controls will be disabled. To enable them, close the program and then restart it.
Solution: Upgrade: Contact Animotion Development Corp at 800-536-4175 or 205-591-5715.

Media Blitz 3.0

After you install MediaBlitz, restart your computer.

Menuworks Total Security

The security features of this product are incompatible with the Windows 95 file system. You should remove this program before you install Windows 95.

MicroHelp Compression Plus 4.0

If you have problems installing this program under Windows 95:

1. Add the word progman to the end of the SHELL= line in your System.ini file. For example:

    shell=explorer.exe progman

2. Restart your computer; then reinstall MicroHelp Compression.
3. Change your System.ini file back to its original setting.

Microsoft Backup DOS 6+

Run it in DOS mode. It's been replaced by the Windows 95 Backup program (which has problems of its own). See the section "Running in DOS Mode" later in this chapter for help.

Microsoft C/C++ Complier

Some development tools may not work.
Solution: Upgrade. Contact Microsoft at 800-426-9400, or see Chapter 10.

Microsoft Fax

Don't try to use Microsoft Fax unless you have at least 8 Mb of RAM.

If you're using an older 16-bit fax program, Microsoft Fax won't work. Turn off your older program. Then, to have Microsoft Fax answer incoming calls, right-click on the fax icon on the taskbar and click Modem Properties. Change the answer mode to Answer After 3 Rings. If this doesn't work as you want, change the setting to 2 or 4 rings.

Microsoft FORTRAN 5.1

To create QuickWin applications under Windows 95, either delete or remark out the APPLOADER_'MSLANGLOAD' line in the FI.DEF file. Then recompile any QuickWin programs that were built under Version 5.1.

Microsoft FORTRAN PowerStation v. 1.0

Run-time errors appear instead of graphics output.

Solution: Obtain the patch FPSFIX.EXE from the Microsoft Software Library.

Microsoft FoxPro 2.5a

The Close icon doesn't work.

Solution: Upgrade. Contact Microsoft at 800-426-9400, or see Chapter 10.

Microsoft Mail 3.2 and Microsoft Schedule+

Upgrade to Microsoft Exchange. Contact Microsoft at 800-426-9400, or see Chapter 10.

Microsoft Productivity Pack 1.0

You can't install this via Windows 95.

Solution: Install under Windows 3.1; then upgrade to Windows 95.

Microsoft Quick C

Doesn't allow debugging; can't run samples with the Run command.

Solution: Get Visual C++ for Windows. Get a "professional" level version if you want to make both Windows and DOS applications.

Microsoft Source Profiler

Doesn't work under Windows 95.
Solution: Contact Microsoft at 800-426-9400, or see Chapter 10.

Microsoft Visual C++ v. 1.5

Upgrade to version 1.52 of MSCV or MSCV 2.1. Contact Microsoft at 800-426-9400, or see Chapter 10.

Microsoft Visual C++ 1.5x

Upgrade to the 32-bit version of MSVC.

Microsoft Windows for Workgroups

Shares aren't maintained when upgrading to Windows 95.
Solution: Reshare the folders you shared under Windows for Workgroups.

Microsoft Word 6.0 DOS

In graphics mode, when using a Diamond Stealth video card or resolution beyond 16-color 640x480, the desktop may not repaint.
Solution: Contact Diamond at 408-325-7100.

Microcom Carbon Copy 2.5

Versions 2.5 and earlier won't run under Windows 95.
Solution: Upgrade. Contact Microcom at 617-551-1021.

Microtek ScanWizard 2.0b7

If you have problems installing this program, add this line to the [Compatibility] section of Win.ini:

Dshell=0x00400000

Restart your computer and then install ScanWizard. Then remove the Dshell line from your Win.ini file.

Nickelodeon Director's Lab

You'll see messages at the end of the Setup program, but it's OK to ignore them. One message makes a difference, though. If you get the message "Setup

Message: Script or DLL has been corrupted. Unable to load dialog template: 'mscuistf.dll: 2'."

1. Press (CTRL)+(ALT)+(DEL).
2. Click the Director's Lab setup program.
3. Click End Task.
4. Restart Windows 95 and Director's Lab.

Norton Antivirus DOS and Windows

Doesn't work under Windows 95.
Solution: Upgrade. Contact Norton/Symantec at 800-441-7234.

Norton Backup

Before you run Norton Backup, delete the Nbackup.pif file located in the Norton Backup directory. If you still have problems, upgrade. Contact Norton/Symantec at 800-441-7234.

Norton Utilities

Contact Symantec for the Windows 95 version. Norton/Symantec: 800-441-7234.

Novell PerfectOffice 3.0

Starting any program in this suite under Windows 95 displays a network login.
Solution: Contact Novell for an upgrade at 800-638-9273.

Novell PerfectOffice 3.0 Standard

WordPerfect Draw isn't updated after you edit OLE objects. GPFs occur at various times, such as when adding to WordPerfect's supplementary dictionary.
Solution: See the Help system in PerfectOffice.

Office Accelerator

Office Accelerator needs Print Manager, which isn't present in Windows 95. Instead, configure your printers by clicking the Start menu, clicking Settings, and then clicking Printers.

Oracle Personal Oracle 7.1 for Windows 3.1

You can't install this program under Windows 95.
Solution: Contact Oracle Corporation at 415-506-7000.

Paint Shop Pro v. 2.0

You can't draw capture areas inside 32-bit programs, because 16-bit programs don't see mouse movements over 32-bit programs.
Solution: Use another mouse capture method.

PCTools v. 7-9

These versions don't support long file names. If you need long file names, upgrade to a Windows 95 version. Contact Symantec at 800-441-7234.

These versions don't automatically create shortcuts after Windows 95 is installed. To create the shortcuts:

1. Click the Start menu, and then click Run.
2. Type **Cpsdos.grp** and press (ENTER).

For the shortcuts to work, you must add the PCTOOLS directory to the PATH statement in your AUTOEXEC.BAT file. You should find it under your Programs folder.

Pixar Typestry

This may have problems printing to a postscript printer.
Workaround: Print to a non-Postscript or UniDriver printer. Obtain a patch from Pixar. Call the product support number that came with your program: 415-258-8100.

PowerSoft PowerBuilder Enterprise 4.0 for NT

Can't create multiline edit controls.
Solution: Use the Windows 3.1 version.

QuarkXPress 3.3, 3.11, 3.31

If you're running Quark XPress 3.3 with Microsoft Client for Netware, using dial-up networking, you may have conflicts with PageMaker 5.0 and

QuarkXPress. If you see the message "Unable to access network [116]," when you start Quark, remove the Dial-up/IPX components. Contact Quark at 800-788-7835 for an upgrade to version 3.32 or later.

If you get an out-of-memory error running the standalone version, upgrade to version 3.32 or later, or obtain a patch from Quark, Inc.

With QuarkXPress 3.11 and 3.31, the Installer may stall. Click Continue.

Quickbooks 2.0

If you have problems running Quickbooks 2.0 with Windows 95, add the following entry to the [Compatibility] section of your Win.ini file:

```
QBW=0x08000000
```

Quickbooks 3.0

Register this product with the manufacturer before you minimize Quickbooks! If it's too late—you've already minimized it and are having trouble, delete the Qbw.ini file.

Quickbooks can't handle long printer names, either. See the CorelDraw entry for a fix.

Quicken

If you were using Quicken with a printer other than the system default printer or with custom fonts, you'll lose these settings when you run it under Windows 95. After Windows 95 is installed, you can restore them.

SoftKey PFS:WindowsWorks Plus 2.5R

GPFs occur when the taskbar is set for Always on Top.
Solution: Don't use Always on Top.

Splice 2.0

You may get GPFs if you try to create an optimal palette with some video files.
Solution: Free upgrade to Digital Video Producer available from Asymetrix at 206-637-1600.

STAC Electronics Multimedia Stacker v. 4.02

Don't use this version of Stacker. Contact STAC for an upgrade at 619-431-6712.

SuperBase 4

Versions 1.21 and earlier don't work under Windows 95.

Solution: Contact Software Publishing Corp. for an upgrade at 800-234-2500.

SuperPrint 2.0

Version 2.0 doesn't work with Windows 95.

Solution: Get SuperQue 95. Call 800-366-7494.

Symantec Norton Antivirus DOS and Windows

Doesn't work under Windows 95.

Solution: Upgrade. Contact Norton/Symantec at 800-441-7234.

Symantec Norton Backup

Windows 95 needs new settings for this program.

Solution: Delete Nbackup.pif in the Norton Backup directory before you run it under Windows 95.

Symantec Norton Backup for Windows

Doesn't work under Windows 95.

Solution: Upgrade. Contact Norton/Symantec at 800-441-7234.

Symantec pcAnywhere 2.0

Doesn't work under Windows 95.

Solution: Upgrade. Contact Symantec at 800-441-7234.

Symantec pcAnywhere 4.5 and 5.0

Require MS-DOS mode.

Solution: Delete or rename the PIF file provided with the program.

Symantec Norton Utilities

Contact Symantec for the Windows 95 version. Norton/Symantec: 800-441-7234.

Symantec Xtree Gold

Undelete and Wipe don't work. Long file names aren't supported. Contact Symantec for the Windows 95 version at 800-441-7234.

Talk-To Plus

Upgrade. Contact Dragon Systems at 800-825-5897 or 617-965-5200.

3D Studio v. 3

3D Studio wants the Pharlap DOS extender. Put

device=pharlap.386

in the [386 enh] section of your System.ini file

Timeline

You may have problems running macros.
Solution: Upgrade. Contact the manufacturer's bulletin board at 415-892-0408.

Traveling Software LapLink 6.0 and 6.0a

Version 6.0 doesn't work correctly.
Solution: Delete the Ll.pif file.
Version 6.0a won't start under Windows 95.
Solution: Contact Traveling Software at 800-527-5465.

Typestry 2.0

May have problems printing to a PostScript printer.
Workaround: Print to a non-Postscript or UniDriver printer. Obtain a patch from Pixar by calling 415-258-8100.

View Software

Long file names don't work.

Solution: Upgrade to the Windows 95 version. Call 800-536-8439; outside the United States, call 415-856-8439.

Wolfram Mathematica

To perform calculations, you'll need to get a patch from Wolfram Research at 800-441-6284.

WordPerfect Presentations 2.0

If you upgrade over Windows 3.1, this program should work correctly. If you install it after Windows 95 is installed, it may not work correctly.

Solution: Contact WordPerfect at 800-638-9273 (this number may change, depending on who buys WordPerfect!).

WordPerfect Windows 6.0

The Network button isn't available in the Open dialog box. Parts of the Coaches may not run correctly.

Solution: Contact WordPerfect/Novell at 800-638-9273 (this number may change, depending on who buys WordPerfect!).

If you have a font problem with WordPerfect (such as WordPerfect fonts not showing up):

1. Double-click on the Fonts icon in the Control Panel Folder.
2. Choose Install New Fonts from the File menu.
3. Select the Windows\System\Color directory.
4. Select the Modern font.
5. Restart your computer.

XtraDrive

To avoid problems, load SETVER before the file Xtradrv.sys loads.

Running in DOS Mode

If you can't get an older program to run correctly under Windows 95, or if you can't get it to run at all, try running it in DOS mode. In this mode, the program "thinks" it has your computer all to itself. Games are particularly notorious for demanding this me-only situation. But you can custom-tailor your DOS environment to whatever your program wants, if you can figure out what that is (it may require hauling out the program's manual). Remember PIFs (Program Information Files)? Well, the following technique replaces PIFs.

To run an MS-DOS-based program in DOS mode, first create a shortcut to the program. Then:

1. Right-click the shortcut icon and choose Properties.
2. Click the Program tab and then click Advanced (Figure 4-8).
3. Make sure that the MS-DOS Mode box is checked.

When the MS-DOS Mode box is checked, you can click the "Specify a new MS-DOS configuration" button and specify a custom configuration for this program to run under (see Figure 4-8). That includes an AUTOEXEC.BAT and CONFIG.SYS with whatever environmental settings you need to run the

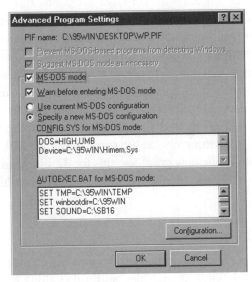

Figure 4-8. Setting up for DOS mode

program—for example, a special PATH statement or a memory manager. You'll usually need to tweak the automatic settings Windows 95 provides. You can take a look at your old AUTOEXEC.BAT and CONFIG.SYS (search for Autoexec and Config to see all the files with any extensions, such as .OLD or BAK), or you can get out the program's manual and see what it wants. You may have to use the SET command in your AUTOEXEC.BAT file to specify exact Sound Blaster settings, for instance. In another example, some users have reported hissing and popping sounds when using action games like TIE Fighter with a SoundBlaster Pro audio card, but have reported vast improvements by loading the old SoundBlaster Pro drivers from a custom AUTOEXEC.BAT.

When you double-click on a program that you've set to run in DOS mode, Windows 95 closes all the other running applications, closes itself, and restarts, running DOS and your program only, using those settings.

For example, to make more memory available to run DOS games, you might want to try these lines in the program's CONFIG.SYS:

```
device=c:\windows\himem.sys
device=c:\windows\emm386.exe noems i=e000-efff
highscan dos=high,umb
```

You can also check the Prevent MS-DOS programs from detecting Windows box. This may make an older program stop looking for certain Windows 3.1 files it thinks it needs to run, but really doesn't because the replacement Windows 95 files are named something else. Don't forget this setting is here! And if you can't get an older Windows 3.1 or DOS program to run, try it. Then again, the simplest solution for many games is to boot the machine, press (F8), and select Command prompt only. That gets you the most DOS-compatible situation short of booting from a disk with DOS on it, and you can run most DOS games this way. You won't be able to run anything else at the same time, but with games this isn't so important. Finally, with the new graphics APIs for 32-bit Windows, a lot of games will be coming out in Windows, and Windows versions of older DOS games will come out.

That's Just a Start

We're not done yet. There are other settings you can change. For example, some programs need special Windows 3.1 files, and if they don't find them but find the Windows 95 equivalent, they may not run. Check the first box to try to stop this

144

Software Purgatory

from happening. The downside of this is that your program may run slower. But the upside is that it may run.

There are other tabs, too, with settings you can tweak. I can't go into them all here (because the publisher insists this is not a "learn how to do Windows 95" book, much less a "learn how to do DOS" book), but I'll hit the ones you'll most likely need to know.

Tweaking the Program tab

The Program tab (Figure 4-9) lets you specify how Windows runs the program. If your program needs to start in a certain directory, fill in the path to that directory in the Working box. If you need to use a batch file, put the path to the batch file (which you've created already) in the Batch file box. This one is great, by the way, for loading a TSR that your program needs to run. That way, it runs only when the program runs.

The Run box lets you specify whether you want to run the program in a normal window, minimized, or maximized. For example, File Director, discussed earlier in this chapter, wants to run in full-screen (maximized) mode.

You can also click Change Icon and pick a new icon for your custom-tailored program. Look in Pifmgr.dll for some neat icons (Figure 4-10).

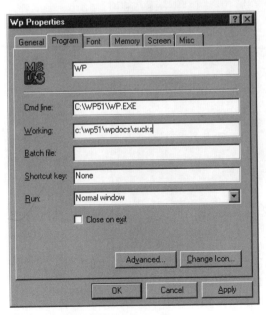

Figure 4-9. The Program tab

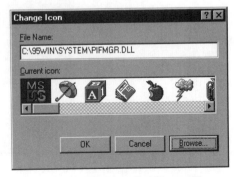

Figure 4-10. Peeking in Pifmgr.dll

145

Tweaking the Memory Tab

You knew you'd have to do this if you started fooling around with programs that Windows 95 refuses to run. Well, here they are, the Memory settings (Figure 4-11). So let's deal with them.

Click on the down arrow next to each setting to see what's available. We'll look at these in order.

The most conventional memory you can get is 615 Kb; there's no point specifying any more than that. If you do, you're fooling yourself.

Windows 95 automatically sets your DOS environment to 1024; you may want to use a larger setting if you've set up a complicated environment in the Advanced tab.

Check Protected if you want Windows 95 to catch memory protection errors when you run this program. It will run slower with this box checked, but it may get a program that needs to access memory directly running.

Now for Expanded memory. I always mix up expanded and extended memory, so here's the difference. Expanded memory comes on a card; extended memory comes built into your computer. One way to see what you've got is to

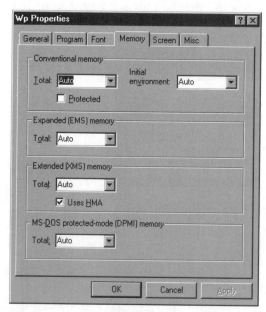

Figure 4-11. The Memory tab

run Microsoft System Diagnostics (MSD). Enter **MSD** in the Run box if you're running Windows 95; otherwise, enter **msd** at the command line. You'll get more accurate results if you run MSD in a DOS box. You'll see a screen with a fairly decipherable allocation of your memory, in terms of conventional memory, extended memory, and expanded memory. Your program may want a specific amount of extended or expanded memory allocated to it; check the manual and change the settings if needed. If you use the Auto setting, Windows 95 will only see the default.

You can leave the last box, DPMI (DOS Protected Mode Interface) memory, alone as Windows 95 normally handles this setting just fine.

Tweaking Screen Settings

The Screen tab (Figure 4-12) also has some memory settings that you might need to tweak. Under Performance, you'll see Fast ROM emulation and Dynamic memory allocation. If you're getting odd-looking screens, mouse cursor trails, bars on the screen, or odd-shaped windows, try unchecking Dynamic memory allocation.

Normally you can leave Fast ROM emulation checked. Basically, this is what was once called "shadow RAM."

Tweaking Misc Settings

The Misc tab (Figure 4-13) has a variety of settings you can experiment with if you can't get an unruly DOS program to run right. We'll go though them in order.

For maximum protection, don't allow a screen saver. If you want to be able to copy and paste with the mouse when you're running in less than a full-screen window, check QuickEdit. Checking Exclusive is a last resort if you have mouse problems with the program. If the mouse isn't working right, try running the program full-screen (use the Program tab) before you check Exclusive. Checking Exclusive means the mouse will *only* work with this program when it's running.

Under Background, there are two settings you can change. You might want to check the "Always suspend" box if the program you're setting up requires constant input, like a game.

But if your DOS-based program slows down or stops when it's running in the background, drag the Idle Sensitivity slider toward Low and make sure "Always suspend"*isn't* checked.

147

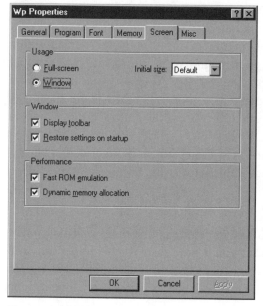

Figure 4-12. The Screen tab

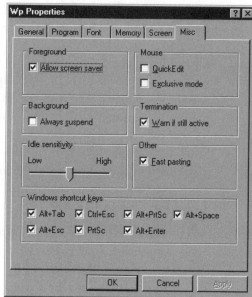

Figure 4-13. The Misc tab

Games

According to Microsoft, most of the games listed here run in DOS mode. If a game has (Windows) next to it, you can run it directly under Windows. Contact the manufacturer to see if a Windows 95 version is available. I've provided extra notes on a couple of games from the information I've gathered.

Blake Stone
Castles 2
Civilization
Corridor 7
Dark Forces
DOOM I 1.6 (1)
DOOM II (1)
Earth Siege
Eniod
Epic Pinball (1)
Eye of the Beholder 1
Eye of the Beholder 1
Full Throttle

Hell

Heretic

Jazz JackRabbit

King's Quest 1

King's Quest 2

King's Quest 3

King's Quest 4

King's Quest 5

King's Quest 6

Kyrandia 3 Malcolm's Revenge (Windows): If you get an EMS memory error:

1. Right-click the Malcolm.pif file, click Properties, and then click the Memory tab.

2. Change the settings for Expanded Memory and Extended Memory to 4096.

3. Click Apply; and then change the same settings back to Auto.

Lode Runner

Master of the Orion

Microprose 1942 Gold (Windows): To run 1942 Gold with Windows 95, copy Command.com in your Windows directory to your DOS directory.

Might & Magic 3

One Must Fall

Privateer

The 7th Guest (Windows): If you're running The 7th Guest with a Pro Audio Spectrum 16 sound card, you either need to enable and use the Sound Blaster compatibility mode or configure your Pro Audio Spectrum card to IRQ 5 and DMA 3.

Sim City DOS

Sim City 2000 (1)

Star Control 2

Star Trek 25th Anniversary

Strike Commander

Syndicate Plus

Theme Park

Tie Fighter

Ultima 6

Ultima 7

Ultima 8

Ultima UnderWorld 1

Ultima UnderWorld 2

Ultima VI: You need to run the Ultima VI CD from your hard drive because Windows 95 doesn't support the JOIN command. You will need approximately 5 Mb of space for Ultima VI.

1. Go to the Explorer or My Computer and double-click on your CD-ROM drive.

2. Click the icon for the folder you want to move and drag it to your hard disk's icon.

3. Run the install program from your hard drive.

Wing Commander 1
Wing Commander 2
Wing Commander CD: You need to run the Wing Commander CD from your hard drive because Windows 95 doesn't support the JOIN command.

1. Go to the Explorer or My Computer and double-click on your CD-ROM drive.

2. Click the icon for the folder you want to move and drag it to your hard disk's icon.

3. Run the install program from your hard drive.

X-Wing
Zone 66

And Next...

Hardware Hell is next. If you're having problems with some device, check out the workarounds in Chapter 5.

Chapter 5

Hardware Hell

What Won't Work with Windows 95:
How to Make It Work. How
to Live Without It.

Hardware Hell

What Won't Work with Windows 95: How to Make It Work. How to Live Without It.

"But what ... is it good for?"

Engineer at IBM's Advanced
Computing Systems Division,
commenting on the microchip, 1968

When you're in Hardware Hell, you know you're there. Hardware problems are usually worse than software problems, because the trouble is that your device (disk drive, CD-ROM, printer, modem, whatever) just *won't work*. With software, often it's only part of it that won't work. And software glitches are generally easier to fix by changing a setting in a dialog box or adding a line to a configuration file, instead of taking the cover off your box and pulling cards and resetting jumpers.

Yes, hardware can go dead in Windows 95 even with Plug and Pray ('scuse me, Play). Sometimes you'll have a device that worked fine until you installed Windows 95. Other times you'll have a new device that you're trying to install under Windows 95 but doesn't work right—or doesn't work at all. In the first case, you probably need a new driver. In the second, you probably have a conflict with another device. Two devices usually can't share the same IRQ (interrupt quotient) or DMA (direct memory access) channel. If both are trying to use the same channel setting, you may, if you're lucky, get an error message. Most times, though, the symptom is that one of the devices won't work, or will work erratically. In the worst case neither of them will work.

Yes, Windows 95 has a Device Manager that theoretically solves hardware conflicts. But it can't physically reset switches that need to be reset on your old ('scuse me again, we don't say *old* any more; we say *legacy*) cards and devices. And more often than you'd like (once is too often for some of us), when you use the Device Manager to troubleshoot your problem, you'll see the dreaded message "See your hardware manual." Some help.

And here's another classic Catch-22. If you can't get Windows started, you can't run the Device Manager!

Welcome to Hardware Hell. There may even be a Plug and Play sticker on the carton of whatever you've got that's not working, but that sticker won't do you much good for troubleshooting. Instead of kicking the carton across the room, check out the workarounds in this chapter.

The Tools You'll Need

You'll need to know:

- How to use the Device Manager
- How to find new drivers
- How to install new drivers
- How to change IRQs and such
- How to run Sysedit

You may need a screwdriver, too.

We'll cover all that first.

Using the Device Manager

Before you despair, give the Device Manager a chance. Windows 95 comes with a sophisticated Device Manager that can automatically detect whether your hardware is working properly. Double-click on the System icon in the Control Panel folder. Click that Device Manager tab and look closely (Figure 5-1). Then click on the plus sign next to each device to see the individual devices (Figure 5-2). Any devices that aren't working and have been disabled will have a red "No way" icon over them. Others may have a yellow exclamation point (Figure 5-3). This indicates a conflict with another device. Either way, double-click on the icon to see a message about what's wrong and how you can fix it (Figure 5-4). A lot of the time, you'll see "See your hardware manual." Very helpful. Be prepared to get the manual out, or check the workarounds in this chapter.

You can also click the View devices by connection button for a different view of what Windows 95 thinks is connected to your computer (Figure 5-5). This may help also.

Reinstalling Drivers

If the error message tells you to reinstall the driver, use the Add New Hardware icon in the Control Panel folder. Follow the instructions on the screen. You may need to locate the manufacturer's installation disk.

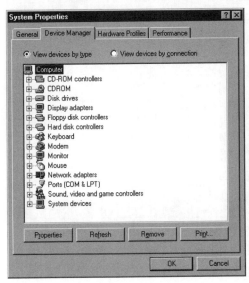

Figure 5-1. The Device Manager

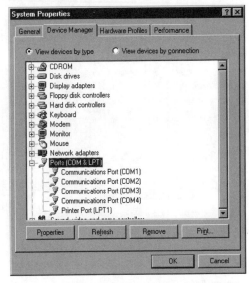

Figure 5-2. Checking individual devices

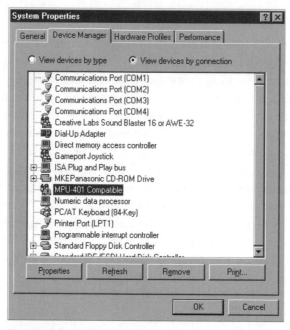

Figure 5-3. Status message

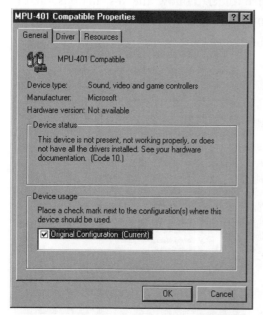

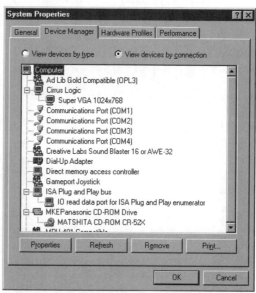

Figure 5-5. Viewing devices by connection

Figure 5-4. Typical message about how to
fix the problem

156

If this doesn't work, or if you can't do it because you don't have the disk and Windows can't find the appropriate driver, check your AUTOEXEC.BAT file. Make sure the line that loads the device hasn't been REM'ed out (preceded with the word *REM*) by Windows' installation program. If it has, delete that REM and any spaces following it, save the file, and restart your computer.

And one more word of advice: Only install one device at a time. You really *will* go crazy trying to troubleshoot if you're trying to install several devices all at once.

Printing a List of Your Devices

While you're there in the Device Manager, turn on your printer (if it's working) and choose Print to get a list of everything connected to your computer. Choose "Print devices and system summary" to get a list of IRQs, DMA channels, I/O addresses, and so forth (Figure 5-6). This summary will tell you which versions of device drivers you're using, your BIOS date (ideally it should be younger than January '94), what type of processor you have, and so forth.

If you've ever hung upside down like a bat over the back of your desk pulling cards and resetting jumpers, you'll value all this technical information. It will come in handy when performing the workarounds in this chapter, or if you need to make a call to a tech support line or bulletin board—which you may indeed

```
System Resource Report - Page: 1

******************* SYSTEM SUMMARY *******************

Windows version: 4.00.950
Computer Name: unknown
Processor Type: 80486DX
System BUS Type: ISA
BIOS Name: American Megatrends
BIOS Date: 01/10/94
BIOS version: unknown
Machine Type: IBM PC/AT
Math Co-processor: Present
Registered Owner: Kay Yarborough Nelson
Registered Company: Herself


******************* IRQ SUMMARY *******************

IRQ Usage summary:
00 - System timer 01
(CONTINUES)
```

Figure 5-6. Sample system summary

need to do if you're using what Microsoft delicately calls "legacy" devices (ones that aren't brand new and therefore up to its Plug and Play standards). If you're using one of these devices, or a device that you or another program specifically configured, Windows won't change the configuration automatically when you install it, so you can still get hardware conflict. That means resetting a jumper or two, which usually entails experimenting until you get something to work. Worst case: You get to do the bat act.

To see the IRQs, I/O addresses, and the like without printing them out, select the icon labeled Computer at the top of the Device Manager list and click Properties. Then click the View Resources tab (Figure 5-7).

If you're using a network interface card (NIC), check your jumper settings for IRQs before installing Windows 95. If you need to change something, it's easier to do it by changing settings through software than by pulling the card and resetting jumpers.

There's one slight drawback. Sometimes, after you print the All devices and system summary from the Device Manager, you'll get a message saying you're out of memory the next time you try to run a DOS program. This happens because the device detection code created a problem for the DOS program. But the workaround's easy. Restart your computer.

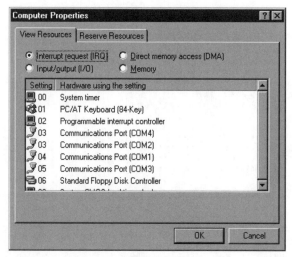

Figure 5-7. Checking IRQs

Changing IRQs

In some cases, Windows 95 lets you change IRQs without resetting DIP switches. Go to the Control Panel folder, double-click the System icon, and click the Device Manager tab. Double-click on the device that has an IRQ you want to change, or highlight it and click Properties. You'll see a dialog box about that device (Figure 5-8). Click the Resources tab, if it has one, and look at the current value for the Interrupt Request (Figure 5-9). Uncheck Use automatic settings and click Change Setting. If the device will allow it (you'll get a message if it won't), you'll be able to change the interrupt, and Windows 95 will tell you if your new choice conflicts with other equipment.

If you know that a "legacy" device (one of your "old" ones that you bought maybe last year) wants to use a certain DMA channel or IRQ, use the Device Manager's Reserve Resources tab (Figure 5-10) and click Add to add a setting to protect from Windows 95's Plug and Play Police. To display that tab, double-click on the Computer icon at the beginning of the Device Manager's list.

But be careful! Don't reserve a setting that a system device (such as the system clock) is using. Your machine will hang, and sometimes you won't even be able

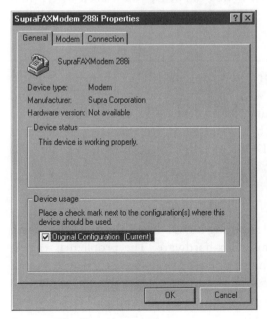

Figure 5-8. Checking devices

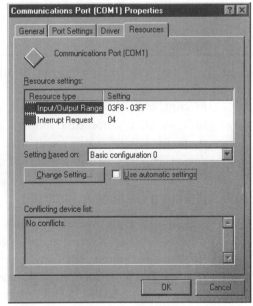

Figure 5-9. Changing IRQs

159

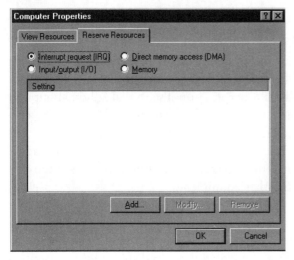

Figure 5-10. Reserving IRQs

Figure 5-11. Running MSD

to get to Safe mode by pressing (F8). If this happens, you'll need to reinstall Windows 95 all over again.

Running MSD

If you can't get Windows to start, you can run MSD (Microsoft Support Diagnostics) instead of the Device Manager. Enter **msd** at the DOS command prompt. It will show you all your functioning devices (Figure 5-11). If a device isn't listed, it's not functioning. That could mean you have to reset some switches. It also could mean that DOS can't find the driver needed for that device. Hey, it's a start!

Picking a Diagnostic Program

You may want to seriously consider getting a DOS-based diagnostic program if you're repeatedly having problems with hardware. The problem is that if Windows is running, the Device Manager doesn't always have total access to all your hardware. Also, if you can't get Windows started, you can't run the Device Manager! So consider a DOS diagnostic program like Norton or PC Tools as a backup to the tools Windows 95 provides.

What's Here and Where to Find More

I've tried to pull together relevant hardware headaches and workarounds from various places, such as the user forums on CompuServe, AOL, Web pages, and the like. If the information is sketchy, that's because it's all I have, but some clue may be better than no clue at all as to what's happening. I've also relied heavily on Microsoft's own information files (hardware.txt, mouse.txt, and printers.txt), which you've got to give them credit for providing. But these files may not be accessible when you can't get your computer or one of its components working right, so I've repeated much of their information here, paraphrased freely. I'm sure Microsoft wants you to have this information, as it's in their best interests that you get your system running.

You may have a problem not covered here; if so, the best place to seek advice is from your hardware vendor (see Chapter 10 for how to get in touch with them, either by phone or via computer, which is faster and usually a lot less hassle), or by asking directly on a user forum on one of the big information services.

If you have access to the World Wide Web, you may be able to do some one-stop shopping for updated drivers and information at any of these sites:

http://oeonline.com/~frankc/up-a-m.html	Drivers and Upgrades, Companies A-M
http://oeonline.com/~frankc/up-n-z.html	Drivers and Upgrades, Companies N-Z
http://www.zdnet.com/~pcmag/1415/pcm00115.ht	PC Magazine—The Driver Manual
http://www.microsoft.com/kb/softlib/windows/windows95/	Microsoft's Driver Library

You can also contact other sources of information:

The Microsoft Network	\Categories\Computers and Software\Software\Microsoft\Windows 95
Internet File Server	ftp://ftp.microsoft.com/Products/Windows/Windows 95
World Wide Web	http://www.microsoft.com/Windows
Gopher	gopher://gopher.microsoft.com
FTP	ftp://ftp.microsoft.com
CompuServe	GO MSL
Genie	Go to Microsoft Roundtable
Microsoft Download Service (MSDL)	In the United States and Canada, call 206-936-6735

Usenet news groups are also a good place to inquire for information. See the listing in Chapter 10.

A word of warning: *don't download drivers directly into your Windows 95 folder*, or you may overwrite some important files.

Installing and Updating Drivers

Use the Add New Hardware wizard in the Control Panel folder to install new drivers. Those you download may be compressed; they'll have an extension of .sea or .zip. If they have an .sea extension, just double-click on them to expand them. If they're .zip files, use a utility like PKUNZIP or WINZIP to extract them.

If you're upgrading to a driver that comes with Windows 95, one that's in the Hardware Compatibility List on the CD-ROM, do this:

1. Right-click on My Computer and choose Properties.

2. Click the Device Manager tab, click on the + next to the device type, and then double-click on the device you're upgrading (Figure 5-12).

3. Click the Driver tab (Figure 5-13). If you don't see a Driver tab, go to the Control Panel folder and double-click on the icon for the type of device you're adding.

Figure 5-12. Upgrading via the Device Manager

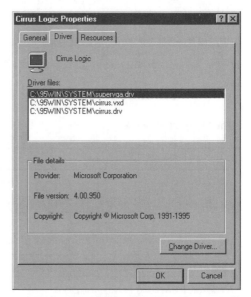

Figure 5-13. Changing drivers

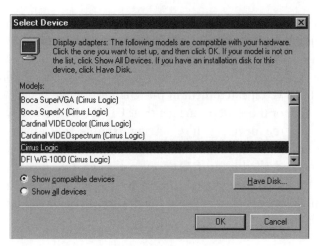

Figure 5-14. Selecting the device

4. Click the Change Driver button to see a screen similar to the one in Figure 5-14. Your device should be selected already.

5. Click Have Disk.

6. Enter the location of the driver file and follow the instructions on the screen.

Using Sysedit

If any of the workarounds in this chapter require you to edit System.ini, AUTOEXEC.BAT, CONFIG.SYS, and the like, use the System Editor for a quick way to edit them. Choose Run from the Start menu, enter **sysedit**, and press (ENTER). All those files will be loaded for you, ready to edit. (For an example of the System Editor's startup screen, look back in Chapters 1 and 4.)

Have Courage

One last word of advice. Hardware troubleshooting is not for the faint of heart. You'll need to know things most users never bother to learn.

What Will Work

What will work with Windows 95 is listed in a file named HCL.TXT (Hardware compatibility) in the Drivers folder on your Windows 95 CD-ROM. However... sometimes things aren't quite as advertised, and a device listed there may not work, especially if it has a conflict with a legacy device. If you want to see the list, look there. Personally I think that if something's working fine, don't mess with it. But the information is there if you need it, or for your amusement. This file *is* valuable because it details instructions for obtaining and installing drivers, but I've repeated them in this chapter for the benefit of those who don't have the CD, or those who can't get their CD-ROM drive to work (the Catch-22).

Look up the device you're having trouble with by category (computer, modem, mouse, and so forth) and then by manufacturer's name. You're not meant to *read* all this stuff! And even though I've provided the voice phone number for most of the manufacturers mentioned in this chapter, remember that it's usually more efficient to get in touch with them via modem if you can. Check out the listings in Chapter 10 for how.

Computers

Here are the known problems with various computers made by specific manufacturers, and their workarounds. Unfortunately, a lot of these solutions require you to acquire something you haven't got, usually a new driver.

Acer Acernotes

If you hear a low tone when you insert your PCMCIA (Personal Computer Memory Card International Association) card, you'll need to edit System.ini and CONFIG.SYS. Use the System Editor; it opens both of these. Delete the EMMExclude line from System.ini and the exclude range data from the EMM386 line in the CONFIG.SYS file.

If you're still getting a low tone, try this:

1. Double-click the PCMCIA icon in the Control Panel folder.
2. Click Global Settings and make sure Automatic Selection *isn't* checked.
3. Set the valid range to start at 000D0000 and end at 000DFFFF.

Compaq Areo

Sometimes there's a problem with the Compaq Aero floppy disk drive card. Make sure the card is already inserted when you start the computer to install Windows 95. After Windows 95 has configured the card, you can take it out.

If you can't access the floppy card, try this workaround:

1. In Control Panel, double-click the System icon; then click the Device Manager tab.

2. Click the plus (+) sign next to Floppy disk controllers.
3. Double-click the floppy disk controller that's not responding.
4. If the Device Status area reports a resource conflict, click the Resources tab, click the Set Configuration Manually button, and click OK.

DEC Hi Note Ultra

If you're having trouble getting your PCMCIA card working with this one, you'll need to update your BIOS to a version later than 3/31/95 (v.1.3). Contact DEC at 508-493-5111.

HP OmniBook 600C

The HP Omnibook's PC card needs special drivers. If you installed Windows 95 from CD-ROM, you can find them in the Drivers directory on the disc.

IBM Thinkpad Models 750 (all 750 series except 750ce)

Get the new BIOS that's available from IBM's bulletin board. Download the latest System Program Service Diskette for the Thinkpad 750 from the BBS. See Chapter 10 for how to access IBM's many bulletin boards.

IBM Thinkpad Models 755cd, cx, ce, cse, cdv (but not 755c)

There were several problems with this computer running Windows 95 at the time of the initial Windows 95 release. By now most, if not all, of them have been resolved with updated drivers. See Chapter 10 for how to access IBM's bulletin boards and download the updated drivers, or how to contact IBM by phone.

Specifically, there were problems with Mwave. If you had more than 8 Mb of memory, Mwave was lost. In fact, if you have a version of Mwave earlier than 1.2, you'll find lots of bugs. Also be aware that if you install Windows 95 over Windows 3.1, the Mwave drivers will be overwritten and you'll need to reinstall them using IBM's Mwave Setup program disk.

The infrared port also causes conflicts with the Device Manager. For a workaround, contact IBM for the updated Infrared VxD driver.

Another problem: If you're having difficulty using docking with this machine and Windows 95, you'll need to get the latest updates to the System Program Service Diskette for your model of Thinkpad. There's no other workaround.

If you're having power management problems with the suspend and resume commands, check to see if you have a 1994 BIOS by printing out a system

summary from the Device Manager (see "Printing a list of your devices" earlier in this chapter). If you're still using a 1994 BIOS, get the latest Flash BIOS revision from IBM.

IBM Thinkpad Dock II

An IBM Thinkpad Dock II will most likely hang on you if you don't disable the BIOS for the Adaptec 1530P SCSI controller in the docking station before starting the docked computer.

To disable the BIOS:

1. Restart your computer while it's docked.
2. Press (CTRL)+(A) to start the Adaptec SCSISelect utility.
3. Choose Configure/View Host Adapter Settings.
4. Choose Advanced Configuration Options.
5. Change the setting for Host Adapter BIOS to Disabled.
6. Press (ESC) to exit and restart your computer.

You can also disable the BIOS entirely, which will enable the adapter to successfully run in Plug and Play mode, but you'll need to reset a DIP switch inside the dock unit. See your Dock II manual if you want to do this.

Micron M5-PI Series

Before you install Windows 95, if you're using a Micron M5-PI series (P-60, P-66) computer you need to make sure the BIOS read/write jumper (W22) is set to the read-only position. If you try to install Windows 95 with this jumper in the read/write position, it may corrupt the BIOS. Your best bet is to contact Micron.

Micron P90/100

Make sure your BIOS version is N15 or later. (Print out that system summary to check.) If it's not, Micron's bulletin board is at 208-368-4530, where you can see how to get the latest BIOS.

NEC Versa M and AT&T Globalyst

If you're using AT&T Globalyst and NEC Versa M, you need to set the BIOS setting for PCMCIA Power to Enabled. First, restart your computer. Then:

1. When the cursor changes to a rectangle, press (F1).
2. When the BIOS configuration program is ready, select Power and change the PCMCIA Power setting to Enabled.
3. Save these settings.
4. In Windows 95, run the PC Card (PCMCIA) wizard by pressing (F3) for Help, choosing Troubleshooting from the Contents tab, and choosing "If you have trouble using a PC card (PCMCIA)".

Change the Mouse Driver, Too

The Omnibook also needs a special mouse driver for Windows 95. You won't have any trouble if you install Windows 95 over Windows 3.1, because it will keep the correct driver. If you install Windows 95 into a different directory, though, you'll need to copy the right mouse driver from your old Windows\System directory. The mouse driver is named Obmouse.drv. Copy it into your new Windows 95\System directory, whatever you've named it. Then change these lines in System.ini:

```
[boot]
mouse.drv=obmouse.drv
[386Enh]
mouse=*vmd
```

If you don't have this driver, you can get it from one of the Windows Drivers Libraries described later, or from Microsoft Support Services.

Packard Bell Legend MultiMedia Machines

If you get a "System Detection Error—BIOS Could Lead to Data Loss" message, contact Packard Bell. Their tech support line is 800-733-4411, or see Chapter 10.

Toshiba Computers: T610 T400 Series, T2100 Series, T2400 Series, T4700 Series, T4800 Series, and the T4900CT and T3600

If you use any of these Toshiba computers, contact Toshiba for an upgrade of your computer's BIOS to version 5.0. Call them at 800-999-4273, or see Chapter 10.

Toshiba T2150 Models

With this model, your computer may hang during suspend or resume operations. If it does, edit CONFIG.SYS and REM out of the line containing the Toscdrom.sys driver, such as:

rem device=c:\cddrv\toscdrom.sys

Winbook XP

If the keyboard stops working, you'll need to disable power status polling:

1. Go to the Control Panel folder, double-click the System icon, and click the Device Manager tab.
2. Click the plus (+) sign next to System Devices.
3. Double-click Advanced Power Management Support; then click the Settings tab.
4. Make sure the Disable Power Status Polling box is checked.
5. Click OK.

Zenith NoteFLEX 486DX and PC Cards

Sometimes PC cards don't work with these machines and the Windows 95 PCMCIA drivers. The workaround is to reserve IRQ 10 and the memory range C000-CBFF:

1. Go to the Control Panel folder and double-click the System icon.
2. Click the Device Manager tab.
3. Click Computer and Properties.
4. Click the Reserve Resources tab.
5. Click Interrupt Request (IRQ) and Add.
6. Reserve IRQ 10; then click OK.
7. Click Memory; then click Add.
8. Reserve the memory range C000-CBFF; then click OK.
9. Click OK again and restart your computer.

Zenith NoteFLEX 486DX

If you're using the NoteFLEX with the Flexshow docking station, you'll need to reserve IRQ 10 (as described above) for the built-in CD-ROM drive to work.

Then open CONFIG.SYS in the Notepad or System Editor and make sure the line loading Mztinit.sys appears before the line loading Pcenable.exe.

Also, to avoid "Bad Command or File Name" errors during startup, copy Rplstr.com from your DOS directory to your Windows directory.

If you're using a PCMCIA hard drive with this computer, you'll need to enable 32-bit PCMCIA support. To do this, go to the Control Panel folder and double-click the PC Card (PCMCIA) icon. Then follow the on-screen instructions.

If you see properties for your PCMCIA socket instead of the wizard, that means Windows' 32-bit support for PC cards is already enabled. If you don't see the PC Card (PCMCIA) icon in the Control Panel folder, double-click the Add New Hardware icon in Control Panel to install the PCMCIA socket.

Motherboards

Got a motherboard problem? Check out the known problems listed in this section, or contact your computer manufacturer (not the manufacturer of your motherboard). The problems listed here are the only ones I've heard of. There are others, no doubt.

Micronics Motherboards with a Flash BIOS

If you're using a Micronics motherboard with a Flash BIOS, before you install Windows you need to be sure the BIOS read/write jumper is set to the read-only position. If you try to install Windows 95 with this jumper in the read/write position, it may corrupt the BIOS. Best here to contact your computer manufacturer (see Chapter 10).

Triton Chipset Pentiums

Some of these are having problems. Best bet: Check with your computer manufacturer (see Chapter 10).

Printer Problems and Workarounds

There are always problems printing. See if your printer is listed here.

Canon Color Bubble-Jet

If you have a Canon BJC-70, BJC-400, BJC-600(e), or BJC-800, get the updated drivers from the manufacturer. Canon's at 800-423-2366, or see Chapter 10.

Fargo Primera and Primera Pro

Until you can get new drivers for these printers, use the Windows 3.1 drivers. The Primera needs version 4.3 or newer; the Primera Pro needs version 2.7 or newer. Fargo: 800-327-4622.

Fax Printing

If you have a portable PC, Windows 95 may assume your fax printer is offline. You need to make sure this isn't the case if you want to send faxes.

1. Click Settings on the Start menu.
2. Click Printers and double-click the icon for the Microsoft Fax printer.
3. On the Printer menu, make sure that Work Offline isn't checked.

Hewlett-Packard DeskJet Printers

Versions 6.1 and earlier of the Hewlett-Packard DeskJet printer drivers won't work with Windows 95. Look at the installation disk that came with your printer to see which version it is. In most cases you can substitute another printer driver (pick a model that's close to the one you have; for example, if you have an 850C, try a 550C, which is the next color model down) until the updates are available from HP. See Chapter 10 for a list of all the HP numbers.

Getting an Extra Page?

If you're using a Hewlett-Packard printer, or a printer that emulates an HP printer, you may be getting an extra page before each print job. To fix this problem, install the Lpt.vxd file on the Windows 95 CD-ROM. Go to the Explorer and:

1. Rename the Lpt.vxd file in the Windows\System folder as Lpt.old.
2. Copy the Lpt.vxd file from the Drivers\Printer\LPT folder on the Windows 95 CD-ROM to the Windows\System folder on your hard disk.
3. Restart Windows 95.

Hewlett-Packard DeskJet 600, 660C, and 850C

If you've just bought a new HP DeskJet 600 or 800 printer, check the label to see if the driver is later than version 6.1. If it is, Windows can automatically detect your printer and install the printer driver. Double-click on the Add New Hardware icon in the Control Panel folder. When you're asked for the manufacturer's disk, insert the HP DeskJet Printer Disk 1 that came with your printer.

If Windows 95 doesn't automatically detect the HP DeskJet printer, install the driver by following the steps listed on the label of the printer installation disk that came with your printer.

If you have an older printer driver (6.1 or earlier), you'll need to get an updated one. See Chapter 10 for how to get in touch with HP. In the meantime, you can still print by installing another printer driver:

1. Click Start, choose Settings, then choose Printers.
2. Click the Add Printer icon; then follow the instructions on the screen.
3. When you're asked to select the printer manufacturer and model and number, choose the HP DeskJet 550C Printer if you have a 660C or 850C printer. Choose the HP DeskJet 540 if you have a DeskJet 600.
4. Click Next and follow the steps on the screen.

Hewlett-Packard LaserJet Printers

If you're adding a LaserJet 4 printer, a Color LaserJet, or a LaserJet 5P/5MP to your Windows 95 system, you can get better results by getting the HP TrueType Screen fonts that match your internal printer fonts. See Chapter 10 for the various ways to contact HP.

Then, to install the screen fonts, find the installation disks that came with your printer.

1. Insert Disk 1 in your floppy drive.
2. Click Start and Run.
3. Click Custom installation, and then click on the printer that you have.
4. Click "HP TrueType Screen fonts". Deselect the Printer Driver, Status Window, and the Travel Guide.
5. Click OK and follow the instructions on the screen.

If you have a HP LaserJet 5P Printer, follow the same steps above, but choose Typical installation instead of Custom installation. For a Color LaserJet, choose Express installation.

If you have a HP LaserJet 4M to 5MP PostScript printer, you'll need to use the PostScript driver that comes with Windows 95, *not* the one on your printer installation disk. But if you have a HP Color PostScript LaserJet, you'll get better results if you *do* use the PostScript Color printer driver that comes with your printer. To install it:

1. Put the HP Color LaserJet Printer disk in your floppy disk drive.
2. Click Start, Settings, and Printers.
3. Click Add Printer, and then follow the instructions on the screen.
4. Click the Have Driver Disk button. If you're prompted to replace or update the driver, say Yes.

HP LaserJet Troubleshooting

Sometimes the HP Status window conflicts with the Windows printer status program. If you have trouble with this, uninstall the HP Status window:

1. Click Start, Programs, and the HP LaserJet folder.
2. Double-click the Deinstall HP Status Window icon.
3. Say Yes when you're asked about restarting Windows.

LaserMaster Printer

The Windows 3.1 printer driver for LaserMaster products won't work under Windows 95. Contact LaserMaster Technical Support (see Chapter 10 for how) and get the updated driver.

Lexmark Printers

Contact the manufacturer for updated drivers especially designed for Windows 95. In the meantime, it's okay to use the Windows 3.1 drivers.

If you have a Lexmark 40x9 laser printer, you may have problems using bidirectional support. To fix this, go to your Windows 95\System folder and make sure it has a file named LEX01.386. If you don't see it, press (F3) and let Find find it. If it's not found, contact Lexmark at 606-232-3000 (also see Chapter 10).

Then open System.ini in the Notepad or the System Editor. In its [386Enhanced] section, add these two lines:

```
*device=lex01.385
WPSLPT#=1
```

where # = 1, 2 or 3, depending on whether your printer is on LPT1, LPT2, or LPT3. If it's on LPT1, for example, the line should read WPSLPT1=1. Save the file and restart your computer.

NEC Silentwriter SuperScript 610

The Windows 3.1 printer driver for NEC SilentWriter SuperScript won't work under Windows 95. Contact NEC Technical Support (800-632-4636, or see Chapter 10) and get the updated driver.

QMS Jetscript Boards

First, contact QMS and see if they've updated the driver yet. In the meantime, if you can't print, you can work around it by creating a port named LPT*x*.DOS, where *x* is LPT1, LPT2, or LPT3, depending on which port your JetScript printer's on:

1. Click Start and choose Settings and Printers.
2. Right-click on the QMS JetScript printer icon and click Properties.
3. Click the Details tab and then click Add Port.
4. Click Other and click Local Port.
5. Click OK.
6. Enter the name of the port you want to add (such as LPT1.DOS).
7. Click OK twice.

Video Cards

The following is the official Microsoft-approved vendor list as of the first commercial release of Windows 95:

Actix Systems	Diamond Multimedia Systems
ATI Technologies	Digital Equipment Corporation
Boca Research	ELSA
Cardinal Technologies	Genoa Systems
Chips & Technologies	Hercules Computer Technology
Cirrus Logic	IBM
Compaq	IIT
DFI	Matrox Graphics

- Number Nine Visual Technology
- Oak Technology
- Orchid Technology
- Paradise
- S3
- Spider Graphics
- STB Systems

- Trident Microsystems
- Tseng Labs
- Video Logic
- Video Seven
- Western Digital
- Windows 3.x Drivers

Windows 95 also supports standard VGA, SVGA, and standard laptop display devices. If you don't see your brand listed here, or if you're getting weird-looking screens, try the Standard Display Adapter and see what results you get.

If your video board manufacturer isn't listed here, and you have the device drivers on your system or on floppy disk, you can select the Manual configuration option in the Hardware Setup Wizard and tell Windows 95 where the appropriate driver is.

There are always other problems, though. For example, even though Windows 95 may recognize your video card, you may need to edit your AUTOEXEC.BAT to set the right refresh rates. Or you may not be getting colors displayed correctly, or windows may not resize right. If this happens, press (F8) at the startup beep and start in Safe mode. Go to the System icon in the Control Panel folder, click the Performance tab, click the Graphics button, and turn down the hardware acceleration setting (Figure 5-15). This sometimes fixes a jumpy or badly colored picture.

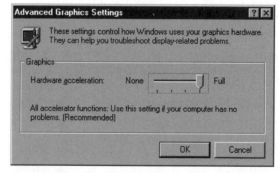

Figure 5-15. Adjusting graphics hardware acceleration

Here are more graphics board problems—and solutions—that I've managed to locate, listed alphabetically by manufacturer.

Advance Logic Display Adapters

Use the updated Windows 95 driver on the Windows 95 CD-ROM in the \Drivers\Display\Advance folder.

Appian Renegade

Windows 95 uses the VGA driver for this adapter. If you preserved your old Windows 3.1 setup, you may still have the Renegade drivers used with Windows 3.1. If you use these drivers instead of the VGA driver, turn off the Device Bitmaps option.

ATI Mach8/32/64

If you're not getting high-resolution modes, run the ATI Install program and make sure you're using the right setting for your monitor type.

If your computer occasionally stops responding on PCI mach32 or mach64 adapters, try adding these lines, one at a time, to the [display] section of System.ini:

```
outengine=0
VAD=1
```

Restart your computer after adding each line.

Chips and Technologies

You may have to manually install this driver. Double-click on the Display icon in the Control Panel folder, click the Settings tab, and then click Change Display Type.

Compaq Presario with Cirrus Logic

If you aren't getting screen resolutions higher than 640 x 480, check your AUTOEXEC.BAT file and see if it has a line like this one:

```
c:\windows\vgautil\clmode.exe t640=60 t800=0 t1024=0 t1280=0
```

If it does, you aren't getting anything higher than 640 x 480 because the higher resolutions are disabled. Restart your computer and press (F8) when you hear the beep. Choose Command Prompt Only, and at the command prompt, type **c:\windows\vgautil\clmode**. Now you can use the Clmode program to choose the correct monitor type and configure it. Restart for the changes to take place.

Diamond Stealth Series

This one needs a little tweaking to work with Windows 95. Basically, you need to install its DOS Utilities into your AUTOEXEC.BAT. Add the S64MON-ITOR line and specify S64DMODE, S64MODE, or GO, depending on the model of your video card. For example, a Stealth 64 card needs a setting of S64MODE in the AUTOEXEC.BAT. You also need to specify the S64 directory in the AUTOEXEC.BAT's PATH statement.

Diamond Stealth and SpeedStar 64/Pro

Use the enhanced drivers found in the \Drivers\Display\Diamond folder on the Windows 95 CD-ROM, or download them from the Windows Driver Library if you don't have the CD-ROM.

Diamond Viper

If you installed Windows 95 over Windows 3.1, the Setup program will keep the Windows 3.1 drivers. If you installed Windows 95 in a different directory, Setup installs the VGA driver.

If you have the Windows 95 CD-ROM, you can find a Windows 95 driver for Diamond Viper VLB and PCI adapters (Weitek P9000 based) in the \Drivers\Display\Diamond folder.

Hercules Graphite, Boca Vortek, Orchid Celsius (IIT AGX)

The Windows 95 Setup program doesn't automatically install these drivers and other adapters that use the IIT AGX controller. Double-click on the Display icon in the Control Panel folder, click the Settings tab, click Change Display Type (Figure 5-16), and choose the correct driver.

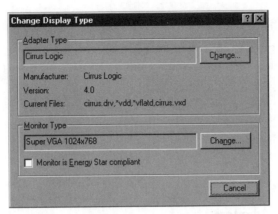

Figure 5-16. Changing the display type

IBM ThinkPad

If you aren't getting 256 colors (and you used to get them), put a line to load the Ibmvesa.com driver in your AUTOEXEC.BAT file.

If you're having cursor or high-resolution problems on a ThinkPad 755cx, open Display properties, click the Settings tab, then click Change Display Type. Change the display type from Western Digital to IBM ThinkPad 755cx.

Matrox MGA

If your computer hangs up while you're trying to install Windows 95, you may have a conflict with a network adapter. Check the settings in the Matrox setup utility on your hard disk in the \Mga\Setup folder as well as your network adapter's settings to see if there's a conflict. If you're not sure what the settings should be, check the manual or contact Matrox.

If you're seeing garbage on the screen, try adding FontCache=OFF to the [mga.drv] section of your System.ini file.

Number Nine Imagine 128

Windows 95 uses the Cirrus Logic driver instead of this one, so your maximum resolution is 800 x 600, 256 colors. Get the Number Nine driver from the Windows Driver Library as discuused earlier in this chapter.

PCI Systems

Getting only VGA video? If both the video and a secondary PCI IDE controller are using IRQ 15, that's what happens. You have two choices for a temporary fix. Either

- Use the Device Manager to disable the secondary PCI IDE controller,

or

- Manually reconfigure the video device's IRQ.

The best solution: Upgrade your BIOS. Contact the manufacturer.

S3 Display Adapters

You'll have a problem if your modem is on COM4. Use the Device manager and put the modem on a different COM port. Or try this: Double-click on the System icon in the Control Panel folder, click the Performance tab, click Graphics, then drag the slider to None.

If you're having trouble with line and shape outline appearance, add

Polygon=0

to the [Display] section of your System.ini file.
For color problems with High Color (16 bit), add

HighColor=15

For color problems with True Color (24 bit), add

TrueColor=24

SPEA Adapters

If your SPEA adapter uses an S3 controller, you need to have a line that loads a VESA TSR in your AUTOEXEC.BAT—for example, V7mepvbe.exe.

Trident Display Adapters

Use the Super VGA driver in the \Drivers\Display\Trident folder on the Windows 95 CD-ROM. Or get it from the Windows Driver Library.

Video Logic 928Movie

If you're using 16-bit color, double-click on the Display icon in the Control Panel folder and make sure your display adapter type is set to Video Logic 928Movie.

Western Digital

If the mouse pointer's changing to colored dots when you switch from a command prompt, double-click the System icon in the Control Panel folder. Click the Performance tab and then click Graphics. Drag the slider left one notch.

Sound Cards

One word of advice: If you haven't bought a sound card yet, make sure it's compatible with Windows 95 before you buy it. Look for that Windows 95 logo on the box. Various generic sound cards can be hidden away in "over-the-counter" computers like Packard-Bells.

If you have a non-Plug and Play sound card and you're having trouble getting it to work, try installing it using the program that came with it instead of using Windows 95's automatic hardware detection.

Advanced Gravis UltraSound Cards

You can use the Windows 3.1 drivers with these cards until 32-bit drivers are available from the manufacturer. Press (F8) when you hear the computer beep on startup. Then go to the command prompt and run the DOS-based installation program for the sound card.

AZTECH 16-bit Sound Cards

You may have one of these cards without knowing it. These cards are used in many computers, such as Packard Bell, Gateway, ACER, and Reveal. You'll want 32-bit drivers for them (to contact the manufacturer, see Chapter 10). You can use the Windows 3.1 drivers with these cards until 32-bit drivers are available from the manufacturer. Press (F8) when you hear the computer beep on startup. Then go to the command prompt and run the DOS-based installation program for the sound card.

DEC Venturis and Media Vision Audio Cards

If you're using a Media Vision sound card on a DEC Venturis, you may have problems. The workaround:

1. Go to the Control Panel and double-click the System icon.
2. Click the Device Manager tab.

3. Under Sound, Video and Game Controllers, double-click Media Vision Pro Audio Spectrum 16/Studio With SCSI.

4. Click the Settings tab and make sure the Enable Warm Boot box is unchecked.

Media Visions Pro Audio Spectrum Sound Cards

Although there are 32-bit drivers for these cards, they still need all of the old AUTOEXEC.BAT information from your Windows 3.1 setup. Open the Notepad and open AUTOEXEC.DOS. Copy any SET commands that involve the sound card; they'll usually have the name or initials of the sound card cryptically embedded in them, like sb for Sound Blaster or Ds for DigiSpeech. Close AUTOEXEC.DOS and open AUTOEXEC.BAT. Paste the SET commands. Restart, and your card should work.

Mozart Sound Card/Canon Innova 550 CD Driver

If you have a problem starting Windows 95 with this card installed, you need a new driver. Contact the Canon Help Desk at 800-423-2366, or see Chapter 10.

Reveal Sound Cards

If you're having problems with a Reveal sound card, it may actually be an AZTECH 16-bit sound card, which has a known problem. See that entry for the workaround.

Soundblaster SCSI-2

May cause IRQ conflicts. Solution: Change the IRQ or set MSDOS.SYS to DoubleBuffer=1.

CD-ROM Drives and Removable Media

Here are some substitute drivers and workarounds you can use until you contact the vendor for updated drivers. The drivers are on the Windows 95 CD-ROM.

Diamond Multimedia Quad Speed

If you have trouble, use the Windows 95 Goldstar drivers.

Iomega Zip Drives

Can't print to the printer attached to your Iomega Zip drive's passthrough port? You need to install the 32-bit ZIP drivers. They're on the Windows 95 CD-ROM in the Drivers\Storage\Iomega directory. The latest drivers (later than the ones on the Win95 CD) come with the Win95 Zip Tools package. Iomega is now including this package standard with new zip drives.

Despite having the latest drivers, if a drive and a printer use the same parallel port, one or the other may not work. That's a problem with the parallel port itself. The workaround: Put the printer and zip drive on different parallel ports (LPTs). If you can't do that, or if you do that and it still doesn't work, buy a new parallel I/O card for your PC (a barebones model costs about $25).

Panasonic 56X Double Speed

If you have trouble, use the Windows 95 Matsushita drivers.

Reveal Double Speed

If you have trouble, use the Windows 95 Matsushita drivers.

Sony Quad Speed

If you have trouble, use the Windows 95 ATAPI drivers.

Sanyo 3-D ATAPI (IDE) CD-ROM Drive

This CD-ROM drive has a three-disk changer. Although all three drives will appear when you are running in protected mode, only one of them will be accessible.

To access to all three drives, remove the REM command from the beginning of the MSCDEX line in your AUTOEXEC.BAT file. You'll also have to disable the Windows 95 protected-mode disk driver:

1. Go to the Control Panel and double-click the System icon.
2. Click the Device Manager tab.
3. Click View Devices by Connection.
4. Click plus signs next to devices until you find the Sanyo drive.
5. Look at the levels above it until you find the parent controller.
6. Click the controller, and then click Properties.

7. In the Device Usage area, uncheck the Original Configuration (Current) box.

Sanyo 3-D ATAPI (IDE) CD-ROM Drive

You need a new driver. Contact Sanyo at 714-724-1505, or see Chapter 10.

Syquest Removable IDE Cartridge

If you're using a SyQuest IDE removable drive, put

Removable IDE=True

in the [386Enbh] section of your System.ini file. You'll need to have a formatted cartridge in the SyQuest drive when Windows 95 starts.

Getting Windows 95 Backup to Work with Your Tape Drive

Here's the thing: Windows 95 doesn't detect tape drives unless they're SCSI drives. It supports only one tape drive format—QIC. Your newer DAT (Digital Audio Tape) tape drive won't work.

But most backup *programs* do detect tape drives, so Microsoft tells you not to worry if your tape drive doesn't appear in Device Manager. Just use a different backup program than the one Windows 95 provides. If you still can't get the thing to work, *then* Microsoft tells you to contact your backup program's manufacturer. In the meantime, read on for some workarounds.

Here's the official squeaky-clean list of supported tape drive manufacturers:

- QIC 40, 80, and 3010 tape drives connected to the primary floppy disk controller, made by the following companies:
- Colorado Memory Systems

  Conner

  IOmega

  Wangtek (only in hardware phantom mode)
- Colorado Memory Systems QIC 40, 80, and 3010 tape drives connected through a parallel port.

The following aren't listed as compatible with Windows 95's Backup utility:

- Drives connected to a secondary floppy disk controller or to an accelerator card
- Archive drives
- Irwin AccuTrak tapes
- Mountain drives
- QIC Wide tapes
- QIC 3020 drives
- SCSI tape drives
- Travan drives
- Summit drives

But as usual, there are plenty of inconsistencies and workarounds. Read on.

Colorado Jumbo

According to reports, it won't work with Windows 95 Backup. It will reportedly work with Norton Backup for Windows 3.0 (but there's no long file name support). It can't back up the Windows System files, either.

Colorado Trakker

If you're having problems with this one connected to the parallel port, get a patch from the manufacturer. Colorado's BBS is at 970-635-0650.

Conner TapeStor

If you're having problems with this one connected to the floppy controller, try disabling any 16-bit screen savers while you back up.

Hard Drives

You can also have problems with hard drives and Windows 95. I've heard of problems with the Adaptec EZ SCSI, Arco AcideJL, EZ-Drive, and Promise 2300+ drivers, but I haven't been able to locate the fixes. If you have one of these, try contacting the manufacturer (see Chapter 10) for the latest information.

Micron PowerServer M5-PE (66 MHz Pentium PCI/EISA Bus)

If you're having trouble with this one and your SCSI devices, contact Micron (their BBS is at 208-368-4530, or see Chapter 10). An updated driver may be available by now.

TrueFFS Flash File System for PCMCIA Cards

The Windows 3.1 version of the TrueFFS driver won't work with the Windows 95 PCMCIA driver. You need to install a new driver.

1. Go to the Control Panel and double-click the Add New Hardware icon.

2. Click Next; then click the option to not have Windows search for your new hardware.

3. Click Hard Disk Controllers and click Next.

4. Choose M-Systems. If you don't see it, click Have Disk (if you have it, that is) and follow the on-screen instructions.

5. Choose your specific Flash Card and click Next.

6. Follow the instructions on the screen.

Modems

Windows 95 works with most high-speed modems. Here's the list of modem manufacturers that had driver support built right into Windows 95, as of its August 24th commercial release:

- Acer
- Angia
- Apex Data, Inc.
- AST
- AT&T
- ATI Technologies
- Avtek
- Banksia
- Best Data
- Boca Research
- Calcom

- Cardinal
- Com 1
- Communicate
- Compaq
- Computer Peripherals, Inc.
- Creative Labs
- Creatix
- Data Race
- DEC
- DFI
- Diamond Multimedia Systems

Diamond Multimedia

Digicom

Digital Equipment Corporation

Digitan

E-Tech

Epson

Exar

Exicom Suatrailia PTY

EXP

Gateway 2000

General DataComm

GVC

Hayes

Hotline

IBM

Infotel

InteCom

Intel

Interlink Electronics

Kingston

Logicode

Macronix

Maestro Digital Communications

Magic RAM

Maxtech

Megahertz Corp.

Metricom, Inc.

Microcom, Inc.

Microfax

Mitsubishi

Motorola

MultiTech Systems

NEC

NetComm

New Media Corporation

Nokia Mobile Phones

Noteworthy

NovaLink Technologies

Ositech

P.N.B.

Pace Micro Communications

Packard Bell

Piceon

Practical Peripherals

Premax

Psion

Puredata

Racal

Reveal

Rockwell

Schmidt Electronic Laboratories

Sierra Semiconductor

Sierra Wireless

Simple Computing

Smart Modular Technologies

Sonix Communications, Ltd.

Spectrum Signal Processing

Supra Corporation

TDK

Telebit

- Teltra
- Texas Instruments
- Toshiba
- Turbomodem
- U.S. Robotics, Inc.
- Ven-Tel
- Victory
- Winbook
- Xircom
- Zoltrix
- Zoom Technologies, Inc.
- Zypcom
- ZyXEL

CAS modems aren't supported. You can use Class 2 fax modems to send and receive traditional Group 3 faxes, but you really need a Class 1 fax modem to take advantage of Windows 95's advanced security features.

This list, of course, doesn't guarantee all models made by these manufacturers will work. If you have an older driver, you may still need to get an updated one.

If you're having trouble connecting with a Standard Modem selected, try choosing a Hayes Compatible modem driver. Double-click on the Modems icon in the Control Panel folder, select Standard Modem, and then click Remove. Then click Add, check Don't Detect My Modem, and click Next. Under Manufacturers, select Hayes and choose Hayes Compatible.

And sometimes the trouble may not be with your modem at all, but with your COM port. To check this out, go to the control Panel folder and double-click the System icon. Click Device Manager and the Ports icon. Make sure the settings are correct. And if you have an internal modem, make sure its IRQs and other settings aren't conflicting with the ones your system's BIOS has requested for your COM port. Check for comflicts between your modem, your mouse, and your serial printer, too. The Device Manager should tell you.

I Can't Get My Modem to Work with Windows 95!

You may need to manually configure your modem in the Control Panel to get it to work. Double-click on the Modems icon, click Properties, and check to see that the connection settings are correct (Figure 5-17). You may need to get out the modem manual, but let's hope not. Windows 95 *should* detect your modem and set it up accurately.

There are known problems with some modems—as you'll see in the next section—which I've tried to keep listed alphabetically. (You'll notice some of these are made by manufacturers listed above as "squeaky clean" with Windows 95.)

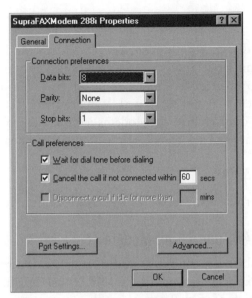

Figure 5-17. Checking modem
connection settings

I've compiled this list from a variety of sources, and this is all the information I have! Check with the vendor (see Chapter 10) to find out if a newer version or upgrade is available.

Digicom Connection Series Modems

These modems use a proprietary program called SoftModem Manager. It doesn't work with Windows 95. You can still use your modem, though. Go to the DOS command line and run Smview.exe, or load your protocols from the command line. Don't run Windows Setup to set up this modem until after you manually set it up (see the next paragraph).

Make sure your AUTOEXEC.BAT file has the smodem directory in the path, plus the appropriate dl command (that's dl followed by a modem driver name). If you run the modem setup program from DOS mode, it will copy the appropriate commands into AUTOEXEC.BAT automatically. It's a good idea to check with Digicom for the latest modem driver files. You can also run Windows setup to make Windows 95 better acquainted with your modem, but you have to have AUTOEXEC.BAT set up "manually" first.

Generic Modems

If Windows 95 detects your modem as a "Standard Modem," or incorrectly detects its make and model, you can use the Change button in the Install New Modem wizard to change the modem type. If you choose the wrong type, though, your modem may not work with Windows 95.

If this happens, double-click the Modems icon in Control Panel, remove the modem, and then add it back as one of the Standard modem types.

Intel Satisfaxion 400i

Contact Intel for new firmware that will convert this modem to Class 1.

Megahertz Em1144T and 16-bit Modem

If you have problems getting this modem running in a real-mode PCMCIA environment, try explicitly setting the COMIRQ and COMBASE parameters in the Megahertz section of your Protocol.ini file.

Minitel in France

Some modems may not be able to connect to French Minitel in HyperTerminal if they're using the Windows 95 default settings. To correct this, get out your modem manual. (What? You left it at home?)

1. Check the modem manual for a command that will let your modem connect to Minitel in V.23 modulation. This is used for the slower 75 bps/1200 bps communication. (If you have a SupraFax 288i modem, the command is %F.)

2. Go to the Control Panel, double-click the Modems icon, click the name of your modem, and then click Properties.

3. Click the Connection tab; then click Advanced.

4. In the Extra Settings box, type the command that enables V.23 modulation.

Racal Modems

Don't let the Install New Modem wizard detect your modem. Click Don't Detect My Modem, and then pick one of the standard modem types. If you've already run detection and your modem isn't responding, turn the modem off and then back on again.

U.S. Robotics Sportster Modems

Make sure you're using the latest BIOS. See Chapter 10 for how to contact the manufacturer.

ZOOM Technologies V.34i

This one drops connections using the ZOOM driver. Use the Generic 28.8 drivers instead.

Keyboards

If your keyboard is locking up on you, you may need the new VKD.VXD file, which is the keyboard driver for Windows 95. Copy it into your Windows95\SYSTEM\VMM32 directory.

Microsoft Natural Keyboard

If you have a Microsoft Natural Keyboard and you've upgraded to Windows 95 over Windows 3.1, IntelliType won't work as well as it did. The workaround is to edit System.ini and delete this line:

taskman.exe=TASKSW16.EXE

Scanners

Scanner problems? The fix for the HP ScanJet II works with a lot of scanners.

HP ScanJet II

If you're having problems with this scanner, add the ASPI manager real-mode driver (Aspi2dos.sys) to your CONFIG.SYS file.

Logitech Scanman

If you're using a hand-held Logitech Scanman on a computer with more than 16 Mb of memory, you may get an "Insufficient system resources" message. If you do, get the updated driver, Scanupt.exe, from the Logitech bulletin board or from one of the sources in Chapter 10.

Mice Difficulties

Try the workarounds in this section if your mouse is acting up.

Logitech Mouse

Don't use the Windows 3.1 Logitech MouseWare Setup program. If it's too late and you've already used it, double-click the Mouse icon in the Control Panel folder. Click the General tab; then click Change. Choose the appropriate Windows 95 Logitech mouse driver.

If you use a Logitech serial mouse and you have a PS/2 mouse port on your computer, your mouse may not work. The workaround: Double-click on the System icon in the Control Panel folder. Click the Device Manager tab and change the PS/2 mouse to Logitech Serial Mouse.

Microsoft IntelliPoint 1.00

If you installed Windows 95 over Windows 3.1, you'll be able to use your mouse, but only in a limited way. Contact Microsoft for a new driver. See Chapter 10 for a listing of Microsoft suport phone and BBS numbers as well as Web addresses.

Microsoft BallPoint Mouse

If you need to adjust settings for your BallPoint mouse, use the Mouse Manager or IntelliPoint control panel icon that came with the mouse. If you don't have either of these, contact Microsoft for an updated version of the mouse software.

Mouse Systems/Genius Mice (3-button)

Use the standard mouse driver with these devices as 2-button mice, or install a new driver. If you have the Windows 95 CD-ROM, you'll find the new drivers in the Drivers directory. You can also get a new driver from the Windows Driver Library online.

And Next...

That's about all the hardware information I've been able to pull together. Your best bet is always to contact the manufacturer (all sorts of different ways are listed in Chapter 10) if you don't see the solution to your problem here, or if the solution described here doesn't work. Or join in the chorus of complaints to be found in any of the Windows 95 user forums on the information services. You may find someone who's solved the same problem you're having! (Again, see Chapter 10 for the list of appropriate JUMP and GO keywords.)

In the next chapter, we'll take a retro look at what you left behind when you went to Windows 95 and see what's salvageable from Windows 3.1. After all this, it's beginning to seem like Windows 3.1 wasn't so bad, after all. In fact, it had some functionality that you're probably wishing you could get back.

Chapter 6

Don't Leave Home Without It!

Keeping the Good

Parts of Windows 3.1

Don't Leave Home Without It!
Keeping the Good
Parts of Windows 3.1

"Everything that can be invented has been invented."

Charles H. Duell, Commissioner, U.S. Office of Patents, 1899

If you used Windows 3.1, you may have found some of it pretty annoying. Like going to one part of the system, the File Manager, for arranging files and going to another part, the Program Manager, for starting programs. Like mysteriously losing icons from your program groups from time to time, for no apparent reason. Like the mouse trifecta you sometimes had to run ("Are you sure?" "Are you really sure?" "Fingers not crossed?"). Version 3.1 wasn't necessarily better than version 95, but it did have features many of us came to depend on. When the designers at Microsoft took out some of Windows 3.1's most annoying features, maybe they took out too much.

Some accessories that you may have come to depend on in Windows 3.1 weren't included in Windows 95. Their absence can be a real disaster if you relied, for example, on a database of Calendars and Cardfiles to manage your schedule and personal contacts. When you install Windows 95 over Windows 3.1, you aren't asked whether you want to keep these accessories. They're just erased.

The new Windows 95 WordPad accessory looks shiny: it even lets you insert OLE objects—data from other programs—so that when you double-click on them, you can use the toolbars and menus from the program that originally created that data. You can insert sounds, graphics, even video clips. You can search and replace. You can even make WordPad mimic the look of other word processors, such as Word 6 or Write. All these features are pretty slick, and you may think you've got a full-featured word processor. But if you open a Word document in WordPad, it will automatically erase fancy formatting that you've spent hours on in Microsoft Word. WordPad doesn't support headers and footers, page numbers, curly quotes, small caps, superscripts, subscripts, or even double spacing! Beware this wolf masquerading in sheep's clothing. You may want to keep Write just because it looks like what it is, a simple no-frills editor, and you don't have to learn anything new to use it.

In other cases Windows 95 can do what Windows 3.1 did, but it does it in a different way, and doesn't always tell you how. Do you miss having two windows open at the same time in the File Manager and being able to drag files from one to the other? You can still do this in Windows 95, but it's not immediately obvious. Do you miss being able to view files with wildcards (to see all the files beginning with *Ch* in a folder at once, for example), copy and rename files at the same time, or copy files by date? You could do all this in Windows 3.1—and although it looks on the surface like you can't in Windows 95, you can. Those workarounds are explained in this chapter, too.

There are ways to get back some of the functionality you may miss from Windows 3.1. Be warned: Some of the workarounds will take you right back to good old DOS!

The Tools You'll Need

For the workarounds in this chapter, you'll need:

 The Windows 3.1 installation disks

A willingness to approach the command line

A devil-may-care attitude about what others think

The System Policy Editor (covered in Chapter 3)

The Applets You Can't Live Without

Windows 95 doesn't have a Cardfile, a scheduler, or a macro recorder, like Windows 3.1 does. Well, you can live without the Windows 3.1 macro recorder. But you may want to keep the Cardfile and the Calendar if you've come to depend on them, especially if you've set up a big database of card files with names, addresses, and phone numbers. Windows 95 doesn't tell you that it's going to erase these applets; it just goes right ahead and erases them when you install it over Windows 3.1.

In addition, you may want to keep Windows 3.1's Paintbrush and Windows Write. Why? Because their Windows 95 counterparts are strangely crippled. The 95 version of Paint won't save .PCX files, so if you try to edit one of these in Paint, you'll have to save it as a .BMP file.

Beware of WordPad!

On the surface WordPad it appears to be almost a full-featured word processor, but lurking below are serious omissions that you won't be aware of until it's too late. For one thing, it lets you save in only three formats—Rich Text Format (.rtf), Text Only (.txt), and Word 6.0. If you use WordPad to open a Windows Write document that you've done a lot of formatting on—and then go to save it, you can't save it as a Write document to give to someone using Windows 3.1.

It's even worse with a fancy-formatted Word document that you open in WordPad. Although WordPad looks sophisticated, with its support of OLE objects and so forth, it actually lacks a lot of rather basic features. Look at what it's missing. Open a Word document in WordPad, and your styles will be gone. Double spacing is removed; there's no double spacing in WordPad. Headers and footers, goodbye. There's no support for them in WordPad, either. No type-setter's quotes (curly quotes), either. No page numbering. No small caps, super-scripts, or subscripts. Nor is there an easy way to force manual page breaks (you can use Print Preview and press (ENTER) to insert blank lines to force page breaks, but there's no Page Break command). You get the idea. A Word document you've spent hours formatting and applying styles to suddenly has no styles, no page numbers, none of the above.

One more potential pitfall in WordPad: What you see on the screen probably isn't what you'll get when you print. The word wrap options in WordPad only affect the screen display, not the printed output. For the printed document, WordPad uses the margin settings specified in the Page Setup dialog box, although it doesn't tell you that. To view on the screen what you'll get when you print, use the "Wrap to ruler" option.

Steer clear of WordPad. As a workaround, rescue Windows Write from your 3.1 installation disks, or install Windows 95 for a dual boot so you can get to Write. Or stick to your regular word processor and Notepad.

To the Rescue

If you read this in time, copy these Windows 3.1 files onto a floppy disk before you install Windows 95: WRITE.EXE, WRITE.HLP, PBRUSH.EXE, PRUSH.HLP, PBRUSH.DLL, as well as CARDFILE.EXE, CARDFILE.HLP, CALENDAR.EXE, and CALENDAR.HLP, if you want them, too. Then after you install Windows 95, copy them from the floppy disk to the Windows 95 folder.

Expanding Compressed Files

But say it's too late. You've installed Windows 95 and the files are gone. Get out your original Windows 3.1 installation disks. Then use the EXPAND.EXE utility on Disk 2 to uncompress the Paintbrush, Write, and other files you want back. Copy EXPAND.EXE into your Windows 95 folder. Then use it, for example, to expand Paintbrush like this:

expand a:pbrush.ex_ c:\windows\pbrush.exe

Here's how the Expand command's syntax works. Compressed files have a _ as the last character of their extension. So enter the path to the compressed file and the path to where you want the uncompressed file to appear, substituting the last character in the real file name for the _.

The Files 95 Nukes

For your information, here are the Windows 3.1 files that Windows 95 gets rid of when you install it, in case you want some of these back:

 Microsoft Antivirus—mwavabsi.dll, mwavdrvi.dll, mwavmgr.dll, mwavtree.dll, mwavdlg.dll, mwav.exe, mwavscan.dll, mwavtsr.exe, mwavdosi.dll, mwav.hlp, mwavsos.dll, mwgrafic.dll

📌 Calendar—calendar.exe, calendar.hlp

📌 Cardfile—cardfile.exe, cardfile.hlp

📌 Clock—clock.exe

📌 Recorder—recorder.dll, recorder.exe, recorder.hlp

📌 Schedule (if you had it)—msremind.exe, schdplus.exe, trnsched.dll, mssched.dll, schdplus.hlp, schedmsg.dll, trnoff.dll

Use the above workarounds to retrieve the files you need.

How to Do What You Could in Windows 3.1 That You "Can't" in Windows 95

If you're willing to be a little adventuresome, you can find ways to do things in Windows 95 that its designers are trying to stop you from doing, like using wildcards and other neat stuff.

You Can't View Files with Wildcards Any More (Yes, You Can)

Here's another way Windows 95 has been made "easier": by taking away your ability to use wildcards. Sure, wildcards can be confusing and you should understand the rules before you use them, but it sure was nice to see, for instance, all the files in a folder whose names or extensions matched a certain pattern. Windows 95 took this away (but there's a workaround) and added a new system of its own (undocumented, of course) in the Find facility.

The Rules

First, a quick review of wildcard rules. The symbol * stands for any number of characters (or none at all), and ? stands for any one character (or none at all). In Windows 3.1, you could see all the files ending in .doc in a directory by specifying *.doc as the file type to view. That was handy for seeing, for example, all the Word documents that were in that folder ('scuse me, directory). If you wanted to see all the files that began with Report, ended with any other character, and had the .doc extension, you'd enter report?.doc and you'd see report2.doc and report.doc, if those were the files that matched that pattern.

This was all really handy, because in addition to seeing the listings, you could press (F8) and copy all the files ending in .doc. Or you could delete files whose names matched a certain pattern. Or move them. Or move and rename them at the same time. Windows 95 won't let you do this. You can display files by File Type, but that isn't the same as the extension, as you saw earlier in this chapter. (You no doubt found this out on your own the first time you tried to display files by File Type.) But there are workarounds.

The New Rules

The second problem, as you'll soon find out, Windows 95 (and its built-in DOS) has a new set of rules for using wildcards. Don't look for them in Help, because they're not documented. Most of the changes involve using the question mark character. But what can really throw you is that Windows 95's Find facility *assumes* you're using wildcards, even if you're not. If you enter chapter, it's as though you entered *chapter*.*, because it will find Shortcut to Chapter, Chapter 4, Chapter1—anything with *chapter* in it (Figure 6-1). This can drive you nuts till you figure out what's going on.

In addition, although it doesn't tell you, in Windows 95 you can use ? to specify the position where the character should match. For example, entering **?x?.*** will find any folder or file name that has x as the second character. Entering **?xy** finds xy anywhere after the first character, either in the name or the extension. Entering **?x?** locates files or folders with an x anywhere in their names, as long as it's not the first or last character of the name. Entering ***xyz*** finds files and folders with xyz anywhere in the name or the extension.

Bewildered by all these rules? Forget them. The practical rule of thumb is *enter as much as you can remember about the name of what you're searching for.*

Displaying Files That Match a Pattern

You're not restricted to using wildcards just in Find, although it seems you are at first glance. You can also use wildcards in applications' Open and Save As dialog boxes. So if you want to see a list of files whose names match a certain pattern, fire up WordPad, choose Open from the File menu, make sure you're looking at All Files (next to Files of type:), and enter your pattern in the File name box. (In my opinion, this is all WordPad's good for; see "Beware of WordPad!" earlier in this chapter.) More sophisticated programs like Word and WordPerfect will let you copy, rename, delete, and move right in their Open and Save As dialog boxes. So even if you don't need to use the program for the purpose it was designed for, you can use it for this kind of file management that

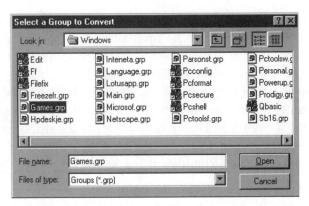

Figure 6-1. Searching in Find

you're used to from the old days. For an even more elegant solution, use the Find command (**F3**). It lets you use wildcards.

You Can't Rename with Wildcards (Yes, You Can)

Now let's look at a couple of other workarounds for typical problems. Although Windows 95 officially doesn't let you rename all the files in a directory at once, there's a way around that. Say that you want to rename all the files in a directory to have the extension .txt or .Doc, or begin with Chap. Windows 95 makes you right-click on each file one by one and rename them one by one. Instead, just sneak out to DOS and use REN, which will accept wildcards. For example, **ren *.* *.txt** renames all the files in a folder to have the extension .Txt. (As you can see, upper- and lowercase don't matter.)

If you try to outwit the system by selecting several files at once and then pressing **F2** for Rename, you're out of luck. It doesn't work.

You Can't Delete with Wildcards (Yes, You Can)

Here's another thing Windows 95 officially doesn't let you do: delete all the files whose names match a pattern. Back in the old File Manager, it was neat to be able to delete, say, all the files beginning with Chap by pressing **DEL** and entering **chap*.*** in the Delete dialog box, then saying Yes to All. In Windows 95, you'll just get asked if you want to send the files you've selected to the Recycle Bin. If you haven't select any files, all you'll get is a beep when you press **DEL**. Another PITA.

However, you can get around this limitation by using a couple of workarounds. First, you can use Find. Entering **A*.*** finds all the files beginning with A in the directory you choose. Then all you have to do is press (CTRL)+(A) to select them all, right-click, and choose Delete (or just press (DEL)).

You can also go to the DOS prompt and delete files by using wildcards, using the DEL command. Remember, though, that files deleted in DOS don't go to the Recycle Bin, and Windows 95 DOS has no Undelete command (see Chapter 3).

You Can't Move/Copy and Rename at the Same Time (Yes, You Can)

Because of the way The Explorer and My Computer are set up, you can't move a file named Girls to another folder and rename it Boys at the same time. You have to move Girls to the other folder, go to that folder, and rename it Boys. This can be a major PITA.

Instead, use this workaround. It's kludgy, but it works. You can do this with the new Windows 95 applications that have Save In boxes, like WordPad (finally, something WordPad's good for!). Open an application's Save As dialog box. Enter a different name for the file in the Save as text box (to rename it); then open the Save in list and double-click on the other folder you want the file saved in.

Or run the DOS XCOPY command. Remember, DOS is still there and can be of real use. To copy a file and rename it at the same time, do it this way:

xcopy c:\doc.txt a:doc.bak.

A more elegant workaround: Get the Windows 95 PowerToys ('scuse me, PowerTools; see Chapter 9 for how to get them) and install the Other Folder utility. Or, if you want to spend money, get the Norton Navigator. Both give you the ability to copy and rename at the same time.

You Can't Specify a Path Name (Yes, You Can)

Likewise, if you want to copy or move files in My Computer/the Explorer, you'll either have to have both folders open (to do it by dragging and dropping) or you'll have to open the folder with the files, select them and (CTRL)+(C) or (CTRL)+(X), and then locate the folder where you want them and paste them there. Again, go to the DOS prompt and use COPY or XCOPY. If you get the PowerTools or Norton Navigator, you can also specify a path name.

An aside: Don't try using the DOS COPY command in the Run box on the Start menu. It's an internal DOS command. Go to the DOS prompt. If you need to go to DOS often, make a shortcut to it and keep it on your desktop. The Run box accepts only the DOS commands listed in the Windows\Command folder or those you enter with a path name, such as **c:\dos\copy**.

However, XCOPY will work in the Run box. To see which DOS commands you can "run," look in your Windows\Command folder.

There's No Way to Copy Files by Date Quickly (Yes, There Is)

Want to copy all the files you worked on since last Wednesday? One way is to view them in the Explorer with details; then click on the Modified column heading to sort them, starting with the most recent file. Select the ones you want and copy them. Then go to the next folder that has files you may have worked with and do the same all over again. PITA. Takes too long.

Another way, which is much faster if your files aren't all in the same folder, is to run the old favorite DOS XCOPY command. For example:

xcopy *.* a: /d:02-16-96 /s

If you're at the top-level directory of your hard disk, this command will pick up all files modified on or after February 16, 1996, including those in any sub-directories (indicated by the /s switch).

Getting Around the Workarounds

If these DOS workarounds are driving you nuts, there's a workaround you can use to work around them: any batch files you create and store in the Windows\Command folder are available to you to use in Windows 95's Run box.

For example, you can create a batch file named F8.bat in the Notepad and save it in that Command folder. It should contain this line:

xcopy %1 %2

Now you can choose Run and enter **F8 test testnew** to make a new copy of the test file named testnew. Why F8? It was the old keyboard shortcut for Copy. For details on creating batch files, dust off a DOS book.

I Can't Stop Windows 95 from Changing My Desktop!

In Windows 3.1, everybody complained because they *wanted* to save their desktops just as they left them. Now Windows 95 does this by default. If a constantly changing desktop (it comes back the same way you left it) is driving you nuts, there's a workaround.

You have to install the Policy Editor if you didn't install it already for the workarounds in Chapter 3. It's on the CD-ROM in the D:\Admin\Apptools\Poledit folder.

1. Double-click on Add/Remove Programs in the Control Panel folder.
2. Select Windows Setup and click Have Disk.
3. Click Browse and enter **D:\Admin\Apptools\Poledit**.
4. Check the System Policy Editor box and click Install.
5. When it's through installing, click OK.

Now you'll find a shortcut to the System Policy Editor in your System Tools folder.

1. Run it, and choose Open Registry from its File menu.
2. Double-click on the Local User icon.
3. Double-click on Shell and Restrictions.
4. Check the "Don't save" settings at exit box.
5. Click OK and exit from the Policy editor, answering Yes when you're asked if you want to save the new settings.

Now your desktop will come back "clean" on startup, with no windows open (unless there's something in your StartUp folder).

Isn't There Any Easy Way to Convert a Windows 3.1 Program Group to Windows 95?

You may have had a program group set up just the way you liked it in Windows 3.1—say, a group with icons for the documents and spreadsheets you work with frequently and maybe an accessory program or two like the Calculator and the Notepad, or even a Games group with icons for your favorite games. You can convert it to a folder in Windows 95 instead of creating a new folder and creating shortcuts to those items. If you're only converting one group, the fastest way is to simply double-click its .grp file to automatically convert it to a Windows 95 folder.

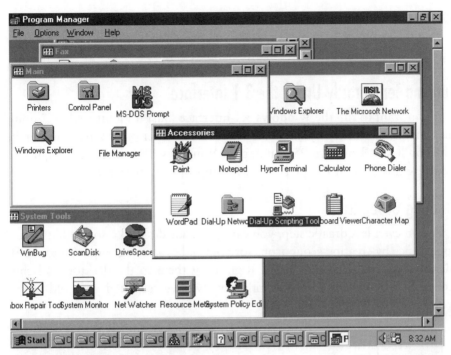

Figure 6-2. Running Grpconv.exe

If you're converting several groups, run the Grpconv command with the /m parameter to display a dialog box that lets you choose the groups you want to convert (Figure 6-2). When it finishes running, you'll find the group in your Windows 95 folder and a shortcut to it in the Programs folder on the Start menu.

If you want to recreate *all* your old Windows 3.1 program groups as folders, go to your Windows folder and rename Setup.old to Setup.ini. Then enter **grpconv /s** in the Run box, and Windows 95 will convert all your old program groups to folders.

I Hate Windows 95. How Can I Make It More Like Windows 3.1?

Edit System.ini in Notepad and change the shell=line from Explorer.exe to Progman.exe, and you'll have Windows 95 running and looking like your old Windows. Groups won't be the same, but you'll get icons for what used to be in them. All Windows 95's 32-bit functionality will be there, though. Pressing

205

(CTRL)+(ESC) brings up the Task List and lets you exit the way you used to, by ending the Program Manager's task. If you want the Explorer, just run Explorer with the Run command (enter **explorer**).

Running Temporarily Under the 3.1 Interface

If you want to run the Windows 3.1 interface "just for a little while," double-click on Progman.exe in your Windows folder or enter **progman** in the Run box, and you'll see Windows 95 running as Windows 3.1's interface (Figure 6-3). You saw this back in Chapter 1, but it's appropriate here, too.

Creating Group Icons

For an even less drastic step, you can give your desktop a somewhat retro 3.1 appearance by creating group icons for your old program groups. Go to the Start Menu folder and click Programs. Right-drag them to the desktop and choose Create Shortcut(s) Here. Keep going until you've recreated your old program groups.

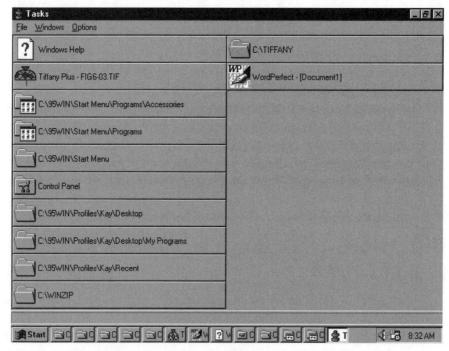

Figure 6-3. Running under the 3.1 interface

Getting the Task List Back

Do you miss the Task List? Windows 95 comes with an improved Task List-type utility called the Task Manager. It's not very well documented. But it's there, and you can do all sorts of stuff with it. If the taskbar and Start menu are driving you bananas, check out Taskman.exe in your Windows 95 directory (enter **taskman** in the Run box to see it in action). The Task Manager (Figure 6-4) lists all the things you have open, and you can switch among them by clicking on them. As extra features, you can run applications and shut down Windows from the Task Manager by using its File menu.

Put a shortcut to the Task Manager in your desktop. Or put it in your Startup group if you really like it, so it's always available on the taskbar. You can also assign it a hot key combination so you can hot-key to it. Or put it on the Start menu so that (CTRL)+(ESC) always brings it up, just as it brought up the Task List in Windows 3.1.

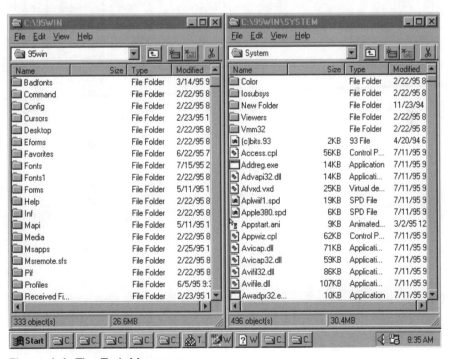

Figure 6-4. The Task Manager

Getting the File Manager Back

Miss the File Manager? If you're missing the File Manager's two-directory view, you can tweak Windows 95 to get something similar. Open two instances of the Explorer, right-click on the Task bar, and choose Tile Vertically (Figure 6-5). Now, when you shut down, leave these folders open so they'll be available the next time you start.

I Want to Get Rid of the Whole Thing. Period.

Recall from Chapter 1 that this is indeed possible, unless you bought a brand-new machine that never had Windows 3.1 on it to begin with (in which case you can install Windows 3.1 and then remove Windows 95). To remove Windows 95, go to the Control Panel and double-click on Add/Remove Programs. Click the Install/Uninstall tab and choose Windows 95 as the thing you want to remove.

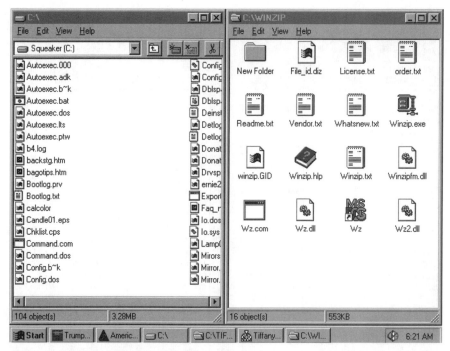

Figure 6-5. Getting a two-directory view

Be careful if you have a brand-new machine configured only with Windows 95! If you remove Windows 95, you'll have no operating system left. Many machines today come with Windows 95 pre-installed, and you get no installation disks or CD, so you can cause yourself a lot of heartache by trying to remove Windows 95. Install Windows 3.1 on your machine; then you can remove 95. Keep that emergency startup disk handy (see Chapter 1), just in case something goes wrong.

And Next...

Want to surf the Internet and crawl the Web? It's sometimes not as easy as Microsoft would have you believe. Check out the pitfalls and procedures in Chapter 7 if you're having trouble with your dial-up connections.

Chapter 7

Lost on the Internet with Windows 95?

Road Kill on the Information Highway

Lost on the Internet with Windows 95?

Road Kill on the Information Highway

"One day you will receive
Web browsers in your cereal box."

Mike Zisman, IBM VP and CEO of Lotus Development, 1996

Windows 95 has one feature that really confuses and annoys folks who've been using the Internet with a service provider other than the Microsoft Network. The gist of the situation is that when you install the Microsoft Network that comes with Windows 95, it goes and steps on the settings of whatever Internet provider you may have been using. Suddenly you can't get on Netscape or CompuServe or AOL any more!

What's happened is that Windows 95 has renamed a very necessary file for communicating with the Internet and has in effect replaced it with its own version of that file.

(In this chapter you'll see exactly which files are affected and how to fix them.) Most providers have provided updates to make their software compatible with Windows 95's by now. But before you can get the update, you have to first figure out what's causing the problem (which is rather mysterious since the only obvious symptom is that a program that was running fine under version 3.1 is suddenly dead in the water under Windows 95) and second, contact the provider's manufacturer and download the latest version (which is rather difficult considering that you can't get on the Internet). A classic Catch-22. There's a way around it, which I'll tell you about in this chapter.

You'll also see how to set up a PPP or SLIP connection, figure out your DNS address, automate dial-up networking, remove the "unremovable" Network Neighborhood icon, add CompuServe to your Internet connection, and many more interesting things that aren't included in the online Help.

The Tools You'll Need

To get on the Internet, you'll of course need:

- A modem
- An Internet service provider account, which can be an account with an information utility like America Online or the Microsoft Network (which comes with Windows 95), or a direct dial-up PPP (Point-to-Point Protocol) or SLIP (Serial Line Internet Protocol) account
- A Web browser such as Netscape or the Internet Explorer included with the PLUS pack or available via download from Microsoft, as well as software for e-mail, ftp, or other desired functions
- Patience, especially if you have a slow modem (14.4 Kps or slower) and you want to browse the World Wide Web

You can get a browser from several different sources:

- The Windows 95 Plus Pack has a Microsoft browser and other tools
- Information services (AOL, CompuServe, and so forth) have buuilt-in browsers (upgrade if you don't have one yet)
- Shareware browsers (Netscape, Mosaic, and so forth) can be found in information services' software libraries as well as in other places

CompuServe (America Online, Prodigy, you name it) Won't Work with Windows 95! It Worked Fine Before!

This is the big problem that almost everybody's complaining about. When you install the Microsoft Network, which comes with Windows 95, it renames your old Winsock.dll so that your programs can't access it any more. As a result, a dial-up connection that was working fine under Windows 3.1 is suddenly dead in the water.

Trumpet Winsock is a special program that lets you dial up the Internet (it looks for a "socket"—that's why it's called Winsock). You may not even know it's there, because your program, like CompuServe, uses it behind the scenes.

First, you need to check to see if you have more than one Winsock file. Some applications that use Winsock copy their own Winsock.dll file into their directory, which may be the cause of your troubles. Having more than one Winsock.dll invites trouble. Use the Find utility (F3) and search your whole hard disk for any Winsocks. Rename each one Winsock.1, Winsock.2, and so forth. Leave the one named Winsock.old alone for the next step.

Second, the Find utility should have found a file named Winsock.old. That's the one your application was using. Windows 95 renamed it. Your application is looking for it and can't find it. Rename it Winsock.dll.

Next, use the Notepad to look at the PATH statement in your Autoexec.bat and make sure the path to the folder containing the real Winsock.dll is there.

Finally, restart Windows. You should be able to use your program now.

Once you get through, contact the application's vendor and ask if they can send you an updated version that will work with Windows 95's Winsock.dll (see Chapter 10).

My New Windows 95 (32-bit Winsock) Program Doesn't Work!

This is a different problem. If you're using the 32-bit version of something like Netscape, you'll need a 32-bit Winsock.dll. Windows 95's 32-bit Winsock is called Wsock32.dll. That's the one you want to use instead of Winsock.dll, so make sure your program can find it and it hasn't been renamed something else. It should be in your Windows 95 \System folder.

If you get the error message "Netscape was unable to create network socket connection (Reason 10047)," that means you're trying to use the 16-bit .dll (Winsock.dll). Make sure it's not in your path. If Windows 95 encounters the Trumpet Winsock.dll file, it can crash.

If you're connecting via SLIP or PPP, you'll need to set up dial-up connections to the Internet.

How on Earth Do I Set up a PPP Connection?

You'll need to install TCP/IP support. Then you'll install the Dial-up Adapter and configure it. Then you'll need to configure your dial-up connection. You'll need patience. You'll also need to know quite a few facts about the connection you're setting up, such as whether you have a static (dedicated) or a dynamic (variable) IP address (most likely, yours is dynamic), your host's domain name, IP (Internet Protocol) subnet mask, gateway IP address, and DNS (Domain Name Server) address.

If you were previously using a dial-up utility such as Trumpet Winsock, the easiest way to find this stuff out is to check its settings (in the case of Trumpet Winsock, choose Setup from its File menu).

This procedure is pretty complex. You can get the Internet Wizard with the Plus! Pack (see Chapter 9), and it will step you through it. But I'll assume you don't have the Wizard, just in case. You can also find more detailed information at http://windows95.com, where Steve Jenkins provides all sorts of Internet connectivity information.

The first step: If Dial-up Networking isn't installed on your computer, you'll have to install it. To install dial-up networking:

1. Double-click on the Add/Remove Programs icon in the Control panel folder.

2. Click the Windows Setup tab and double-click Communications.

3. Choose Dial-Up Networking (Figure 7-1) and OK and follow the instructions on the screen.

Now check whether everything's okay. Double-click the Network icon in the Control Panel folder. You'll see a dialog box like the one in Figure 7-2.

Click the Configuration tab and make sure that the Dial-Up Adapter and TCP/IP are there. If they aren't:

1. To add the Dial-Up Adapter, click Add, double-click Adapter, scroll down, and select Microsoft.

2. Choose Dial-Up Adapter and OK.

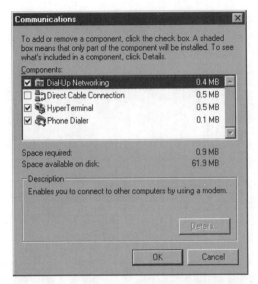

Figure 7-1. Installing Dial-up Networking

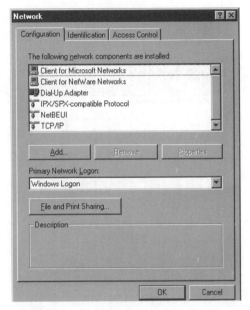

Figure 7-2. Checking the network configuration

3. If you need to install TCP/IP, click Add, double-click Protocol, and select Microsoft, then TCP/IP.

4. Click OK.

Now your Network Configuration page should contain both Dial-Up Adapter and TCP/IP, as in Figure 7-2.

5. Now double-click on the Dial-Up Adapter, click Properties, click Bindings, and make sure the TCP/IP box is checked (Figure 7-3). Click OK.

Now you need to configure the TCP/IP protocol. This is where all that stuff you need to know comes in. What you do depends on whether you get your IP address dynamically or not. If you don't know, you can try one way and then the other to see which works. Most folks get it dynamically, so try that first.

1. Back at the Network Configuration sheet, click TCP/IP and then click Properties.

2. Wow! You need to fill all this stuff out (Figure 7-4). Click each tab in turn.

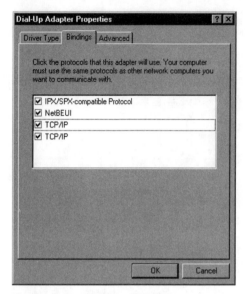

Figure 7-3. Checking TCP/IP

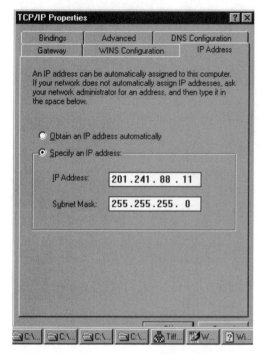

Figure 7-4. Configuring TCP/IP (dynamic)

- IP Address—If you get your IP address dynamically, select the "Obtain an IP address automatically" option. If you don't, select the "Specify an IP address" option. Then type in your IP address, which was assigned to you by your provider, and fill in the Subnet Mask text area, which is probably 255.255.255.0.

- WINS Configuration—Select Disable WINS Resolution (Figure 7-5).

- Gateway—Enter the gateway for your access provider (Figure 7-6). Try 0.0.0.0 if you don't know it. Click Add.

- Bindings—Keep Client for Microsoft Networks option checked.

- Advanced—No changes needed.

- DNS Configuration—Select Enable DNS. Enter your user name in the Host box (Figure 7-7). For Domain, enter the name of your provider, such as net.net.

  1. In the DNS Server Search Order section, enter the IP address of your provider's name server. Click Add.

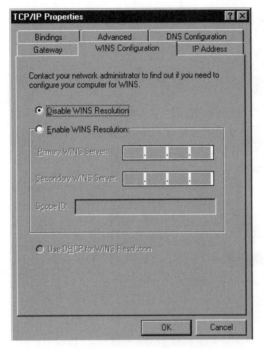

Figure 7-5. The WINS Configuration tab

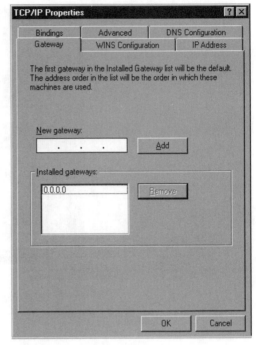

Figure 7-6. The Gateway tab

2. In the Domain Suffix Search Order section, enter the domain suffix (it's usually the same as the domain). Click Add.

3. Click OK until you're asked whether you want to restart (the taskbar may be covering up an OK); say Yes.

After you restart, you're ready to configure your dial-up connection.

1. Double-click the Dial-Up Networking icon. It's on the Start menu; look in Programs and Accessories.

2. Double-click the Make New Connection icon (Figure 7-8) and follow the instructions on the screen (Figure 7-9).

Here are some notes to keep in mind:

Name the icon you're creating for your dial-up connection anything you want, such as To the Internet! It doesn't matter what you name it. If you have more than one dial-up connection, you'll need to go through this process again and create an icon for it, too. Be descriptive.

219

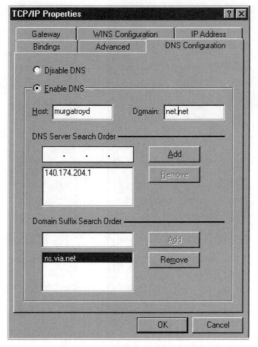

Figure 7-7. Configuring your DNS
(Domain Name Server)

Figure 7-8. Starting
to configure a dial-
up connection

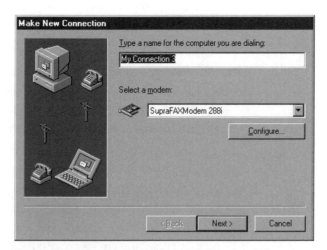

Figure 7-9. The Make a New Connection Wizard

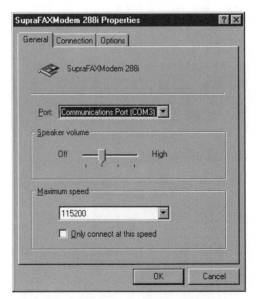

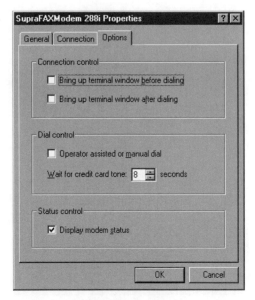

Figure 7-10. Configuring the modem   Figure 7-11. Setting options

🖈 Click Configure to configure your modem. On the General tab (Figure 7-10), choose a fast speed for your modem. If you have a 28.8 Kps modem, for example, set the speed to 115200; *Don't* check "Only connect at this speed," so that your modem will adjust its speed as necessary.

🖈 On the Options tab, your best bet is to leave the "Bring up terminal window after dialing" unchecked (Figure 7-11). You can go back and change it to "Bring up terminal window after dialing" if you can't get through the first time. Click OK.

🖈 When you're asked for a phone number, add ***70,** (be sure to include the comma) at the beginning if you have call waiting. This code disables call waiting.

Now you need to set the dial-up properties. Right-click on your new icon and choose Properties. In the dialog box you see (Figure 7-12), click Server Type. In the Type of Dial-Up Server section, choose PPP from the list (Figure 7-13). Keep "Log on to network" (in the Advanced options section) unchecked for now. Click OK twice.

Now (theoretically) all you need to do to connect is double-click the connection icon, enter your name and password, and click Connect.

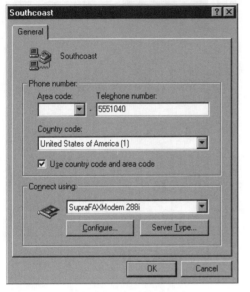

Figure 7-12. Configuring dial-up
properties

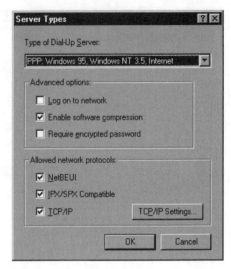

Figure 7-13. Choosing a server type

If you don't log on, go back and adjust that "Bring up terminal window after dialing" setting. You'll see a screen to fill out, and it will tell you what number you're connecting to. Write that number down and click Continue. When you're asked for a PPP Connection IP Address, enter the number you wrote down.

You should be done. I am. But other stuff may go wrong, so read on.

I Can't Figure out How to Set up a SLIP Connection!

When Windows 95 first shipped, it seemed to allow only PPP connections, not SLIP. But you can set up for SLIP if you know where to look and you have Windows 95 on CD-ROM.

First, you'll need to install dial-up networking if it isn't already installed. See the preceding technique for how to do that. Next, install SLIP support.

1. Double-click on the Add/Remove Programs icon in the Control Panel folder.

2. Click Windows Setup and Have Disk.

3. Browse to locate the \Admin\Apptools\Dscript folder and then click on the Rnaplus.inf file. Click OK twice.

Figure 7-14. Installing SLIP support

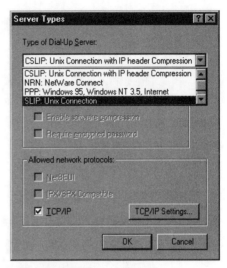

Figure 7-15. Selecting SLIP

4.   Check the SLIP and Scripting for Dial-Up Networks box and click Install (Figure 7-14).

When you're done, restart your computer.

Now you need to double-click on Dial-Up Networking and create a new connection (see the preceding technique). When you're done with that, right-click on the new connection's icon and choose Properties. Click Server Type and choose SLIP (or CSLIP) (Figure 7-15).

Now click TCP/IP Settings and fill out all the TCP/IP information your host computer needs. Again, see the preceding technique for details.

When you're all done, double-click on your connection icon, enter your name and password, and click Connect.

Help! I Can't Find out What My DNS Address Is!

To find this number, you can log into your provider with a Windows terminal and type **nslookup**. Your provider's server will return the DNS address. If that doesn't work, try using 128.95.1.4. That's the Microsoft default. If you were previously using Trumpet Winsock, the DNS address is the Name server value in the Trumpet Winsock Setup dialog box.

Is There Somewhere I Can Find out About What All Those IP Numbers Are?

There's a program called Winipcfg.exe in your Windows 95 directory. Double-clicking on it brings up information about your IP connection, if it's already set up on your computer (Figure 7-16).

If you were using Trumpet Winsock, you can check its Setup dialog box, where you'll find the PR address, the Netmask values, the Default Gateway, and other numbers.

Is There Any Way to Automate Dial-up Networking? I Hate Having to Enter My Name and Password by Hand.

If you got Windows 95 on CD-ROM, look in the Admin\Apptools\Dscript folder. There's a program called Scripter there. It will log you into the Internet automatically. Or you can get Robodun, a freeware automated scripting program for SLIP/PPP connections at ftp.southwind.net//users/l/leeb/rdun61.zip (just one of many locations that has it). Or you can get the Plus! Pack, which comes with dial-up scripting. See the neat Internet tools you can download in Chapter 9.

Is There Any Way to Automatically Redial?

Yes, but it's turned off by default. Weird. To turn it back on, double-click the Dial-Up Networking icon and choose Settings from the Connections menu. Check Redial (Figure 7-17) and choose the settings you want. Click OK.

If you keep getting disconnected, get the freeware program RTV_Reco. See the "Other Goodies" section in this chapter.

I Go Nuts Looking for My Dial-up Networking Connections. Is There an Easy Way to Access Them?

If you have several dial-ups, you can make a folder for them and put it on the Start menu. Right-click on the Start button and choose Explore. You should wind up in the Start Menu folder. Right-click the Explorer's right pane and choose New and Folder. Type the following and press (ENTER):

Dial-Up Net.{992CFFA0-F557-101A-88EC-00DD010CCC48}

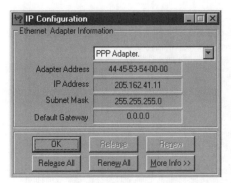

Figure 7-16. Checking Winipcfg.exe

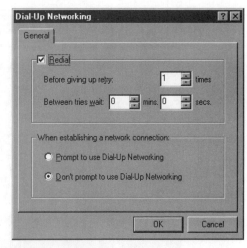

Figure 7-17. Turning on Redial

This gives you a Dial-Up Net folder on the Start Menu with all your network dial-up connections in it (Figure 7-18).

I Can't Get That *** Network Neighborhood Icon off My Desktop!

If you're "networked" with a SLIP or PPP dial-up connection, you may not want that Network 'Hood icon on your desktop. Dragging it to the Recycle Bin doesn't delete it. You gotta hack the registry.

1. Run the Policy Editor. You may need to install it first. It's on the CD-ROM in the D:\Admin\Apptools\Poledit folder.

2. If you're asked to Open a template file, select Admin.adm.

3. Choose Open Registry from the File menu.

4. Double-click on the Local User icon.

5. Open Local_User Shell Restrictions.

6. Check Hide network neighborhood. Then click OK, save the file, and exit.

7. Click on the desktop and press (F5) to refresh it.

One word of caution: If you remove the Network Neighborhood icon, you won't be able to use UNC notation (such as \\server) to access network resources. If you want to be able to access them, you should map network resources to a local

Figure 7-18. Creating a Dial-Up Net folder on the Start menu

drive letter before you take out the Network Neighborhood icon. (To do this, right-click on My Computer and choose Map Network Drive.) Direct Cable Connection will always display an error message about not being able to open the server, but it will run OK.

The Little Flashing Modem Icon Is Driving Me Nuts!

You can get rid of the modem on the taskbar that flashes whenever you make a dial-up connection. It can indeed drive you nuts. The problem is that you have to do it for all your dial-up connections.

1. Open the shortcut to Dial-Up Networking. It's on the Start menu under Accessories, and I recommend that you put a shortcut to it on the desktop. This is one of those "mystery" accessories whose original is safely hidden away.

2. Right-click on the first connection (you'll need to do this for all of them, one by one) and choose Properties.

226

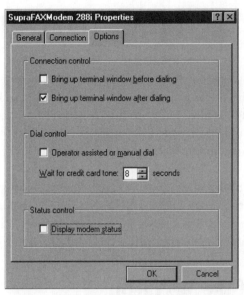

Figure 7-19. Nuking the modem icon
on the taskbar

3. Click Configure.
4. Click the Options tab (Figure 7-19) and uncheck Display Modem Status.
5. Click OK till you get back to the desktop.

I Can't Get Through to MSN!

There's a Signup and Access Troubleshooter you can use. Right-click the Microsoft Network icon on your desktop, and then click Connection Settings. Click Help.

Sometimes your modem will try again and again without success. If this happens, you might be in an area code that isn't accessible to Microsoft's toll-free signup number. If this happens, go to the Connection Settings dialog box, click Access Numbers, click Change, and choose a number in your calling area. Now click Try Again.

If all else fails, you can call Microsoft Customer Service. Right-click on the MSN icon and choose Properties; then scroll to find the number to call.

Every Time I Try to Get Through to MSN, It Disconnects!

The first time you try to get on MSN, the network looks for a special file that may have the wrong name on your hard drive. Go to the Explorer and make sure you're showing all files. Find the file named 800950.dat and rename it to 800950.da_. It should be in your Microsoft Network folder.

If this doesn't work and you still can't connect to MSN, try turning off error correction.

You may wonder why there's not more here on MSN. It's slow, that's why. It takes you through too many dialog boxes without giving control back to you. I don't like it. Netscape is better. You can get the 32-bit version at ftp://ftp.mcom.com/pub/netscape/windows/n32e122.exe.

I Can't Get Rid of the MSN Icon!

There's one good way... remove the Microsoft Network. Use the Add/Remove Programs control panel.

My Modem Settings Are All Screwed Up!

You need to change properties for the modem you're calling MSN by double-clicking the MSN icon on your desktop, clicking Settings, and then clicking Modem Settings. MSN overrides some Control Panel modem settings, so if you try to change settings via the modem's Control Panel, they don't always "take."

Help! I Want to Add CompuServe to My Internet Stuff!

The easiest way to do this is to use the Microsoft Internet Wizard. It's in the Microsoft Plus! Pack, or you can download it directly from Microsoft at http://www.windows.microsoft.com/windows/download/msie10.exe.

When you run the Wizard, answer the prompts this way:

1. Choose "I already have an account with a different service provider".
2. Choose your default modem.
3. For service provider, type **CompuServe**.
4. For phone number, enter your CompuServe access phone number. You may want to add at the beginning of the number ***70,** (with the comma) to disable call waiting.

5. Choose "Bring up terminal window" after dialing.

6. Enter your CompuServe user name and password.

7. For IP Address, choose "My Internet Service Provider automatically assigns me one."

8. For DNS Server, enter 149.174.211.5 and enter 149.174.213.5 for Alternate DNS Server.

9. Enable the Use Internet Mail option.

10. In the Your Email Address box, enter your CompuServe user number (use a period to separate the two numbers instead of a comma), followed by @compuserve.com.

11. Enter **mail.compuserve.com** as the CompuServe mail server.

12. Click Finish, and Windows makes your new connection icon.

Finished, hah! Now you've got to configure it.

1. Right-click on the new icon and choose Properties.

2. Click Server Type.

3. In the Type of Dial-Up Server section, choose PPP:Windows 95, Windows NT Internet.

4. Uncheck Log on to network.

5. Check TCP/IP in the Allowed network protocols section.

6. Don't allow software compression.

7. To dial up, double-click on your new icon. Leave the User ID and Password box blank. Click Connect. When CompuServe answers, press (ENTER) and type **cis**. Then press (ENTER) and type your user id and password, pressing (ENTER) after each. Finally, type **go pppconnect** and press (ENTER).

8. Click Continue or press (F7).

Now you should be on CompuServe.

Connecting to AOL via Windows 95

Setting up for CompuServe is Byzantine; AOL isn't a problem, but I'll mention it here in case you're wondering. You need to be using at least version 2.5 of AOL, and you only have to do this once. Within AOL, go to the Set Up and Sign on Screen, click Setup, and click Create Location. Give your new location a name and fill out all the boxes, such as those about your modem speed, outside prefixes, Touch Tone, and so forth, except the one for the phone number;

leave it blank. As your network, choose TCP/IP (click to see the pop-up list). Save the information and exit from AOL. From then on, all you have to do is connect to your service provider via Windows 95 and then double-click on the AOL icon. When you sign on, choose the location you just created (click Setup to select it) if you don't see the new location's name after Current Location just above your screen name.

It Doesn't Remember My Password!

Windows 95 is supposed to remember your password if you use dial-up networking or shared network resources (as discussed in Chapter 8). But sometimes it doesn't. This is because you probably bypassed the log-in dialog box by pressing (ESC) or clicking Cancel, so Windows 95 hasn't opened your password cache.

To get around this, log onto Windows 95. If you aren't normally asked for a log on, double-click on the Passwords icon in the Control Panel folder, click the User Profiles tab, and check the "Users can customize their preferences and desktop settings" button. The next time you start Windows 95, you'll be asked to log on. Don't press (ESC) or click Cancel. If you don't have a password, create a new one by typing one in the Password box, or create a null password by clicking OK. Creating a null password tells Windows 95 to open the password cache when you log on, which saves your dial-up networking password from one session to another.

Help! I Can't Get Netscape 1.1 for Windows NT to Work!

There are dial-up networking problems with this version. Solution: Add this line to the [Main] section of Netscape.ini:

DDEhosted=Yes

I Got Internet Explorer. I Don't Like It. How Can I Get Rid of It?

The Internet Explorer can make you furious by changing all the associations to URLs you'd set up while previously using Netscape or some other browser. This alone may make you want to get rid of the Internet Explorer. But it ain't simple.

First, drag the Internet Explorer's icon and its folder to the Recycle Bin. Empty the Recycle Bin.

Then run Regedit, choose Find from the Edit menu, and search for URL and Internet. If you find text that's associated with Internet Explorer, delete its entry in the Registry. If you're not using MSN, you can also get rid of any entry containing the word Favorites. Then restart your computer to get rid of the Favorites folder.

Other Goodies

You may want to supplement your Windows 95 Internet package with some other goodies once you get connected to the Net. Here are some ideas, but these are just the tip of the iceberg! Look at Chapter 9, too. And don't forget to get Netscape and some of the other goodies mentioned in this chapter.

Many of these are available at Randy's Windows 95 Resource Page (http://www.cris.com/~randybrg/win95.html); highly recommended for one-stop shopping. For other interesting Internet sites to visit for information about Internet applications, try Windows 95 Internetworking Headquarters at http://nearnet.gnn.com/gnn/wic/windows.15.html or Dial-up Networking at http://www.wwa.com/~barry/win95slip.html.

- Eudora Lite (freeware)—a Windows mail reader program. Get it at ftp://ftp.qualcomm.com/quest/eudora/windows/eudor152.zip

- Craig's Connect Time Monitor—keeps track of how much time you spend online. *Do you want to know?* Get it at ftp://papa.indstate.edu/winsock-l/time_log/ccm281.zip

- RTV_Reco—if your dial-up networking connection keeps timing out, this will reconnect you. Put it in the Startup group and you won't need to worry about losing connections. It's freeware or donation-ware. Get it at Randy's: http://www.cris.com/~randybrg/win95.html as rtv_reco41.zip

- Dial-up Scripter—automates your remote access. Includes a Help file, too. Get it at http://www.windows.microsoft.com/windows/download/dscrpt.exe

- KeepGoin'—an alternative to RTV_Reco. Now you won't have to click Connect each time you try to dial up the Internet. Get it at http://www.cris.com/~randybrg/win95/keepgoin12.zip

- Mail Notify—Retrieves e-mail headers for you from your POP3 server and notifies you when new mail is arriving. Shareware. Get it at

  http://olympe.polytechnique.fr/~zic/english/notify.html

- Fingerer/32 (also named InterSnoop)— a Finger client, Whois Client, CCSO Ph client, Name Server Lookup client, and ICMP Pinger. Get it at

  ftp://papa.indstate.edu/winsock-l/Windows95/Finger/fing031b.zip or

  http://www.akiss.lm.com/ISnoop.ZIP

- Internet Explorer—Microsoft's web browser. Get it at

  http://www.windows.microsoft.com/windows/ie/ie.htm

- HotJava Win32—"a prototype of a dynamic, extensible World Wide Web browser that provides the unique feature of 'executable content.' HotJava brings interactivity to Web pages and showcases many of the capabilities of the Java language." Free.

  Get it at

  http://java.sun.com/

  No doubt a newer version is available by now. You need Netscape 2.0 to use it.

- NCSA Mosaic—the original WWW browser. Free. Get it at

  http://www.ncsa.uiuc.edu/SDG/Software/WinMosaic/HomePage.html

- Internet Assistant—lets you create HTML documents from Word for Windows 95 documents. Free from Microsoft. Get it at http://198.105.232.6/msoffice/freestuf/msword/download/ia/ia95/default.html

And Next...

We'll look at some network problems in the next chapter. Some of what's there may be relevant to you if you're connecting to the Internet but not really as part of a network.

Chapter 8

It's Not Speaking to Me!
Networking Issues

It's Not Speaking to Me!
Networking Issues

"This 'telephone' has too many shortcomings to be seriously considered as a means of communication. The device is inherently of no value to us."

Western Union internal memo, 1876

The most popular game in town seems to be sneaking Windows 95 past your company's MIS administration and onto your office computer, despite the administration's dire threats of what will happen to you and your paycheck if you do this. They have their reasons—most notably that the company's custom applications they paid outside programmers megabucks for may not run as well as they used to, or may not run at all. Also, providing technical support for several different operating systems is something they probably don't want to jump into right away. MIS managers are known to be prone to doing things the long, slow, "good old" way. And they're worried about Windows 95's lack of security, too, as well they might be (see "There Ain't No Such Thing as Desktop Security" in Chapter 3 in case you skipped this hot topic).

Using Windows 95's long file names on a network can cause troubles for those still running Windows 3.1, with its limitation of eight characters plus a three-character extension. The non-Windows 95 users on the net aren't seeing your long file names at all, but are seeing Windows 95's truncated version of them. Plus, using Windows 95's new long printer names on a mixed network of 3.1 and 95 machines can lose a print job before you know it, because the system can't figure out to which printer you want to send the job. And your favorite shortcuts, to non-Windows 95 network users, are simply empty files with a .LNK extension—if they try to open them, there's nothing there. So you may not be seeing Windows 95 at work yet.

But it doesn't matter whether you're connecting two computers, such as your notebook and your desktop machine, or two thousand in a large company—networking issues can be a hassle. It's one thing to be a network user; it's a completely different thing to be a system administrator and have to install and maintain a network. Obviously that topic alone could fill several books, each one about a specific network. So this chapter will address some common networking problems, and hopefully point you toward other resources that can bail you out when it seems like the ship is going down.

I'm a System Administrator, and I Need All the Help I Can Get!

It's not immediately obvious, but Windows 95 comes with a set of tools on the CD-ROM, in \Admin\Nettools\Netsetup (Figure 8-1). There's a utility named Netsetup.exe that lets you write a script for installing Windows 95 on your network (a "push" installation). You'll have to install it separately, because it's not automatically installed when you install Windows 95.

It's beyond the scope of this book to tell you all the how-to's of using NetSetup, but the tool is there, ready and waiting for you. With a lot of luck, you can edit its sample script to meet your needs.

By all means, don't overlook the extensive Help and tour files in \Admin\Reskit\Helpfile (Figures 8-2 and 8-3). You'll find detailed discussions of

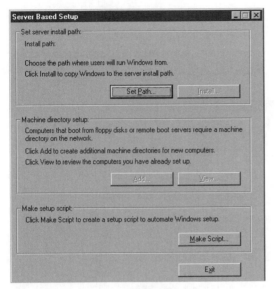

Figure 8-1. Running Netsetup

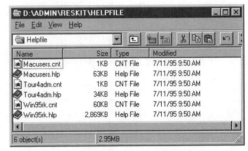

Figure 8-2. Getting network help

Figure 8-3. Help contents

237

technical networking issues (Figure 8-4) as well as specific instructions about individual products (Figure 8-5).

On the Web, visit sites like the Unofficial Question and Answer Database (QUAID) at http:whidbey.net/~mdixon/win40001.htm and the Windows 95

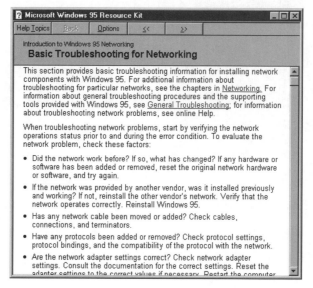

Figure 8-4. Technical discussion

Figure 8-5. Help on a specific product

Networking FAQ at http://www-leland.stanford.edu/~llurch/win95net-bugs/faq.html (a really good one). And Microsoft itself publishes known problems and workarounds at The Windows Knowledge Base, http://www.microsoft.com/kb/indexes/windows.htm.

Installation Woes

Be sure to remark out any TSRs before you install Windows 95. Also REM out ANSI.SYS. If you're on a real-mode network, disable it before installing Windows 95. Also disable any drive mappings, so that Windows Setup can locate your real startup drive. If you're on a peer-to-peer network like LANtastic, use the Custom installation so Windows 95 won't detect your network adapter. (If it detects a network adapter, it tries to install a Microsoft network.) Then restart! Lots of folks forget that you need to restart so *these settings can take effect*.

Some administrators have found the best way to install Windows 95 over a network is to install Windows 3.1 (if it isn't already installed on the network). Then install the real-mode network and then Windows 95, so that any 3.1 files the network installation program needs are findable.

I'm Trying to Do a Remote Administration of Windows 95 from My NT 3.5 Server, and It Won't Work!

Try installing \Admin95\Nettools\Remotreg\Regserv.exe from the CD-ROM. Use the Add/Remove programs icon in the Control Panels folder. This should update your Registry with the right files.

Also, make sure you've allowed user-level access control (check the Network icon's Access Control tab). Then check its Configuration tab and make sure file sharing is enabled.

As a last step, go to the Passwords icon in the Control Panel folder, click the Remote Administration tab, and check Enable Remote Administration of this server. And make sure the right server is listed in the Administrator box.

My Password Got Screwed Up, and It's Driving Me Crazy!

If you're trying to make a dial-up connection and you suddenly find a whole lot of resources mysteriously unavailable, Windows 95 may have screwed up your password. This has been known to happen over NT and NetWare servers.

The workaround: Delete your .PWD or .PWL (password) files; then try to reconnect. You'll be asked for a new password.

I Hate Going Through the Network Neighborhood to Find Another Computer.

There's an easier way. Use the Run command and type the path to the computer you want to connect to, like this: *ervername*.

How Can I Be More Secure on a Network?

Turn off print and file sharing for TCP/IP! That way, anybody on the Net can't access your files at will. Double-click on the Network icon in the Control Panel folder. Click the Configuration tab; then choose your network. Click File and Print Sharing and uncheck the boxes for sharing (Figure 8-6).

It Seems to Me That Everybody on the Network Has Access to All My Files!

If you're on an IP network, Windows 95 warns you about this and asks if you want to disable file sharing. But on a peer-to-peer network, where you're simply connected to other PCs running Windows 95 (or Windows for Workgroups, or Windows NT, or OS/2), everybody does have access to all your files unless you do something about that.

Here's the catch. If you're not on a NetWare network, you can share either all your files or none of them. So let's assume you're on a NetWare network.

First, double-click on the Network icon in the Control Panel folder; next, click Access Control. Then decide whether you're going to specify exactly what

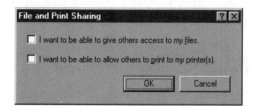

Figure 8-6. Turning off file sharing for everybody on the net

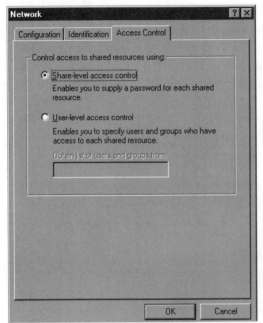

Figure 8-7. Configuring access control

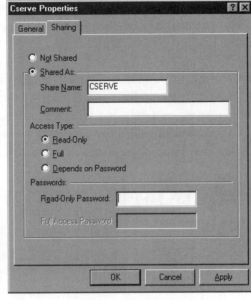

Figure 8-8. Specifying access control

folks can share (share-level access control), or who can access your shared resources (user-level access control) (see Figure 8-7).

To pick which files you want to share, go to My Computer, right-click on the folder or printer to which you want to control access, and choose Properties. Click the Sharing tab; then click Shared As and set the access you want to give (Figure 8-8). If you don't see the Sharing tab, you haven't enabled file and printer sharing yet (see the preceding paragraph).

If you're a network administrator who's concerned about security, set up your folks so they can't share files. If users don't have access to the Network control panel, they can't share files (see Chapter 3's discussion of "There's No Such Thing as Desktop Security").

Network Security Seems Pretty Puny, or Is That Just My Imagination?

It's not your imagination. Although there are a few things administrators can do to restrict access to the network, the local desktop running Windows 95 is wide open. A casual user can simply press (ESC) to bypass the opening log-on dialog, or boot from a floppy (see "There Ain't No Such Thing as Desktop Security" in Chapter 3 if you missed it). A user without a network password can't get access to network resources, but a determined hacker with a decryption key could conceivably crack the stored password.

As a network administrator, you can use the Policy Editor to disable password caching; that will stop random users from cracking the stored NetWare passwords. Open the Registry and double-click on Local Computer, Network, and Passwords; then check the "Disable password caching" box.

Yow! The Log-on Goes Past on the Screen Too Fast to Follow!

Sometimes you'll need to diagnose what's going on at log-on if you're having problems logging on the net. But the text flies passed on the screen too quickly for the human eye to follow.

The workaround: To be able to see what's going on, put a Pause command in the user script. Then you can edit the user script by running NetWare's Syscon utility.

By the way, you may have a problem if you use lowercase letters for drive letters in a NetWare script. Change drive letters to uppercase. Commas may not be recognized, either; try using ANDs instead.

I Can't Change My NetWare Password!

Windows 95 doesn't tell you this up front, but you can't use the Passwords icon in the Control Panel folder to change your NetWare password. This to me is not logical. You can go berserk trying to figure out why your new password didn't "take."

The workaround: Use the NetWare SETPASS command at the DOS prompt. If you change your password often (didn't Cliff Stoll say "treat your password like your toothbrush: use it every day and change it frequently"?), use the Notepad to make a batch file of the SETPASS command and put a shortcut to it on your desktop.

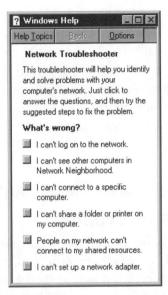

Figure 8-9. The Network troubleshooter

Help! I'm Having Network Problems Not Covered Here!

There is a Network Troubleshooter. Press (F1) for Help; then use the index to go the shared folders. Click troubleshooting, and you'll see it (Figure 8-9). This can get you out of lots of network trouble.

My Network Printer Won't Print!

There are as many network printing problems as there are network printers. Here are a couple of common problems I've managed to collect:

> Network paths (also known as UNC names) in Windows 95 are often longer than their Windows 3.1 equivalent and can include spaces, so sometimes the network can't find a printer. They're in the format *server**share*. See your system administrator about changing the

path so it's shorter and doesn't contain spaces. Or assign a local name
to the network resource, such as assigning one of your LPT ports to a
network printer. Or assign a drive letter to a remote disk drive. This was
the way Windows 3.1 worked, and you can still do it in Windows 95.

If you're on a NetWare network and having problems printing with
Postscript printers, often this is because banner pages aren't config-
ured correctly. Solution: Disable banner page printing (uncheck the
Banner Pages box in the Capture printer property sheet).

I'm on a Mixed Network, and Those Long File Names Are Causing All Kinds of Trouble.

That's because some networks "see" long file names and some don't. Say you
have a file you've named MarchSalesFigures, and that's what it looks like to
you. But your coworkers using Windows for Workgroups will see Marcha~.doc,
and it won't make any sense! Stick to the old 8.3 convention until everybody's
using the same stuff.

You can lose data on a non-mixed network, too, especially on earlier versions
of NetWare. If you want to safely use long file names on a NetWare network,
you'll need to use version 3.1.2 or later. If you're a network administrator, to
avoid upgrading your whole network, simply turn off long file name support by
adding these two lines to the Win.ini file:

```
[NWRedir]
supportLFN=0
```

See the discussion in Chapter 3 of why you should steer clear of long file
names on a network, too.

I'm on a Mixed Network, and Those Shortcuts Are Driving Everybody Crazy, Too.

To a non-Windows 95 user, a shortcut is simply a file with a .LNK extension.
If they try to copy this file, they'll get the .LNK file, not the original file it points
to. And it won't have anything in it. Sorry; there's no way around that except to
tell non-Windows 95 users to beware of anything ending in .LNK.

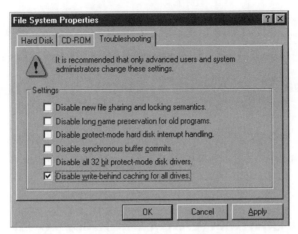

Figure 8-10. Disabling write-behind caching

I'm Losing Data over the Network!

Double-click on the System icon in the Control Panels folder. You'll notice there are Advanced settings at the bottom of the Performance tab. Click File System; then click its Troubleshooting tab (Figure 8-10). If you're losing data over a network—if, for example, some database records are missing—check the "disable write-behind" caching box.

Is There a Quick Way to Temporarily Disable Networking in Windows 95?

Yep. Press (F8) on startup and go into Safe mode.

I Can't Get to Safe Mode!

Sometimes, if you're on a network, you can't get anywhere by pressing (F8) on startup. This is because your network administrator has restricted access to the system. You can start your machine from a floppy—that is, if you've had the foresight to make an emergency startup disk.

I Keep Getting the Message "Error occurred while loading device: VNETSUP: Error 6102. The string specified by the Workgroup keyword in the registry is too short."

This is usually caused by an incomplete network installation. You need to remove (uninstall) the network and then reinstall it. Use the Add/Remove Programs icon in the Control Panel folder.

I Just Want to Connect One Computer to Another, but I Can't Figure Out How!

Windows 95 comes with a Direct Cable Connection that lets you connect two or more computers as a peer-to-peer network so you can share files and printers. This feature was greatly touted in the press (Macintoshes have had it a long time), but it isn't automatically installed when you choose a Typical installation. If you go looking for it, you won't find it. You'll need to use the Add/Remove programs icon in the Control Panel folder to install it (click Windows Setup and Communications). You'll need a NIC (Network Interface Card) in each computer. You'll also, obviously, need a cable to connect the computers. You can use a LapLink-type cable; an EPC cable via the parallel port; or a serial cable, a null modem, and a gender changer. Tell the folks at the computer store what you're up to so you have a better chance of getting the right cable. And make sure you use the same port on both computers.

Once you have it set up (there's a DCC Wizard to help you), you can attach your laptop to your desktop computer and quickly transfer files, or attach other PCs and share files and printers.

Actually, in some cases you have more security on a peer-to-peer network than you have on a "real" network where you share everything or nothing. This is because, when you run the DCC Wizard, you're asked to specify what resources you want to share. To specify resources you want to share, go to the Explorer, right-click on each folder you're willing to share, choose Properties, click the Sharing tab (Figure 8-9), and pick an option. On the other hand, you can't set specific access rights for individual users; everybody either gets access to what you share or nobody gets it.

Specific Problems and Solutions

Here are all the glitches and fixes that I've managed to collect. You may very well indeed have a problem not listed here. Remember to consult the resources in Chapter 10 for other ways to get in touch with manufacturers and obtain files quicker than a regular phone call.

Arcada Network Backup

You'll need to use version 5 or later of this program with Windows 95 so that it will recognize backup and tape databases. Contact Arcada at 407-333-7500.

ArtiSoft LANtastic

You can't install Windows 95 when the LANtastic server is running. You need to disable the server either by removing the Server.exe file from your Autoexec.bat or by typing this at the command line: **server /remove**.

If you have a mapped or shared setup drive, Setup won't finish. Solution: Stop sharing your startup drive or disable mapping before running Setup.

Network Neighborhood in Windows 95 won't see your LANtastic resources. Workaround: Use your LANtastic network Windows utilities to remap drives, change printers, and so forth. You may have to tell Windows your printer is local.

Don't install either a network adapter or a protocol if you're on a LANtastic network.

You won't be able to create a login script unless you use Startnet.bat in LANtastic to create one before Windows 95 starts.

If you need to run TSRs, you have another problem. You can't do this from a script, either. If you need one, say, for a backup agent, put it in the Autoexec.bat. You can run in a DOS session that allows a custom Autoexec.bat.

Be sure to use version 5 or later.

Attachmate Extra! 4.1

If you have difficulties with this program, add entries to map the workstation name and the user name to the workstation's IP address in the host name table.

Banyan VINES

If you get a message that your VINES version isn't the latest, edit Vines.ini to include these statements: (make statements bold for user entry)

[NEWREV]
dontcopy=1
vines.version=5.5x (where x is your version number)
windows.version=3.95

Cheyenne ArcServe Network Backup Agent

Requires ARCServe version 5.10F. Contact Cheyenne at 800-243-9462.

Cheyenne ArcServe 4.0, 5.0

Problems in these versions can cause data loss. Upgrade: 800-243-9462.

Cheyenne ARCSOLO 3.02

This has problems recognizing Client for NetWare Networks (Nwredir.vxd) and Client for Microsoft Networks (Vredir) mapped drives.
Solution: Add this line to the [boot] section of your System.ini file:

network.drv=commctrl.dll

CorelSCSI 2.04

The LASTDRIVE statement added to Config.sys may cause Client for NetWare mapped drives to fail.
Solution: Remove the LASTDRIVE line from Config.sys.

DEC IrmaSuite/3270 Connection

If you have printing problems, redirect printing to an LPT port.

DEC Pathworks

Run Pathworks before trying to install Windows 95; otherwise Pathworks components won't be upgraded and startup problems will occur.
Long file names don't work correctly on versions 5.0b and earlier. Upgrade to version 5.00 EC01 and later.

Windows 95 doesn't support Pathworks NetWare client licenses.
Solution: Get FPS licenses. Contact DEC at 508-493-5111.

Frye Computer Systems Statistics Display Rack for NetWare (StatRack), et al.

This won't run under Windows 95 unless you:

1. Upgrade to a Wfwnet.drv dated 7/24/93 or later (available with Windows NT 3.1 and later).
2. Copy the Wfwnet.drv file into your Windows 95 folder.
3. Add the following line to the [boot] section of your System.ini file:

   network.drv = wfwnet.drv
4. Use the Notepad to create a file called Fryenet.ini consisting of the following lines:

   [network]

   protocol = ipx
5. Save this file in your Windows 95 folder.

Frye NetWare Early Warning System 1.51D

Won't run under Windows 95.
Solution: Start WinPopUp manually or place it in the StartUp group.

Frye Software Metering and Resource Tracking 1.50A-

Doesn't accurately meter file usage on NetWare servers. Solution: Place the DOSSMART command in Winstart.bat.

Frye Software Update and Distribution System 1.50B

Reboot commands in login scripts won't reboot Windows 95. Solution: Upgrade. Contact Frye Computer Systems at 617-451-5400.

Frye Statistics Display Rack 1.0 for NetWare

Shows incomplete network statistics. Contact Frye at 617-451-5400.

Frye Utilities for Networks 2.00B

Shows incomplete network statistics. Contact Frye at 617-451-5400.

Funk Wanderlink 1.0

You can't control the host remote from your local PC.
Solution: Contact Funk for an upgrade at 800-828-4146.

Helix Netroom v. 3

If Windows 95 setup fails, check to see that the CACHECLK line in your Autoexec.bat is disabled. If Windows 95 won't start after setup, look at the Readme.txt file in your Netroom directory and run the CUSTOMIZE program.

If Windows 95 still won't start, there may be a specific hardware incompatibility. Check Netroom's Readme.txt file.

IBM AS/400 Client Access

Won't run under Windows 95.
Solution: Update APAR II08704. Contact IBM at 800-274-0015.

1. Press 1 for support line; then enter your customer number.
2. Press 1 for new call.
3. Press 6 for PTF and ask for APAR II08704.

Intel LANDesk 2.0

May cause Windows 95 to stop responding.
Solution: Upgrade to version 2.01. Intel faxback: 800-538-3373.

Lotus Notes Windows Client 3.2

If you're using the NetBIOS interface over IPX and the NetBUI protocol stacks, you need to configure the port for NetBIOS to use port 6 or 7 if NetBUI uses 0. To change the port, choose Setup from the Tools menu in the Lotus Notes Windows client, then click Ports.

McAfee LAN Automatic Inventory

Your list of network servers may become corrupt under Windows 95.
Solution: Upgrade. Contact McAfee at 408-988-3832.

McAfee NETremote 5.21

Doesn't run correctly under Windows 95.
Upgrade: Contact McAfee at 408-988-3832.

McAfee NetTools 5.1, 5.2

Both versions contain Appman.exe, a Program Manager replacement that may not run correctly under Window 95.

Solution: Upgrade. Contact McAfee at 408-988-3832.

McAfee Site Meter version 4.0

Doesn't run correctly under Windows 95.

Solution: Upgrade to Version 5.2. Contact McAfee at 408-988-3832.

Meridian CD Net Plus Software 5.0

You may have problems running with Microsoft Client for NetWare.

Solution: Include the line NETSTART NWLINK in your Autoexec.bat. Mount the CD with Mount.exe in real mode.

Microsoft Client for NetWare, Running with Dial-Up Networking

May cause problems with Aldus Pagemaker 5.0 and Quark Xpress 3.3.

If you see the message "Unable to access network [116]" when starting QuarkXpress 3.3, remove the DIAL-UP\IPX components or connect to a valid network. Upgrade to QuarkXPress 3.32 or later.

Microsoft NetFax

If your computer is being used as a Microsoft NetFax server, don't shut down Windows 95 or Microsoft Exchange with faxes still in the queue, or you may lose them.

Microtest LAN Assist 4.10

Doesn't work under Windows 95.

Solution: Upgrade. Contact Microtest at 800-526-9675.

Netsoft NS/3270

You won't be able to recognize the NetBIOS connection to an Adapt SNA LAN Gateway running this program under Windows 95.

Solution: Upgrade. Get an updated version of Tixwx.dll from Netsoft at 800-352-3270.

Netsoft NS/Midrange Bundle

Shared folders don't work.
Solution: Upgrade. Contact Netsoft at 800-352-3270.

Norton Lambert Closeup/LAN 6.0

Works with Windows 95 as remote but not as host.
Solution: Upgrade. Contact Norton at 805-964-6767.

Novell GroupWise 4.1

The Coaches may fail because the menu system under Windows 95 uses a different font.
Solution: Contact Novell at 800-638-9273.

Novell LAN Workgroup 4.2

This program fails under Windows 95.
Solution: Upgrade. Contact Novell at 800-638-9273.

Novell NetWare 3.12, 4.01 Servers

If packet burst is turned on, Windows 95 with Microsoft Client for NetWare can have problems with NetWare 3.12 and 4.01 servers.
Solution: Contact Novell for the patch PBURST.EXE (ftp:Novell.com, or 800-638-9273).

Novell NetWare 3.11 Servers

Programs that open multiple files may have problems opening files on NetWare 3.11. You may get "file not found", "sharing violation", and "unable to open file" messages. Solution: Get a patch at /pub/netware/nwos/nw311 and run 311ptd.exe to extract the file Os20pnfx.nlm. Load the NetWare Loadable Module.

Also, you can't use long file names on network servers for Windows 95.
Solution: Disable long file name support in the client for NetWare.

Also, if you install a network that doesn't use protected-mode protocols, you may see a warning next to your network adapter in Device Manager. If everything's working fine, just ignore it.

Novell QuattroPro 6.0

Dragging a file's icon to the printer doesn't print the file.

Solution: Install a NetWare server from a computer running Windows 95. Add this line to the [Boot] section of System.ini:

secondnet.drv=netware.drv

ON NoteWorks 3.5 for NetWare Networks

Can't install with Microsoft Client for NetWare.

Solution: See the release notes accompanying this product.

Palindrome Network Archivist v. 3.1A

Doesn't work right when accessing workstations running Microsoft Client for NetWare.

Solution: Get Version 4.0. Contact Palindrome at 800-288-4912.

Reflection 4 v5.0 for DOS

Run this in DOS VM mode. It requires the manufacturer's TCP/IP stack, so make sure Microsoft's TCP/IP isn't bound to the network adapter.

Reflection X 4.1

Won't run under Windows 95.

Upgrade: Contact Walker, Richer & Quinn at 206-217-7508.

Rumba Office 2.0

The shared folders feature causes installation problems when it's turned on. To turn it off, when installing Rumba:

1. Select Custom.
2. Select AS/400.
3. Make sure the check box titled Shared Folders And Client API's isn't checked.
4. Continue the installation.

Saber LAN Workstation 2.0e

Saber Software no longer supports this version.
Upgrade. Saber's BBS is 214-361-1883.

SPSS 6.1 for Windows

Doesn't recognize UNC names on network print jobs.
Solution: See Windows 95 Help.

Windows for Workgroups 3.11

You'll find that network fax clients can't connect to a Windows 95 NetFax
server.
Solution: Get a patch from Microsoft Product Support at 800-426-9400.

And Next...

In the next chapter we'll take a look at all sorts of good tools, utilities, and
add-ons you can get to fill the gaps that Microsoft left in Windows 95.

Chapter

9

Gotta Haves! Shareware,
Freeware, and Band-Aids

...And Where to Find Them on the Web

Gotta Haves! Shareware, Freeware, and Band-Aids
...And Where to Find Them on the Web

"Why would anyone need a computer of their own?"

Ken Olsen, chairman of Digital Equipment Corporation, 1974

O f course, no operating system has everything, but Microsoft left several things out of Windows 95. For example, there's no antivirus program included with Windows 95. If you don't have one from another source, you may be vulnerable to virus attacks, especially from boot sector viruses, because Windows 95 boots in a different way from Windows 3.1. There's no Calendar and no alarm clock, either. These may seem frivolous, but not if you've come to rely on them for scheduling. The new Windows 95 HyperTerminal doesn't have scripting, so you can't automate your dial-ups, and it won't let you create messages offline in a separate window to save connect time charges.

In addition to the stuff that was left out, you'll want some other goodies, too. How about some graphics utilities and more games? While you're at it, get some Internet utilities for creating your own Web pages. You'll need a Web browser, too. And a backup program that works. You can't duplicate the disks Windows 95 comes on because they're in a special format, and the Copy Disk command won't work on them. So if you want a backup set of installation disks for safe-keeping, you'll need to get a new disk-copying utility. You probably really need an irreverent Bill Gates screen saver also, and I'll tell you where to get one.

Here are some ideas for things to get to fill the gaps left in Windows 95, and where to find them. These are mostly shareware and freeware, not commercial software, but a few commercial products are mentioned, too—whatever you need to get the job done. Remember, you can try shareware for free; if you like it, send in the modest registration fee (usually $10–$40).

The Tools You'll Need

- Access to the Internet (for ftp) or the Web
- *Or a friend who has access to the Web*
- *Or an account on CompuServe or AOL or another information service*

Anti-Virus Programs

Gotta Have (something, at least)! Windows 95 doesn't have a built-in antivirus program. You need to get one. Your old ones won't fix boot sector viruses because of the way Windows 95 uses interrupt routines. They won't know what to do with your long file names, either. And if your antivirus program is an automatic TSR, it may not work at all with Windows 95. Go to http://www.mcafee.com for McAfee's virus scanner.

Communications

Yes, HyperTerminal is better than Windows 3.1's Terminal, and it has ZMODEM. Plus, it's faster and easier to set up. But it doesn't have scripting or the ability to create messages offline in a separate window. So you'll need to get something for that. HyperAccess for Windows 95 is available from Hilgraeve, 800-826-2760, and it provides all the above plus virus detection for your downloaded files.

Disk Tools

Although Windows 95 comes with a disk defragmenter, ScanDisk for repairing disks, and DriveSpace, a disk compression utility, these are stripped-down versions of commercial packages, and you'll be better off getting the "real thing"— Norton Utilities for Windows 95 (Symantec, 800-441-7234). For an inexpensive solution to disk compression, you might consider the Microsoft Plus Pack, discussed later in this chapter.

Disk Duplicators

Need to be able to copy those new DMF disks, the kind that Windows 95 comes on? To get Disk Duplicator, which both formats and copies DMF disks, go to http://download.netex.net/w95/windows95/utils/dskdupv5.zip.

Or try Copyqm, at SimTel mirror ftp.oak.oakland.edu, in the SimTel/msdos/diskutil/ directory.

Another DMF disk utility is copyq318.zip, which duplicates disks in one pass. You might also want to get Vgacopy, which, although it isn't a DMF disk utility, has a nice graphical interface and lets you diskcopy 1.2 Mb disks to 1.44 Mb disks. You can get either of these from BBS, the Web, and most online services. Search for them.

File Compression

Gotta Have! If you send files to anybody else or get files from anywhere else, you need WinZip for Windows 95. Get it at ftp.winzip.com/winzip/winzip95.exe. It's an excellent 32-bit compression utility with internal support for PKZIP, TAR, and GZIP compression format, with optional support for ARJ, ARC, and LHZ files.

Drag And Zip 95 is good, too. Get it at ftp.canyonsw.com/DZ95.EXE. Get both and see which one you like best.

Backup

Windows 95 Backup doesn't work. It doesn't work with most tape drives. Get another backup program. A commercial one that works with most is Colorado Backup for Windows 95, from Colorado Memory. 800-416-8569.

Web Browsing

Gotta Have—Netscape Navigator's 32-bit version! Get it at ftp://ftp.netscape.com/. There's nothing like it.

Microsoft Plus!

Do you want it? Do you need it? Microsoft Plus! adds a System Agent, which is basically an event scheduler that performs routine tasks for you at set times, like scan for disk errors (if you leave your computer on). It also offers a 3-D pinball game and an optimized version of DriveSpace that compresses a disk better than Win95's own disk compression, and gives you more control over how much and when to compress things. The desktop patterns and sounds ("schemes") take up a lot of space, and frankly I don't like them. Having Full Window Drag is kind of nice. It makes what's going on easier to see, but it's not necessary, and I kind of wonder why they named it that. It also includes Internet Explorer, which could be quite useful if Microsoft gets the Microsoft Network running faster.

One other rather neat feature that Plus! adds is font smoothing in high resolutions so you don't see jagged edges in extra-large fonts on the screen. If you work with large fonts, you may want to get Plus! for this reason alone. To use this feature once you've installed the Plus! pack, right-click on the desktop and choose Properties. Click the Plus! tab and check the Smooth edges of screen fonts box (Figure 9-1).

The PowerToys

This is a collection of useful utilities (they're really officially called the Power Tools, but their file name says *powertoys*), available from Microsoft itself. Get it free at http://www.microsoft.com/windows/software/powertoy.htm.

Here's what's in the package:

CabView — Lets you look in .CAB compressed files on installation disks and drag files in and out of them instead of using the mysterious EXTRACT command to get the individual files you want.

CD AutoPlay Extender	Makes Autorun work on non-audio CDs.
Contents Menu	Gives you access to files without opening folders.
Explore From Here	Opens the Explorer, rooted anywhere you want.
FlexiCD	Controls your audio CDs from the taskbar.
DPI	Changes screen resolution on the fly, without rebooting.
Round Clock	A retro-style analog clock.
Shortcut Target Menu	Lets you right-click to get the properties for a shortcut's target.
Mouse	Forces the focus to follow your mouse without clicking.

Installing and Uninstalling the PowerToys

Before you download the PowerToys, create a new folder for them and name it something clever like PowerToys. Then:

1. Download the PowerToys from
   http://www.microsoft.com/windows/software/powertoy.htm
   and save the file in your PowerToys folder.

Figure 9-1. The Plus Properties tab

2. Open that folder and double-click on Powertoy.exe.

3. Right-click on each .INF file in that folder and choose Install.

To uninstall the toys if you decide you don't want them, use the Add/Remove Programs utility in the Control Panel folder.

A Better Notepad

Gotta Have (one of these)! Trust me; avoid WordPad! (Look back to "Beware of WordPad" in Chapter 6 for why.) Programmer's File Editor is excellent for editing large text files beyond Notepad's limit. Get it at ftp.pcix.com/pub/win95_apps/pfe0601i.zip. Or there's another enhanced Notepad, called Textpad, at http://download.netex.net/w95/windows95/utils/txp32130.zip.

Textpad's a full-featured text editor that lets you open multiple files at once. You can even search for text in several files at the same time. Try ftp://ftp.zdnet.com/zdi/software/textpd.zip if the first site's busy.

Screen Capture Utilities

If you need to crop screen shots instead of taking the entire active window, try SnapShot/32 at ftp://192.149.1.51/anon/snap241.zip. Or try GrabIt Pro 4.1, which saves your screen captures as small files (good if you're low on disk space). Or there's PrintScreen95, at http://download.netex.net/w95/windows95/graphics/prtscr95.zip.

Calendar/Cardfile/Alarm Clock Substitutes

If you need a replacement for a scheduler, try some of these inexpensive solutions. Or see Chapter 3 for how to preserve your old Windows 3.1 originals.

ftp.cdrom.com/.22/cica/nt/alt35b.zip	Almanac v.35b, a 32-bit personal information manager. Includes a calendar, daily schedule, to-do list, phone book, and notes.
http://download.netex.net/w95/windows95/utils/nt-vip.zip	Simple address manager.
http://download.netex.net/w95/windows95/utils/bput95.zip	
	Barry Press's utilities for Windows 95: a pop-up monthly calendar, digital clock, ASCII printer, Runner (adds a Run command to the right mouse button), and more.
http://download.netex.net/w95/windows95/utils/alarm32.zip	Flexible alarm program.

http://download.netex.net/w95/windows95/utils/wmlpb_60.zip	Windows 95 "My Little Phone Book" upgrade 6.0.
http://download.netex.net/w95/windows95/utils/ntz31n.zip	32-bit Notes-style program.

File Utilities

Get one or the other of these, or both.

ftp://ftp.zdnet.com/zdi/software/dv96.zip	Drag and View. Excellent alternative to QuickView. You can search, view, and print most any file.
ftp.canyonsw.com/DF95.ZIP	Drag and File. PC Magazine's shareware utility of the year, now in a Windows 95 version. File manager plus utilities for formatting and copying floppies. Good for managing multiple drives.

Internet Utilities

Try out these freeware and shareware products to create your own Web pages, find a better newsreader, and more.

http://www.halcyon.com/webwizard/webwiz32.zip	WEB Wizard 32-bit. Lets you create your own home page on the Web. For beginners.
ftp.ksc.nasa.gov/pub/winvn/nt/winvn_99_06_intel.zip	WinVN 32-bit, a 32-bit newsreader.
ftp.usma.edu/pub/msdos/ws_ftp.zip	32 bit FTP client; supports long file names.
papa.indstate.edu/winsock-l/winirc/mirc36.zip	mIRC32, the number-one Windows IRC client, now in a 32-bit version.
ftp.vandyke.com/pub/vandyke/ntcrt10.zip	CRT, a good Telnet/remote login app.

Graphics

These are just a sampling of the many graphics utilities available on the Web. Just a note: MPEGS are movies; JPEGs, BMPs, and GIFs are still images.

ftp://papa.indstate.edu/winsock-l/Windows95/Graphics/vmpg17.exe	Mpeg (video) player w/sound!
ftp://papa.indstate.edu/winsock-l/Windows95/Graphics/polyv217.zip	PolyView, a multi-threaded, 32-bit GIF/JPEG/BMP viewer.
ftp.std.com/ftp/vendors/mmedia/lview/lviewpro.zip	LView Pro for Win95. Good for making transparent/interlaced GIFs.

Just Plain Fun

Want animated cursors or a Recycle Bin that flushes? Try some of these.

ftp.cdrom.com/pub/cica/nt/anicurs1.zip and anicurs2.zip	Animated cursors.
ftp://ftp.zdnet.com/zdi/software/dsktlt.zip	Desktop Toilet replaces your Recycle Bin with a Guess What, complete with flushing sound.
ftp://ftp.zdnet.com/zdi/software/zgdw95.zip	An irreverent screen saver. Bill Gates smashes your old Windows 3.1 desktop.
http://www.netex.com/w95/windows95/misc/psych10.zip	Weird screen savers.
http://download.netex.net/w95/windows95/graphics/mchang10.zip	Media Changer for system sounds, screen savers, and wallpaper.
http://download.netex.net/w95/windows95/graphics/bn.zip	Background Noise 1.52, a multiple media player.
http://download.netex.net/w95/windows95/utils/trayqt.zip	Lets you quick-quit from the taskbar. Free! Left-double-click to exit; right-double-click to restart.
http://download.netex.net/w95/windows95/games/hwsol.zip	Solitaire in full color.
http://download.netex.net/w95/windows95/games/solcon95.zip	More solitaire!
ftp.cdrom.com/.22/cica/nt/bog2.zip	Bog 2, computerized Boggle.
http://download.netex.net/w95/windows95/games/vortex95.exe	Vortex, a strategy board game.
http://download.netex.net/w95/windows95/games/bombs2.zip	Bomb squad game.
http://download.netex.net/w95/windows95/games/nt_hang.zip	32-bit Hangman.

For Programmer Types

Try some of these helpful utilities to fill the holes Microsoft left.

http://download.netex.net/w95/windows95/utils/pfe601i.zip	Programmer's file editor.
http://download.netex.net/w95/windows95/utils/regsearch.zip	Registry search and replace.
http://download.netex.net/w95/windows95/utils/unix95.zip	Unix command-line utilities for Windows 95.
http://download.netex.net/w95/windows95/utils/grep-32.zip	Gives you 32-bit Unix-style grep capability.
http://download.netex.net/w95/windows95/utils/wpack32d-v80.exe	WinPack 32 Deluxe -Zips, Gzip, Uuencode, Binhex, Tar, and ARJ.
http://download.netex.net/w95/windows95/utils/fileview.zip	ANSI/hex file viewer for Windows 95.

More Interesting Utilities, Defying Categorization

A lot of these are at Net Ex's Unofficial Windows Page. That doesn't mean they're not at other sites, too. If the Net Ex site's busy, do a Lycos search for other sites. Hint: don't include ".zip" in your search, or you'll find a lot of sites you don't want.

ftp://papa.indstate.edu/winsock-l/Windows95/Graphics/vuepro41.zip	View-Print Pro 4.1. Graphics, video, sound, uuencode, zip, slideshow, screensaver, and more!
http://download.netex.net/w95/windows95/utils/clckr12a.zip	32-bit mouse button programmer. Assigns PgUp, PgDn, function, and Alt keys to mouse buttons.
ftp://ftp.zdnet.com/zdi/software/excbe.zip	CAB Extractor. Extracts Microsoft's compressed CAB files.
http://download.netex.net/w95/windows95/utils/memstat.zip	Provides graphical memory statistics.
http://download.netex.net/w95/windows95/utils/tskpro20.zip	Task Pro 2.0. A Taskman replacement.
http://download.netex.net/w95/windows95/utils/launch09.zip	Launchpad for Win95.
http://download.netex.net/w95/windows95/utils/smi95v11.zip	Smiler Shell 95. Essentially a command line for Win 95. Change directories in SmilerShell 95, and you go to that directory in Explorer. Adds custom function keys to Windows 95, too.
http://download.netex.net/w95/windows95/utils/widen14.zip	Wide Open for Word 6.0. Adds long file name support.

Windows 95 Software Pages

Want more? Go to these sites for the latest and greatest of the available shareware and freeware. New postings are made daily, so check them out.

http://biology.queensu.ca/~jonesp/win95/software/software.html	Windows 95 Page Selection of the "Best" Windows 95 Software.
http://cwsapps.texas.net/win95.htm	CWSApps List—Windows 95 Apps.
http://fub46.zedat.fu-berlin.de:8080/~banshee/win95/apps.html	Windows 95 Software.
http://gfecnet.gmi.edu/software/window95.html	Windows 95 Software.
http://sage.cc.purdue.edu/~xniu/winsock/win95.html	Xiaomu's Windows 95 Winsock software archive.

http://www.cris.com/~randybrg/win95.html	Randy's Windows 95 Resource Page.
http://www.csusm.edu/cwis/winworld/winworld.html	Windows World Shareware Archives.
http://www.netex.net:80/w95/	Net Ex Unofficial Windows 95 Page.
http://www.pcix.com/win95/software.html	The Windows 95 Software Archive.
http://www.process.com/win95/win95ftp.ht	Windows 95 Software.
http://www.windows95.com/win95aps.html	Windows 95 Applications.
http://www.winternet.com/~rgraner/win95.html	Windows 95 Links & 32-Bit Shareware.
http://www.zdnet.com/~zdi/software/win95/apps.html	Windows 95 Applications.
http://www.zdnet.com/~zdi/software/win95/utils.html	Windows 95 Utilities.
http://www.zdnet.com/~zdi/software/win95/comm.html	Windows 95 Communication.
http://www2.pcix.com/win95/win95/software.html	Hot Windows 95 Software.
http://www.viper.net/~parker	ViperNet Unofficial Windows 95 Software Archive.
http://cwsapps.texas.net/win95.html	Stroud's CWSApps List—Windows 95/NT Winsock Apps.
http://www.process.com/win95	Process Software's Windows 95 Page.

And Next...

If you need something else, you can undoubtedly use Chapter 10, "As a Last Resort," to find it. You'll find tech support sites and BBSes, vendor phone numbers and URLs, and other ideas about where to go for help.

Chapter
10

As a Last Resort...
Other Resources

As a Last Resort...
Other Resources

"The Edsel is here to stay."

Henry Ford II to dealers, 1957

You're not alone, struggling with Windows 95 and maybe saying a few bad words about it after midnight, with the late-late movie blasting away and a 9 a.m. deadline to face. There are literally millions of other users out there, and they're probably having the same kinds of problems you are.

Remember, it is in the best interest of millions of computer product manufacturers to keep you and your programs and equipment up and running. In fact, there's a wealth of information out there that can bail you out of trouble, and it's yours for the asking.

Here's your guide to the rest of the world. This chapter may even be the reason you bought this book!

Really, all you need is a phone to get information from lots of sources mentioned in this chapter. If you have a modem, too, you can get even more information, a lot quicker. With a modem and an account on an information utility like AOL, you'll have access to even more. And if you can get on the Internet or the Web, that's great! You'll find URLs in this chapter that let you contact most computer and computer-related manufacturers directly.

You'll also find great Windows 95 support sites on the Web. If you're not Web-walking yet, or can't find the tech support Web site you're looking for, this chapter has BBS numbers and even plain old voice phone numbers to help you. A list of manufacturers have fax-back lines where you can ask questions and receive faxes of "white papers" (general information), FAQs (fcrequently asked questions), or even specific answers to specific problems.

Keep hunting. It *should* be here in this chapter...

The Tools You'll Need

- Telephone
- *or a modem and a phone*
- *or a modem, a phone, and access to the Web*
- *or a friend with the above.*

Using the Information Services

Here's where to find relevant information on Windows 95 products and vendors using the commercial online services:

America Online	Keyword: win95
Compuserve	GO MSL
FTP	ftp.microsoft.com/Products/Windows/Windows95/
Genie	Go to Microsoft Roundtable or MOVE to PAGE 95
Microsoft Network	Categories -> Computers and Software -> Software ->Microsoft -> Windows 95
Prodigy	JUMP WINNEWS

Later in this chapter you'll find listings for specific Web sites for vendors of computer-related products, not just Microsoft itself. However, you may want to use your online information service instead of the Web, because you can usually search for vendor names directly. In addition, CompuServe and other services have well-stocked shareware and freeware libraries. You may find these easier to use if you aren't comfortable browsing the Web or if the site you need is always too busy.

Computer User Groups on the Web

Go to http://www.melbpc.org.au/others/index.html for an index of PC user groups around the world, where you may find someone nearby, really nearby, to help you.

Mailing Lists

Want to be on a Windows 95 mailing list? Here are a few. Warning: Your mailbox will fill up quickly.

- win95-l. A "give & take" forum for general discussions and problem-solving related to win95 (users helping users). To subscribe, send an email message containing this line to win95-l@peach.ease.losft.com: **subscribe win95-l** firstname lastname. If you would like the list in *digest form*, add the following command: **set digest win95-l**

- Win95-NET forum discusses networking issues related to win95. To subscribe, send

- email to Listserv@ntb9.cdc.gov. In the body of the letter, include **subscribeWin95-net**.

Also, Micro$oft offers a free email newsletter, WinNews. To subscribe, send email to enews@microsoft.nwnet.com. In the body of the letter, write **subscribe winnews firstname lastname.**

Newsgroups

There are lots of newsgroups! Here are a few...

alt.os.windows95.crash.crash.crash
comp.infosystems.www.browsers.ms-windows

comp.os.ms-windows.win95.misc

comp.os.ms-windows.win95.setup.

comp.os.ms-windows.apps.winsock.mail

comp.os.ms-windows.apps.winsock.misc

comp.os.ms-windows.apps.winsock.news

comp.os.ms-windows.apps.utilities

comp.os.ms-windows.misc

comp.os.ms-windows.apps.misc

comp.os.ms-windows.advocacy

IRC Chat Channels on Windows 95

Internet Relay Chat, or IRC, lets people from around the world join in "chats," or real-time conversations, either in groups or privately. To use IRC, you need a client program to connect you to the network via a server that passes messages from user to user over the network. You can read about the basics, obtain a client, and get a list of IRC servers at either of these two sites:

http://www2.undernet.org:8080/~cs93jtl/IRC.html

http://www.main.com/dms/irc.html

Once you get set up for IRC, here are some of the channels that discuss Windows 95:

- #win95-net—using Microsoft client for networks and file-sharing capabilities over the Internet.
- #Windows95— general Windows 95 chat.
- #workgroup— creating workgroups on the Internet using Windows 95 and TCP/IP.

Windows 95 FAQ Sites

These FAQs (Frequently Asked Questions) are full of tips and troubleshooting techniques:

http://www.pcix.com/win95/win95faq.html

http://www.primenet.com/~markd/win95faq.html

http://www.whidbey.net/~mdixon/win40001.htm

http://www.windows.microsoft.com/windows/qa/qa.htm

Windows 95 Pages on the Web

I've tried to put together an eclectic combination of all sorts of Windows 95 Web resources for you. You'll find all sorts of sites to visit here—everything from sophisticated commercial pages to home-brewed Web pages, worldwide. Remember, the Web changes all the time!

1,001 Windows 95 Shortcuts	http://www.zdnet.com/~pccomp/1001tips/index.html
ADL'S Windows 95 Corner	http://www.univaq.it:81/~antdilor/Windows95/win95cor.html
Analysis of Windows 95, OS/2 Warp and Mac System 7 from The Computer Paper	
	http://www.tcp.ca/April95.rtfhtml/Showdown.html
Andrew Tan's Page	http://www.alumni.nus.sg/nussu/SIG/Win95/
Arri's Home Page - Windows '95 Links	http://www.advantage.co.za/~rip/win95.html
Arrow Windows 95 Connection	http://home.ptd.net/~arrow
Backstage: Tips and Hints for Win95	http://fub46.zedat.fu-berlin.de:8080/~banshee/win95/soft.html
Backstage Windows 95	http://fub46.zedat.fu-berlin.de:8080/~banshee/win95/backstg.html
Barb's Help Page for Windows 95	http://pages.prodigy.com/Confusion/barb/barb95.html
Barry A Barr's Home Page	http://www.wwa.com/~barry
BenZ Windows95 Page	http://www.webcom.com/~hywan/bcheong/win95/win95.html
Bob Cerelli's Home Page	http://www.halcyon.com/cerelli/
Brian MacDonald's Windows 95 Page	http://www.wsu.edu:8080/~bryan/
Buster's Windows 95 Page	http://moose.erie.net/~rweidner
Charles Kelly's Home Page	http://cpcug.org:80/user/ckelly/
Chromee's Corner & Millenium Studios	http://www.iaw.on.ca/~robemell
Clueless Inkorporated: Windows 95	http://www.xmission.com/~eheintz/Win95/
CMS' Windows 95 Help Page	http://www.neosoft.com/~gregcms
CompuHelp's Windows 95 Page	http://www.viper.net/~parker
Configuring SLIP in Win 95	http://www.southwind.net/~leeb/95slip.html
Configuring TCP/IP in Windows 95	http://www.wwa.com/~barry/wn95slip.html
Configuring TCP/IP in Windows95 by Barry Barr	http://www.mcs.net/~barry
Connecting Win95 to the InterNet	http://www.Luna.net/Home/Documentation/Windows95.html
Connecting Windows 95 to the Internet	http://www.Luna.net/Home/Documentation/Windows95.html
Craig's Windows 95 Page	http://www.bucknell.edu/~cbonsig/win95.html
Creating Workgroups on Internet using Windows95	http://www.algonet.se/~aarto/wishare.html
Cutter's Windows 95 Crossroads	http://www.io.com/~kgk/win95.html
Darwin Brewer's Homepage	http://www.ionet.net/~dbrewer/
Dave's Win95 Page	http://www/cityscape.co.uk/users/cf49
Derk's Nifty Web Page	http://www.cris.com/~Derk/win95.html
Doc's Windows 95 Page	http://www.webcom.com/~docline/win95.shtml
Dylan Greene's Windows 95 Home Page!	http://www.wam.umd.edu/~dylan/win95.html
Frank Condron's Windows 95 Page	http://oeonline.com/~frankc/fjcw95.html
Getting the Most from the Windows 95 Registry	http://www.usa.net/~rduffy/registry.htm
Global Computing, Inc.- Windows 95 - Links, Links, and more Links...	http://www.planet-hawaii.com/global/win95.html
Hendry's HomePage	http://www.geopages.com/SiliconValley/1612/

HelpWin95 page	http://www.helpwin95.com
Holy Temple of Bill	http://www.mc2-csr.com/~dmorford/holytemplebill.html
How To Setup Windows 95 - Achilles Internet	http://www.achilles.net/~tkolsen/ms95how2.html
Hutch's Windows 95 Page	http://www.iea.com:80/~hutching/win95.html
IAC - Win95/Canary Islands/HomePage	http://www.iac.es/galeria/ronald/wingrp.ht
Info on Windows 95	http://www.wineasy.se/ove/win95.ht
Internet Assistant Support Page	http://www.microsoft.com/msword/ia/support.htm
InterNet Direct Win95 HelpDesk	http://www.idirect.com/win95/index.html
Internetworking HQ	http://nearnet.gnn.com/gnn/wic/widows.15.html
InterNetworking Headquarters	http://www.windows95.comW
Jason's Windows '95 Page	
	http://www4.ncsu.edu/eos/users/j/jgbright/WWW/Win95/Windows95.html
John's Cool Windows95 Page	http://www.mcs.net/~jlueders/windows95.html
Keele's Win95 Page	http://www.usask.ca/~keele/
Kegs Page!	http://www.indirect.com/www/kgamard/
Kenneth Fowler's Home Page	http://www.access.digex.net/~rfowler/home.html
KJ King's Windows 95 WWW Page	http://www.execpc.com/~kjking
LWNET- Windows 95 Web Page	http://www.innotts.co.uk/~leewilko/index.html
MarkG's Win32 Programming Page	http://www.epix.net:80/~markga/index.html
Microsoft Windows Inquirer	http://www.haywire.com/inquirer
Microsoft Plus! Frequently Asked Questions	http://www.pcix.com/win95/plusfaq.html
Microsoft Slackville	http://www.avenue.com/the/forum/win95.html
Microsoft Windows '95	http://www.contrails.com/knapen/win95.ht
Microsoft Windows 95 Home Page	http://www.windows.microsoft.com
Makoto's Windows 95 Home Page (Japanese)	http://www.bekkoame.or.jp/~makots/win95/index.html
Mike Wood's Home Page	http://www.bdt.com/home/mwood/homepage.html
Mikie's Win95 Net Page	http://oeonline.com/~mrenick/win95.html
MIT Win'95 Home Page	http://web.mit.edu/win95/
NetEx Win95 Software Archive and Discussion Forums	http://www.netex.net/w95
Network Specialist Windows 95 Page	http://newtoy.kumc.edu/win95/
NussuWeb Win95 Special Interest Group	http://www.nussu.nus.sg/nussu/SIG/Win95/
One-stop Home page	http://www.win95.com/win95users.html
OS/2 Warp vs. Windows95	http://www.austin.ibm.com/pspinfo/os2vschg.html
Patrik Hall's Windows 95 Page (Finnish)	http://www.vtyh.fi/~phall/win95/index.html
Paul Hammat's Win95 Page	http://203.15.24.1/members/hammat/paulpage.html
Probers' Windows95 HelpDesk	http://www.idirect.com/win95/index.html
Process Windows95 Page	http://www.process.com/win95
Preston's Picks	http://www.zdnet.com/~zdi/software/win95/prespick.html
Randy's Windows 95 Resource Page	http://www.cris.com/~randybrg/win95.html
Richard's Home Page - Windows 95 Information Links	http://www.winternet.com/~rgraner/win95.html
Ryan's Page	http://www.net-connect.net/~ryan/index.html
Slip, Internet with WIN95	http://www.wwa.com/~barry/wn95slip.html
Slovenia's Win95 Page	http://ripl.fovref.uni-mb.si/~igor/windows95.html
Stroud's CWSApps List - Windows 95/NT Apps	http://cwsapps.texas.net/win95.html
Subliminal Messages in Windows 95 ?	http://www.tcp.ca/gsb/PC/Win95-subliminals.html
Sven Sajet's, Windows '95 Page	http://www.euronet.nl/users/ssajet/win95.html

Tan Tat Eang's Win95 Page	http://www.iscs.nus.sg/~tantatea
Taylor's Site List	http://wimsey.com/~taylor/general/sites.html
TBP's Home Page	http://www.welch.jhu.edu/homepages/tbp/html
TechFile	http://techweb.cmp.com:80/techweb/techweb/win95/win.html
The Best Windows 95 Software	http://www.pcix.com/win95/software.html
The Cavern's Windows 95 Page	http://www.iag.net/~mgoetz.win95.html
The Not-even-close-to-comprehensive-but-trying Win95 Links Page	http://www.engin.umich.edu/~jslandau/win95.html
The Official Windows95 FAQ	http://www.windows95.pcd.net/faq/index.html
The Official #Windows95 Home Page	http://www.windows95.pcd.net
The One-Stop Windows 95 Spot	http://www.win95.com
The PUTZ Windows 95 Homepage	http://www.shore.net/~mpcd/win95.ht
The (Unofficial) Windows 95 Home Page	http://www.southwind.net/~leeb/win95.html
The Win95 FAQ	http://www.primenet.com/~markd/win95faq.html
The Windows 95 FAQ	http://www.pcix.com/win95/win95faq.html
The Windows 95 Page	http://uptown.turnpike.net/W/Windows95/index.html
The Windows 95 Page!	http://darwin.biology.queensu.ca/~jonesp/
The Windows 95 Page!	http://biology.queensu.ca/~jonesp
The Windows 95 Rulez Page	http://www.cs.mcgill.ca/~big/
The Windows Source	http://metro.turnpike.net/M/mphacker
The Windows95 TCP/IP Setup FAQ	http://www.aa.net/~pcd/slp95faq.html
Tip of the Week	http://www.process.com/Win95/win95tip.ht
Tips and Tricks	http://www.execpc.com/~kjking/kjkpage2.html
Tips and Tricks	http://www.netex.net/hyper95/get/tricks.html
Tips and Tricks	http://www.netex.net/w95/tips.html
Unofficial ClubWin Home Page	http://www.supernet.net/~edtiley/win95/
Ventana: Windows 95 Online Companion	http://www.vmedia.com/vvc/onlcomp/win95/win95 .html
ViperNet Unofficial Windows 95 Software Archive	http://www.viper.net/~parker
Welcome to the Windows 95 Page on the NET	http://uptown.turnpike.net/W/Windows95/index.html
Welcome to WINHQ	http://www.windows95.co
WfW	http://www.uni-giessen.de/~g093/win95.ht
What's New with Windows95	http://windows95.lrs.stcloud.msus.edu/whatsnew.ht
White's Win95-Home	http://www.interaccess.com/users/gwhite/win95.html
Win32 Freeware/ Shareware on the World-Wide-Web	http://www.access.digex.net/~rfowler/software.html
Win32 Programming Features for Windows 95	http://www.iftech.com/classes/nt/nt0.htm
Win95 Homepage Swiss	http://www.isbiel.ch/~lienf/win95/win95.html
Win 95 in Dutch	http://www.euro.net/ecompany/ijme.html
Win 95 Links to Info	http://www.euronet.nl/users/ries/w95links
Win95-NET	http://www.pcix.com/win95/win95home.html
Win95-Page	http://www.planet-hawaii.com/global/win95.html
Win95-L Windows 95 FAQ	http://walden.mo.net/~rymabry/95winfaq.html
Win95-Page Germany	http://fub46.zedat.fu-berlin.de:8080/~banshee/win95/soft.html
Windows 95	http://www.pcworld.com/win95
Windows 95	http://GFECnet.gmi.edu/Software/window95.html
Windows 95	http://www.csra.net/jononkeyz/win95/win95.ht
Windows 95	http://www.io.prg/~mani/win95.html

Windows 95 Annoyances	http://ocf.berkeley.edu/~daaron/win95ann.html
Windows 95 Apps (Winsock Apps List...)	http://www.itu.ch/CWSApps/win95.html
Windows 95 Dial-Up Networking White Paper	http://www.wwa.com/~barry/wn95slip.html
Windows 95 Event Page	http://www.mcp.com/que/win95/
Windows 95 FAQ	http://www.primenet.com/~markd/win95faq.html
Windows 95 from Slovenia	http://www.rip1.fovref.uni-mb.si/~igor/windows95.html
Windows 95 Internetworking Headquarters	http://www.windows95.com
Windows 95 Home Page	http://www.ksu.edu/~plw/pages/win95.html
Windows 95 Home Page	http://www.phoenix.net/~dspyre/windows95.html
Windows 95 Home Page	http://www.isbiel.ch/~lienf/win95/win95.html
Windows 95 Homepage	http://www.windows95.pcd.net#
Windows 95 Info Page	http://www.tiac.net/users/snipe/win95home.html
Windows 95 Info Page	http://www2.pcix.com/~snipe/win95home.html
Windows 95 Information Page	http://www.mbnet.mb.ca/win/Window95.html
Windows 95 Links	http://www.refdesk.com/win95.html
Windows 95 Links	http://www.voicenet.com/~johnston/peter/win95.html
Windows 95 Links to Information	http://www.euronet.nl/users/ries/w95links.html
Windows 95 Preview Home Page	http://soho.ios.com/~pzurek/index.html
Windows 95 Question/Answer/Information Database	http://www.whidbey.net/~mdixon/qaid0001.htm
Windows 95 Reseller Training in South Africa and Windows 95 Tips	http://win95.is.co.za
Windows 95 Software-archive	http://www.idiscover.co.uk/tucows/window95.html
Windows 95 Start	http://www.txdirect.net/users/wolsefer/start.ht
Windows 95 Tip Sheet - A ClibWin Site	http://www.cs.umb.edu/~alilley/win.html
Windows 95 - Tom Jansen	http://www.hooked.net/users/tjansen/win95/
Windows 95 Utility Page	http://www.shadow.net/~wolverin/win95.ht
Windows 95 Web Page	http://windows95.lrs.stcloud.msus.edu/
Windows95(tm) Dial-Up Networking Tutorial	http://www.castle.net/~ace/cwin95.html
Windows95 FAQ	http://walden.mo.net/~rymabry/index.html
Windows95 Home Page	http://www.windows95.pcd.net/
Windows95 Rulez Page	http://www.cs.mcgill.ca/~big/
Windows95 Winsock Shareware	ftp://papa.indstate.edu/winsock-l/Windows95
Windows95 TCP/IP Setup HOW-TO/FAQ	http://www.aa.net/~pcd/slp95faq.html
Windows and Windows95 Page	http://miso.wwa.com:80/~tyocum/
Windows and Windows95 Page	http://www.mcs.net/~tyocum/dospp.html
Windows in the Jungle Tutorial to download	http://www2.csn.net/~medlin
Windows Computing Home Page	http://antares.prodigy.com/wincoi.ht
Windows Support Assistant	http://198.105.232.5:80/windows/support/assist.htm.
Winserve - Windows Internet Services	http://www.winserve.co
Winsock- und Win95-Software (German)	http://staff-www.uni-marburg.de/~sander/win95.h
X Avenue: Microsoft Slackville	http://www.avenue.com/the/forum/win95.html
Xima's SLIP FAQ	http://www.wolfe.net/~vector/slp95faq.html
ZD Net	http://www.zdnet.com/~cobb/win95/

Getting Microsoft Support

Windows 95 comes with 90 days of free support. The first time you call Microsoft (206-637-7098), the clock starts running. This number connects you with a person (ultimately) between the hours of 6 a.m. to 6 p.m. Pacific time. For free recorded advice, call the Fast Tips line at 800-936-4200. If you're really in trouble after hours, you can call 800-936-5700, but it'll cost you $35 per incident. Sometimes it's worth it, though. If you call (anybody!), be sure to have these things handy:

- Your product ID number.

- Your computer's configuration—size of your hard disk, how much RAM you have, what kind of CPU you have, what devices you're using, and so forth. It's a great idea to run MSD (Microsoft Support Diagnostics) and print out the results while your computer's still running, before any trouble occurs. That way, you'll have a record of what you have. Or run the Device Manager and print all your devices and a system summary (see "Printing a list of your devices" in Chapter 5) for an incredible amount of technical detail about your computer.

- The wording of any error messages you've gotten (write them down).

After 90 days, you can buy technical support, either from Microsoft or from other tech support companies like Corporate Software (800-556-7549), Unisys, or DEC (all prices vary, but you can usually get charged either by the minute or by the incident). Microsoft charges $1.95 per minute or $35 per incident.

Phone and BBS numbers

1STREADER BBS   615-230-8822

3Com BBS   408-980-8204 9600bps
3Com CardFacts   408-727-7021
3Com T/S   800-876-3266
3Com Faxback   800-638-3266

3Com Anonymous FTP	ftp3comcom
3D Microcomputer Sales	905-479-8822
3D Microcomputer Service	905-479-3668
3D Microcomputer Tech Support	800-846-7655
3rd Planet Software, Inc BBS	213-841-2260 2400bps

 9

#9 General	800-438-6463
#9 General	617-674-0009
#9 FAX	617-674-2919
#9 BBS	617-862-7502 288

 A

AIR Fax	408-428-0950
AIR Voice	408-428-0800
Abacus Concepts BBS	616-698-8106 2400bps
Abaton Technology BBS	415-438-4650 2400bps
Accolade BBS	408-296-8800 2400bps
Acculogic BBS	714-454-8124
Acculogic Fax	714-454-8527
Acculogic Product Support	714-454-2441
Acer America BBS	408-428-0140
Acer America Tech Support	800-445-6495
Acer Technologies Corp Tech Support	408-922-0333
ACS Computer	408-481-9988
Actix Systems BBS	408-970-3719 14400bps
Actix Systems Sales	800-927-5557
Actix Systems Service	408-986-1625
Adaptec Automated Fax	408-957-7150
Adaptec BBS	408-945-7727 14400bps
Adaptec General	800-959-7274
Adaptec General	408-946-8600
Adaptec Internet	support@adapteccom
Adaptec Literature Request	800-934-2766
Adaptec Tech Support	408-945-2550
Addstor BBS	415-324-4077 14400bps
Adobe Systems BBS	206-623-6984 14400bps
Adobe Systems Fax Back	206-628-5737
Adobe Systems FTP Site	ftpadobecom
Adobe Systems Tech Support	206-628-2757
Advanced Digital Corp BBS	714-894-0893 2400bps
Advanced Gravis	604-431-5020
Advanced Logical Research BBS	714-458-6834 14400bps
Advansys	408-383-9400
Ahead Systems General	415-623-0900
Alacrity Fax	908- 813-2490 BBS 908-813-2495

Aldus, Also see Adobe	800-288-6832
All Computer BBS	416-960-8679 2400bps
Allied Telesis BBS	415-964-2994 2400bps
Alloy Computer Products BBS	508-460-8140 2400bps
Alpha Software Corp BBS	617-229-2915 2400bps
Alpha Software Corp General	800-451-1018
ALR T/S	714-458-1952
Altima BBS	510-356-2456 2400bps
Altima T/S	800-356-9990
Altos Computer Systems General	408-258-6787
Altsys BBS	214-680-8592 2400bps
Always Technology BBS	818-597-0275
Always Technology Sales/Tech Support	818-597-1400
AMD Literature	800-222-9323
AMD Main	800-538-8450
AMD Tech Support	800-292-9263
Amdek Corporation BBS	408-922-4400 2400bps
Amdek T/S	800-722-6335
American Data echnology	818-303-8567
American Megatrends (AMI) BBS	404-246-8781 14400
American Megatrends (AMI) BBS	404-246-8782 V32bis
American Megatrends (AMI) FaxBack	404-246-8787
American Megatrends (AMI) T/S	404-246-8600
American Training Int'l General	800-955-5284
AMIPRO Cust Service	404-399-5505
AMIPRO (Upgrade to 30) Upgrading	800-872-3387
Andataco C/S	800-443-9191
Andataco Fax	619-453-9294
Antex Electronics	800-338-4231
APCUG (Association of PC User Groups) BBS	408-439-9367
Apogee Software BBS	508-365-2359 16800bps
Appian Main	408-730-5400
Appian Tech Support	800-422-7369
Apple Computer Fax Back	800-SOS-APPL
Apple Computer T/S USA Only	800-SOS-APPL
Applied Engineering BBS	214-241-6677 2400bps
Arcada	407-333-7500
Archive Corporation General	714-641-0279
Areal Technology Inc General	408-436-6800
Artisoft BBS	602-884-8648
Artisoft Sales	800-TINY-RAM
Artisoft T/S	602-670-7000
Artist Graphics BBS	612-631-7669 2400bps
Asante Technologies BBS	408-432-1416 144N81
Asante Technologies E-mail	support@asantecom
Asante Technologies Fax	408-432-6018
Asante Technologies Fax Back	800-741-8607
Asante Technologies FTP	ftpasantecom
Asante Technologies Voice	800-622-7464
Ashton-Tate BBS	213-324-2188

279

Ask Sam Systems BBS	904-584-8287 2400bps
AST Research BBS	714-727-4723
AST Research BBS(>9600)	714-727-4132
AST Research T/S	800-727-1278
Asus motherboard (Aorta) BBS	408-956-9084
Asus motherboard (Aorta) General	408-956-9077
Asymetrix BBS	206-451-1173 14400bps
AT&T Computer Systems BBS	908-769-6397 2400bps
AT&T Paradyne Modems	800-482-3333
AT&T Tech Support	800-247-1212, 800-582-3333, 800-242-6005
Atari General	408-745-2000
ATI Technologies BBS	416-764-9404 14400bps
ATI Technologies BBS	905-764-9404 9600bps
ATI Technologies Customer Service	905-882-2626
ATI Technologies Fax	905-882-2620
ATI Technologies Sales	905-882-2600
ATI Technologies Tech Support	905-756-0711
Autodesk General	415-332-2344
Automated Design Systems BBS	404-394-7448 2400bps
AVM	800-880-0041
Award (Bios) BBS	408-556-9084
Award (Bios) Tech Support	415-968-4433
Aztech Labs	510-623-8988

 B

Beagle Bros BBS	619-558-6151 2400bps
Below Zero General	403-547-0669
Below Zero Mail Order	800-461-2777
Bestgift Service BBS	813-978-3044 2400bps
Best Data Products	818-773-9600
Big State Doors BBS	512-398-7346 14400bps
Black Box Sales/Tech Support	412-746-5500
Blackmond Software BBS	505-589-0319 96H00bps
Boca Research BBS	407-241-1601 14400bps
Boca T/S	407-241-8088
Borland Automated Support	800-524-8420
Borland BBS	408-439-9096 2400bps
Borland Corporate Sales	800-331-0877
Borland Fax Back	800-822-4269
Borland General	404-431-5250
Borland Sales	800-331-0877
Borland T/S	408-438-5300
Borland T/S	800-252-5547
Boston Computer Society	BBS 617-964-6939
Bourbaki BBS	208-342-5823 2400bps
Box Hill Systems General	800-727-3863
Brightbill Roberts BBS	315-472-1058 2400bps

Brightwork Development	BBS 914-667-4759 2400bps
Brother BBS	514-685-2040
Brother General (Canada)	514-685-0600
Brother T/S	800-284-4357
Brown Bag Software BBS	408-371-7654 16800bps
Buerg Software BBS	707-778-8944 2400bps
BusLogic FTP f	tpbuslogiccom
BusLogic Main Phone	408-492-9090
BusLogic Prod Info	info@buslogiccom
BusLogic Tech Support	408-654-0760
BusLogic Tech Support	techsup@buslogiccom
BusLogic Tech Support FAX	408-492-1542
BusLogic WWW	wwwbuslogiccom
Buttonware BBS	206-454-7875 14400bps
Byte (magazine) BBS	617-861-9764

 C

Cabletron BBS	603-335-3358 14400bps
Cabletron Systems	FTP 13414119725
Cabletron Systems internet	sales@ctroncom
Cabletron Systems internet	support@ctroncom
Cabletron Systems T/S & Sales	603-332-9400
Cadworks General	800-545-4223
Calcomp T/S	800-CAL-COMP
Calcomp BBS	714-821-2359 2400bps
Calera Recognition Systems BBS	408-773-9068 9600bps
Campbell Services BBS	313-559-6434 2400bps
Canon Main Office	516-488-6700
Canon Printer (Italy) BBS	9-2-58010997 16800bps
Canon Printer Division BBS	714-438-3325 9600bps
Canon Tech Support	800-423-2366
Cardexpert Technology	510-252-1118
Cardinal 144 modem Tech Support	717-293-3124
Cardinal Technologies BBS	717-293-3074 14400bps
Cardinal (Techs) Tech Support	717-293-3135
CBIS, Inc BBS	404-446-8405 2400bps
cc:Mail BBS	415-691-0401 2400bps
CCT Inc General	612-339-5870
CD Publishing Corp FAX	604-874-1431
CD Publishing Corp General	604-874-1430
CD Publishing Corp General	800-333-7565
CD-ROM Inc Fax	303-526-7395
CD-ROM Inc General	303-526-7600
Celestica Modems	416-448-4689
Central Point Software BBS	503-690-6650 14400bps
Central Point Software PC Tools Tech Support	503-690-8090
Central Point Software T/S	503-690-8080
Certus BBS	216-546-1508 2400bps

Cheyenne Software BBS	516-484-3445 2400bps, 800-243-9462
Chicony Tech Support	714-771-9067
Chipsoft BBS	619-453-5232 2400bps
Chips and Technologies General	800-323-4477
Ciprico Fax	612-551-4002
Ciprico General	612-551-4100
Cirrus Logic BBS	510-440-9080
Cirrus General	800-272-1135
Cirrus Logic General	510-623-8300
Citizens America Corp BBS	310-453-7564 2400bps
Citizen America General	800-477-4683
Citrix Fax	305-341-6880
Citrix General	305-755-0559
Citrix General	800-437-7503
Citrix Systems BBS	305-346-9004 2400bps
Clarion Software BBS	305-785-9172 2400bps
Claris Corp BBS	408-987-7421 14400bps
Clark Development Corp BBS	801-261-8976 16800bps
Clear & Simple General	203-658-1204
Clear Software BBS	617-965-5406 2400bps
CMS Enhancement, Inc T/S	714-222-6000
CNET BBS	408-954-1787 2400bps
Coconut Computing Inc BBS	619-456-0815 14400bps
Codenoll BBS	914-965-1972 2400bps
Colorado Memory Systems BBS	303-635-0650 (8N1)
Colorado Memory Systems BBS	970-635-0650 14400bps
Columbia Data Products BBS	407-862-4724 2400bps
Commodore Business Mach Tech Support 2	15-431-9100
Communications Research BBS	504-926-5625 2400bps
Command Software BBS	407-575-1281 14400bps
Command Software Fax	407-575-3026
Command Software General	407-575-3200
Compaq Computer Systems BBS	713-378-1418 14400bps
Compaq General	713-370-0670
Compaq FTP Site	ftpcompaqcom
Compaq T/S	800-888-5858
Compaq Tech Support	800-345-1518
Compaq Tech Support	800-652-6672
Compati Tech Support	815-756-3411
Compex Fax	714-630-6521
Compex Voice	714-630-7302
Compuadd Tech Support	800-456-3116
CompUSA General	703-821-7700
CompUSA Training Dept	800-TRAIN-80
CompuServ Info Serv General	800-848-8199
Computer Associates General	800-225-5224
Computer Connections	800-438-5336
Computer Peripherals Inc BBS	805-499-9646 14400bps
Computer Peripherals Inc Tech Support	805-499-5751
Computer Support BBS	214-404-8652 14400bps
Computers International BBS	213-823-3609 14400bps

Computone Corp BBS	404-343-9737
Computone Corp BBS	404-664-1210
Computone Corp General	404-475-2725
Computone Corp Tech Support	404-475-2725 x250
Comtrol BBS	612-631-8310 288K
Comtrol BBS	612-639-1502 144K
Connectsoft	206-827-6467
Conner Peripherals BBS	408-456-4415 V32
Conner Peripherals Fax Back	408-456-4903
Conner Peripherals Tech Support	408-456-3388
Conner Peripherals Tech Support	800-421-1879
Conner Peripherals Tech Support	800-426-6637
Control Data Corp (CDC) General	800 345-6628
Core International BBS	407-241-2929 2400bps
Core International Tech Support	407-997-6044
Corel General	800-836-7274
Corel System BBS	613-728-4752 14400bps
Cornerstone Technology BBS	408-435-8943 2400bps
Cornerstone Technology T/S	408-435-8900
Corvus System, Inc BBS	408-972-9154 2400bps
Covox Corpoartion BBS	503-342-8261 14400bps
CPI T/S	800-235-7618
Creative Labs BBS	405-742-6660 14400bps
Creative Labs C/S	800-998-1000
Creative Labs ftp	ftpcreafcom
Creative Labs T/S	405-742-6622
Cross Communications BBS	303-444-9003 14400bps
Crosstalk Communications BBS	404-740-8428
CTX (monitors) BBS	909-594-8973
CTX (monitors) Repair (East Coast)	800-342-5289
CTX (monitors) Repair (West Coast)	800-289-2189
CTX (monitors) Service Center	800-888-2012
Cumulus BBS	216-464-3019 2400bps
CYRIX BBS	214-994-8610 14400bps
CYRIX General	800-FAS-MATH
CYRIX T/S	800-327-6284
CYRIX T/S	800-GO-CYRIX
CYRIX Technical Support	800-848-2979 x325

 D

D-Link Systems, Inc BBS	714-455-1779 14400bps
D-Link LAN adaptors/cards	800-361-5265
DAC Software BBS	214-931-6617 2400bps
DAK Online Resource Center BBS	818-715-7153 14400bps
Dallas (chip) Tech Support	510-796-6100
Dariana Technology Group BBS	714-994-7410 2400bps
Darwin Systems BBS	301-251-9206 14400bps
Data Access BBS	305-238-0640 2400bps
Data Shield T/S	312-329-1601

Data Technology Corp BBS	408-942-4010
Data Technology Corp Tech Support	408-262-7700
Datadesk/Prometheus BBS	503-691-5199 9600bps
DataEase Int'l BBS	203-374-6302 2400bps
Datapoint General	210-593-7000
Dataproducts Corp BBS	818-887-8167 9600bps
Datastorm (Procomm) BBS	314-875-0503 14400bps
Datastorm (Procomm) Business	314-443-3282
Datastorm (Procomm) Fax	314-875-0595
Datastorm (Procomm) Tech Support	314-875-0530
David Systems BBS	408-720-0406 2400bps
Dayna Communications BBS	801-535-4205 2400bps
DCA BBS	404-740-8428 9600bps
Dell Computer BBS	512-728-8528
Dell Computer Customer Service	800-624-9897
Dell Computer FTP Site	ftpdellcom
Dell Computer Sales	800-879-3355
Dell Computer Tech Fax	800-950-1329
Dell Computer Tech Support	800-624-9896
Delphi BBS	800-365-4636 2400bps
Delrina Technology Inc BBS	416-441-2752 16800bps
Delrina Technology Inc General	416-441-3676, 800-268-6082
DeltaComm Development BBS	919-481-9399 16800bps
DeltaComm Development FAX	919-460-4531
DeltaComm Development General	919-460-4556
Describe General	800-448-1586
Development Technologies General	803-790-9230
Diamond BBS	408-730-1100 2400 bps
Diamond BBS	408-325-7175 9600-1440 bps
Diamond Fax	408-773-8000
Diamond Fax Back	800-380-0030
Diamond Tech Support	408-325-7100
Diconix T/S	513-259-3100
Digiboard Inc BBS	612-943-0812 2400bps
Digiboard Inc Tech Support	612-943-9020
Digicom Systems, Inc BBS	408-262-5629
Digicom Systems, Inc Voice	408-262-1277
Digital Communications BBS	513-433-5080 2400bps
Digital Equip Corp(DEC) General	508-493-5111
DEC ordering by fax	800 234-2298
DEC ordering by fax	800-524-5694
DEC ordering by modem	800-234-1998
DEC ordering by phone	800 PC BY DEC
DEC Product info	800-DIGITAL
DEC Tech Support	800-354-9000
Digital Research BBS	408-649-3443 2400bps
Digital Research Tech Support	408-646-6464
Digital Vision BBS	617-329-8387 14400bps
Digitrend Systems Corp General	818-772-0190
Dilog General	408-241-3192
Disk Technician Corporation BBS	619-272-9240 2400bps

DNA Networks, Inc BBS	215-296-9558 2400bps
Dove Computer BBS	919-343-5616 14400bps
DPT (Dist Process Tech) BBS	407-831-6432
DPT (Dist Process Tech) General	407-260-3566
DPT (Dist Process Tech) Tech Support	407-830-5522
DSI (Digicom Systems) BBS	408-262-5629
DSI (Digicom Systems) Sales	800-833-8900
DSI (Digicom Systems) Tech Support	408-262-1277
DTC BBS	408-942-4010
DTC Fax	408-942-4052
DTC Fax Back	408-942-4005
DTC General	408-942-4000
DTC Tech Support	408-262-7700
DTK Main	818-810-8880
DTK Tech Support (GA)	800-746-4386
DTK Tech Support (FL)	305-597-8888
DTK Tech Support (IL)	800-804-8048
DTK Tech Support (NJ)	908-562-8800
Dudley Software BBS	615-966-3574 2400bps
Durant Technologies T/S	800-451-4813
Dynamic Microprocessor BBS	516-462-6638 2400bps
Dysan Corp Tech Support	408-988-3472

 E

EagleSoft BBS	812-479-1310 16800bps
Eastman Kodak T/S	800-255-3434
Elek-Tec, Inc General	800-395-1000
Elite Business App's BBS	410-987-2335 2400bps
Elitegroup Computer Systems	510-226-7333
Elitegroup BBS	510-683-0928
ELSA BBS	408-565-9630
ELSA Inc.	408-565-9669
Emac/Everex BBS	510-226-9694 2400bps
Emerald Systems BBS	619-673-4617 2400bps
Emerald Systems T/S	800-366-4349
Enable Software BBS	518-877-6316 2400bps
Ensoniq General	610-647-3930
Envisions BBS	415-259-8145
Epson T/S	800-922-8911
Epson Tech Support	213-539-9955
Epson America, Inc BBS	310-782-4531 9600bps
Equinox Systems, Inc BBS	305-378-1696 2400bps
eSoft Inc BBS	303-699-8222 16800bps
Ericsson Mobile Comm	800 268 1887
Etech Research	408-988-8108
ETS Incorporated BBS	801-265-0919 14400bps
Everex Systems BBS	510-438-4650
Everex Systems Tech Support	510-498-1115

Exabyte BBS	303-447-7100
Exabyte Sales	800-445-7736
Exabyte T/S	303-447-4323
Exabyte Direct Srvce Admn Fax	303-447-7199
Excalibur BBS	408-244-0813 14400bps
Exis BBS	416-439-8293 14400bps
Expert Graphics	404-320-0800
Expert Graphics BBS	404-315-7646
EZX Publishing BBS	713-280-8180 14400bps

 F

Family Scrapbook BBS	904-249-9515 16800bps
Fargo Electronics	800-327-4622
FaxWorks	800-345-4329
Fidelity International	908-417-2230
Fifth Generation Systems BBS	504-295-3344
Fifth Generation Systems BBS	504-295-3344 2400bps
Fifth Generation Systems T/S	800-766-7283
Fifth Generation Systems T/S: Mace, Fastback	800-873-4384
Flashllink BBS	717-293-3074
FlashTek BBS	208-883-3859
FlashTek Email	flashtek@protocom
FlashTek England	44-476-74108
FlashTek General	208-882-7275
FlashTek Orders	800-397-7310
Focus Information Systems	510-657-2845
Folio BBS	801-375-9907 2400bps
Footprint Works General	416-860-0477
Footprint Works T/S	800-465-8470
Foresight Resources BBS	816-891-8465 2400bps
Frederick Engineering, Inc BBS	301-290-6944 2400bps
FreeLance Cust Support	800-223-1662
Fresh Technology BBS	602-497-4235 2400bps
Frye Computer Systems	617-451-5400
Fujitsu America, Inc BBS	408-894-2950 9600bps
Fujitsu America, Inc FaxBack	408-428-0456
Fujitsu America T/S	408-432-1300
Fujitsu America, Inc Tech Support	800-826-6112
Funk	800-828-4146
Future Domain BBS	714-253-0432 2400bps
Future Domain Tech Support	714-253-0400
Future Domain Update Center	800-879-7599
FutureSoft Engineering BBS	713-588-6870 2400bps
Galacticomm BBS	305-583-7808 14400bps
GammaTech General	405-359-1219
GAP Development Company BBS	714-493-3819 14400bps
Gateway General	800-846-2000
Gateway BBS	605-232-2109 14400bps
Gateway T/S	714-553-1555

Gateway Tech Support	800-846-2301
Gateway Communications BBS	714-863-7097 2400bps
Gazelle Systems T/S: Optune	800-233-0383
Gazelle Systems BBS	801-375-2548 2400bps
GEcho BBS	316-263-5313 16800bps
General DataComm Ind BBS	203-598-0593 14400bps
GEnie Information Services BBS	800-638-8369 2400bps
Genoa BBS	408-943-1231 2400bps
Genoa Tech Support	408-432-9090
Genovation Fax	714-833-0322
Genovation General	714-833-3355
Gensoft Development BBS	206-562-9407 2400bps
GeoClock BBS	703-241-7980 14400bps
GeoWorks T/S	415-644-3456
Gibson Research BBS	714-362-8848 2400bps
Gibson Research Sales-T/S: Spinwrite	714-362-8800
GigaTrend, Inc BBS	619-566-0361 2400bps
Global Village Comm BBS	408-523-2403 14400bps
Global Village Comm General	408-523-1000
Global Village Comm Tech Support	408-523-1050
GoldDisk	905-602-0395
Goldstar T/S	800-777-1192
Goldstar Tech Support	408-432-1331
Goldstar Technologies BBS	408-432-0236 14400bps
Graphic Workshop BBS	416-729-4609 14400bps
Gravis BBS	604-431-5927
Gravis Tech Support	604-431-1807
Great American Software BBS	603-889-7292 2400bps
Gupta Technologies, Inc BBS	415-321-0549 2400bps
GVC Technologies BBS	201-579-2380 14400bps
GVC Technologies General	800-289-4821

 H

HardDrives Intl Sales?	800-998-8093
Hayes T/S	404-441-1617, 404-441-0896
Hayes Microcomputer BBS	404-446-6336 14400bps
Hayes Microcomputer BBS	800-874-2937 14400bps
Hayes On-line BBS (product info)	800-874-2937
Hazard Soft BBS	405-243-3200 16800bps
HDC Computer BBS	206-869-2418 2400bps
Headland General	510-656-0503
Headland Technology BBS	415-656-0503 2400bps
Headstart T/S	800-722-6224
Hercules Computer BBS	510-540-0621 2400bps
Hercules Computer Tech	BBS 510-623-7034
Hercules Computer Tech Tech Support	510-623-6030
Hewlett-Packard Co BBS	408-553-3500
Hewlett-Packard Co Customer Information	800-752-0900
Hewlett-Packard Co Fax Back	800-331-1917

287

Hewlett-Packard Co Tech Support	800-858-8867
Hitachi T/S	224-785-9770
Houston Instruments T/S	800-444-3425
Hyundai Electronics Tech Support	800-234-3553

i-link General (Germany)	+4930-216-20-48
IBM PC Users Group BBS	404-988-2790
IBM Automated Fax	800-426-3395
IBM BBS	919-517-0001 14400bps
IBM BBS Information	800-848-8199
IBM BBS (Montreal, Canada)	514-938-3022
IBM BBS (Toronto, Canada)	905-316-4255
IBM BBS (Toronto, Canada)	416-492-1823
IBM BBS (Vancouver, Canada)	604-664-6464
IBM BBS (Victoria, Canada)	604-380-5441
IBM BBS (Winnipeg, Canada)	204-934-2798
IBM Cust Relation (Canada)	800-465-6600
IBM Defect Support	800-237-5511
IBM General	800-426-3333
IBM General	800-426-2468
IBM General (USA)	800-547-1283
IBM General (Canada)	800-465-7999
IBM PS/2 HelpCenter	800-772-2227
IMC Networks BBS	714-724-0930 2400bps
IMSI Software BBS	415-454-2893 2400bps
Indelible Blue Fax	919-878-7479
Indelible Blue General	800-776-8284
Indelible Blue General	919-878-9700
Infinity Computer Services BBS	215-965-8028 2400bps
Infochip Systems BBS	408-727-2496 2400bps
Informix BBS	913-492-2089 2400bps
InfoShare BBS	703-803-8000 96H00bps
Innovative Data Concepts	BBS 215-357-4183 2400bps
Inset Corporation BBS	203-740-0063 14400bps
Inset Systems, Inc.	800-DR-INSET
Insignia Solutions BBS	415-694-7694 2400bps
Integrated Inf Tech BBS	408-727-0952
Integrated Inf Tech Mathco T/S	800-448-5033
Integrated Inf Tech XtraDrive T/S	408-727-1676
Intel Application Support BBS	916-356-3600 14400bps
Intel BBS	503-645-6275 14400bps
Intel Cust Support/FaxBack	800-538-3373
Intel FaxBack	800-525-3019
Intel FaxBack	503-629-7576
Intel Fax	503-629-7580
Intel Fax	800-458-6231
Intel Sales	800-538-3373
Intel Sales	503-629-7354

Intelligent Graphics Corp BBS	408-441-0386 2400bps
Intracorp BBS	305-378-8793 2400bps
Intuit	800-624-8742
Iomega BBS	801-778-4400 2400bps
Iomega T/S	800-456-5522
Irma DCA T/S	404-740-0300
Irwin T/S	800-421-1879
Irwin Magnetics BBS	313-930-9380 9600bps
ITAC Systems, Inc General	214-494-3073

 J

JDR Microdevices BBS	408-559-0253 2400bps
Jetfax BBS	415-324-1259 2400bps
Jetform BBS	613-563-2894 2400bps

 K

Kalok (HDD) BBS	408-738-4258
Kalok (HDD) FAX	408-747-1319
Kalok (HDD) Voice	408-747-1315
Kaypro Tech Support	619-481-3900
Kensington Microware T/S	800-535-4242
Kent Marsh BBS	713-522-8921 2400bps
Keytronics Tech Support	800-262-6006
Kodiak Technology BBS	408-452-0677 2400bps
Kodiak Technology Tech Support	800-777-7704
Kurta T/S	800-645-8782
Kurta Corp BBS	602-243-9440 2400bps
Kyocera Unison Inc General	415-848-6680

 L

LAN (magazine) BBS	415-267-7640
LAN Master BBS	817-771-0233 16800bps
LAN Systems BBS	801-373-6980 2400bps
LAN Works BBS	416-238-0253 2400bps
Landmark Research International	800-683-0854
Laser Go BBS	619-450-9370 2400bps
Lattice BBS	708-916-1200 2400bps
Leading Edge BBS	508-836-3971 14400bps
Leading Edge Customer Service	800-874-3340
Leading Edge Tech Support	800-245-9870
Lexmark BBS	606-232-5238
Lexmark BBS	800-453-9223 2400bps
Lexmark Fax	606-232-2380
Lexmark Voice	606-232-3000

Liant Software BBS	508-626-0681 9600bps
Liant Software Tech Support	508-875-2294
Liberty Systems	800-774-5044
Lightning Communications BBS	714-457-9429 9600bps
Logical Connection BBS	504-295-3344 2400bps
Logicode Technology	805-388-9000
Logitech BBS	510-795-0408 14400bps
Logitech Tech Support	510-795-8100
Lotus BBS	404-395-7707 2400bps
Lotus BBS	617-693-7000 2400bps
Lotus Cust Support	800-223-1662
Lotus Development General	617-577-8500
Lotus Tech Support Support	404-399-5505
Lucas Games BBS	415-257-3070

 M

Mace, Paul Software BBS	714-240-7459
Mace, Paul Software BBS	503-482-7435 2400bps
Mace, Paul Software Tech Support	800-523-0258
Macronix Tech Support	800-468-4629
Macronix California Tech Support only	408-453-8088
Madge Networks BBS	408-441-1340 2400bps
Magee Enterprises, Inc BBS	404-446-6650 16800bps
Magitronic Technology BBS	516-454-8262 14400bps
Magnavox BBS	310-532-6436 14400bps
Magnavox T/S	800-722-6224
Main Lan BBS	407-331-7433 2400bps
Mannesman Tally BBS	206-251-5513 2400bps
Mansfield Software Group BBS	203-429-3784 14400bps
Manx Software Systems BBS	201-542-2793 2400bps
Matrix Technology BBS	617-569-3787 2400bps
Matrox Graphics	514-969-6300
Maxi Host Support BBS	209-836-2402 2400bps
Maxis Software BBS	510-254-3869 14400bps
Maxtor/Miniscribe BBS	303-678-2222 14400bps
Maxtor/Miniscribe Fax	303-678-2618
Maxtor/Miniscribe General	303-651-6000
Maxtor/Miniscribe Tech Support	800-356-5333
Maxtor/Miniscribe T/S	800-262-9867
Maxoptics T/S	800-848-3092
Maynard Electronics BBS	407-263-3502 2400bps
Maynard Electronics General	800-227-6296
McAfee Assoc BBS	408-988-4004 16800bps
McAfee Assoc Fax	408-970-9727
McAfee Assoc General	408-988-3832
MediaTrix Peripherals	800-820-8749
Media Vision BBS	510-770-0968 14400bps
MediaVision BBS	510-770-0527

MediaVision General	800-684-6699
MediaVision Sales	800-845-5870
MediaVision Tech Support	510-770-9905
Megahertz Corp Sales	800-LAPTOPS
Megahertz Corp T/S	800-527-8677
Metheus T/S	503-690-1550
Micro Design	800-228-0891
Micro Display Systems BBS	612-438-3513 2400bps
Micro Solutions BBS	815-756-9100 14400bps
Micro Solutions	800-890-7227
Microbotics Tech Support	214-437-5330
Microcom BBS	617-762-5134 2400bps
Microcom, Inc	617-551-1021
Microdyne BBS	703-739-0432 2400bps
Microid Research FAX	408-727-6996
Microid Research Voice	408-727-6991
Micro Labs	214-234-5842
Micrographics	214-234-1769
Micron Technology BBS	208-368-4530 2400bps
Micronics BBS	510-651-6837 14400bps
Micronet General	714-837-6033
Micronics General	510-651-2300
Micropolis Corp BBS	818-709-3310 2400bps
Micropolis Corp Tech Support	818-709-3325
MicroProse BBS	301-785-1841 2400bps
Microrim BBS	206-649-9836 2400bps
Microscience Int Tech Support	408-433-9898
Microsoft Access	206-635-7050
Microsoft Basic PDS	206-635-7053
Microsoft BBS	206-646-9145
Microsoft BBS 9600	206-936-6735
Microsoft BBS Canada	905-507-3022
Microsoft C Compiler	206-635-7007
Microsoft COBOL	206-637-7096
Microsoft Corporate Switchboard	206-882-8080
Microsoft Cust Support	800-426-9400
Microsoft Customer Sales & Service	800-426-9400
Microsoft DOS 5	206-646-5104
Microsoft DOS 5 recordings	206-646-5103
Microsoft Excel for Macintosh	206-635-7080
Microsoft Excel for Windows & Excel for OS/2	206-635-7070
Microsoft FORTRAN Compiler	206-635-7015
Microsoft General (Toronto)	416-568-0434
Microsoft LAN Manager for UNIX	206-635-7021
Microsoft Macro Assembler	206-646-5109
Microsoft Mail for Windows & Mail for Macintosh	206-637-9307
Microsoft Money for Windows	206-635-7131
Microsoft Mouse, BallPoint, & Hardware	206-637-7096
Microsoft Pascal	206-637-7096
Microsoft PowerPoint for Windows	206-635-7145
Microsoft PowerPoint for Macintosh	206-635-7145

Microsoft Profiler   206-635-7015
Microsoft Project for Windows and Macintosh   206-635-7155
Microsoft Project for MS-DOS   206-635-7155
Microsoft Publisher for Windows   206-635-7140
Microsoft Quick Assembler   206-635-7010
Microsoft QuickC Compiler   206-635-7010
Microsoft Test Tools for Windows   206-635-7052
Microsoft Visual Basic Startup   206-646-5105
Microsoft Windows Applications   206-637-7099
Microsoft Windows Applications for OS/2 ver 20   206-635-7247
Microsoft Windows Environment   206-637-7098
Microsoft Word for Macintosh   206-635-7200
Microsoft Word for MS-DOS   206-635-7210
Microsoft Word for OS/2   206-454-2030
Microsoft Word for Windows   206-462-9673
Microsoft Works for Macintosh   206-635-7160
Microsoft Works for MS-DOS   206-635-7150
Microsoft Works for Windows   206-635-7130
ALL Microsoft OTHER PRODUCTS   206-454-2030
MICROSOFT STARTUP AND INSTALLATION SUPPORT
    Microsoft LAN Manager Startup (first 30 days only)   206-635-7020
    Microsoft MS-DOS 50 (first 90 days only)   206-646-5104
    Microsoft QuickBASIC Startup   206-646-5101
    Microsoft SQL Server Startup (first 30 days only)   206-637-7095
    Microsoft Visual Basic Startup   206-646-5105
    Microsoft Windows Entertainment Pack   206-637-9308
    Microsoft Windows Software Development Kit (SDK)   206-635-3329
MICROSOFT FAST TIPS SERVICES
    Microsoft Excel for Macintosh   206-635-7081
    Microsoft Excel for Windows   206-635-7071
    Microsoft Fast Tips General   800-936-4100
    Microsoft MS-DOS 50   206-646-5103
    Microsoft Project for Windows   206-635-7156
    Microsoft Visual Basic   206-646-5107
    Microsoft Windows   206-635-7245
    Microsoft Word for Macintosh   206-635-7201
    Microsoft Word for MS-DOS   206-635-7211
    Microsoft Word for Windows   206-635-7231
MICROSOFT INCREMENTAL FEE-BASED SUPPORT
    Microsoft OnCall for Basic $2/min   900-896-9999
    Microsoft OnCall for Basic $20/call   206-646-5106
    Microsoft OnCall for MS-DOS $2/min   900-896-9000
    Microsoft OnCall for MS-DOS $20/call   206-646-5108
    Microsoft OnCall for Visual Basic $2/min   900-896-9876
    Microsoft OnCall for Visual Basic $20/call   206-646-5106
    Microsoft Network Support $175/call   206-635-7022
Microsystems Software BBS   508-875-8009 2400bps
Microtech BBS   203-469-6430 2400bps
MicroTek BBS   310-538-4032 14400bps
Microtest BBS   602-996-4009 2400bps, 800-526-9675
Mirage Multimedia Computers   800-228-3349

miro Computer Products	415-855-0940
Mitsubishi Inc T/S	800-344-6352
Mitsubishi Inc Tech Support	213-515-3993
Mitsubishi BBS	714-636-6216 2400bps
Mitsumi	800-648-7864
Mitsumi BBS	415-691-4469
MitsumiSales	516-752-7730
MitsumiTech Support	408-970-9699
MitsumiTech Support	408-970-9730
Motorola	800-487-1456
Motorola BBS	800-843-3451
Motorola BBS	512-891-3733
Motorola BBS	512-891-3733
Mountain Computer, Inc BBS	408-438-2665
Mountain Computer, Inc General	800-458-0300
Mountain Computer, Inc Tech Support	408-438-7897
Mouse Systems (MSC) BBS	510-683-0617 14400bps
Mouse Systems Tech Support	510-656-1117
Multi-Tech Systems BBS	612-785-9875 14400bps
Multiwave Innovation	408-379-2900
Mustang Software BBS	805-395-0650 16800bps
Mustang Software FAX	805-873-2599
Mustang Software MSI HQ BBS	805-873-2400
Mustang Software OFFICE	805-873-2500
Mustang Software SALES	800-999-9619
Mustang Software T/S	805-873-2550
Mustek BBS	714-250-4263
Mutant Group BBS	405-372-6621 16800bps
Mylex	800-776-9539
Mylex BBS	510-793-3491
Mylex Technical Support	510-796-6100

 N

National Design	800-253-8831
National Semiconductor BBS	408-245-0671 2400bps
NCR BBS	719-596-1649
NCR Video Chip Support	800-543-9935
NEC Sales & Info	800-632-4636
NEC T/S	708-860-0335
NEC Tech Support BBS	508-635-4706
NEC Tech Support fax	708-860-5475
NEC Tech Support faxback	800-366-0476
NEC Tech Support General	800-388-8888
Netsoft	800-352-3270
Network Products Corp BBS	818-441-6933 14400bps
NetWorth BBS	214-869-2959 2400bps
New Media Corp	714-453-0100
New Media Corp General	800-227-3748

New Media Graphics BBS	508-663-7612 14400bps
NeXT Answers automated email	nextanswers@nextcom
NeXT Answers Fax Back	415-780-3990
NeXTT/S General	800-848-NEXT
Night Owl BBS	716-881-5688 16800bps
NISCA BBS	214-446-0646 2400bps
Nokia Sales/Service	800-296-6542
Norton Tech Support	213-319-2020
Norton-Lambert BBS	805-683-2249 14400bps, voice 805-964-6767
Norton/Symantec	800-441-7234
Norton/Symantec BBS	408-973-9598 2400bps
NovaStor Fax	818-707-9902
NovaStor Sales	818-707-9900
Novell Tech Support	800-638-9273
Nuiq Software Inc BBS	914-833-1479 14400bps
Number Nine	617-674-0009
Number Nine BBS	617-497-6463 9600bps
Nth Graphics	800-624-7552

 O

OCR Systems BBS	215-938-7245 2400bps
Okidata BBS	800-283-5474 9600bps
Okidata T/S	800-634-0089
Okidata Tech Support	609-235-2600
Olivetti Office USA General	201-526-8200
Omen Technology BBS	503-621-3746 9600bps
OPTi, Inc BBS	408-980-9774
OPTi, Inc Voice	408-980-8178
Ontrack Computer Systems BBS	612-937-0860
Ontrack Computer Systems Data Recovery	800-872-2599
Ontrack Computer Systems Sales Dos utils	800-752-1333
Ontrack Computer Systems Sales: Disk Manager	800-752-1333
Ontrack Computer Systems Tech Support	612-937-2121
Open Network BBS	718-638-2239 2400bps
OPTi, Inc Voice	408-980-8178
Orange Micro T/S	714-779-2772
Orchid Technology BBS	510-683-0327
Orchid Technology General	510-683-0300
Orchid Technology Sales	800-767-2443
Orchid Technology Tech Support	510-683-0323
Origin BBS	512-328-8402 2400bps
Ositech Communications	519-836-8063

 P

Pacific Data Products BBS	619-452-6329 2400bps
Pacific Data Product T/S	619-597-3444

Packard Bell BBS	818-773-7207 2400bps
Packard Bell BBS - Canada	416-542-7359
Packard Bell BBS USA	801-250-1600 2400bps
Packard Bell Tech Support	800-733-4411
Packard Bell Tech Support	801-579-0160
Palindrome BBS	708-505-3336 2400bps, 800-288-4912
Panasonic T/S	800-222-0584
Panasonic Communica'n Sys BBS	201-863-7845
Panasonic Printers Cust Support	708-468-5440
Paperback Corporation BBS	415-644-0782 16800bps
Paradise Tech Support	800-832-4778
Paradise Systems BBS	714-753-1234 14400bps
Patton & Patton Software BBS	408-778-9697 2400bps
PC Power and Cooling	619-931-5700
PC Power and Cooling	800-722-6555
PC User Groups) BBS	408-439-9367
PCubid (CPU fans) General	916-338-1338
Pentax Technologies BBS	303-460-1637 16800bps
Perstore BBS	602-894-4605
Perstore Tech Support	602-894-4601
Philips BBS	719-593-4081
Phoenix (Bios) BBS	405-321-2400 14400bps
Phoenix (Bios) Tech Support	617-551-4000
PIICEON, Inc	800-366-1517
Pinnacle Publishing BBS	206-251-6217 2400bps
Pinpoint Publishing BBS	707-523-0468 2400bps
Pioneer New Media	800-444-6784
Pixar	415-258-8100
PKWare BBS	414-354-8670 16800bps
PKWare Voice	414-354-8699
PLI BBS	510-651-5948 2400bps
Plexor	800-886-3935
Plus Development BBS	408-434-1664
Plus Development Tech Support	900-740-4433
Plus Development Tech Support Calif	800-826-8022
Power Pixel Technologies	408-748-0246
Practical Peripherals BBS	805-496-4445 14400bps
Practical Peripherals General	800-442-4774
Practical Peripherals T/S	805-496-7707
PraeoTek	612-785-9717
Priam Systems BBS	408-434-1646 2400bps
Priam Systems Tech Support	408-954-8680
Prime Solutions Tech Support Disk Tech	800-847-5000
Princeton Graphic Systems BBS	404-664-1210 2400bps
Princeton Graphics T/S	404-664-1010
Pro Engineering Inc FAX	613-738-3871
Pro Engineering Inc General	613-738-3864
ProComm Support BBS	314-474-8477
Programmer's Workshop General	216-494-5260
Programmer's Workshop General	216-494-8715
Programmer's Workshop General	800-336-1166

295

Prometheus Products BBS	503-691-5199 14400bps
Promise Technology General	408-452-0948
Promise's Technology BBS	408-452-1267
Promise's Technology Tech Support	408-452-1180
Proportional Software General	800-666-4672
Proteon BBS	508-366-7827 2400bps
Proteon T/S	508-898-3100
Public Brand Software BBS	317-856-2087 14400bps
Pure Data BBS	214-242-3225 14400bps
Pure Data Sales	905-731-6444
Pure Data T/S	800-661-8210

 Q

Q+E Software BBS	919-851-1381
Q+E Software Sales	800-876-3101
Q+E Software Technical Support	919-851-1152
QIC Standards Inc Fax	805-962-1541
QIC Standards Inc General	805-963-3853
Qmail BBS	901-382-5583 16800bps
QMS BBS	205-633-3632
QMS FAX	205-633-3145
QMS General	205-633-4300
QNX Fax	613-591-3579
QNX T/S	613-591-0941
Quadram BBS	404-564-5678 2400bps
Qualitas BBS	301-907-8030 14400bps
Qualitas FaxFacts	301-718-6066
Qualitas General	301-907-6700
Qualitas Tech Support	301-907-7400
Qualitas T/S FAX	301-718-6061
Qualitas Toll Free	800-676-6386
Quantum BBS	408-894-3214 2400bps
Quantum T/S (end user)	800-826-8022
Quantum T/S	408-894-4000
Quantum T/S	408-944-0410
Quark	800-788-7835
Quarterdeck BBS	310-314-3227 V32bis
Quarterdeck BBS	310-396-3904 14400bps
Quarterdeck Customer Service	800-354-3222
Quarterdeck Fax	310-314-3217
Quarterdeck Sales	310-392-9851
Quarterdeck Tech Support	310-392-9701
Quarterdeck Tech Support DeskView	310-392-9851
Quarterdeck Tech Support - Fax	310-399-3802
Quarterdeck Tech Support Manifest	310-392-9851
Quarterdeck Tech Support - UK	+4471 973-0663
Quercus Systems BBS	408-867-7488 14400bps
Quess Micro BBS	719-597-8670 14400bps

Quick Link II SW General 144 Modem	714-362-5800
QuickBBS BBS	407-896-0494 16800bps

 R

Racal Interlan/Rabbit Soft BBS	508-264-4345 2400bps
Race BBS	305-271-2146 2400bps
Rams' Island Software BBS	303-841-6269 16800bps
Rancho Technology Tech Support	714-987-3966
RC Electronics General	714-375-3791
RelayNet National BBS	301-229-5623 16800bps
Remote Control Int BBS	619-431-4030 2400bps
Reveal	800-473-8325
Revelation Technologies BBS	206-641-8110 2400bps
Ricoh Corp General	201-882-2000
Rix Softworks BBS	714-476-0728 2400bps
Rodime Inc General	407-997-0774
Roland Corporation	213-685-5141
Rybs Electronics BBS	303-443-7437 2400bps

 S

S3 General	408-986-8144
S3 BBS	408-654-5676
Saber Software BBS	214-361-1883 14400bps
Safetynet, Inc BBS	201-467-1581
Safetynet, Inc Sales	800-851-0188
Safetynet, Inc Tech Support	201-467-1024
Salt Air BBS BBS	801-261-8976 16800bps
Samsung Info Systems BBS	201-691-6238 2400bps
Samsung Info Syst BBS	408-434-5684
Samsung Info Syst Tech Support	800-446-0262
Santa Cruz Operation (SCO) Tech Support	800-347-4381
Santronics Software BBS	305-248-7815 16800bps
Sanyo Storage Products General	714-724-1505
SEAboard BBS	201-473-1991 9600bps
SeaFax Automated Fax Back Serv	408-438-2620
Seagate Technology BBS France	33-1-40-67-1034 2400bps
Seagate Technology BBS Germany	49-89-140-9331
Seagate Technology BBS Singapore	65-227-2217
Seagate Technology BBS UK	44-628-478011
Seagate Technology BBS USA	408-438-8771 14400bps
Seagate Technology Customer Service	800-468-3472
Seagate Technology General	408-438-6550
Seagate Technology Sales	408-438-8111
Seagate Technology Tech Support	408-438-8222
Searchlight Software BBS	516-689-2566 9600bps
SemWare BBS	404-641-8968 9600bps

Sharp BBS	404-962-1788 16800bps
Sharp T/S	708-759-8555
Shiva Corporation BBS	617-621-0190 2400bps
Shugart Tech Support	714-770-1100
Sierra Online BBS	209-683-4463 14400bps
Sigma Design BBS	510-770-0111 2400bps
Silicon Valley Computers BBS	415-967-8081
Silicon Valley Computers General	415-967-1100
Sitka Corporation BBS	415-769-8774 2400bps
Sitka BBS	510-769-8774 2400bps
SMC BBS	714-707-2481 V32
SMC T/S	800-992-4762
SMS Technology BBS	510-964-5700 9600bps
Sofnet BBS	404-984-9926 14400bps
Sofnet Fax	404-984-9956
Sofnet Sales	800-FAXWORKS
Sofnet Voice	404-984-8088
SoftArc Inc BBS	416-609-2250 14400bps
Softklone BBS	904-878-9884 14400bps
Softlogic Solutions Tech S Disk Optimize	800-272-9900
Softlogic Solutions BBS	603-644-5556 2400bps
Softronics BBS	719-593-9295 2400bps
Softronics Fax	719-548-1878
Softronics T/S	719-593-9550
Software Products Intl BBS	619-450-2179 2400bps
Software Publishing	800-234-2500
Software Security BBS	203-329-7263 2400bps
Software Venture BBS	510-849-1912 2400bps
Solutions Systems BBS	617-237-8530 2400bps
Sony Customer Relations	800-282-2848
Sony Sony CD-ROM BBS	408-955-5107
Sony Sony CD-ROM hotline	408-894-0555
Sony Faxback	800-961-SONY
Sony faxback service	408-955-5505
Sparco Communications General	800-840-8400
Sparco Communications General	601-323-5360
SparkWare BBS	901-382-5583 16800bps
Specialix Inc General	408-378-7919
Specialix Inc UK	44-0-932-354254
Spectra Publishing BBS	408-730-8326 2400bps
Spectrum Signal Processing	604-421-5422
Spider Graphics	408-526-0535
SprintNet BBS	800-546-1000 2400bps
SPSS BBS	312-836-1900
SPSS Sales	800-543-2185
SPSS Tech Support	312-329-3410
Stac Electronics BBS	619-431-5956 14400bps
Stac Electronics Tech Support	619-431-6712
Star Micronics BBS	908-572-5010 14400bps
Star (Printers) T/S	908-572-3300
STB Systems BBS	214-437-9615 16800bps

STB Systems BBS UK	44-181-897-1008
STB Systems Fax	214-234-1306
STB Systems Fax France	33-144-647687
STB Systems Fax UK	44-181-897-1006
STB Systems General	800-234-4334
STB Systems General	214-234-8750
STB Systems General	France 33-144-647685
STB Systems General	UK 44-181-897-1003
Storage Dimensions BBS	408-944-1220 14400bps
Storage Dimensions Tech Support	408-395-2688
Summagraphics T/S	203-384-1344
Summagraphics T/S	800-729-7866
Sun Express	800-USE-SUN
Sun Main Helpline	800-USA-4SUN
Sundial Systems General	310-596-5121
Sunrise Software BBS	404-256-9525 2400bps
Sunriver BBS	512-835-8082 2400bps
Supermac Software BBS	408-773-4500 2400bps
Supra	360-604-1400
Supra Corp BBS	503-967-2444 14400bps
Swan Technologies BBS	814-237-6145 14400bps
Sydex BBS	503-683-1385 2400bps
Symantec	800-441-7234
Symantec BBS	408-973-9598 14400bps
Symantec BBS	503-484-6669 14400bps
Symbios Logic Tech Support	719-573-3016
Symbios Logic BBS	719-573-3562
Syquest	415-226-4000
Syquest BBS	510-656-0473 9600bps
Syquest Fax Back	800-245-2278
Sysgen BBS	408-946-5032 2400bps
Sysgen T/S	800-821-2151
Systems Compatibility BBS	312-670-4239 2400bps

 T

TAG BBS BBS	313-582-6671 16800bps
Tandon Corp General	805-523-0340
Tandy Corp General	817-390-3011
Tandy Corp Tech Support	817-878-6875
Tangram Enterpise Soln's General	919-851-6000
Tatung Co of America Tech Support	213-979-7055
Teac America, Inc Fax Back	213-727-7629
Teac America, Inc Tech Support	213-726-0303
TEAMate BBS	213-318-5302 14400bps
Tech Data BBS	813-538-7090
Tech Data Tech Support	800-553-7977
Tech Tools BBS	603-888-8411
Tech Tools General	603-888-8400
Tech Tools Tech Support	603-888-6721

Tech Works	512-794-8533
Tecmar BBS	216-349-0853 14400bps
Tektronics BBS	503-685-4504
Tektronics General	800-835-6100
Tektronics Service	800-547-8949
Tektronics Tech Support	800-835-6100
Telebit BBS	408-745-3803 14400bps
Telebit Corp Tech Support	800-835-3248
Telix Support BBS	416-439-9399
Telix Support BBS	416-439-8293 16800bps
Template Garden Software BBS	212-627-5089 9600bps
Texas Instruments BBS	512-250-6112 2400bps
Texas Instruments Tech Support	512-250-7407
TheComplete PC BBS	407-997-9130 14400bps
TheComplete PC Fax	407-997-9621 14400bps
TheComplete PC Tech Support	407-997-8062 14400bps
TheSoft Programming BBS	415-581-3019 2400bps
Thomas-Conrad Corp BBS	512-836-8012 14400bps
Thomas-Conrad Corp T/S	800-334-4112 24 hour
Thomas-Conrad Corp T/S Canada	800-654-3822
Thumper Technologies BBS	918-627-0059 2400bps
Thunderbyte USA BBS	615-442-2833 14400bps
Tiara Computer Systems BBS	415-966-8533 14400bps
Timeline Software BBS	415-892-0408 2400bps
Timeslips BBS	508-768-7581 2400bps
Tops microsystems BBS	510-769-8774 2400bps
TOPS Support BBS	415-769-8874
TopSoft Software BBS	502-425-9941 16800bps
Toshiba America BBS	714-837-4408
Toshiba America Tech Support	800-999-4273
Toshiba Printer Products BBS	714-581-7600 2400bps
Trantor BBS	510-656-5159
Trantor FAX	510-770-9910
Trantor Systems BBS	415-656-5159 2400bps
Traveling Software	800-527-5465
Traveling Software BBS	206-485-1736 14400bps
Trident BBS	415-691-1016
Trident Tech Support	415-691-9211
Tripplite T/S	312-329-1601
Trison Electronics/Pronets Technology & Ancilla	905-238-9251
Trius BBS	508-794-0762 16800bps
True Vision BBS	317-577-8783 2400bps
Tseng Labs Fax	215-860-7713
Tseng Labs General	215-968-0502
TSR Systems BBS	516-331-6682 2400bps
Turbo Tax BBS	619-453-5232 2400bps
TurboCom BBS	503-482-2633 14400bps
Turtle Beach	717-767-0200
Turtle Beach BBS	717-845-4835 14400bps

U

USRobotics FaxBack	800-762-6163
USRobotics Sales & Marketing	800-342-5877
USRobotics T/S	800-982-5151
USRobotics T/S Fax	708-933-5552
USRobotics Voice	708-982-5151
Ultrastor BBS	510-623-9091
Ultrastor General	714-581-4100
Ultrastor Tech Support	510-623-8955
UMAX	800-562-0311
Unicore General	508-686-6468
Unicore General	800-800-2467
Unicorn Software BBS	317-784-2147 2400bps
UNIFACE Corp General	510-748-6145
UNIFACE Corp Support	510-748-6445
UniNova Service Corp BBS	509-925-3893 16800bps
US Sage BBS	417-331-7433 2400bps
USNO Time of Day BBS	202-653-0351
UUNET	800-488-6386

 V

Ven Tel BBS	408-922-0988 14400bps
Ventura Software BBS	619-673-7691 14400bps
Vermont Microsystems BBS	802-655-7461 2400bps
VESA FAX	408-435-8225
VESA General	408-435-0333
VideoLogic	800-578-5644
Video Seven BBS	510-656-0503 14400bps
Video Seven T/S	800-248-1850
View Software	800-536-8439
Virex BBS	919-419-1602 14400bps
Visual Business Systems BBS	404-953-1613 2400bps
Volkswriter BBS	408-648-3015 2400bps
Vortex Systems BBS	412-322-3216 2400bps

 W

Wacom BBS	415-960-0236 2400bps
Walker,Richer, & Quinn BBS	206-324-2357 9600bps, 206-217-7500
Walnut Creek (CDROM) FAX	510-674-0821
Walnut Creek (CDROM) General	510-674-0783
Walnut Creek (CDROM) General	800-786-9907
Walt Disney Software BBS	818-567-4027 2400bps
Wangtek BBS	805-582-3370 2400bps
Wangtek BBS	805-582-3620 9600b

Wangtek Fax	805-583-8249
Wangtek Fax Back	805-582-3381
Wangtek Voice	800-992-9916
Wangtek Voice	805-583-5255
Wantree Development BBS	913-441-0595 14400bps
Washburn & Co FAX	716-381-7549
Washburn & Co General	716-248-3627
Wearnes Peripherals	408-423-1888
Weitek BBS	408-522-7517 2400bps
Weitek Corp Fax	408-738-1185
Weitek Corp General	408-738-8400
Weltec T/S	714-669-1955
Western Digital BBS	714-753-1068 14400bps
Western Digital BBS	714-753-1234 2400b
Western Digital Fax Back	714-932-4300
Western Digital France	331-69-85-3914
Western Digital Germany	49-89-922006-60
Western Digital Tech Support	714-932-4900
Western Digital Tech Support	800-832-4778
Western Digital UK	44-372-360387
White Water Systems BBS	708-328-9442 2400bps
Wolfram Research	800-441-6284.
WordPerfect / Novell Fax	801-229-1566
WordPerfect/Novell Tech Support	800-638-9273
WordPerfect Corp BBS	801-225-4414 14400bps
WordPerfect Corp Tech Support DOS ver	800-541-5096
WordPerfect Corp T/S Mac ver 21	800-336-3614
WordPerfect Corp T/S Mac ver 30	800-228-2875
Wordtech BBS	415-254-1141 2400bps
Wyse Technology BBS	408-922-4400
Wyse Technology Tech Support	408-435-2770

 X

Xebex General	702-883-4000
Xerox Computer Serv General	213-306-4000
Xircom/Keating Technologies	416-479-0230
Xircom BBS	818-878-7618 14400bps
Xircom Tech Support	800-874-4428
XTree BBS	805-546-9150 2400bps
Xyquest BBS	508-667-5669 2400bps

 Y

Y-E Data General	714-898-3677
Young Micro Systems General	800-365-VEGA

Z

Zenith T/S	708-808-4300
Zenographics BBS	714-851-3860 2400bps
Zeos International Customer Service	800-848-9022
Zeos International Sales	800-423-5891
Zeos International T/S Fax	612-633-4607
Zeos International Tech Support	800-228-5390
Zeos International Upgrade Sales	800-874-2943
ZEOS Online Graphics BBS BBS	612-633-0815
Zoltrix	510-567-1188
Zoom Telephonics (24HR) BBS	617-423-3733 28800bps
Zoom Telephonics Sales	800-666-6191
Zsoft BBS	404-427-1045 14400bps
Zyxel Communications BBS	714-693-0762
Zyxel Communications Service Center	714-693-0804

Web Sites

Note: these URLS were complied from a variety of sources. For a one-stop source to check for updated and new URLs, go to Yahoo: http://www.yahoo.com/Business_and_Economy/Companies/Computers/. Another good souce can be found at http://www.tile.net/tile/vendors, which lists vendors by product, zip code, and other categories. If you don't find a vendor listed here, try one of those URLs, which are constantly updated.

1

1PCiTech Computers	http://www.pcitech.com/
1st Facilities Group Inc.	http://www.altcom.net/1stfacilities/
1st Solutions, Inc.	http://www.firstsol.com/

2

20/20 Sofware Inc.	http://www.twenty.com/~twenty/
21 TORR medienDesign GmbH	http://www.multimedia.de/

3

3Com	http://www.3com.com
3D Realms Entertainment	http://swcbbs.com/apogee/3drealms.htm
3D Scanners Ltd	http://www.3dscanners.com/
3D/EYE Inc.	http://www.eye.com/
3DO	http://www.3do.com/
3k Associates	http://www.3k.com/
3Space Virtual Reality and Interactive Graphics	http://www.io.org/~3space

4

4-Sight (International) Ltd.	http://www.four-sight.co.uk/4-sight/
4-Sight LC (USA)	http://www.4Sight.com/
4GL Computing Ltd	http://www.demon.co.uk/4gl/

7

7th Wave Productions	http://www.speakeasy.org/~herc/

A

A & M Consulting	http://www.niagara.com/~anna/
a la mode, inc.	http://www.alamode.com/
A New Perspective	http://www.cwo.com/~randjm/
A&M Networking Inc.	http://www.bei.net/amni/
A+ Computers	http://www.teleport.com/~aplus/
A-ARVIN Laser Resources	http://www.shore.net/~adfx/laser/top_page.htm
A-Link CD-ROM	http://www.a-link.com/
A.A.C.S. Computer Wholesale	http://www.cybergate.net/~raistlin/
A.C.E. Inc.	http://vipersoft.com/
A2Z Computers & Software	http://www.a2znet.com/
AA Computech, Inc.	http://www.gus.com/emp/aac/aac.html
AAA Computer Depot	http://www.nashville.com/member/depot.html
Aangstrom Precision	ftp://ftp.neosoft.com/pub/users/a/apc/html/homepage.html
AApex Software Corporation's Master Series	http://io.com/user/aapex/
Abacus Niagara	http://www.niagara.com/~abacus/
Abacus Research and Development, Inc.	http://www.ardi.com/
Abel Computers Ltd.	http://www.abelcomputers.com/
Ablaze Business Systems, Inc.	http://www.radix.net/~ablaze
Able Data Corporation	http://emory.com/~emory/able.html
Absoft Corporation	http://www.absoft.com/
ABSolute Best Systems	http://www.channel1.com/business/abs/
Absolute Media	http://www.maui.net/~absolute/am.htm
Abstract Software	http://www.abstractsoft.com/
Abstract Technologies	http://www.abstract.co.nz/
ABT, Inc.	http://www.abtcampus.com/
Abut Oy - Technical Multimedia	http://www.ttl.fi/abut/
Academic Systems P/L	http://www.ozemail.com.au/~cosmocom/cosmo.html
Academy of Learning	http://www_wol.info-mine.com/aol/
ACC Corp., Inc.	http://www.acc-corp.com/
ACC Systems Inc.	http://www.sys.acc.com/
Accelerated Computer Training, Inc.	http://www.earthlink.net/~actinc/
Accelerated Technology, Inc.	http://www.atinucleus.com/ati/
Accent	http://www.accentsoft.com/
ACCESS Computer Hardware	http://www.electriciti.com/~access/
Access First	http://www.inforamp.net/~access/af1.htm
AccessManager	http://www.icl.co.uk/access
Access Multimedia Technology	http://nol.net/amt/

Accidental Software	http://www.primenet.com/~accident/accident.html
Accounting MIS	http://www.excelco.com/mystery/
Accsys Corporation	http://info.acm.org/~rkaplan/homepage.html
AccuFACTS9000 Shop Floor Control Software	http://www.smartdocs.com/~bmcd/accufacts9000
Accugraph	http://www.accugraph.com/
ACD Systems	http://vvv.com/acd/
ACE Contact Manager for Windows	http://www.genphysics.com/ACE/
Acer America	http://www.acer.com/aac/
Acer America On-line Technical Support	http://www.acer.com/aac/support/
Acer America Product Information	http://www.acer.com/aac/products/
Acer America What's New	http://www.acer.com/aac/whatsnew.htm
Acer America Windows 95 Information	http://www.acer.com/aac/win95/
Acer Computec Latin America	http://www.acer.com.mx/
Acer Group	http://www.acer.com/index.htm
ACEware Systems, Inc.	http://www.aceware.com/
Achieve Technology	http://www.mv.com/biz/achieve-tech/
Ackley Industries	http://www.ackind.com/
Acomsoft-Software div. of Infinity Computer Systems	http://acomsoft.com/
ACS Custom Manufacturing	http://www.btsweb.com/cable/
Action Technologies	http://www.actiontech.com/
ActivCard	http://www.francenet.fr/activcard/
Active Information Management	http://www.activeinfo.com/
Activision	http://www.activision.com/
ACTS Production	http://www.scsn.net/~pfrmimpr/
Acumart	http://www.acumart.com/
Acumen Systems	http://www.iu.net/acumen/
Adaco Services Inc.	http://nwlink.com/~adaco9/
Adaptek Systems	http://branch.com/adaptek/adaptek.html
Adaptiv Software	http://www.adaptiv.com
ADD+ON Software, Inc.	http://www.gmcclel.bossnt.com/addon/
Adept Scientific plc	http://www.adeptscience.co.uk/
Adept Scientific plc	http://www.adeptscience.co.uk/
ADEPT, Inc.	http://205.199.112.21/~adept/
Adjile Systems	http://www.klws.com/adjile/adjile.html
Admins Inc.	http://www.admins.com/
Adobe	http://www.adobe.com/
ADOSEA Technologies Corporation	http://www.adosea.com/
Adriano Abbado	http://www.planet.it/freewww/abbado.html
ADSTAR Distributed Storage Manager (ADSM)	hardsoft/software/html/adsmhome.htm
AdvanceComp	http://rampages.onramp.net/~advcomp/index.html
Advance Network Solutions	http://www.halcyon.com/routers/
Advance Systems	http://www.asl.com/
Advanced CAD/CAM	http://www.adcadcam.com/
Advanced Computer Technologies	http://www.mountain.net/hp/act/
Advanced Computing Systems Company	http://acsc.com/
Advanced Cultural Technologies	http://www.ACTinc.bc.ca/

Advanced Image Management, Inc	http://firstnations.ca/~aim/
Advanced Instruments Corporation	http://www.ai.com/
Advanced Logic Research	http://www.alr.com/
Advanced Network Technologies	http://www.advancednet.com/
Advanced Networking Concepts, Inc.	http://www.adv-net.com/
Advanced Paradigms, Inc.	http://www.paradigms.com/
Advanced Personnel Systems	http://www.aps.com
Advanced Quick Circuits, L.P.	http://www.iu.net/aqc/
Advanced Real Estate System for ACT!	http://www.well.com/user/lexnet/ares1.html
Advanced Software Technology, Inc.	http://www.aescon.com/asti/index.htm
Advanced Storage Concepts	http://www.eden.com/~asc/
Advanced Technology Enterprises	http://www.ateshop.com/
Advanced Visual Systems	http://www.avs.com/
Advantage Business Computer Systems, Inc.	http://www.coconet.com/abc.html
Advantage Computers Ltd.	http://www.advantage.com/
ADVANTIS Networking Technology Services	http://www.ibm.com/globalnetwork
Advox AB	http://www.advox.se/default.htm
Aeon Technology	http://www.aeon.com/
AeroHydro, Inc.	http://www.netins.net/showcase/aerohydr/
AFL Consulting	http://www.interport.net/~aflcons/
AFP Solutions	http://www.gold.net/users/bw06/index.html
After Hours Media - CD-Backup Services	http://www.afterhours.com/cd-backup.html
After Hours Media - Disk Duplication	http://www.afterhours.com/disk.html
After Hours Media Duplication Service	http://www.afterhours.com/
AG Group, Inc.	http://www.aggroup.com/
AGE Logic, Inc.	http://www.age.com/
AgentCentral	http://www.mindspring.com/~jon-tom/AgentCentral.html
Agorics, Inc.	http://www.agorics.com/~agorics/
AHK & Associates	http://www.value.net/ahk/html/
AIC Software	http://www1.usa1.com/~aic/2.html
AIM Flight Simulation Network	http://pages.prodigy.com/SC/aimhomepage/aimhomepage.html
Ainsworth Group of Companies	http://wchat.on.ca/ainsworth/ati.htm
Ainsworth Keyboard Training Systems	http://www.qwerty.com/
AIPS (Classic, not aips++)	http://info.cv.nrao.edu/aips/aips-home.html
Air Havoc Controller for Windows	http://com.primenet.com/rainbow/
AIT - Applied Information Technologies, Inc.	http://access.digex.net/~solson/
Al Hasseb Corporation	http://www.kuwait.net/~alhasseb/
Aladdin Knowledge Systems Ltd.	http://www.hasp.com/
Aladdin Software	http://www.aladdin.no/
Alantec Corporation	http://www.alantec.com/
Alberta Printed Circuit Boards	http://www.apcircuits.com/htmls/apc/apdef2.html
ALCAD	http://www.infi.net/~aleonard/
Alchemy Mindworks, Inc.	alchemy/html/alchemy.html
Alden Computer Consultants	http://www.io.com/~alden/acc.htm
ALG Systemcorp	http://www.systemcorp.com/
Algorithms Corporation	http://www.everest.com/algorithms/

Aliah, Inc.	http://www.aliah.com/
All About Computers, Inc.	http://www.magic.mb.ca/~allabout/
All-Internet Shopping Directory	http://www.webcom.com/~tbrown/hardware.html
Allegro Consultants, Inc.	http://www.allegro.com
Allegro New Media	http://www.allegronm.com/
Allen & Associates, Ltd.	http://www.radix.net/~eallen/
Allen Communication Multimedia	http://www.allencomm.com/
Allon Computer, Inc.	http://www.promedia.net/allon/allon.html
Allstar Systems Inc.	http://www.phoenix.net/USERS/allstar/
AllWare Internet	http://www.allware.com/
Aloha Toner Cartridge	http://pete.com/toner/
Alpha Microsystems	http://www.alphamicro.com/
Alpha Printed Circuit Board Designs	http://www.mcs.net/~netdezin/alpha/home.html
Alpha Products	http://www.shore.net/~icorporate/dci/alpha.html
Alps Electric USA	http://www.alpsusa.com/
Alt-imedi@	http://www.ee.net/hsearles/
Alta Group	http://www.altagroup.com/
AltaVista Technology, Inc.	http://www.altavista.com/altavista/
Alteris Business Management System	http://www.pic.net/olympic/alt.html
Alternate Image	http://www.suspects.com/AlternateImage
Alternate Source Components, Ltd.	http://www.alternatesrc.com/
ALVE Software Engineering	http://www.alve.com/
ALWIL Software	http://www.anet.cz/alwil/alwil.htm
Amadeus Consulting	http://www.wolfgang.com/
Amass Systems Inc.	http://www.supernet.ab.ca/Mall/Computer/amass.html
Ambrosia Software, Inc	http://www.digitmad.com/ambrosia/ambrosia.html
AMCC	http://www.amcc.com/
Amdahl Open Enterprise Systems	http://www.amdahl.com/doc/products/oes.html
Amecon Inc.	http://www.tiac.net/users/amecon/index.html
American Compusystems	http://www.summitmedia.com/acs/
American Computer Consultants	http://www.ionet.net/~accokc/index.shtml
American Computer Express	http://www.acexpress.com/
American Computer Resources, Inc.	http://www.the-acr.com/
American Intelligent Systems	http://www.aisworld.com/
American Megatrends (AMI)	http://www.megatrends.com
American Power Conversion	http://www.apcc.com/
American Research Group	http://www.arg.com/arg/
American System Integrators, Inc.	http://www.cybernetics.net/users/asiinc/homepag
American Technologies	http://www.uscyber.com/virtual/landnet/
American Technology Labs	http://fred.net/atl/
American Teleprocessing Corporation (ATC)	http://atchou.com/
AmeriData, Inc.	http://www.ameridata.com/
AmeriNet	http://amerinet.com/
Ameritech Library Services	http://www.amlibs.com
Amherst Computer Group	http://www.niagara.com/nerds/homepage.html
AMI-Microage	http://www.ami.qc.ca/

Amivar Computers	http://www.tiac.net/users/amivar/index.html
AMRAM Memory Devices	http://dtc.net/~amram/
Amulet Consulting	http://www.cygnus.nb.ca/amulet2/amulet1.html
Analytical Graphics	http://www.stk.com/stk/
Analytical Software & Services	http://www.acsinfo.com/
Analytical Software Packages, Inc.	http://www.emi.net/~asp
Anark	http://www.anark.com/
Anchor Consulting	http://www.anchorcon.com/anchor.html
AND Idenfication	http://www.and.nl/corporate_review/identification/
Andresen Data	http://www.oslonett.no/home/adsystem/
AngelWorks	http://www.alaska.net/~angelwrk/index.html
ANGOSS Software International	http://www.angoss.com/
AniCom, Inc.	http://www.spadion.com/interweb/spadion/anicom/index.html
AniCom, Inc.	http://www2.interpath.net/anicom/
AnimaTek, Inc.	http://www.animatek.com/
Animax Multimedia, Inc.	http://www.isisnet.com/mm/
Anixter	http://www.anixter.com/
ANO Office Automation	http://infoweb.magi.com/~anoott/index.html
ANT Limited	http://www.ant.co.uk/
Anzen	http://www.tesser.com/anzen/
Apache Digital Corporation	http://www.apache.com/
Apcon	http://www.apcon.com/
Apex Data, Inc.	http://warrior.com/apex/index.html
Apex Group	http://www.apexgrp.com/
Apogee Software Ltd.	http://swcbbs.com/apogee/apogee.htm
Apollo Digital, Inc.	http://www.cris.com/~kiriakis/apollo.shtml
App Foundation, Inc.	http://www.onthego.com/taf/
Apparel Retail Information Management Systems	http://pages.prodigy.com/NY/cbsys/
Applied Computer Services, Inc.	http://www.acsil.com/
Applied Computer Systems	http://www.apcom.com/
Applied Computing Systems, Inc.	http://www.acsys.com/
Applied Microsystems Corp.	http://www.amc.com/
Applied Parallel Research - APR	ftp://ftp.netcom.com/pub/fo/forge/home.html
Applied Testing and Technology	http://www.aptest.com/
Applix, Inc.	http://www.applix.com/
Apple Computer	http://www.apple.com
Apple Computer World Wide Technical Support	http://www.support.apple.com
Appraisal Group, The	http://www.citysource.com/Services/TAG/
APTE,Inc.	http://birl.nwu.edu/apte/
Apunix Computer Services	http://infolane.com/infolane/apunix/apunix.html
AquaNet	http://www.finite-tech.com/fti/aquanet.htmld
Arawak CD Solutions	http://www.icis.on.ca/homepages/arawak/
ARC Computers	http://www.infoark.com/arc/
Arcada Software	http://www.arcada.com/
ArchaeoMation Instrument and Data Systems	http://www.crl.com/~archaeo/
ArchiTECH Information Designs, Inc	http://www.architech.com/

Architext Software	http://www.atext.com/
Archtek Telecom Corp.	http://www.archtek.com.tw/
Arcland, Inc.	http://www.xensei.com/flowmodel/
Arcus Inc.	http://www.arcus.nyc.ny.us
Arena Logistics	http://www.arena.com.au/
ARGUS - Census Map USA	http://www.tcel.com/~argus/
Aris	http://www.aris.com.sg/
Aristo-Soft, Inc.	http://www.aristosoft.com/
ARSoftware	http://www.clark.net/pub/arsoftwa/
Artifice, Inc.	http://artifice.com/foyer.html
Artisan Software	http://www.ibmpcug.co.uk/~artisan/home.htm
Artisoft	http://www.artisoft.com
Arvore	http://www.arvore.pt/arvore/
Arztec Computer Resources	http://www.Arztec.COM/Arztec/
ASA Net	http://www.moscow.com/homepages/anpili@freenet.hut.fi.html
ASANET	http://emporium.turnpike.net/~ASANET/bella.htm
Asante Technologies	http://www.asante.com/
ASAPc Direct Inc.	http://204.7.36.94/
Ascolta	http://www.ascolta.com/
Ascom Timeplex	http://www.timeplex.com/
ASH WARE, Inc.	http://www.primenet.com/~klumpp/index.html
Ashlar Inc.	http://www.ashlar.com
Ashmor MicroComputer Recyclers	http://www.koyote.com/as/a.html
Ashmount Research	http://www.ashmount.com/
Ashton ITC	http://www.webpress.net/itc/
Asia PC Yellow Pages	http://206.17.44.3/pcasia/pcasia.htm
Asklepios - New Media for Scientific Publishing	http://www.asklepios.com/
askSam Systems	http://199.44.46.2/askSam.htm
ASLAN Computer	http://www.gus.com/emp/aslan/aslan.html
Aslan Computing Inc	http://www.aslaninc.com/
Aspect Software Engineering	http://www.aspectse.com/
Aspect Telecommunications	http://www.aspect.com/
Aspen Technology, Inc.	http://www.aspentec.com/
Assert Ltd.	http://www.assert.ee/
ASSET - Asset Source for Software Engineering Technology	http://source.asset.com/
Assistive Technology	http://www.execpc.com/~labres/
AST Computers	http://www.sdd.com/support/ast/index.html
Astrobyte	http://www.astrobyte.com/
Astrodynamic Visualization Software	http://www.jsci.com/
Astute	http://lethe.leeds.ac.uk/staff/JonesRG/astinfo.html
ASUS	http://asustek.asus.com.tw/
Asymetrix Corporation	http://www.asymetrix.com/
AT&T Enterprise Modelling	http://www.edd.co.uk/em/intro
AT&T Global Information Solutions	http://www.attgis.com/
AT&T Paradyne	http://www.paradyne.att.com/

Athosfax	http://www.uni.net/datalink/
ATI - Advertising Technologies Inc.	http://www.whistler.net/ati/
ATI Technologies	http://www.atitech.ca/
Atlantic Information Systems, Inc.	http://www.learning.com/AIS/AISHome
Atlantic Scientific Corporation	http://www.iu.net/atlsci/
Atlantic Systems Group	http://www.ASG.unb.ca/
Atlantic Systems Group	http://www.ASG.unb.ca/
Atlantis Cyberspace	http://vr-atlantis.com/concept.html
Atlantis Interactive	http://www.atlantisint.com/
Atomic Dog Software	http://atomicdog.com/
Atomic Games	http://atomic.neosoft.com/Atomic.html
Attachmate	http://www.atm.com
Audio Help Systems	http://apollo.co.uk/a/audiohelp/
Auricle Control Systems	http://www.webcom.com/~auricle/
Aurora Products Company	http://www.cybergate.net/~aurorapr/
Auspex Systems	http://www.cimteg.ists.ca/corp/hcci/auspex/auspex.htm
Austin Software Foundry	http://www.foundry.com/
Authorware/CBT/Interactive Presentations/Multimedia/Training	
	http://www.ccnet.com/in-house/home
Auto-Graphics Inc.	http://www.agfx.com/
Automata	http://www.automata.com/
Automata Design, Inc. (ADI)	http://www.adiva.com/
Automated Business Systems, Inc.	http://www.awod.com/gallery/business/abs/
Automated Design Systems - AutoCAD Dealer	http://www.niagara.com/autodes/autodes.html
Automated Facilities Management Inc	http://www.interlog.com/~afm/afmhome.htm
Automated Solutions Incorporated	http://www.tiac.net/users/asisales/
Automated Training Systems	http://www.ibmuser.com/
Automation Soecialists	http://www.cyberport.com/mall/autospec/
AutoSimulations	http://www.autosim.com/
Autotime Corp.	http://www.teleport.com/~autotime/
AutoWeb	http://www.kbt.com/knowledge/products.html
AVA Instrumentation, Inc.	http://www.aimnet.com/~avasales/
Avaika Networks Corporation	http://www.io.com/~webpub/avaika/index.html
Avalan Technology Inc.	http://www.ultranet.com/~dtemple/
Avazpour Systems	http://www.tyrell.net/~avazsys/
Avcom Systems	http://www.avcom.com/
AVCOM Systems	http://www.best.com/~avcom/avcom.htm
AVerMedia Inc.	http://www.aver.com/aver/
Avista Design Systems	http://www.avista.com/avista/
AVM Summit	http://www.well.com/www/manatee/summit.html
AXENT Technologies	http://www.axent.com/
Axil Computer, Inc.	http://www.axil.com/
Axiom (UK) Limited	http://www.axiom.co.uk/
Axis Communications AB	http://www.axis.se/
AXOS Computer GmbH Germany	http://www.axos.com/Welcome.html
Aydelu Computer inc.	http://www.magi.com/~aydelu

Aztech Labs Inc.	http://www.aztechca.com/
Azteq SuperStore	http://www.azteq.com/

B

B & C CompuSoft, Inc.	http://www.southwind.net/~ccustine/
B & E Technology Group	http://www.cnct.com/~bgriffin/
B&B Computer	http://www.cris.com/~bnbcomp/
B-Plan	http://www.elron.net/bplan/
B. Richardson & Assoc.	http://mindlink.net/br/br2r1.html
B.M. Software Solutions	http://www.interlog.com/~bmynarsk/BMSolutions.html
Baccalieu Consulting	http://www.databits.com/baccalieu/bacc.html
Bacher Systems	http://www.sun.co.at/sun/
Bachman Information Systems	http://www.novalink.com/bachman/index.html
Baker Consulting Inc.	http://www.baker.com/
Bananas Software Inc.	http://www.ios.com/~banana/
BancTec Technologies	http://www.bti-ok.com/bti/index.html
Banyan Networking	http://warp.agroup.com
Banyan Vines	http://www.banyan.com
Barlow Wilson PowerBuilder Consultancy	http://www.ibmpcug.co.uk/~jtyndale/
Barnett's Computers	http://www.kern.com/~cwmarket/biz/barnett/index.html
Basic Skills Educational Software	http://www.skillsbank.com/
Basin Office SystemS	http://www.owt.com/boss/
Batesole, Robert D.	http://www.batesole.com/
BATS, Inc.	http://www.bats.com/bats/
Baustert Engineering	http://otisnt.baustert.com/
Bayleaf Software Inc.	http://www.bayleafsw.com/
Beacon Hill Software	http://world.std.com/~bhs/
Beedee Corporation	http://www.beedee.com/beedee/
BekArts International	http://ak.planet.gen.nz/bekarts/
Belgasoft	http://www.belgasoft.com/
Belhaven	http://www.owt.com/belhaven/
Bell Microproducts, Inc.	http://www.bellmicro.com/
Below Zero	http://www.wimsey.com/PacificaBlue/belowzero/
Benaroya	http://www.portal.com/~sedit/rexxgrph.html
Bentley Systems	http://www.bentley.com/
Berkeley Integration Group, Inc.	http://www.dnai.com/~big/
Bernstein & Associates, Inc.	http://www.b-and-a.com/
Best Computer Service	http://www.winternet.com/~wcdc/bcs.html
BETACORP Multimedia	http://www.betacorp.com/
Bevelstone Production I/S	http://www.login.dknet.dk/~bvlstone/
Beyond 2000 Systems	http://www.beyond2000.com/
BGS Systems	http://www.bgs.com/
BI-TECH Software	http://www.bi-tech.com/index.html
Big Noise Music Software	http://www.icba.com/bignoise/index.html
Binary Media	http://www1.mhv.net/~ssmith/
BindView Development Corporation	http://www.lsg.com/

Binomial International	http://www.binomial.com/
Biomechanics, Inc.	http://www.crl.com/~biomech/
Birds-of-Prey The Total Point of Sale Solution	http://www.netaxs.com/people/bsc/index.html
BIS Process Manager	http://www.bis-us.com/
Bismarck Group	http://www.bismarck.com/
BiTools	http://www.bitools.com/
Bitronics, Inc.	http://www.infop.com/bitron/index.html
BitWise Solutions, Inc.	http://www.bit-wise.com/bitwise/
Black Belt Systems, Inc.	http://www.blackbelt.com/blackbelt/bx_top.html
Black Box Corporation	http://www.blackbox.com/
BlackMagic Enterprises	http://www.blackmagic.com/
Blue Cat Design	http://www.eagle.ca/bluecat/
Blue Line Communications Warehouse, Inc.	http://www.bluecomm.com/blueline/
Blue Sky Information Technologies	http://www.sestran.com/sestran/cityscape/promenade/bluesky/
Blue Sky Research	http://www.bluesky.com/
Blue Sky Software Corporation	http://www.blue-sky.com/
Blue Star Systems	http://www.interaccess.com/users/ka9dgx/bluestar.html
Bluestone, Inc.	http://www.bluestone.com/
Blumer LeVon Online	http://www.blumer.com/
Blyth	http://www.crocker.com/~pistrang/bcsOmnis.html
Blyth Software	http://www.blyth.com/
BMG Ariola Studios	http://www.bmgstudios.de/
BMT Micro	http://www.wilmington.net/bmtmicro/
Boca Research	http://www.boca.org/
Bonsai Software	http://www.bonsai.com/
BookLink Technologies	http://www.booklink.com
Borland	http://www.borland.com/
Born Information Services Group	http://www.born.com/
Boss Net	http://www.isisnet.com/jeff/index.html
Boston Business Computing	http://www.bbc.com/
Boston Microcomputer Consulting	http://turnpike.net/emporium/B/bmc/index.html
Bouquet Multimedia	http://www.bouquet.com/
BPE Technologies	http://www.wta.com/bpe/
Bradbury, Kristin, Business Systems Design Ltd.	http://www.cityscape.co.uk/users/et92/kbbsd.htm
Brainstorm Computer Solutions	http://www.brainstorm.co.uk/
Brainwave	http://www.bart.nl/~brainwav/
Braun Science and Engineering, Inc.	http://www.bseng.com/
Bredex GmbH	http://www.bredex.de/
Bremmer & Walen Consultancy	http://www.euronet.nl/users/bwc/index.html
Briccetti, Dave	http://www.davebsoft.com/
Brickell Research	http://www.shadow.net/~roland/homepage.html
Brightware Corporation	http://www.brightware.com/
Brimm, Troy	http://www.prgone.com/tbrimm/
Bristol Technology Inc.	http://www.bristol.com/
Broadcast Management Plus	http://www.bmp.com/
BroadVision, Inc.	http://www.broadvision.com/

Broadway Video, Inc.	http://www.broadwayvideo.com/
Brocade	http://www.herald.co.uk/clients/B/Brocade/brocade.html
Bryant Software	http://www.bryant.com/
Buczek Consulting	http://www.best.com/~jbuczek/
BUDS (Bath University Distribution Services)	http://www.buds.co.uk/
BuggySoft(tm) Development	http://uptown.turnpike.net/~poot/BSD.html
Bulldog Group	http://bulldog.ca/
Bullfrog	http://www.bullfrog.co.uk/
Bullseye Software	http://www.bullseye.com/
Bullseye Software	http://www.eskimo.com/~bullseye/
Bureau of Electronic Publishing, Inc.	http://www.bep.com/
Business Automation Associates	http://www.busauto.com/
Business Computer Products	http://www.america.com/mall/store/dcw.html
Business Edge	http://pcixous.deltanet.com/behomepage.html
Business Machine Services	http://www.demon.co.uk/bms/index.html
Business Systems of America Inc.	http://www.webcom.com/~bsa/
BusLogic, Inc.	http://www.buslogic.com/
Buss Ltd.	http://www.buss.co.uk/buss/
Buy-Rent.Exe Mortgage Analysis	http://tribeca.ios.com/~millevoi/test2.html
BVM - VMEbus IndustryPacks and OS-9 Operating System	http://www.bvmltd.co.uk/welcome/
BVM Limited	http://www.bvmltd.co.uk
BwanaK's Software Super Store	http://www.mindspring.com/~bwanak/bwanaks/bwanaks.html
Byte by Byte	http://bytebyte.com/
Byte Elaborazioni Srl	http://www.ats.it/byte/index.html
ByteBox Computer Enclosures	http://www.bytebox.com/bytebox/
Bytewide	http://www.america.com/mall/store/bytewide.html

C

C & C d.o.o. Maribor	http://lite-sun.eunet.si/cc/index.html
C I Technologies	http://www.trinet.com/ashwin.html
C&T Laser Services	http://www1.mhv.net/~intercity/c&tlaser.htm
CabiNet Systems Inc.	http://www.cabinet-sys.com/
CabiNet.ISO	http://www.cabinet-sys.com/iso/disowht.html
CableMaster	http://www.cablemaster.com/cablemaster/
CACI Company	http://www.caciasl.com/
Cactus Brand Software Inc.	http://www.cactusbrand.com/cactus/
Cade Consulting	http://www.tech-comm.com/customer/cade/
Cadkey Corp.	http://www.cadkey.com/
CADlink Technology Corporation	http://www.cadlink.com/
CadSoft Online	http://www.CadSoft.DE/
CadWhiz Computer Consulting	http://www.ravenet.com/cadwhiz/
Caema Ltd.	http://www.sci.fi/~tsuomine/caema.htm
CalComp AB	http://www.calcomp.se/
Caldera Inc.	http://www.caldera.com/
California Components	http://www.calypso.com/pcparts/

California Computer Options	http://ntweb.cco.com/
California Software Incorporated	http://www.calsoft.com/
Callhaven Computing	http://www.londonmall.co.uk/callhav/
CalTech Software Systems, Inc	http://www.webstar.net/~caltech/
Calydon Technology	http://www.cuug.ab.ca:8001/~hummelg/calydon.html
Cambridge Computer Corp.	http://cam.com/~cam
Cambridge Quality Management	http://www.avonibp.co.uk/cqm/
Cambridge Technology Partners	http://www.ctp.com/
Camellia Software Corporation	http://www.halcyon.com/camellia/
CAMO Computer Aided Modelling, Inc.	http://www.aksess.no/camo/
Campbell Micro Distributors	http://www.traveller.com/cmd/
Campus Network Solutions	http://www.halcyon.com/routers/campus/
Can Tech Computer Services	http://merlin.magic.mb.ca/~rickm/adanac/cantech/
Candle Corporation	http://www.candle.com/
Capella Networking	http://plaza.xor.com/capella/
Capilano Computing Systems Ltd.	http://www.wimsey.com/capilano/
Capital Data, Inc.	http://www.arrownet.com/capdat/
Capital Equipment Corporation	http://www.cec488.com/~cec/cec.html
CapMed Systems	http://www.capmed.com/
Capstone Software	http://www.gate.net/~intracor/capstone.html
Cara Informatique Inc.	http://www.carainfo.com/
Caravelle Networks Corporation	http://www.caravelle.com/
Career Blazers Learning Centers	http://www.cblazers.com/
Caribou Codeworks	http://www.winternet.com/~jottis/
Carl Yaffey Computer Consulting	http://www.infinet.com/~clydss/
Carnation Software	ftp://ftp.netcom.com/pub/ca/carnation/HT.Carn.Home.html
Carnegie Group, Inc.	http://www.cgi.com/CGI/
Carney, Hood, and Pancost, Inc.	http://www.halcyon.com/tomas/welcome.html
Carolina Computer Systems	http://www.netside.com/ccshome.html
CARS Information Systems Corporation	http://www.carsinfo.com/
Cartagena Software Limited	http://inforamp.net/~carta/
Cartridge Care and Inks Direct	http://www.londonmall.co.uk/ccare/
Casady and Greene	http://www.casadyg.com/
Cascade Consulting	http://www.omix.com/sites/cascade/home.html
Cascadilla Press Linguistics Titles	http://www.shore.net/~cascadil/linguistics.html
CastCAE	http://www.castech.fi/
Castle Computers	http://www.castlec.com/
Castle Rock Computing	http://crc.castlerock.com/
Castle Software	ftp://ftp.netcom.com/pub/da/danberke/html/cs.html
Catalink Direct	http://www.catalink.com
Catapult, Inc.	http://www.aa.net/pbt/
Catfish Software	http://anytime.cs.umass.edu/~jgrass/catfish.html
Catron Custom Software	http://www.tiac.net/users/cgb/catron/
CATS Software	http://www.cats.com/cats/
Cayman Systems	http://www.cayman.com/
Cayuga Computers	http://light.lightlink.com/cayuga/

CB-Byte Computersolutions	http://www.worldport.co.at/worldport/cb_byte/cb_home.htm
CCAT Limited	http://www.hk.linkage.net/~cat/index.html
CCI World	http://cciworld.com
CD Archive, Inc.	http://www.cdarchive.com/
CD ROM Paradise Srl - CD ROM Publishing Company	http://www.cdrom-paradise.com/
CD Solutions	http://www.cdsolutions.com/cdsolutions/
CD Solutions, Inc.	http://www.cdarchive.com/cd_solutions/welcome.htm
CD SourceLine	http://www.omix.com/cds/
CD-Production Gruenberger	http://www.austria.eu.net/aishop/cdprod/
CD-ROM Multimedia Access	http://www.cdma.com/home.html
CD-ROM Shop	http://www.cdromshop.com/cdr/home.html
CD-ROM Software	http://www.tignet.net/pav/omni/crs/cdr-soft.htm
CD-ROM Software by Telecentral	http://www.a1.com/tlcental/
CD-ROM-WORKS	http://www.teleport.com/~cdromwks/
CDE Technologies	http://www.ipac.net/cde/cdehome.html
CDG Systems	http://www.peganet.com/cdgsys/cdg.html
CDM Distributors	http://www.iquest.net/cdm/index.html
CDROM Plus+	http://rampages.onramp.net/~powerv/
CdRoms R Us	http://cdsrus.midwest.net/
CDS, Inc.	http://www.compdisk.com/
CE Software	http://www.cesoft.com/
CEL Corporation	http://www.celcorp.com/
Center for Software Development	http://www.teleport.com/~cci/
Center for Software Development	http://www.service.com/csd/home.html
Center for the Application of Information Technology	http://www.cait.wustl.edu/cait/
Centerline Computers	http://www.centercomp.com/
Central Data	http://www.cd.com/
Centro Multimedia	http://phortos.inesc.pt/
Century 23 Computers	http://www.intermind.net/c23/
Century Computing, Inc.	http://www.cen.com/
Century III at Universal Studios Florida	http://www.digital.net/~century3/
CEO Software	http://www.the-wire.com/usr/ceo/
CERA Research	http://www.cera.com/
Ceram Inc.	http://www.csn.net/~stinger/
Cerberus Development	http://picard.transy.edu/~cerbdev/
Certified Network Educators	http://www.comnet.com/cne/cnehome.html
CFC Computers, Inc.	http://www.cfc.net/
CFX Technologies	http://cfx.com.au/
CG2	http://ro.com/~cg2/
CGI Group Inc.	http://www.tor.cgigroup.com/
CGI Systems, Inc. - An IBM Company	http://www.cgisystems.com/
Chaco Communications	http://www.chaco.com/
Chameleon Concept Inc.	http://www.lizardlink.com/home.html
Changing Technologies	http://www.mindspring.com/~cti/home.html
Channels - Internet-Based Discussion Forum and Chat software	
	http://www.channels.com/team/

Chariot Technologies	http://os2.iafrica.com/chariot/
Charles View Software	http://www.charlesview.com/
CharterHouse Software Corporation	http://www.earthlink.net/~charterhouse/
Cheap Memory	http://www.goworldnet.com/cheap.htm
Chemical Safety	http://www.portal.com/~austin/chemsafe/index.html
Chesapeake Computer Consultants WWW Server	http://www.ccci.com/
Cheyenne Software	http://www.chey.com/
Chick Enterprises Ltd.	http://www.infomatch.com/~chick/chick.htm
Chips and Bits Australia	http://www.chips.com.au/
Choice Medical, Inc.	http://choicemed.com/
Chordboard MIDI Controller Musical Instrument	http://www.chordboard.com/
Chrysalis Symbolic Design, Inc.	http://www.chrysalis.com/
CIAO Software Solutions, Inc.	http://www1.usa1.com/~jurgen/
Cinax Designs Inc.	http://www.cinax.com/
Cincom Systems, Inc.	http://www.cincom.com/
Circa Informatique	http://www.globale.net/~circa/
Circle Computer Center	http://www.circlecc.com/circlecc/www/home.htm
Circuit Cellar	http://www.primenet.com/~circuit/
Circuit Technology, Inc.	http://www.halcyon.com/sverne/home.html
Circuit Works	http://www.localweb.com/circuitworks/test1.html
Cirrus Consulting	http://www.singnet.com.sg/customers/cirrus/cirrus1.htm
Cisco	http://www.cisco-futures.com/
Cisco Information Online	http://cio.cisco.com/
Citac Corporation	http://www.wta.com/citac/
Claret Software,Inc.	http://www.valley.net/~claret/
Clarion for Windows	http://www.io.com/~hanover/cw.html
Clark Graphics Corp.	http://www.traveller.com/~pgrafix/
Clarus AB	http://www.clarus.se/
Clayton Wallis	http://www.crl.com/~clwallis/
Clean Machine	http://wchat.on.ca/cleanmch.htm
Cleo Products	http://www.rock.cleo.com/
Clever Managment Systems	http://www.expressnet.com/clever.html
Client Check Software	http://www.infowest.com/clientchek/index.html
Client Systems, Inc.	http://www.clientsys.com/
Client-Server Software Testing (CSST) Technologies	http://www.icon-stl.net/~djmosley/
Clipper Expert Group	http://www.ceg.co.za/ceg/ceg.htm
Cloud Seven, Inc.	http://www.cloud7.com/
clySmic Software	http://www.albany.net/~rsmith/
CMB Software - Development and consulting	http://www.xnet.com/~cbone/cmbsoft.htm
CMEA Multimedia Group	http://www.lb.com/~cmea/
CMS Technologies	http://www.chrimar.com/
CN Software	http://www.cns-nj.com/cnsoft/
CNA Computer Systems Engineering	http://www.tacoma.net/~larrymc/cna.htm
Cobotyx	http://www.cobotyx.com/
Coconut Info	http://www.dublclick.com/coconutinfo
Cogent Data Technologies, Inc.	http://www.cogentdata.com/

Cogent Technology Training	http://www.halcyon.com/cogent/
Cognitive Technology Corporation	http://www.well.com/user/ctc/
Cognitive Technology Corporation	http://www.well.com/user/ctc/
Cognoscente Software International Inc.	http://www.cognoscente.com/csi/
Cohesive Systems	http://www.cohesive.com/
Coleman Consultants	http://www.gold.net/users/ab70/index.html
Collaborate Strategies	http://www.collaborate.com/
Collabra Software, Inc.	http://www.collabra.com/
Collage Communictaions, Inc	http://www.collcomm.com/
College Sports Tracking Software	http://www.mindspring.com/~sophos/sophos.html
Collideascope Digital	http://collideascope.com/empire/
Colorgraphic Communications Corporation	http://www.colorgfx.com/
Colorocs	http://www.nav.com/colorocs/colorocs.html
Columbia Data Products, Inc.	http://www.magicnet.net/cdpi/
Columbus Micro Systems	http://www.ee.net/
Com Tech Communications Pty	http://www.comtech.com.au/
COMCOM Systems	http://www.intbc.com/comcom/
Comdisco Inc.	http://www.comdisco.com/
Command Corp - Speech Recognition on the Web	http://www.commandcorp.com/incube_welcome.html
Commax Technologies, Inc.	http://www.commax.com/
Common Ground Software, Inc.	http://www.commonground.com
Commonwealth Data Systems,Inc.	http://www.mnsinc.com/bradshaw/cds_inc1.html
CommQuest Unlimited	http://www.commquest.com/
CommTech Systems, Inc.	http://www.ctsystems.com/commtech/
Commtech Systems, Inc.	http://www.websrus.com/websrus/commtech/
CommTouch Software, Inc.	http://www.commtouch.com/
Communications Modeling	http://tieo.saic.com/russo/models.html
Communitype Communications Ltd.	http://www.atlas.co.uk/ccl/
Compact Disc Authoring	http://www.ph.kcl.ac.uk/cd/
CompAdept Corporation	http://www.compadept.com/
Compass Computer Group	http://www.hiway.co.uk/compass/ccghome1.html
Compass Point Software, Inc.	http://www.cais.com/aevans/cpsi/cpsi.html
Compaq Computer Corporation	http://www.compaq.com/
Compatible Systems	http://www.Compatible.COM/
CompCo Incorporated	http://cu.comp-unltd.com/~brett/compcohp.html
ComPeters Consulting Services	http://www.mgl.ca/~competer/
Competitive Computing	http://www.modulations.com/cc/cc.htm
Complete Business Solutions, Inc. (CBSI)	http://www.cbsinc.com/index1.htm
Component Graphics, Inc.	http://www.cginc.com/
Comport Consulting Corporation	http://www.comport.com/
Compression Technologies, Inc.	http://compression.com/
Compris Inc.	http://infoweb.magi.com/~compris/
ComPro Technology and Imaging Services	http://www.charm.net/~compro/
Compu Team Systems	http://www.mbnet.mb.ca/~ayre/
Compu-Save International	http://www.compu-save.com/
CompuGraph International	http://www.cybergate.com/~marc/cg/index.html

CompuHelp	http://www.panix.com/~joseph/home.html
CompuHelp Online	http://www.connix.com/~shpilber/
Compumedia Inc	http://www.compumedia.com/~control/comtrol/index.html
CompuNet USA	http://www.compunetusa.com/cnet/
CompuOffice Software Inc	http://www.compuoffice.com/
CompuShare, Etc...	http://www.wp.com/cshare/
CompuSmart (Ottawa)	http://infoweb.magi.com/~compsmrt
Compusource International, Ltd.	http://www.awa.com/cus/cush.html
Compusult Limited	http://www.compusult.nf.ca/
Computational Mechanics Company	http://www.comco.com
Computer Aid	http://www.computeraid.com:3088/
Computer Attic SuperCenter	http://netsmart.com/attic
Computer Bay	http://www.netzone.com/computerbay/
Computer Channel	http://www.compchannel.com/
Computer Chrome Presentation Graphics	http://www.compchrome.com/
Computer City Supercenters	http://www.catalogue.com/ccity/
Computer Clinic	http://www.supernet.net/~pvignola/
Computer Clinic	http://www.vistech.net/users/pvignola/clinic.html
Computer Clinic Corporation	http://www.memphisweb.com/ccc/default.html
Computer Coach	http://www.star.net/People/~romorris/coach.htm
Computer Company Belgium	http://www.coco.be/
Computer Concepts	http://www.pernet.net/~concept/
Computer Concepts Corporation	http://www.pb.net/~dbexpress
Computer Consulting Company	http://www.tech.net/c3/
Computer Consulting Group	http://www.scsn.net/~ccg/
Computer Consumables Buyer's Club	http://www.inforamp.net/~ccbc
Computer Crime Research Laboratories	http://crimelab.com/
Computer Data Archival Services (CDAS)	http://www.mbnet.mb.ca/~cdas/
Computer Direct	http://www.worldgate.com/compdirect/
Computer Discount Warehouse	http://www.cdw.com/
Computer Discounters	http://www.intergate.com/sjbp/disc.html
Computer Discovery Corporation	http://www.computerdiscovery.com/
Computer Ease - training, consulting, programming	http://www.computer-ease.com/ce/
Computer Engineering Technologies, Ltd.	http://www.cet.net/
Computer Gate	http://www.aimnet.com/~cgate/cgate.htm
Computer Goldmine	http://www.csn.net/~fmills/
Computer Graphics Systems Development Corporation	http://www.cgsd.com
Computer Guy, The	http://www.mcn.net/~bdavies/comguy.html
Computer Hardware	http://netcenter.com/yellows/hardware.html
Computer Hardware & Software Co's Phone Numbers	http://mtmis1.mis.semi.harris.com/comp_ph1.html
Computer Hardware Page - The MegaMall	http://infotique.lm.com/cgi-bin/phpl.cgi?comphard.html
Computer Highway	http://pacificnet.net/~erebuni/index.html
Computer House/ISMAX	http://emanate.com/ismax/
Computer Information Services, Inc.	http://www.ultranet.com/~cdenman/
Computer Language Arts, Inc.	http://www.cla.com/
Computer Marketplace, Inc.	http://www.mkpl.com/

Computer Max	http://www.NeoSoft.com/users/c/cmptrmax/cmptr.htm
Computer Network Services	http://www.cns-nj.com/
Computer Network Solutions	http://www.maui.net/w3/js_beyer/public_html/
Computer Physicians	http://www.main.com/~comphy/
Computer Power Group	http://www.cpsg.com.au/cpg/welcome.html
Computer PREP Software Training Materials	http://cybermart.com/cprep/
Computer Price Cruncher	http://www.killerapp.com/
Computer Products, Inc.	http://cpi.navsea.navy.mil/
Computer Recycler	http://www.coolsville.com/recycler/
Computer Renaissance	http://www.ro.com/pages/computer_renaissance/
Computer Revolution	http://www.infinet.com/~jnthomas/computer_revolution/
Computer Salvage Company	http://www.charm.net/~creative/salvage/index.html
Computer Savvy	http://www.hom.net/~jps01/index.html
Computer Sciences Corporation	http://www.csc.com/
Computer Shopper Magazine [zdnet.com]	http://www.zdnet.com/~cshopper/
Computer Software	http://netcenter.com/yellows/softcity.html
Computer Solutions	gopher://ftp.std.com/11/vendors/compsol
Computer Solutions GSD, Inc.	http://www.csgsd.com/
Computer Store, The	http://surf.rio.com/~apples/
Computer Supply Company of Virginia	http://www.infi.net/csc/
Computer Swami, Inc.	http://www.srv.net/~bia/swami.html
Computer System Architects	http://itchy.itsnet.com/commercial/csa/public_html/
Computer System Specialists	http://www.peganet.com/css/css.html
Computer Systems Advisers, Inc.	http://www.silverrun.com/
Computer Talk Inc.	http://www.gpl.net/itcb/cti/
Computer Technology Applications, Inc.	http://www.dnaco.net/~dhbrown/
Computer TeleVision	http://www.ozemail.com.au/~davidh/ctv/cthome.html
Computer Trading	http://www.widdl.com/tucson/ct/ct.html
Computer Tutors, U.S.A.	http://www.freenet.scri.fsu.edu/ctusa/
Computer Warehouse	http://usashopping.com/cgi-win/cw/cwnet.exe
Computer Way Pty Ltd.	http://www.computerway.com.au/
ComputerClinic, Inc.	http://www.southwind.net/~rwweeks/
ComputerDen, Inc.	http://www.gate.net/~compden/
Computerized Data Management	http://www1.minn.net/~cdm/
Computermaster, Inc.	http://www.primenet.com/~johnw/cm.htm
ComputerPeople/Dci	http://www.computerppl.com/
Computers and Learning A/S	http://www.oslonett.no/html/adv/Candle/candle.html
Computers Plus	http://www.cris.com/~jayalan/cplus.html
Computersmith	http://www.wp.com/computersmith/
ComputerTutor, The	http://www.linex.com/comtut/
Computervision Corp.	http://www.cv.com/
ComputerWare Belgium	http://www.webhaus.be/cwb/
CompuType Computer Services	http://basenet.net/~geopersh/cti.html
Compuware Corporation	http://www.compuware.com/
CompuWave Computer Sales	http://www.rain.org/~cland/wave.htm
Comstar	http://www.comstarinc.com/

ComStar Company	http://www.gy.com/
Concorde Group, Ltd.	http://www.concorde.com/
Concurrent Engineering	http://www.mor.itesm.mx/EVENTOS/CERG/CERG.html
Conetic Software Systems Inc.	http://www.conetic.com/
Config.Sys	http://www.apk.net/1/cdrom
Congruent Technologies	http://vannevar.com/congruent/
CONNECT, Inc.	http://www.connectinc.com/
Connectivity	http://www.tminet.com/~connectivity/connect/connect.html
Connectivity Custom Controls	http://www.toupin.com/~etoupin/ccc.html
Connectix!	http://www.connectix.com/
Connector GmbH	http://www.connector.de
Connectworld	http://www.connectworld.net/
Conner Peripherals	http://www.conner.com/
ConPro	http://204.227.128.14/
Consensus Development	http://www.consensus.com:8300/
Consolidated Computer Services, Inc.	http://www.viper.net/clients/CCSI/
Constant Synthesis Project	http://www.sanctuary.com/haven/consynpro/
Consultimate Technologies	http://www.tiac.net/biz/consultimate/
Continental Resources, Inc.	http://www.conres.com/
Continuum Information Services	http://pages.prodigy.com/GA/continuum_is/continuum_is.html
Contraste Canada Inc.	http://www.contraste.com/
Convergence Consulting	http://www.docker.com/~BROWNJ/conv.htm
Convergence Systems, Inc.	http://www.convergence.com/
Conway Professional Consulting	http://www.rtt.ab.ca/rtt/karry/cpc.htm
CooperSoft	http://www.getnet.com/~joeco/
CoPilot	http://www.leadgroup.com/
Copley Systems Educational Services	http://copley.mv.com/copley/edserv/
Coptech, Inc.	http://www.oai.com/coptech/
Core Systems	http://www.corsys.com/core/
Core Systems	http://www.infosystems.com/homeworld/
Core Technology Corporation	http://www.ctc-core.com/
CoreLAN Communications, Inc	http://www.corelan.com/
Cornelius Concepts	http://www.teleport.com/~concepts/
Cornell Computer Consulting	http://www.numedia.tddc.net/jcornell/
Cornerstone Computers	http://www.cornerstone.com.au/
Cornerstone Software, Inc.	http://www.corsof.com/
Cornett & Associates, Inc.	http://www.accunet.com/cornett.htm
Corporate Computer Centers, Inc.	http://204.94.70.7/
Corporate Data Analysis	http://www.avonibp.co.uk/cqm/analysis.html
Corporate Disk	http://www.disk.com/
Corporate Raider	http://www.rothnet.com/corpraid/corpraid.html
Corporate Software Integration Services	http://www.csis.csof.com/
Cosmic JamStain	http://uptown.turnpike.net/~Makari/CJS/
CP Software Group	http://www.cpsg.com.au/
CP Systems	http://www.connix.com/~cps/
CPLEX Optimization, Inc.	http://www.cplex.com/

CPsoft Consulting	http://www.azstarnet.com/~cpsoft/index.html
CPU Collections	http://www.st.rim.or.jp/~seaside/
CQ Computer Communications, Inc. WWW Site	http://www.cq-comm.com/
CRAK Software	http://www.getnet.com/crak/
Cray	http://www.cray.com/PUBLIC/product-info/
Crazy Dave's Used Computers	http://www.csi-infinet.com/daves.htm
Crazy Dave's Used Computers	http://www.csiworld.com/hutchnet/daves.htm
Creative Concepts	http://www.tyrell.net/~hawkenet/
Creative Electronic Systems	http://www.eunet.ch/CES_info/Welcome.html
Creative Innovations Computer Services	http://vsmith.fast.net/
Creative Labs Europe	http://www.demon.co.uk/cluk/
Creative Programming Consultants Inc.	http://www.onramp.net/~cpc/home.html
Creative Software Technologies	http://www.cst.com.au/
Creative Technologies	http://www.creativetech.com/
Credit Manager, Version 1.0	http://www.xmission.com/~rexm/tsb.html
CREN ListProcessor	http://www.cren.net/.www/listproc.html
Crescent Division	http://www.progress.com/crescent/
Crisis Software	http://www.dcs.warwick.ac.uk/~phid/Crisis/
Croft Computers	http://www.exp.ie/Ireland/croft.html
Cross International	http://www.aescon.com/cross/index.htm
CrossComm Corporation	http://www.crosscomm.com/
CrossTarget	http://www.ozemail.com.au/~pdavidso/
CrossWind Technologies,Inc.	http://www.crosswind.com/
Crystal Data Systems	http://www.crystaldata.com/cds/
CSI.NET, Inc.	http://www.csi.net/
CSR Systems South	http://www.cais.com/cytex/csr/csr.html
CTE Computer Training Center	http://www.ctetrain.com/cte/
CText Inc.	http://www.ctext.com/
CubicTek	http://www.cubic.re.kr/
Cunningham & Cunningham, Inc.	http://www.c2.com/
Custom Innovative Solutions (CIS)	http://www.cisc.com/
Custom Microprocessor Software Systems Inc.	http://www.cmss.com/
Custom Technology Corp.	http://www.ctech.co.jp/
CutterNet Network Software Specialists	http://InetBSystems.us.com/CUTTERNET/CutterNet.html
CutterNet, Inc.	http://inetbsystems.us.com/CUTTERNET/CutterNet.html
CVS Bubbles	http://www.loria.fr/~molli/cvs-index.html
Cxsoft	http://www.convex.com/prod_serv/cxsoft/
cyber exchange	http://www.chattanooga.net/cyberx/index.html
Cyberian Outpost	http://www.cybout.com/
CyberMedia	http://www.internet-is.com/cybermedia/in-iis.html
CyberMedia, Inc.	http://www.internet-is.com/cybermedia/
CyberMeridian	http://www.cybermeridian.com/
CyberMind Interactive	http://www.cybermind.com/
Cybernautix	http://electriciti.com/~harnold/
CyberSearch Foundation	http://www.halcyon.com/maulf/Index.html
CyberStar	http://www.vistech.net/users/cstar/

CyBerTech Corporation	http://www.u-net.com/cybertech/
Cybertzara	http://www.webcom.com/~cybertza/
CyberWarehouse Discount Computers and Electronics	http://marketplace.internetMCI.com/market/cyber/
Cybex Corporation	http://www.cybex.com
Cyborg Systems	http://www.cyborg.com/
Cyclades	http://www.calyx.net/cyclades/
Cycle Company	http://www.cyclenet.com/
Cyclic Software	http://www.cyclic.com/
CygnaCom Solutions, Inc.	http://www.cygnacom.com/
Cygnus Support Information Gallery	http://www.cygnus.com/
Cynosure Computer Technologies	http://www.cynosure.kosone.com/
Cyphertech	http://www.cypherscan.com/
Cypress Consulting, Inc.	http://www.cycon.com:8080/
Cytopia Software Incorporated	http://www.cytopia.com/

D

D&R Software Innovations	http://www.at-data.ns.ca/drsoft/default.htm
D-Best Computer Center	http://fs.cei.net/dbest/
DAC Micro Computing	http://www.ultranet.com/~ward/
DAIS	http://www.icl.com/dais
DAKCO PC Products Division Inc.	http://dakco.lm.com/
Dakota Software, Inc.	http://www.indirect.com/www/vaughn
Dalmatian Group, Inc.	http://www.jagunet.com/dalmatian/
Dalton Maag	http://www.demon.co.uk/trash/DaltonMaag/type.html
Damar Enterprises	http://www.damar.com/
Damar Group	http://www.dgl.com/
Dan's Sound & Music	http://www.cyserv.com/dans/
Daniel Crowder Consultant	http://www.ticllc.net/home/whitehurst/HOME.html
Danpex Corporation	http://sweb.srmc.com/danpex/
Dansys Consultants	http://www.ican.ca/dansys/
Darim Vision Co.	http://darvision.kaist.ac.kr/
Dark Unicorn Productions	http://www.mcd.on.ca/longbow/dup/
Dart Communications	http://www.dart.com/
Darwin Micro Systems	http://www.deltanet.com/users/darwin/
Darwin Open Systems	http://www.uunet.ca/darwinsys/
DASCO Marketing Group	http://www.mindspring.com/~dasco/homepg.htm
Data Exchange Corporation	http://www.dex.com/
Data Fellows	http://www.datafellows.fi/
Data General Corporation	http://www.dg.com/
Data Image Systems	http://bigweb.com/mall/don/index.html
Data Logic	http://www.datlog.co.uk/
Data Modeling Web Site	http://www.fred.net/mandalay
Data Site Consortium	ftp://ftp.indirect.com/user/www/dschome.html
Data-Doc Electronics, Inc.	http://www.datadoc.com/
Database Consultants, Inc.	http://www.realworld.com/
Database Excelleration Systems	http://www.desdbx.com/

DataBoat	http://www.mpcs.com/databoat/
Databyte Corporation	http://www.databyte.com/home.html
DataByte Systems	http://www.dbsmb.com/
DataCAD	http://www.cadkey.com/datacad/
Datacom Limited	http://www.inforamp.net/~datacom/
Dataflex Corporation	http://www.dataflex.com/
Dataflight Software	http://concord.lax.primenet.com/
Dataflux/Genetec	http://www.dataflux.com.mx/
Datalink Direct	http://www.datalinkrdy.com/
Dataman Programmmers Ltd.	http://www.dataman.com/
Datamini Systems	http://www.net1.net/comm/datamini.html
Datanet	http://www.iw.net/datanet/
Datarutin AB	http://www.datarutin.se/datarute.html
Datascape, Inc.	http://datascape.com/
dataserv Employees	http://www.sky.net/~kkuehl/welcome.html
DataSoft	http://pulse.datasoftbus.com/
Datasurge	http://www.usa1.com/datasurg/
Datatek International Inc.	http://datatek.com/datatek.html
DataTools, Inc.	http://www.datatools.com/
DataVault Corp.	http://access.digex.net/~dvcorp/
DataVision	http://www.primenet.com/~dvnet
DataViz	http://199.186.148.129/
Dataware Technologies, Inc.	http://www.dataware.com/
DataWave Technologies	http://usa.net/datawave/
DataWire	http://www.datawire.com/
Dataworld	http://www.datawld.com/
Datel Systems, Inc.	http://www.cts.com/cts/market/datel/
Daum Communications Co. Ltd.	http://www.daum.co.kr/
David Rose Design / Multimedia	http://www.drdesign.com/
David Whitt & Associates, Inc.	http://www.gate.net/~pdwhitt/
Davidson & Associates, Inc.	http://www.davd.com/
Davis Studios	http://www.sirius.com/~jdavis/
Dawn Designs	http://www.mind.net/dawndesign/dawn.htm
Daylight Software	http://www.netins.net/showcase/dsshow/
DAYO Multiuser Business Applications	http://www.dayo.com
DayStar Digital, Inc.	http://www.daystar.com/
DCC, Inc.	http://www.dcc.com/
DDIX, Inc.	http://www.charm.net/~iscape/packview.html
DeannaSoft	http://www.directnet.com/~spiegel/
Deepwoods Software	http://netmar.com/mall/shops/heller/
DejaView	http://bigmac.gmg.com/
Dell Computer	http://www.dell.com/
Dell Computer's Technical Support Pilot Project	http://www.dell.com/techinfo
Delphi Information Systems	http://www.delphinfo.com/~delphi/
Delphic Medical Systems	http://www.delphic.co.nz/
Delta Tao Inc. (Unofficial)	http://www.cis.yale.edu/~casper/deltatao/deltatao.html

deltaComm Development	http://delta.com
DeltaPoint Web Site	http://www.deltapoint.com/
Delvin	http://www.grfn.org/~tilo/
Demand Systems	http://fishnet.net/~drumbra/
Denmac Systems	http://www.denmac.com/denmac
DentalMac Practice Management Software	http://north.pacific.net/~bma/DentalMac.HTML
Descartes Solutions	http://www.u-net.com/descartes/
Descartes Systems Group	http://www.descartes.com/
Design Science, Inc.	http://www.mathtype.com/mathtype/
Design Software	http://www.whytel.com/home/design/
Design Visualization Partners	http://www.desviz.com/~desviz/
DesignAvenue Software	http://www.ozemail.com.au/~designav
Designed Information Systems Corporation	http://www.aurora.net/disc.html
Desktop Innovations	http://www.misha.net/~desktop/
Desktop Miracles	http://rampages.onramp.net/~desktop/
Desktop Multimedia Solutions	http://www.dmsolutions.com/
Develcon - Ethernet and Token-Ring Products	http://www.develcon.com
devSoft Inc.	http://www.dev-soft.com/devsoft/
Dexedream Productions	http://www.york.ac.uk/~mad5/dex/
DGA	http://www.dga.co.uk/
DGI Multimedia	http://www.hiwaay.net/mm/dgi.htm
DGS Group	http://www.edensys.com/edensys/dgs/index.html
DiAcoustics	http://www.iquest.com/~diac
Diamond International Systems Ltd.	http://www.hk.net/~drummond/diammain.html
Diamond Multimedia Systems	http://www.diamondmm.com/
Diamond Optimum Systems, Inc.	http://www.diamondos.com/
Dickens Data Systems, Inc.	http://www.dickens.com/
Dickinson Consulting Services	http://village.ios.com/~rtd/
DICO-SOFT GmbH	http://www.dicosoft.co.at/dicosoft/
Digicore	http://digimall.com/digicore/i.html
DigiCraft Software	http://yallara.cs.rmit.edu.au/~s9312630/digicraft.html
Digidesign	http://www.oz.is/digidesign/
Digidraft, Inc.	http://www.maf.mobile.al.us/business/b_dir/digi/
Digiphone	http://www.ikon.com/digiphone/
Digital brokers inc.	http://www.nav.com/dbius/
Digital CafQü	http://www.skypoint.com/members/digitalc/
Digital Cinema	http://www.dcinema.com/
Digital Collections, Inc.	http://www.ipac.net/dci/dcihome.html
Digital Creations, L.C.	http://www.digicool.com/
Digital Creators	http://www.digitalcreators.com/dc/
Digital Design Group Limited	http://www.interact.lm.com/
Digital Dimensions	http://quasar.fastlane.net/homepages/lantz/digital.htm
Digital Dreamshop	http://www.indirect.com/www/steelep4/ddi.html
Digital Dynamics Inc.	http://branch.com/dd/dd.html
Digital Equipment Corporation	http://www.sna.com/cpass/index.html
Digital Equipment Corporation - High Performance Computing	
	http://www.digital.com/info/hpc/hpc.html

Digital Information Gallery	http://www.digallery.com/
Digital Insight	http://www.csn.net/digins/
Digital Link Corporation	http://www.dl.com/
Digital Pathways, Inc.	http://www.digpath.com/
Digital Product and Service Information	http://www.dec.com/info/info.home.html
Digital Sound	http://www.dsc.com/
Digital Tools	http://www.digit.com/dt/dt1.html
Digital Vision, Inc.	http://www.digvis.com/digvis/
DigitalFacades	http://www.dfacades.com/
DigiTar Corporation	http://www.hooked.net/users/williams/digitar.htm
Digitool, Inc.	http://www.digitool.com/
Dilan	http://www.dilan.com/
Dillon Technology Group, Inc	http://www.fentonnet.com/dillon/
Dimension Specialist, Inc.	http://www.dspecialist.com/
Dimensions Micro, Inc.	http://rampages.onramp.net/~dmisales/index.html
Dinamika Computers s.r.l.	http://oasi.shiny.it/Firms/Dinamika/
DIOSS Corp.	http://www.in-tech.com/
Direct Connections	http://www.owplaza.com/dc/
Direct Data Storage	http://www.harddisk.com
Directmedia CD-ROM	http://www.infopark.de/directmedia/
DirectWARE	gopher://gopher.nstn.ca/11/e-mall/Computer/odyssey
Dirigo Incorporated	http://www.dirigo.com/
Discount Computer Service	http://www.adtek.com/~dcs/
Discovery	http://www.gus.com/emp/discover/discover.html
Discovey Networks	http://www.shopping2000.com/shopping2000/discovery/
Disk-O-Tape, Inc.	http://branch.com/disko/disko.html
Display Tech Multimedia, Inc.	http://www.ccnet.com/~dtmi/
Distinct Corporation	http://www.distinct.com/
Distinctive Solution	http://www.cfonline.com/cli/factors/distinc/distinc.htm
Division Ltd.	http://www.division.co.uk/
DK Multimedia!	http://www.helix.net/dk/dk-home.html
DNA Multimedia Corp.	http://www.wimsey.com/~robhan/dna-hp.html
DNS Worldwide	http://www.dnsww.com/users/dnsww/
Dog Computer Systems	http://hamton.eng.ua.edu/college/home/mh/grad/jtong/dog/
Dokken Consulting Inc.	http://imt.net/~dokken/
Domark Software	http://www.domark.com/domark/
Don Barth Consulting	http://www.atw.fullfeed.com/~dbarth/
Dorling-Kindersley	http://www.main.com/~waynew/
DOS Invoicing for Self-employed Professionals	http://www.magic.ca/~wsblady/JOB/JOBAD.HTML
Double P Software	http://www.sentex.net/~ppytlik/
Doug Cates Consulting	http://www.wimsey.ca/~jdcates/gis
DPE Computers	http://www.direct.ca/dpe/
DPI	http://www.digprod.com/
Dr. Computer	http://infomatch.com/~townsend/drc.html
Dr. Computer Logick	http://www.barint.on.ca/rcsmith/drlogick.html
Dr. Mac, inc.	http://www.magpage.com/drmacinc/

DragInstall	http://www.sauers.com/draginstall/
Dragon's Eye Software	http://rampages.onramp.net/~desoftw/
Dragonvision Animation & Video Editing Services	http://www.azc.com/client/rti/htmls/anima.html
DreamLight WebSite	http://www.shore.net/dreamlt/
DreamPark Development	http://www.xmission.com/~dp/
Dreams.com	http://www.dreams.com/welcome
DS Diagonal Systems	http://www.diagonal.com/
DSI Datatrak	http://www.datatrak.com/
DSP Development Corporation	http://www.dadisp.com/
DSP Group, Inc.	http://www.dspg.com/
DTK Computers Inc.	http://www.gan.net/dtk/
Dubl-Click Software Corporation	http://www.dublclick.com/
Due North	http://www.icw.com/duenorth/duenorth.html
Due North CD-ROM's	http://www.vianet.on.ca/comm/duenorth/index.html
Due North Earth Science Shareware	http://www.vianet.on.ca/comm/duenorth/geology.html
Dun & Bradstreet Software	http://www.dbsoftware.com/
Dunedain Multimedia	http://www.magic.ca/~dunedain/
Durand Communications Network	http://www.durand.com/
Durango Computer Classroom	http://animas.frontier.net/~mkatz/

E

E.T.C.S. Computer Consulting	http://www.brainlink.com/~etcs/etcs.html
Eagle Consulting Group	http://www.eaglecg.com/
Eagle Nest Intelligence	http://kaleidoscope.bga.com/eaglenest/eaglenest.html
Eagle Technology, Inc.	http://execpc.com/~eagle/
Early Solutions - Client-Server/PeopleSoft Consulting	http://emporium.turnpike.net/O/OnRamp/earlysol.htm
Earth Resource Mapping	http://www.connectus.com/~aztech/ermapper/emuindex.html
East Coast Computer Systems, Inc.	http://dino.worldpub.com/2/b/east-coast/
Easy Software Products	http://www.easysw.com/
Easy-Door Library	http://www.qbc.clic.net/~sincom/easydoor/
ECCS Inc.	http://www.eccs.com/
Ecobyte Technology	http://krenet.it/expo/ecobyte/index.htm
edell	http://www.ios.com/~edell/
Eden Systems	http://www.edensys.com/edensys/eden/edentmr.html
Eden Systems Corporation	http://www.edensys.com/edensys/eden/
EDGE Interactive Media, Inc.	http://www.well.com/www/edgehome/
Edgewood Engineering	http://edgewood.portland.or.us/
EDI - Essential Data, Inc.	gopher://marketplace.com/11/essential.data
Edifika	http://ournet.clever.net/edifika/hp.html
Editorial Experts, Inc. (EEI)	http://www.eei-alex.com/
Edom Technology	http://www.netindex.com/edom.htm
EDS Unigraphics Division	http://www.ug.eds.com/
Education Data Inc.	http://www.southwind.net/~edi/
Education Innovations	http://www.globalx.net/ei/index.html
Educom OnLine	http://www.educom.com.au/
EduSelf Multimedia Publishers	http://www.webscope.com/eduself/homepage.html

EduSoft, LC	http://www.i2020.net/edusoft/
EDV-Markt	http://www.edvmarkt.de/
EER Systems	http://www.netline.net/eer/index.html
Efficax Systems	http://pages.prodigy.com/CA/steele/es.html
Egghead Software	http://www.egghead.com/
Eicon Technology	http://www.eicon.com/
Einstein Investments & Trading	http://www.cyberpages.com/db/company&1&229
EIS International	http://www.eisintl.com/
Elan Computer Group	http://www.elan.com/
Electric Gypsy Software & Consulting	http://www.tyrell.net/~elecgpsy/
Electric Magic Company	http://www.emagic.com/
Electronic Arts	http://www.ea.com/Electronic Arts
Electronic Arts FTP Server	ftp://ftp.ea.com/
Electronic Banking Systems, Inc.	http://www.cityscape.co.uk/users/es45/
Electronic Book Developer	http://www.cnj.digex.net/~vozzaj
Electronic Book Technologies	http://www.ebt.com/
Electronic Frontier Ltd.	http://www.elecfron.com/
Electronic Learning Systems, Inc.	http://www.vector.net/~elstech/
Electronic Mailbox	http://www.cris.com/~videoguy/
Electronic Product Catalog Systems	http://www.intbc.com/ibc2/csad.html
Electronic Publishing Systems Integration	http://www2.csn.net/~kassj/
Electronic Resources Ltd.	http://www.singnet.com.sg/~yllow/
Electronic Systems, Inc.	http://www.esr.com/
Electronics and Networking Services, Inc.	http://www.ip.net/ENS/home.html
Elegance Network	http://www.netrunner.net/elegance/
Elek-Tek, Inc.	http://www.elektek.com/
Elektropost HQ	http://www.ep.se/
Elementrix Technologies, Inc.	http://www.elementrix.co.il/
Elite Computer & KC Vale	http://trojan.neta.com/~kc/
Elite Software	http://www.elitesoft.com/
Ellison CD-ROM	http://www.mordor.com/ellison/cdkiosk.html
Elonex	http://www.elonex.com/
Eloquent Technology, Inc. (Eloquence)	http://www.fcinet.com/eti/index.html
Eltec International	http://www.ibmpcug.co.uk/~eltec
Emagic (Notator) Logic	http://www.mcc.ac.uk/~emagic/emagic_page.html
EMAX Solution Partners	http://www.emax.com/
EMD Armor Plus	http://www.almac.co.uk/business_park/mis/emd1.html
EMD Enterprises	http://www.iis.com/emd/
Emergent Corporation	http://emergent.com/
Emerging Technologies, Inc.	http://www.etinc.com/
Emily Clarke	http://www.ior.com/~eeclarke/
EMJ Data Systems Limited	http://www.emj.ca/
Emory Computer Consultants	http://emory.com/~emory/index.html
emotion, Inc.	http://www.emotion.com/emotion/
EMPaC International Corp.	http://www.empac.com/
Employment	http://www.zds.com/htdocs/zds/htm/zjobs.htm

EMpower Corporation	http://www.empower-co.com/index.html
Empress Software Inc.	http://www.empress.com/
EMS Professional Shareware	http://www.wdn.com/ems
Emulex Network Systems	http://www.emulex.com/
Enabling Technologies Corp.	http://www.techarchitects.com/
Encore Computer Corporation	http://www.encore.com/
Engage Communication	http://www.engage.com/engage/
Engaging Media	http://www.engaging.com/
Engineering and Graphics Systems, Inc.	http://nol.net/EGS/
Engineering Consulting	http://www.earthlink.net/~engcon/
Engineering Graphical Solutions	http://www.tiac.net/users/eazl/egs/
Engineers' Club, The	http://www.engineers.com/tec.html
Ensemble Information Systems, Inc.	http://www.ensemble.com/
Ensemble Software	http://www.esisolutions.com/
Ensemble Systems Inc.	http://www.ansa.com/ensemsys.html
EnSight, CEI, Inc.	http://www.ceintl.com/
Ensoniq	ftp://ftp.ensoniq.com/
Enterprise Network Solutions	http://www.lanology.com/
Entrata Electronic Services	http://www.ic.ncs.com/
EnviroAccount Software	http://wheel.dcn.davis.ca.us/go/earthaware/
Environmental Laser	http://www.toners.com/welcome.html
Environmental Systems Research Institute	http://www.esri.com/
Envision	http://www.envisionit.com/
Envisions Solutions Technology, Inc	http://www.ocm.com/envisions/default.htm
Eolas Technologies Incorporated	http://www.eolas.com/
Epic MegaGames	http://www.epicgames.com/
Epilogue Technology Corporation	http://www.epilogue.com/
EPMOD Consultants, Inc.	http://www.ibp.com/pit/epmod/
Eprom Inc.	http://www.redwing.on.ca/eprom/index.html
Equinox Computer Graphics	http://www.equinox.ie/equinoxweb/
ERCorporation	http://www.netrep.com/global/biz/erc/erc.html
ERDAS	http://www.erdas.com/
Erol's Electronics	http://www.erols.com/erols/
Escape	http://www.shasta.com/~escape/
ESCAtech Media, Inc.	http://www.escatech.com/
ESD USA, Inc.	http://www.iu.net/esd/
ESDX	http://www.esdx.org/esdhome.html
ESH, Inc.	http://www.esh.com/
eSoft, Inc.	http://www.esoft.com/
Essential Data, Inc.	http://netmar.com/mall/shops/edi/
Essential Technical Services, Inc.	http://www.etsinc.com/
Essex Computers, Inc.	http://haven.ios.com/~essex/
Etak Incorporated	http://www.etak.com/
ETG Inc.	http://www.tyrell.net/~etg/
Eton Solutions	http://www.primenet.com/~etonsol/index.html
Evans & Sutherland Computer Corporation	http://www.es.com/

EveryWare Development Corp.	http://www.everyware.com/
Evolution Computing	http://www.evcomp.com/evcomp/
Evolving Technologies Corporation	http://www.evolvingtech.com/
Ex Machina, Inc.	http://www.nyweb.com/exmachina/
Excalibur Technologies Corporation	http://www.xrs.com/
Exceller Software Corporation	http://www.infomall.org/exceller/
Excellink, Inc.	http://www.excellink.com/
eXclaim! - X Windows Spreadsheet	http://www.unipress.com/cat/exclaim.html
Execusoft, Utah Wired!	http://www.utw.com/execusoft/homepge.html
Executive Software	http://www.earthlink.net/execsoft/index.html
Exide Electronics	http://www.exide.com/exide/
Expert Database Systems	http://www.edb.com/index.html
Expert Graphics	http://www.expertg.com
Expert Macintosh Consulting	http://www.efn.org/~machelp/
Expert PC	http://www.xmission.com/~wwwads/expsales.html
ExperTelligence	http://www.expertelligence.com/
Explorer Communication	http://www.explorercomm.com/
Express Star Systems, Inc.	http://www.xstar.com/
Extended Systems Inc.	http://www.extendsys.com/
Extreme/Mountain Biking CD-ROM	http://www.c21media.com/extreme/
EZ Systems	http://register.com/drives/
EZBAK Remote Backup Service	http://www.indirect.com/www/nirkman/
eZemail	http://www.ezemail.com/~vista/

F

F. F. Tronixs	http://www.fftron.com/fftron/
F. H. A.	http://www.thehost.com/fha/
F/X Studios Inc.	http://www.io.org/~fx/
Fairgate Technologies	http://www.iquest.com/~fairgate/
Falcon BBS Systems	http://www.consulan.com/falcon/falcon.html
Falcon Microsystems, Inc.	http://www.falconmicro.com/
Falcon Systems	http://www.falcons.com/
Faludi Computing	http://www.faludi.com/
FAQ - FLEXlm	http://www.globetrotter.com/faq.htm
Farallon	http://www.farallon.com/
Far East Exporter	http://www.sino.net/export/computer/index.html
Fargo Electronics, Inc.	http://www.fargo.com/
Farr Design	http://www.farrdesign.com/farrdesign/
FastComm Communications Corp.	http://www.fastcomm.com/
Fauve Software	http://www.fauve.com/
FAX SCANNER	http://www.goldsword.com/pc-signs/pro-scan/pro-scan.html
Faximum Software, Inc.	http://www.faximum.com/
FCR Software	http://www.fcr.com/homepage.html
Federated Software Group	http://www.federated.com/
Felsina Software, Inc.	http://www.crl.com/~felsina/
Fenestrae, Inc.	http://www.america.net/com/fenestrae/fen.html

FFV Testsystems AB	http://www.ts.ffv.se/
Fiber Optic Marketplace	http://fiberoptic.com/
Fiber Optic Technologies Inc.	http://www.teleport.com/~fottrain/
Financial Dynamics Inc.	http://www.findyn.com/findyn/
Finisar Corporation	http://www.Finisar.com
Finital Informatica Srl	http://www.ats.it/finital/index.html
Finite Systems Consulting	http://www.finite-systems.com/fsc/
Finite Technologies Incorporated	http://www.finite-tech.com/fti/home.htmld
Fintronic USA, Inc.	http://www.fintronic.com/
Firewalls R US, Inc.	http://www.frus.com/
Firmware Design Pty Ltd	http://www.firmware.com.au/
First Byte	http://www.firstbyte.davd.com/
First Floor Software	http://www.firstfloor.com/
First Line Services	http://skyecom.com/f1.html
First Step Research	http://www.fsr.com/
First Tech Computer	http://www.firsttech.com/
FirstBase Software	http://www.firstbase.com/
Flashpoint, Inc.	http://www.flashpt.com/
FlatCracker Software	http://www.fiber.net/flatcracker/
FLEXlm end-user manual	http://www.globetrotter.com/manual.htm
Floppy Drive Repairs	http://www.goldsword.com/pc-signs/floppy/floppy.html
Florida Atlantic University - CNE in 4 Weeks	http://www.fau.edu/academic/cont-ed/cneip.htm
Fluent Incorporated	http://www.fluent.com/
Flying Muffin Enterprises	http://www.cris.com/~Flymuff/
Focal Point Training & Development	http://www.halcyon.com/connectivity/fp/
Focus GbR Software	http://www.liii.com/~louiev/focusgbr.html
Folio Corporation	http://www.folio.com/
Folkstone Design Inc.	http://www.sunshine.net/folkstone/
For-to-Win	http://weber.ucsd.edu/~rtrippi/for2win.htm
Forcom Computer Services	http://fcadmin.kosone.com/forcom.html
FORE Systems, Inc.	http://www.fore.com/
ForeFront Group, Inc.	http://www.ffg.com
Forman Interactive Corp.	http://www.forman.com/fic/c0.htm
Formtek	http://www.formtek.com
FortQ	http://www.forteinc.com/forte/forte.htm
FourGen	http://www.fourgen.com/
Fourth Dimension Software, Inc.—Southwestern Region	http://www.airmail.net/~fourd/
Fox Computing	http://www.edplaza.com/fox/fox.html
Fractal Design Corp.	http://www.fractal.com/
Franz Inc.	http://www.franz.com/
Freedom System Integrators Inc.	http://southwind.net/fsi/
Frick, Thaddeus	http://www.accesscom.net/tfrick/
Friedman Greene & Associates, Inc.	http://www.fga.com/
Friendly Software Store	ftp://ftp.netcom.com/pub/ca/campagna/www/friendly.html
Front Room	http://www.interport.net/~thefront/index.html
Frostbyte Computer Consultants	http://www.frostbyte.com.au/~frostbyt/index.html

FRS Associates Training and Education Division	http://www.frsa.com/frs.shtml
FS Consulting	http://www.fsconsult.com/
Fujitsu Resale	http://www.fujitsu.com/FCPA/resale.html
Fulcrum Technologies Inc.	http://www.fultech.com/
Full Serv Software	http://www.ro.com/customers/fullsrv/
Full Spectrum Communications	http://www.fsc.com/fsc/
Fundamental Software	http://www.funsoft.com/funsoft.html
Funk Software	http://www.funk.com/
Further Vision	http://gaia.gn.apc.org/comsites/vision/home.html
Future Computer Industries, Inc.	http://futureci.isdn.inch.com/
Future Enterprises, Inc.	http://www.fei.com/fei.html
Future Reality	http://www.com.au/future/
Future Vision Multimedia	http://www.fvm.com/
FutureSkills Computer Learning Centers	ttp://www.intersource.com/~future/
FutureTel, Inc.	http://www.ftelinc.com/
Futuristic Computing	http://media1.hypernet.com/futuristic.html
Futuristic Software & Computing Group	http://www.entrepreneurs.net/futuregroup/

G

G & G Cable, Inc.	http://www.eskimo.com/~gremark/
G & R Data Group, Inc.	http://www.grdata.com/
G.A. Parks Consulting Group, Inc.	http://www.gaparks.com/
G.A.C. Computer Services	http://rampages.onramp.net/~campbel/
Galaxy Systems Inc.	http://www.interport.net/galaxy/
Gallagher & Robertson A/S	http://www.gar.no/
Galt Technology	http://www.galttech.com/
Game Link	http://laonline.com/cdrom/
Gamma Productions, Inc.	http://www.gammapro.com/
GammaLink	http://www.gammalink.com/
Gandalf Systems Corporation [vector.com]	http://www.vector.com/gandalf.html
Ganson Engineering, Inc.	http://www.ganson.com/gei/
Garbee and Garbee	http://www.gag.com/
Garrett Communications, Inc.	http://www.garrettcom.com/index.html
GartnerGroup	http://www.gartner.com/
Gary Bergman Associates, Inc.	http://www.castle.net/~gbergman/
Gateway 2000 Computers	http://netcenter.com/netcentr/mall/techmart/gateway1.html
Gateway 2000	http://www.gw2k.com/home/gw2k.html
GAUSS GmbH Co.	http://www.gauss.de/
GCD Wholesale Computer Parts	http://www.ip.net/shops/GCDWholesaleComputerparts/
GCR Computers Llc.	http://198.87.118.50/bus/gcr/pages/gcr.htm
GE Rental	http://www.ge.com/gec/pcrental.html
Gebala Systems, Inc.	http://www.geopages.com/SiliconValley/1500/
Gel-Pro Analyzer	http://www.mediacy.com/gppage.htm
Geli Engineering	http://www.geli.com/
GEMCOM Services Inc.	http://www.gemcom.bc.ca/
Gemini Systems Software, Inc.	http://www.chataqua.com/GSSI/GSSI.html

Genasys II, Inc.	http://www.genasys.com/
GeneCraft	http://www.genecraft.com/vectdir/
General Software Solutions	http://gencom.com/gss/gss.htm
Generator	http://www.iea.com/~stevem/brochure.html
Genesys	http://www.teleport.com/~genesys/index.shtml
GeneSYS Informatica	http://www.genesys.cosulich.it/
Genetic Algorithm Solver for Excel(tm)	http://www.iea.com/~stevem
Genicom Corporation	http://www.concom.com/GENICOM/
Genoa Technology	http://www.gentech.com
GenText, Inc.	http://www.metronet.com/~gentext/homepage.htm
Geo Computers	http://www.connectus.com/~geocomp/
Geodesic Systems	http://www.geodesic.com/
Geographic Designs	http://www.geodesigns.com/
Georg Heeg	http://www.heeg.de/
George C. Wang - InterWeb Computer Solutions	http://www.relay.net/~gcw/
GeoSystems	http://www.geosys.com/
Gerber Information Systems	http://www.pic.net/gis_tech/index.htm
Gestalt Systems	http://www.gestalt-sys.com/
Gestalt Systems, Inc.	http://www.clark.net/pub/gestalt/
GFCT CompTech Switzerland	http://www.datacomm.ch/gfctmain.html
Gholkars INC.	http://www.vivanet.com/~gholkars/
GIC	http://www.gicorp.com/
GIS\Solutions, Inc.	http://www.gisedm.com/gisedm/gisedm.html
Glen Herbert Consulting	http://www.biddeford.com/~gherbert/ocs1.html
Global Computing, Inc.	http://www.planet-hawaii.com/global/
Global Technology Associates, Inc.	http://www.gta.com/
Global Technology Solutions	http://www.castle.net/~rvary/global.html
Global Village Communication, Inc.	http://www.globalcenter.net/
Global Village Consulting	http://espresso.cafe.net/gvc/
Global Visions Software	http://pages.prodigy.com/CO/gviscmr/gviscmr.html
GLOBEtrotter Software, Inc.	http://www.globetrotter.com/
Glyphic Technology	http://www.glyphic.com/glyphic/welcome.html
GNK Programming, Inc.	http://www.io.org/~gosho/gnk_web.htm
GNP Computers	http://www.gnp.com/
Godin London Incorporated	http://www.godin.com/godin/
Gold Canyon Multimedia	http://www.goldcanyon.com
Gold Standard Multimedia	http://inca.gate.net/~gsm/
Golden Diamonds	http://haven.ios.com/~cbsa/
GoldTek	http://www.village.com/business/goldtek.html
Government Computer Sales, Inc.	http://useattle.uspan.com/services/gcsi/
GPC Consulting	http://www.globalserve.on.ca/~gpc/
GrafTek Inc.	http://www.labelview.com/graftek/
GrafTek, Inc.	http://www.graftek.com/
Graphic Simulations Corporation	http://www.computek.net/graphsim/gsc.html
Graphical Imaging Corporation	http://www.gicorp.com/
Graphics Development International, Inc.	http://www.gdisoft.com/

Gravitational N-Body simulation for Windows 95/NT	http://mnnt1.hep.umn.edu/nbody1.htm
Gray Design Associates	http://delta.com/gda.com/gda.htm
Great Computer	http://www.a2z.com/a2z/cr00001a.html
Great Lakes Data Systems, Inc.	http://www.glds.com/
Greenline	http://www.greenline.com/
GreenSpring Computers	http://www.greenspring.com/
Grey-Tech Computer Inc.	http://www.inforamp.net/~greytech/
GriffTax	http://www.episet.com/bus/b1020.html
GroLen Communications	http://busstop.com/grolen.htm
GroupTalk (Collaborative Strategies)	http://www.collaborate.com/index.html
Groupware Technologies, Inc.	http://gtisrv1.grouptech.com/home.htm
GroupWise Information	http://www.dws.net/groupwise.html
Gruppe Telekom, Inc	http://www.interaktiv.com/
Gryphon Software Corporation	http://www.gryphonsw.com/
GSA Training, Inc.	http://bizserve.com/GSA.Training.Inc/
GST/Micro City	http://www.primenet.com/~gst/index.html
guideWorks	http://katz.guideworks.com
Guru Technologies, Inc.	http://www.gurutech.com/
Gus Communications Inc.	http://www.direct.ca/gus/index.html
GW Hannaway & Associates Home Page	http://www.gwha.com/

H

Habia Cable AB	http://www.habia.se/
HADCO Corporation	http://www.hadco.com:8080/
Halo Network Management	http://www.commerce.com/halonet/
Hamilton Rentals Place	http://www.hamilton.co.uk/
Hamrick Software	http://www.primenet.com/~hamrick/
Hand Held Computer Applications, Inc.	http://www.chattanooga.net/HHCA/index.html
Happy Puppy Software	http://happypuppy.com/games/link/index.html
Harder Technologies	http://www.earthlink.net/free/bigbee/webdocs/index.html
Hardware Headquarters	http://iglou.com/hardware_hq/
Hardware Store, The	http://www.demon.co.uk/market/hstore.html
Harlequin Group, Ltd.	http://www.harlequin.com/full/products/
Harlequin's Watson(TM)	http://www.harlequin.com/full/products/apps/watson.html
Harley Street Software	http://www.islandnet.com/~harley/homepage.html
Harmonic Software Inc.	http://world.std.com/~harmonic/
HarperCollins Interactive	http://www.delphi.com/harpercollins/hcinteractive/
Harris Computer Systems	http://www.csd.harris.com/
Harris Network Management	http://neptune.corp.harris.com/HNM/
Harter Image Archives	http://www.tddc.net/geo/harter/
Harts Systems Ltd	http://www.harts.com/info/
Harvard Design & Mapping	http://www.harvardnet.com/hdm/
Hauppauge Computer	http://www.hauppauge.com/hcw/index.htm
hav.Software	http://www.NeoSoft.com/~hav/
hav.Software	http://www.neosoft.com/~hav/
HawkNet, Inc.	http://www.hawknet.com/~netinfo/

Hayes Mucrocomputer Products	http://www.hayes.com/
HBR Enterprises	http://www.diginetmktg.net/diginet/hbr/ibmhtm1.htm
HCCI - Hardware Canada Computing Integration	http://www.cimteg.ists.ca/corp/hcci/hcci.htm
HCL Consulting	http://hclggn.hcla.com/
HD Industries	http://www.Infoservice.com/HDIndustries/
Hearne Scientific Software	http://www.hearne.com.au/
Hebel Computer	http://www.wco.com/~hebelcom/
Hegyi Geotechnologies International	http://www.globalx.net/hegyi/
Heizer Software	http://www.webcom.com/~heizer
Helios Software	http://www.helios.de/
Help Desk Institute	http://www.HelpDeskInst.com/
Help for the Help Desk	http://haven.ios.com/~jimmoore/helpdesk/helpdesk.html
Hernblad Technology Consulting	http://futures.wharton.upenn.edu/~hernbl08/htc.html
Herzog System of Computer Keyboarding	http://www.tucson.com/herzog
Heurikon	http://www.heurikon.com
Hewlett-Packard	http://www.hp.com/
HP Supportline	http://support.mayfield.hp.com/support/
Hewlett-Packard Education Services	Http://www.dmo.hp.com/edserver/edserver.html
HFSI	http://www.hfsi.com/
Hi-Tech	http://www.internet-cafe.com/hi-tech/
High Performance Cartridges	http://www.netpoint.net/hpcart/hpcart.html
High Performance Software Forum	http://www.valley.net/~hps/hps.html
High Techsplanations, Inc.	http://www.ht.com
High-Performance 16/32 Bit ODBC Drivers	http://www.openlink.co.uk/
HighTech Mart	http://netcenter.com/netcentr/mall/techmart/hightech.html
Hijinx	http://www.hijinx.com.au/
Hirschmann, Richard, Network Systems	http://www.hirschmann.de/WELCOME.HTM
Hitachi	http://www.hdshq.com
Hitech Computers	http://www.mktmkt.com/hitech.html
Hitech Digital	http://www.hitechdigital.com/
HJF Digital Media	http://www.aloha.com/~redmond/
HMS Software	http://www.wst.com/hms
HNR Computers	http://www.hnr.com/
Hochtief Software	http://www.ppgsoft.com/ppgsoft/uc_main.html
HockWare	http://www.nando.net/ads/hockware
Holophonics	http://www.xmission.com/~gastown/imaginative/holo.html
Honeysuckle Computing	http://pages.prodigy.com/GA/honeysoft/honeysoft.html
Horizon Software	http://users.aol.com/HorizonSft/
HOT Inc., Canada	http://www.io.org/~hot/
hot-n-GUI	http://www.hotngui.com/
House of Blues - Summer Preview Website	http://underground.net/HOB/
House of CD ROM	http://www.demon.co.uk/house-of-cd-rom/
Houston Crest Co.	http://www.houston.com.hk/
HP Printer Index	http://www.dmo.hp.com/peripherals/printers/main.html
HPI	http://www.instalit.com/
HPS Simulations	http://www.cris.com/~sturmer/

HSF Computers	http://www.europa.com/~surfwave/hsf.html
HSiN Semiconductor Pte Ltd	http://www.singnet.com.sg/~hx1008/
HTR	http://www.htr.com/
Hughes Training/ LINK Division	http://flcsvr1.bgm.link.com/
Hull Speed Data Products	http://www.hullspeed.com/
Human Designed Systems	http://www.hds.com/
Humble Beginnings	http://rhumble.beginnings.com
Hummel and Associates, Inc.	http://192.189.118.114/
Hummingbird Software	http://www.primenet.com/~awong/legaudit.html
Hundred Acre Consulting	http://www.pooh.com/
Huronia Technologies	http://www.bconnex.net/~hurotech/
Hydromantis, Inc.	http://www.hydromantis.com/
HYNET Technologies, Inc.	http://www.hynet.com/
HyperContract	http://www1.usa1.com/~pcohen/aw.html
HyperDesk Corp.	http://www.hyperdesk.com/
HyperGlot, The Foreign Language Software Company	http://www.hyperglot.com/hyperglot.html
Hyperparallel Technologies	http://www.ppgsoft.com/ppgsoft/hc_main.html
HyperSoft MedWorks Inc.	http://infoweb.magi.com/~hypersft
Hyphen Incorporated	http://www.hyphen.com/
Hyundai Information Technology	http://hyangdan.hit.co.kr/

I

I-Cubed Design, Inc	http://www.i3design.com/i3design/
I-Kinetics, Inc.	http://www.i-kinetics.com/
I-Link, Inc.	http://i-linkcom.com/
I.C.S., Inc.	http://www.ics-driveshop.com/
I/NET, Inc.	http://www.inetmi.com/
I/PRO Internet Profiles Corporation	http://www.ipro.com/
iambic Software	http://www.iambic.com/iambic/
Ian Freed Consulting, Inc.	http://www.ifc.com/
IBEX Servicios Informaticos	http://www.ibex.es/ibex
IBM	http://www.pc.ibm.com/products/c30034.html#modem
IBM	http://www.software.ibm.com/
IBM Client/Server Computing	http://www.csc.ibm.com
IBM Lakes Collaborative Networking Architecture	http://www.hursley.ibm.com/p2p/Lakes.html
IBM Mainframe Software Helpers	http://pages.prodigy.com/MA/acs/acs.html
IBM PC Software DIRECT	http://www.issc1.ibm.com/pcdirect/
IBM Person to Person Conferencing	http://www.hursley.ibm.com/p2p/P2P.html
IBM Storage Management Software	http://www.storage.ibm.com/storage/hardsoft/software/
IBVA Technologies, Inc.	http://www.opendoor.com/Pagoda/IBVA.html
ICE	http://www.iced.com/
Ice-9 Publications and Computers	http://info.pitt.edu/~depst8/
IceCube Software	http://www.vnet.net/users/iceman/
ICEM Technologies	http://www.cdc.com/icem.html
ICON Computing Limited	http://www.icon.hu/
Iconovex Corporation	http://www.iconovex.com/

ICS	http://www.relay.net/~gcw/memory.html
ICS PC Repair Center	http://199.234.216.35/homepage.htm
IdeaGraphix	http://ideanet1.ideanet.com/~idea/
IDEAL Communication Technology	http://tribeca.ios.com/~ideal/
Ideal Point	http://www.ipoint.com/
IDEAL Scanners & Systems	http://www.ideal.com/
IdeSYS	http://www.idepro.fr/
Idiom Consulting	http://www.idiom.com/
IDM	http://www.jaring.my/at-asia/idm/id_hpage.html
Iler Networking & Computing	http://teal.csn.net/~kenti/
Illustra Information Technologies, Inc.	http://www.illustra.com/
ILOG	http://www.ilog.com/
Image Club Graphics	http://www.adobe.com/imageclub/
Image Interactive Music	http://www.mindspring.com/~flip/ImageInt.html
Image Manipulation Systems	http://www.imageman.com/
Image Reduction and Analysis Facility	http://iraf.noao.edu/iraf-homepage.html
Image Technologies	http://www.fest.com/Products/features/imagetec/imagetec.htm
Image, The	http://www.lainet.com/image/
ImageFast	http://www.charm.net/~ibc/ibc2/image.html
ImageFX	http://www.imagefx.com/imagefx/
ImageFX	http://www.supernet.net/~jbraatz/
Imagen Communications Inc.	http://www.imagen.net/default.htm
Imagenation Graphics & Multimedia	http://www.primenet.com/~mactalk/imgntn.html
Imageware	http://www.msen.com/~imagewar
ImagiNation Network	http://www.imaginationnet.com/
Imaginative Entertainment	http://www.xspot.com/IE/
IMAGinE+ Multimedia Productions, Ltd.	http://www.imagine.pt/imagine/
Imagix	http://www.teleport.com/~imagix
Imaja	http://www.woodwind.com/Imaja/
Imaja Home Page	http://www.imaja.com/imaja/
Imatek, Inc.	http://www.imatek.com/
ImAtrex Corporation	http://www.imatrex.com/
IMC Networks Corp	http://www.imcnetworks.com/
imedia	http://www.imedia-sf.com
Immedia Systems	http://www.netwest.com/~immedia/
Immedia Technologies	http://infoweb.magi.com/~immedia/immedia.html
Immortal Software Productions	http://www.synapse.net/~immortal/
Impediment, Inc.	http://www.impediment.com/
IMS Communications Ltd	http://www.demon.co.uk/imsc/
IMT Systems	http://mfginfo.com/comp/imtsystems/imt.htm
In Private Practice - Software	http://www.sccsi.com/smg/privprac.html
In The Chips	http://www1.mhv.net/~inthechips/
Inacom Corp.	http://www.inacom.com/
Inch Cumali Software	http://www.attila.com/icsoft/
Incite	http://www.incite.com/
InContext Systems	http://www.incontext.ca/

Indelible Blue	http://www.indelible-blue.com/ib
Indian Fonts	http://clarksville.mc.utexas.edu/~alim/Vijay/vijay.html
Industrial Communication Sweden	http://www.indcom.ideon.se/
Industrial Peer-to-Peer	http://www.callamer.com/~pfahey/
Industrial Simulation by Rapid Modeling	http://www.holli.com/rapid/
Inference	http://www.inference.com/
Infinite Technologies	http://www.ihub.com/index.html
Infinity Software, Inc.	http://www.io.com/~isi_info/
InfoArt!	http://www.highwayone.com/blkbear1/
Infodata Systems, Inc.	http://www.infodata.com/
Infodemco	http://www.netaxis.qc.ca/infodemco/
InfoGestion JFM Ltd	http://www.cam.org/~infojfm/
Infogroup S.p.A.	http://infogroup.iunet.it/
Infoline	http://www.es.co.nz/~sdunbar/home.html
infoLink Communications	http://www.ilcom.com/~infolink
InfoMagnet: LISTSERV tool for Windows	http://www.clark.net/pub/listserv/imag.html
InfoMotion, Inc.	http://bb.iu.net/infomotion/
InfoQuest	http://www.charm.net/~ibc/ibc2/infoq.html
INFORIUM, The Information Atrium Inc.	http://www.e-commerce.com/inforium.htm
Informatik Inc.	http://www.execpc.com/~infothek/
Information Age, Inc.	http://www.informationage.com/
Information Broker	http://infobrkr.com/IB/DTP.htm
Information Builders	http://www.ibi.com/
Information Concepts, Inc.	http://www.infoconcepts.com/
Information Data Products Corp.	http://www.planet.net/idpc/
Information Electronics	http://www.ie.com/
Information Management Group	http://www.imginfo.com/
Information Networks International	http://www.clearfield.co.nz/ini/
Information Solutions Center, Inc.	http://www.spectracom.com/imsc-cad/
Information Technology Design Centre	http://cortona.itdc.utoronto.ca/
Informatique RF	http://www.saglac.qc.ca/inforf/welcome.html
InfoScan	http://www.machinasapiens.qc.ca/machina/infoscanang.html
InfoService	http://www.infoservice.com/
InfoSource	http://www.gate.net/~pctrain/
InfoSource, Inc.	http://www.gate.net/~pctrain/isihome.html
InfoSouth	http://fly.hiwaay.net/~beangl/infosouth.html
InfoStructure Services & Technologies	http://www.netins.net/showcase/infostructure/
InfoTrends Group, Inc.	http://www.infotrends.com/system.htm
InfoWave	http://www.inet.co.th/cybermall/infowave/
Ingram Micro	http://www.ingram.com/
Ingres Consultant - Shaun Bliss	http://www.cris.com/~Sb/cv.html
Inherent Technologies	http://www.inherent.com/
init AB	http://www.init.se/
Inlab Software GmbH	http://www.inlab.com/
Inline Corporation	http://www.inlinecorp.com/inline/
Inmar	http://www.inmar.com/

Innervation Technology Corporation	http://www.innervation.com/inner/
Innosoft International, Inc.	http://www.innosoft.com/
InnoSys Inc.	http://www.ten-io.com/itta/innosys
Innovation Group	http://innovation.com
Innovative Computer Associates, Inc.	http://www.icai.com/icai/
Innovative Computer Technologies, Inc.	http://www.9to5.com/9to5/Diskview/DVHome.html
Innovative Systems of New York, Inc.	http://ison.com/
Innovention Systems Integrators	http://www.innovent.com/innovention/index.html
Insight Designs, Inc.	http://www.phoenix.net/~insight/
Insight Direct, Inc.	http://www.insight.com/
Insignia Solutions	http://www.insignia.com/
InSite Software	http://www.primenet.com/~insite/
Insitu Inc.	gopher://ftp.std.com/11/vendors/insitu
Inspiration Software	http://www.rdrop.com/
inspired arts, inc.	http://www.cts.com/~inspired/
Install Systems, Inc	http://www.interstar.com./corporte/installs/install.html
Instance Corporation	http://www.halcyon.com/instance/instance
Instant Commtact	http://www.rust.net/~instacom/
Instruction Set, Inc.	http://www.inset.com/
Instructional Systems Company, Inc.	http://www.iscinc.com/
Instrumental, Inc.	http://www.instrumental.com/
Intaglio	http://www.intaglio.com/intaglio/
Intangible Assets Manufacturing	http://www.iam.com/iam/
Integrate Communication & Entertainment (ICE)	http://www.iceinc.com/
Integrated Communications	http://www.intcom.net/
Integrated Consulting Group, Inc.	http://www.icg-inc.com/~icg/index.html
Integrated Quality Dynamics, Inc.	http://www.iqd.com/quality/
Integrated Research	http://www.zdepth.com/integ/
Integrated Research Technologies	http://www.intersec-consulting.com/intersec/
Integrated Systems Solutions Corporation	http://www.issc.ibm.com/
Integrated Technical Software	http://www.itswa.com.au/
Integrated Technologies, Inc. (InTech)	http://204.17.76.3/intech.html
Integrix	http://www.miracle.net/integrix/integrix.html
Intek Technologies, Inc.	http://www.intekinc.com/
Intel	http://www.intel.com
Intel Smart Network Devices	http://www.intel.com/comm-net/index.html
InteleNet	http://www.intelenet.com/
Intellectics	http://www.austria.eu.net/intellectics/
Intelligent Business Solutions	http://www.ols.net/users/ibs/ibshomep.htm
Intelligent Business Solutions	http://www.ols.net/users/ibs/index.htm
Intelligent Market Analytics	http://www.marketmind.com/
Intelligent Software Professionals	http://phoenix.phoenix.net/~isp/
INTERACT Multimedia, Inc.	http://www.datanet.net/interact/interact.htm
Interactive Computer Systems Ltd	http://www.discribe.ca/ics/icshome.htm
InterActive Computing	http://www.mind.net/ic/
Interactive Data Systems, Inc.	http://www.idsinc.com/

Interactive Digital Intelligence Group	http://www.microweb.com/idig/
Interactive Effects	http://www.webcom.com/~ie/index.html
Interactive Effects Web Outpost	http://www.irc.umbc.edu/~ie/
Interactive Media Corporation (IMC)	http://www.imcinfo.com/
Interactive Software Engineering	http://www.eiffel.com/
Interactive Systems, Inc.	http://www.teleport.com/~isi/
Interactive Television [IBM]	http://www.raleigh.ibm.com/itv/itvprod.htm
Interactive Voice Applications	http://www.tc.net/voice/
InterActivity Inc.	http://www.synapse.ca/
InterActual Technologies, Inc.	http://www.interactual.com/
INTERCAT	http://www.intercat.com/
Intercom Pacific	http://ipacific.net.au/
Interface Consult	http://www.interface.co.at/interface/
Interface Electronics Inc.	http://www.interface.com/
interGlobe Networks, Inc.	http://www.interglobe.com/
Intergraph Corporation	http://www.ingr.com/
Intergraph Corporation	http://www.intergraph.com/tim.shtml
InterLAN Consulting Inc.	http://www.interlan.ca/~jzaidman/
Interlink Network Group, Inc. Live Network Training	http://lnt.inc-g.com/
InterMind	http://www.intermind.com/
International Business Center	http://www.niagara.com/blmc
International Computer Programs, Inc.	http://www.icp.com/softinfo/
International Data Products	http://www.clam.com/clamweb/idp.html
International Industrial Intelligence	http://international.com/
International Software Systems Inc.	http://www.issi.com/issi/issi-home_page.html
International TechneGroup Incorporated	http://www.iti-oh.com/
International Transware	http://www.metawire.com/transware/
International Typeface Corporation	http://www.esselte.com/itc/
Internet Audit Bureau	http://www.iaudit.com/
InterNET Computer Store	http://inetstore.com/
Internet Database Consultants	http://www.clark.net/infouser/endidc.htm
Internet Pilots	http://www.xmission.com/~ip/ip.html
Internet Resources Group	http://www.helpline.com/
Internet Security Systems	http://iss.net/~iss/
Internet Shopping Network	http://www.internet.net/index.html?source=DYHO
Internet Technologies Group	http://www.magi.com/itg/
Internet Training & Consultancy	http://www.bitz.co.nz/itc/
Internet-LAN Services	http://www.tiac.net/users/mvangel/index.html
Interphase	http://www.iphase.com/
Interplay	http://www.interplay.com/
Interpretive Software	http://www.execpc.com/~isi/
InterSoft International, Inc.	http://starbase.neosoft.com/~zkrr01/
IntersQ Corporation	http://www.interse.com/
Intertech Computers	http://www.leonardo.net/intertech/home.html
Intertex	http://www.algonet.se/~intertex/
InterVision Systems, Inc.	http://www.intervisionsystems.com/wearable/

InterVista Software, Inc.	http://www.intervista.com/
InterWorking Labs	http://ftp.cavebear.com/IWL/HomePage.html
InTEXT Systems	http://www.intext.com/
IntraCoastal Consulting	http://softec.digital.net/user/dgc/intrcstl.html
InTransNet Services Japanese Information Page	http://www.intransnet.bc.ca/engmen.html
Introduction to Neural Networks	http://www.mindspring.com/~zsol/nnintro.html
IntuMediaWorks, Ltd.	http://www.intumedia.com/intumedia/
Investor's Advantage	http://cyber-active.com/appwrite/iawin.htm
Invoice Store	http://www.interbahn.com/pub/softwstor/
InVzn Development Corporation	http://www.invzn.com/
INX_UTIL Tool Kit: Tim Schaefer : The Computer Business Company, Inc.	
	http://www.gate.net/~tschaefe/
Iomega Corp.	http://www.iomega.com/
Iomega Jaz and Zip Drive	http://www.stern.nyu.edu/~jwu/iomega.html
IP Systems	http://www.io.org/~ipsys/
IPC Technologies, Inc.	http://www.ipctechinc.com/
IPL	http://www.iplbath.com/
IQ Technologies, Inc.	http://www.blarg.net/~iq/
Irenyx Data Group	http://www.ark.com/irenyx/info.html
Iris Development Coporation	http://irisdev.com/
Ironstone Technologies	http://www.ironstone.mb.ca/infopage/iron1.html
IRRISOFT	http://fserv.wiz.uni-kassel.de/kww/irrisoft/irrisoft_i.html
ISA Informationssysteme GmbH	http://www.isa.de/
ISC Consultants Inc.	http://www.iscinc.com/
ISDN Systems	http://www.infoanalytic.com/isc/index.html
ISG Technologies, Inc.	http://www.isgtec.com/
ISIS International	ftp://ftp.netcom.com/pub/is/isis/home.html
Islamic Computing Centre U.K.	http://www.ummah.org.uk/icc/
ISOCOR	http://www.isocor.com/
isoma	http://www.ozonline.com.au/TotalNode/isoma/
ISOTRO Network Management, Inc.	http://www.isotro.ca/
ISPW	http://www.ispw.com/
Israel Engineering Software Ltd.	http://www.macom.co.il/ies.jsi/index.html
ITI Software	http://www.cam.org/~ggagnon/

J

J P Mclaughlin & Associates Inc.	http://www.uidaho.edu/~hend881/jpma.html
J&M Computers	http://www.wp.com/J&MCOMPUTERS/
J-MAC System Inc.	http://www.j-mac.co.jp/
J.D. Koftinoff Software,Ltd.	http://www.xmission.com/~seer/jdksoftware/
J.E.Clark Systems Software Consulting	http://www.sentex.net/~jeclark/
Jack - Univ. of Penn. HMS	http://www.cis.upenn.edu/~hms/jack.html
Jack of all Trades	http://www.dnai.com/~penny
Jackson-Reed, Inc.	http://www.halcyon.com/prreed/jackreed.html
Jacobus Technology	http://jacobus.com/
Jamcom Communications	http://chiba.netxn.com/Jamcom.html

James River Group	http://www.jriver.com
JAMMER by Soundtrek	http://www.soundtrek.com/
Jandel Scientific Software	http://www.jandel.com
Janus Interactive	http://www.teleport.com/~janus/
JASC, Inc.	http://www.winternet.com/~jasc/
Javiation	http://www.demon.co.uk/javiation
JCA TQlQmatique	http://www.jca.fr/jca/
JCC Consulting, Inc.	http://www.jcc.com/
JCN Computer Systems	http://www.jcn.nl/
JcS Canada	http://www.cam.org/~jcs/index.html
JCS Computers	http://www.vpm.com/jcs/jcscomp.html
Jegher Computer Consultation	http://www.accent.net/jegher
JEM Computers, Inc.	http://www.jemcomputers.com/biz/bargains
Jenkins Consulting Services, Inc.	http://www.mcs.com/~mjenkins/HTML/jcs.html
JES & Associates, Inc.	http://www.deltanet.com/jes/
Jewell, Chris - Jewell Consulting Software Systems	http://www.wco.com/~jewellcj/
JimWare Inc.	http://www.prairienet.org/~jdpierce/homepage.html
JM Consulting and Cheap Advice	http://pages.prodigy.com/IL/jomoor/
JMG Compushoppe	http://jmg.on.ca/
JMI Software Consultants	http://www.pond.com/~jmi/
JobHuntÖ 6-in-1 for Windows«	http://amsquare.com/america/amerway/jobhunt/jobhunt.html
JOBSCOPE Manufacturing Management System	http://web.sunbelt.net/~jobscope
JobSoft Design & Development	http://www.jobsoft.com/jobsoft/jobsoft.html
John Mayes & Associates	http://www.jma.com/
Johns Creek Software	http://www.inter.net/jcs/
Johnson Computer & Consulting	http://www.ionet.net/mall/jcs/jcc_com.shtml
JourneyWare Media	http://www.journeyware.com/
JP McLaughlin & Associates	http://www.uidaho.edu/~hende881/jpma.htm
JPS Computers	http://jps.ns.net/
JRL Systems, Inc.	http://www.jrl.com/jrl/
JSoft Technologies	http://www.mcs.com/~jsoft/home.html
JTM Enterprises	http://www.jtment.com/
Jubilee Computers	http://www.demon.co.uk/jubilee/index.html
Jubilee Computers	http://www.demon.co.uk/jubilee/index.html
Jumbo Computer International	http://www.xmission.com/~wwwads/jumbo/home.htm
JunkYard, The	http://www.thejunkyard.com/junk/
Jutastat	http://www.os2.iaccess.za/jutastat/index.htm

K

K and M Engineering	http://www.kme.com
K&P Computers	http://www.mainelink.net/~pdieppa/k&p.html
K-Net Ltd	http://www.k-net.co.uk/
K2 Enterprises	http://www.k2e.com/~k2e/index.html
KAB Konsult AB	http://www.dataphone.se/~kab/index.html
Kagi Shareware	http://198.207.242.3/gregko/winregis.htm
KAN Distributors'	http://www.widdl.com/Kan/

Kantara Development	http://www.xgroup.com/kantara/html/kantara.html
KAPS, Inc.	http://www.xmission.com/~wwwads/kaps.html
KarlBridge	http://www.demon.co.uk/kbridge/index.html
Kat Electronic Percussion	http://www.mw3.com/kat
Katalina Technologies	http://www.ozemail.com.au/~katalina/
Kaua`i Media	http://www.electriciti.com/~bbal/
Kaycon	http://www.liberty.com/home/kayconxx/Welcome.html
Kennewick Computer Company Inc.	http://www.kcc-computers.com/
Kenton Lee: X and Motif Consulting	http://www.rahul.net/kenton/
Kernel Productions, Inc.	http://www.kernel.com/
Kewill-Xetal EDI Services	http://www.cityscape.co.uk/users/ew48/index.htm
Key Computer Services	http://www.dfw.net/~jlocke/
Keyser, Charles H.	http://home.aol.com/CHKeyser
KeyStone Learning Systems Corp.	http://www.keylearnsys.com/
Keystone Technology	http://www.keytech.com/
KI NETWORKS	http://www.ki.com/index.html
Kids Universe Toys And Software	http://supermall.com/kids/page1.html
Kim Franchise	http://www.kimsoft.com/fran.htm
Kinesix	http://www.kinesix.com/
Kinfonetics Technology	http://www.io.org/~cyourth/
Kintronics: CD-ROM Technology	http://www.kintronics.com/
Kiowa Creek Resources	http://www.webtex.com/kcr/
Kirchoff, Leif	http://weber.u.washington.edu/~leif/homepage.html
KL Group	http://www.klg.com/
Klever Computers	http://www.klever.com/
Knighted Computers	http://www.knighted.com/
Knowledge Adventure	http://www.adventure.com/
Knowledge Engineering Pty Ltd.	http://www.ke.com.au/
KNX (UK)	http://www.knx.co.uk/~knx/
Kodak Color Printers	http://www.kodak.com/productInfo/officeImaging/output/
Konami	http://www.wtinet.com/wti/konami.htm
Korea.com	http://korea.com/
KPD	http://www.bart.nl/~kpd/
Kratzer Computer Consultants	http://www.greatbasin.net/~kratzer/kratz.htm
Kreative Kids Computer Camp	http://merkury.saic.com/kkids/kkids.html
KRON Computers	http://www.icon.net/commercial/kron/kron.html
KT International, Inc.	ftp://ftp.connix.com/pub/users/k/ktintl/ktmain.htm
Kuck & Associates, Inc.	http://www.kai.com/
Kyushu Matsushita Electric Co.,Ltd. Corporate Engineering Division	
	http://www.kme-lab.co.jp/

L

L & H Computers	http://www.citivu.com/rc/lnh/index.html
L M Software	http://www.infowest.com/lmsoftware/index.html
L.C.P. Company Computer Sales	http://www.upstate.net/lcp.html
LabTop Computers Inc.	http://mindlink.bc.ca/labtop/

Laitron Computers	http://www.vistapnt.com/laitron/
Laitron Computers Inc.	http://www.webquest.com/laitron/
Lamb International	http://ideal.ios.net/~hevans/home2.html
Lambda Systems Ltd.	http://www.wimsey.com/~andy/
LAN Performance Labs - LPL	http://www.ftel.com/t100/lpl_home.html
LAN Solutions	http://www.aimnet.com/~yungi/lansol.html
LAN to Internet Gateways	http://www.tic.net/
Lan-Tech Systems Pty Ltd	http://www.iinet.net.au/~lantech
LandWare	http://www.planet.net/landware/
LANframe Inc. Software Applications and Consulting	http://www.lanframe.com/
Language Engineering Corporation	http://www.lec.com/
Language Systems Corp.	http://www.langsys.com/langsys/
Language Systems Corp.	Vhttp://www.langsys.com/langsys/
Lanis - Internet Classroom	http://www.v-net.com/directory/lanis.html
Lanminds	http://www.lanminds.com/
Lanop Corp.	http://www.maestro.com/lanop/lanop.html
LANtek Computer, Inc.	http://www.gus.com/emp/lantek/lantek.html
LapTECH Systems	http://www.worldweb.com/Laptech/
Lara Consulting Group	http://www.lara.com/lara/welcome.htm
Larscom	http://www.larscom.com/
Lascomm	http://www.rain.org/~eds/
Laser Express	http://emporium.turnpike.net/D/dcservice/wg/krantin.htm
Laser Products and Services Group	http://www.infoanalytic.com/laser/
Laser Pros International	http://www.inmarket.com/laserpro/
Laser Renewal	http://www.infi.net/~elspence/
Laser Today International, Inc.	http://www.best.com/~laserto
LaserByte	http://www-leland.stanford.edu/~hanno/laserbyte/
Lasermoon Ltd.	http://www.lasermoon.co.uk/
LaserSaver	http://rampages.onramp.net/~laser/
LaserSaver	http://www.sundaypaper.com/www/lsrsvr.htm
Lasertone Computers	http://www.lasertone.com/
Latitude Group, The	http://www.latgroup.com/
LavaMind	http://www.lavamind.com/
Law Courseware Consortium	http://ltc.law.warwick.ac.uk/lcchome.html
Law Enforcement/Police Software	http://www.augusta.net/alert1.htm
Lawson & Reay, Inc.	http://www.lri.com/
Learn iT	http://www.hooked.net/learnit/
Learning Edge Corp.	http://www.io.org/~tle/
Learning in Motion	http://www.learn.motion.com/
Learning Quest, Inc.	http://www.peak.org/~labquest/index.html
Learning Spectrum	http://myhouse.com/lspec/
Learning Tree International	http://www.lrntree.com/
Learnix	http://www.learnix.ca/
Ledger Systems	http://www.best.com/pub/ledger/public_html/ledger1.htm
Legal Computer Solutions	http://www.lcsweb.com/
Legato Systems, Inc.	http://www.legato.com

Lemma Inc.	http://www.tiac.net/users/lemma
Leo Electronics	http://www.earthlink.net/~leoelex/
LEVEL5 Info Center	http://www.l5r.com/
Lexmark	http://www.lexmark.com
Lex Systems	http://www.link.ca/~lex/
Lexitech, Inc.	http://www.lexitech.com/
Liant Software Corporation	http://www.liant.com/lpi/
Liberty Stats	http://www.webcom.com/~liberty/
License Management Articles	http://www.globetrotter.com/articles.htm
Lieberman, Harvey M.	http://pages.prodigy.com/PA/harvey/
LifeGuide	http://www.compuoffice.com/lg.html
Lightbulb Factory, Inc.	http://www.lightbulb.com/
Lighten, Inc.	http://www.lighten.com/lighten/
Lighthouse Software, Inc.	http://www.lighth.com/~lighth/
Lightscape Technologies, Inc.	http://www.lightscape.com/
Likom Corporation	http://www.likom.com.my/
Lilly Software Associates, Inc.	http://mfginfo.com/cadcam/visual/visual.htm
Limit X	http://dino.ccm.itesm.mx/AM3/pageengl.html
Lingsoft Products	http://www.lingsoft.fi/products.html
Lingsoft, Inc.	http://www.lingsoft.fi/
Linguistic Technology Corp.	http://world.std.com/~engwiz/
Link Technologies, Inc.	http://www.batnet.com/linktech/
LinkStor	http://www.linkstor.com/
LinksWare hypermedia for Mac	http://www.linksware.com/
Liquid Image	http://www.mbnet.mb.ca/~havelk/
Little Pines Multimedia	http://www.capecod.net/lpines/lpines.htm
Littlejohn Keogh	http://www.littlejohn.com/~ljk/index.html
Live Picture, Inc.	http://www.livepicture.com/
LiveDV	http://livedv.com
Livingston Enterprises, Inc.	http://www.livingston.com/
ljg	http://www.kaiwan.com/~ljg/
LMB Microcomputers	http://www.lmb.iquest.net/
LMSoft	http://geoserver.lmsoft.ca/
Locatech	http://www.venture.net/locatech/
Lockheed Austin	http://www.lmsc.lockheed.com/LAD/lad.html
Lockheed Martin REAL3D	http://www.mmc.com/real3d/real3d.html
LockTite Security Software	http://www.linknet.net/vdi/lockt.htm
Locus Computing Corporation	http://www.locus.com/
Locus, Inc.	http://iglou.com/lp
Lodestone Research, L.L.C.	http://www.aescon.com/lodeston/index.htm
LOGAL Software, Inc.	http://www.logal.com
Logan Industries	http://www.lii.com/
Logic	http://www.logic.be/
Logic Approach	http://www.eden.com/~logic/
Logic Link Co.	http://logiclink.com.tw/
Logic Works	http://www.logicworks.com/

Logica	http://www.img.logica.com/
Logica Documentation Library	http://www.clark.net/pub/tile/home.html
Logical	http://www.logical.iunet.it/
Logical Operations	http://www.logicalops.com
LogicVision	http://www.lvision.com/
Logix Consulting	http://www.lgx.com/
Logos Research Systems, Inc.	http://islander.whidbey.net/~logos/welcome.html
Longbow International Corp.	http://www.panix.com/~longbow/
LOOK Software	http://www.globalx.net/look/
Look Software Systems Inc.	http://look.com/
Looking Glass Technologies	http://www.lgt.com/
Looking Glass Technology (Placer County, CA USA)	http://www.psyber.com/~apierce/lgt-main.html
Loral ADS - Advanced Distributed Simulation	http://www.camb-lads.loral.com:8080/
LOTS Technology, Inc.	http://www.win.net/~lasertape/
Lotto Master	http://www.intex.net/rockware/lotto.html
Lotus Development Corporation	http://www.lotus.com/
Loviel Computer Corporation	http://www.loviel.com/
LPI	http://www.liant.com/lpi/
LucasArts Entertainment Company	http://www.lucasarts.com/menu.html
Luminair Multimedia	http://www.luminair.com/
Lyle Musical ScreenSavers	http://slip23.nb2.usu.edu/~sl323/index.html
Lynx Geosystems Inc.	http://www.info-mine.com/products/lynx/
Lyons Digital Media	http://pd.net/ldmedia/

M

M&S Hourdakis SA	http://www.stepc.gr/~sweetie/hourd.html
M.A.K. Ltd.	http://www.mak.lviv.ua/
M/B Interactive	http://mbinter.com/
Mabry Software	http://www.halcyon.com/mabry/
Mac Classroom	http://198.53.16.194/TMC.html
Mac Education Software: Chemistry Math Latin Greek French Spanish	http://www-leland.stanford.edu/~lefig/index.html
Mac Station	http://www.macstation.com/
Mac Zone and PC Zone	http://www2.pcy.mci.net/marketplace/mzone/
Mac Zone Internet SuperStore	http://www.maczone.com/maczone/
MacByte Computers	http://smartworld.com/macbyte/macbyte.html
Mach 5 Software	http://205.164.234.18/
MacInsight	http://www.sover.net/~ecrelin/
MacLine	http://www.atlas.co.uk/macline/maclinehp.html
MacMedic	http://www.pacificrim.net/~macmedic/
MacNeal-Schwendler Corporation	http://www.macsch.com/
MacPlay	http://www.macplay.com/
MacProducts USA	http://www.dgr.com/mp/planet_mp_l.html
MacService	http://www.sonic.net/~geo/
MacTalk, Inc.	http://www.primenet.com/~mactalk/
MacToolKit	http://www.vsinet.com/mactoolkit/

MacWarehouse	http://www.warehouse.com/micro/
MacWarehouse Australia	http://www.macwarehouse.com.au/
Mad Opal Pseudo Corporate Page	http://www.mcs.com/~madopal/home.html
Madge Networks	http://www.madge.com/
MAEstro Software	http://www.mae.com/
Magellan Interactive	http://www.magellan.net/
Magic Tracks Electronic Media	http://www.intercom.net/biz/magic_tracks/
Magical Fox Interactive	http://www.magicalfox.com/
Magma Software	http://www.cais.com/bryan/
Magna Computer Corp.	http://magna.magna.net/
Magnacom Data Products, Inc.	http://www.webscope.com/magnacom
Magnet Interactive Studios	http://www.magnet.com/
Magnet International	http://www.onlink.net/community/twhitley.html
Magnetic Technology Incorporated	http://argus-inc.com/MagTech/MagTech.html
Mahoney, John	http://www.star.net/People/~jmahoney/
Mainframes, Mins, & Micros	http://www.kern.com/mmm.html
MaK Technologies	http://www.mak.com/
Make Systems, Inc.	http://www.makesys.com/makesys
Malachite	http://www.csua.berkeley.edu/~alexz/
Malibu Software Group, Inc.	http://www.Malibu.com/
MalSoft	http://www.usis.com/~draconis/
Man's Best Friend Software	http://www.mbfs.com/
Man-Made Systems Corporation	http://www.charm.net/~mms/
Management Concepts Incorporated	http://www.MgmtConcepts.com/
Management Graphics, Inc. USA	http://www.mgi.com/
Management Information Solutions	http://www.connix.com/~jlcotter/mishome.html
Management Information Technologies, Inc.	http://www.vyp.com/miti/miti.html
Manager's Desktop	http://os2.iafrica.com/marksman/dt.htm
Mango New Media, Inc.	http://www.halcyon.com/mangoweb/welcome.htm
Mann Consulting	http://www.mann.com
MAPLE	http://www.maplesoft.com/
Maplehurst Productions	http://www.infi.net/~maplhrst/
Mapware Corporation	http://www.mapware.com/
MARATHON Digital Publishing	http://www.tiac.net/users/lenb/
Marc International Inc.	http://www.marx.com
Marcam Corporation	http://www.marcam.com/
MARCorp	http://www.aimnet.com/marcorp/home.html
Marcus Associates	http://branch.com/marcus/marcus.html
Maritime Information Systems	http://www.boatman.com/maritime/
Marketing Masters	http://surveysaid.ostech.com:8080/
Marketing Masters	http://surveysaid.ostech.com:8080/
MarketWare Computer Systems	http://www.mware.com/
Marner International, Inc.	http://www.marner.com/
Massey Development	http://supernet.net/~tmassey/
Master Series Illustraion CD Library	http://www.xmission.com/~wwp/master.html
MasterMind Technology, Inc.	http://www.telepath.com/mmti/

Mastersoft Inc.	http://www.chaco.com/~mastersoft/
Matheson & Associates	http://www.hookup.net/~infobit/
MathSolutions	http://smc.vnet.net/MathSolutions.html
Mathware	http://www.xmission.com/~mathware/
Matrix Computer Consulting, Inc.	http://ios.com/~matrixbb/index.html
Maxi-Vision	http://www.odyssee.net/~pmv/
MAXIT Corporation	http://www.maxit.com/
Maxperts, Inc.	http://www.maxperts.com/
Maxtor	ftp://ftp.maxtor.com/index.html
Maxum	http://www.maxum.com/maxum/
MaxVision Online	http://www.maxvision.com/
MaxWare	http://users.aol.com/maxware1/maxware.html
Mayflower Software	http://www.maysoft.com/
Mazer Corporation	http://www.shore.net/~mazer/
MBG Multimedia	http://www.netaxis.qc.ca/mbg-group/
MBS Industries, Inc.	http://www.mbsii.com/mbs/
MCAE Inc.	http://www.ppgsoft.com/ppgsoft/inertia.html
McAfee Associates	http://www.mcafee.com/
McDonnell Douglas Human Modeling System	http://pat.mdc.com/LB/LB.html
McDonnell Information Systems	http://www.mdis.com/
McLaurin, Chris	http://edge.net/~cmclaur/
MCS Computer Systems	http://www.infi.net/~mcspc/
MDL Information Systems	http://www.mdli.com
Med2000	http://www.digimark.net/vmr/
Media Architects	http://www.teleport.com/~mediarch/
Media Cybernetics Image Analysis	http://www.mediacy.com/
Media Plus, Inc.	http://www.aloha.net/~mpi/mp.htm
Media Range	http://www.mediarange.com/media/welcome.htm
Media Solutions International	http://www.msi-usa.com/
Media Vision, Inc.	http://www.mediavis.com/
Media-Pro Children's Software	http://www.widdl.com/MediaPro/
MediaLogic, ADL Inc.	http://www.adlinc.com/adlinfo/
MediaMagic Solutions	http://mediamagic.inter.net/mediamagic/
MediaPro	http://www.widdl.com/MediaPro/
MediaShare Corporation	http://www.mediashare.com/mshare/
MediaSoft Telecom	http://www.cam.org/~mst/
Mediastorm Multimedia Solutions	http://www.io.org/~mediast/
Mediatrix	http://www.fmmo.ca/mediatrix
Medical Multimedia Systems	http://www.webcom.com/~medmult/
Medlin Accounting Shareware	http://community.net/~medlinsw/
Megahertz Corporation	http://www.xmission.com/~mhz/
Megascore, Inc.	http://www.interactive.net/~jgm/megascore.html
MegaSoft, LLC	http://www.megasoft.com/
Meiko	http://www.meiko.com/
Melange Online	http://www.icenet.it/melange/home.html
Melange Online	http://www.icenet.it/melange/home.html

Memex	http://www.memex.co.uk/
Memorex Telex	http://www.mtc.com/
Memory USA	http://www.mu.com/
Memory World	http://www.memoryworld.com/
Mentor Graphics Corporation	http://www.mentorg.com/
MentorNet - The Internet Learning Center	http://www.mentornet.com/mentornet/
MentorPlus Software, Inc	http://www.webcom.com/~criteria/mentorp/
MentorPlus Software, Inc.	http://www.webcom.com/~criteria/mentorp/
Mercury Interactive	http://www.merc-int.com/
Meridian Computers and Consulting, Inc.	http://WWW.MeridianInc.com/
Merisels Sun Division	http://www.merisel.com/
Merlin Software	http://www.deltanet.com/merlin/
Mesa Net	http://www.mesa.net/
Mesquite Software, Inc.	http://www.mesquite.com/
Messaging Systems Group	http://webmall.com/msg/msg.htm
Messaging Systems Group	http://webmall.com/msg/msg.htm
Meta Software Corporation	http://www.tiac.net/users/metasoft/
Meta-Software, Inc.	http://www.metasw.com/
MetaCase Consulting	http://www.jsp.fi/metacase/
MetaInfo, Inc.	http://www.metainfo.com/
Metalabs	http://www.metalabs.com/vision/
MetalMan Corp.	http://www.unm.edu/~baltz/
MetaSolv Software Inc.	http://www.metasolv.com/
Metatec Corporation	http://www.metatec.com/
Metatec's NautilusCD	http://www.metatec.com/~nautiluscd/
MetaWare Incorporated	http://www.metaware.com/
Metaware Technologies Inc.	http://www.hookup.net/~mti/
METEX Systems Inc.	http://www.wji.com/metex/mxhome.html
Metroline Direct	http://www.mlinedirect.com/
Metrostar Computer Center	http://media1.hypernet.com/metrostar.html
Metus Systems Group	http://www.paltech.com/metus/metus.htm
MEX Multimedia Experts	http://www.mex.com/
Meyer Consulting	http://www.phone.net/
mFactory	http://www.mfactory.com/
MFD Consult	http://login.dknet.dk/~mortenf/
MiBAC Music Software	http://www.winternet.com/~mibac/
Micro 2000, Inc.	http://www.micro2000.com/
Micro Computer Systems, Inc.	http://www.mcsdallas.com/
Micro Consultant Group	http://i-linkcom.com/mcg/mcg.html
Micro Designs Corporation	http://www.microdesigns.com/
Micro House International	http://www.microhouse.com/
MICRO Machines	http://www.gus.com/emp/microm/microm.html
Micro Madness, Ltd.	http://www.madness.net/
Micro Planning International	http://www.microplanning.com/plan/
Micro Service & Training	http://www.ici.net/cust_pages/jsouza/jsouza.html
Micro Visions Plus	http://www.microvisions.com/

Micro-Frame Technologies, Inc.	http://www.microframe.com/
Micro-Rent Corporation	http://www.deltanet.com/micro-rent/
Micro-Vision	http://www.trib.com/service/microv.html
Micro/Station at UIC	http://www.MicroStation.uic.edu/
MicroAge Computer Centers, Inc.	http://www.mid.com/
MicroAssist	http://www.tech.net/microassist/
MicroBench Computer Training and Education	http://rampages.onramp.net/~microben/
MicroBiz	http://www.carroll.com/microbiz/
Microcom Inc.	http://www.microcom.com/
MicroExcel Software	http://www.microexcel.com/mxsoft/mxweb.htm
Micrografix	http://www.micrografix.com/
Microguild, Inc.	http://www.microguild.com/
Microline Software	http://www.mlsoft.com/
Microlytics	http://www.microlytics.com/
Micromath	http://www.micromath.com/~mminfo/
Micromatix Distributing	http://www.atlnta.com/mmatix.html
MicroMedium Inc.	http://www.micromedium.com/
Micromuse	http://www.micromuse.co.uk/
Micron	http://www.micron.com/
Microplex Systems Ltd.	http://www.microplex.com/
Micropolis Corp.	http://www.microp.com/
Microport	http://www.infopoint.com/sc/market/computers/microport.html
Microprose	http://www.microprose.com/
Microsoft Corporation	http://www.microsoft.com/
Microsoft Online Institute	http://www.microsoft.com/MOLI/
Microstar Laboratories	http://www.mstarlabs.com/mstarlabs/
Microstar Software Ltd.	http://www.microstar.com/
Microsystems Engineering Company	http://www.interaccess.com/products/
Microsystems Software	http://www.microsys.com/
Microsystems Software	http://www.microsys.com/
Microtec Research (MRI)	http://www.mri.com/
MicroTool	http://www.ppgsoft.com/ppgsoft/objectif.html
Microtrader	http://www.magic.mb.ca/~microt/
MicroTutor	http://www.uco.es/grupos/ecoagra/
MicroWarehouse, Inc.	http://www.warehouse.com/
MIDI Mark	http://www1.usa1.com/~kandisky/
Midi Mart	http://www.infohaus.com/access/by-seller/Midi_Mart
MIDI2CS	http://www.snafu.de/~rubo/songlab/midi2cs/
MidiMan's Official Web Site	http://www.midifarm.com/midiman/
Midnight Computer	http://www.buyit.com/midnight/
Midware Technologies (SA)	http://www.os2.iaccess.za/midware/index.htm
Midwest Micro	http://www.mwmicro.com/
Migration Software Systems, Ltd.	http://www.migration.com/
Mike Salitter Consultant Services	http://knet.flemingc.on.ca/~msalitte/mscs.html
MIKSoft, Inc.	http://www.cnj.digex.net/~mik/
Milestone Technologies, Inc. (MTI)	http://www.spadion.com/spadion/mti/

Military Simulations Inc.	http://www.military-sim.com/
Milkyway Networks Corporation	http://www.milkyway.com/
Millennium Communications	http://www.webcom.com/~milcom/welcome.html
Millennium Data Systems	http://www.io.org/~pdbmds/
Miltec Electronics Inc.	http://www.miltec.com/miltec/
Mimesis Technology	http://rampages.onramp.net/~mimesis/
Mind Logic	http://www.xmission.com/~wwwads/mind/logic.html
MindQ Publishing, Inc.	http://www.mindq.com/
Mindstreet Multimedia	http://mindstreet.com/mindstreet
Minerva Technology	http://www.minerva.ca/
MiNET Net3D	http://www.minet.com/net3d/
Minicom Data Corporation	http://www.minicom.com/minicom/
Minitab, Inc.	http://www.minitab.com/
Minnesota Datametrics Corporation	gopher://gopher.mndata.com:2074/
Minuteman Software	http://www.ppgsoft.com/ppgsoft/gpssmain.html
mIRC	http://huizen.dds.nl/~mirc/index.htm
Miros	http://www.miros.com/biz/miros/
miro Computer Products	http://www.mirousa.com/
Mirus Industries Corporation	http://www.mirus.com/
Mission Electronics Corporation	http://www.DRAM.com/
Mitek Systems, Inc	http://www.cts.com/browse/mitek/
Mitron Corporation	http://www.mitron.com
Mixware	http://www.mixware.se/
MJC Inc. Computer Services	http://www.holonet.net/mjc/
Mj°lner Informatics ApS	http://www.mjolner.dk/
MKS Source Integrity Product	http://www.mks.com/si/mkssi.htm
MLH Consulting	http://www.aloha.com/~mlh/
MLL Software and Computers	http://www.ppgsoft.com/ppgsoft/wz_main.html
MMI Computing	http://www.mmi-co.com/users/mmi
MMR Software	http://www.execpc.com/~mmrsoft/
Moai Technologies, Inc.	http://www.moai.com/
Mobile Planet	http://www.mplanet.com/
Mobile Training Services Inc.	http://www.ccia.st-thomas.on.ca/~mobile/
MobileWare Corporation	http://www.mobileware.com/
Modern Media Systems	http://www.modernmedia.com/~pedlowl/
Modular Software Corporation	http://www.primenet.com/~modsoft/
Moldflow	http://www.moldflow.co.uk/moldflow/
Monnet, Inc.	http://www.monnet.com
Montage	http://www.montage.skill.com/
Moon Valley Software	http://www.moonvalley.com/
Moondog Multimedia	http://www.moondog-multimedia.com/
Moonlite Software	http://www.synapse.net/~moonlite/home.htm
Moreira Consulting	http://www.moreira.com/
Morse Telecommunication, Inc.	http://www.morse.net
Mosaic Information Technologies	http://www.videoconferencing.com/
Mosaic Multisoft Corporation	http://www.cts.com/~mosaic/

MOSES	http://linus.socs.uts.edu.au/~cotar/moses.html
Motorola Information Systems Group	http://www.motorola.com/MIMS/ISG/
Motorola ISG	http://www.mot.com/MIMS/ISG/
Mount Baker Software	http://www.swcp.com/~bminor/MtBaker.html
Mountain CAD Inc.	http://www.montana.com/MtCAD/MtCAD.html
Mountain CAD Inc. [mountian.net]	http://www.mountain.net/hp/mtncad/
Mountain Lake Software	http://www.woodwind.com/mtlake/index.html
Mountain Software	http://www.mountain.net/hp/mtnsoft/
Mountain Visions Multimedia	http://www.primenet.com/~mtvsion/
MR Mac Software	http://www.ip.net/shops/MR_Mac_Software/
Mr. Upgrade	http://www.primenet.com/~jimb/mrupgrad.html
MSI Communications	http://www.msic.com/
MSS	http://www.gold.net/ifl/mss/
MTC - Training and Support Services	http://osiris.sunderland.ac.uk/mtc/mtchome.htm
MTW Network Solutions	http://web.sunbelt.net/~mtwsolutions
Multi-Media Communications	http://fuji.ixl.net:8000/MultiMedia/
Multi-Media Design, Inc.	http://www.evansville.net/~mmd/
Multi-Tech Systems, Inc.	http://www.multitech.com/
MultiGen Inc.	http://www.sbwinc.com/MultiGen/
Multimedia & Video Center	http://macav.chautauqua.com/mvc.html
Multimedia 4D	http://www.beyond2000.com/webcent/4dstudio/multi.htm
Multimedia Computing Corp.	http://asearch.mccmedia.com/
MultiMedia Dimensions	http://www.cybercom.com/~mediaman/mmdimen.html
MultiMedia Enterprises	http://www.world-wide.com/multimedia/
Multimedia Hotline	http://www.multihot.com/
Multimedia Learning Inc.	http://www.media.com/default.html
Multimedia Solutions	http://www.noumenon.com/
Multimedia Solutions, Inc.	http://www.tcel.com/~mms/
Multimedia Technologies Ireland	http://www.mti.ul.ie/
MultiThread Consultants	http://www.multithread.co.uk/
Murray MultiMedia	http://www.murraymedia.com/murray/
Musitek	http://www.musitek.com/
Mustang Software Inc.	http://www.mustang.com
MVS Training, Inc.	http://www.pittsburgh.net/MVS/
MWA Custom DOS and Windows Programming	http://205.138.166.1/mwa/
MyMail	http://www.mymail.com/
Myriad Logic	http://www.access.digex.net/~myriad/
Myricom, Inc.	http://www.myri.com/
Myrinet Gigabit Switched Network	http://www.myri.com/myricom/myrinet.html
Mystech Enterprises	http://www.primenet.com/~valenti/index.html
Mystic Consulting Group	http://mystic.extern.ucsd.edu/business/mystic.html

N

Nash-Media	http://www.nash-media.co.uk/
Nashoba Networks, Inc.	http://www.nashoba.com/nashoba/
National Computer Systems	http://www.ncslink.com/

National Instruments	http://www.natinst.com/
National Parts Depot	http://www.megasoft.com/npd/
National Pixel Products	ftp://ftp.netcom.com/pub/na/natpix/html/natpix.html
National Service Network, Inc.	http://natserve.com/
National Software Testing Laboratories	http://www.nstl.com/
Nationwide Computer Support	http://navishow.web.aol.com/lab/n/ncs/index.htm
Native Guide - Computer Enhancement of Vocabulary Memory	
	http://www.NativeGuide.com
Natural Graphics	http://www.naturalgfx.com/
Natural Intelligence	http://www.natural.com/
Natural Software	http://www.computan.on.ca/~ksmith/
NaviSoft	http://www.navisoft.com/
NBase Switch Communications	ftp://ftp.netcom.com/pub/nb/nbase/nbase.html
NBG INC.	http://www.winternet.com/~nbgusa
NCD Software	http://www.ncd.com/
NCX Technology, Inc.	ftp://ftp.netcom.com/pub/nc/ncx/home.html
NDS Distributing	http://www.netrep.com/global/biz/nds/nds.html
Neat Software Company	http://www.cs.umanitoba.ca/~changl/neat/neat.html
NEC Corporation	http://www.nec.com/
nekotech SOFTWARE	http://www.nekotech.com/
NeoLogic Systems	http://www.neologic.com/~neologic/
Neon Software, Inc.	http://www.neon.com/
Neptune Interactive Designs	http://www.injersey.com/Clients/NID/
Net Computers International	http://www.netcomputers.com/
Net Design Technology, Inc. St.Louis MO USA	http://walden.mo.net/~netd/
Net Express	http://www.tdl.com/~netex/
Net Guru Technologies, Inc.	http://www.internet-is.com/netguru/
Net Nanny	http://www.netnanny.com/netnanny/
Netbase	http://www.edb.com/nb/index.html
NetCasters Inc.	http://www.netcasters.com/
NetComm UNIX Training and Consultancy	http://sarah.ucd.ie/
NetConsult Computer Systems GmbH	http://www.intershop.de/
NetCount	http://www.digiplanet.com/DP1/netcount.html
netCS	http://www.netcs.com/
NetEdge Systems	http://www.netedge.com/
NETiS Technology, Inc.	http://www.netistech.com/
NetMagic, Inc.	http://www.aristosoft.com/netmagic/company.html
netMAINE	http://backup.maine.net/
Netmare 1	http://netmare1.channel.co.uk/
NeTpower, Inc.	http://www.netpower.com/
NetPro Computing	http://www.netpro.com/
Netsoft	http://voyager.bei.net/amni/netsoft/elite.html
NetSoft	http://www.netsoft.com/
NetSolve	http://www.netsolve.net/
NetStar, Inc.	http://www.netstar.com/
NETSYS Technologies, Inc.	http://www.netsystech.com/

Nettech Engineering	http://www.ebtech.net/users/nettech/
Network Communication Computers and Arrays	http://tribeca.ios.com/~ideal/index.html
Network Computing Devices, Inc.	http://www.ncd.com/xt.html
Network Consulting Group	http://www.comland.com/~mnorth
Network Data Services, Inc.	http://www.gate.net/~nds/index.html
Network Express, Inc.	http://branch.com/netexpress/netexpress.html
Network General	http://www.ngc.com/
Network Masters, Inc.	http://www.rmii.com/~fritts/
Network Performance Institute	http://anshar.shadow.net/~npi/npipage.html
Network Support Inc.	http://www.globalx.net/nsi/
Network Systems Corporation	http://www.network.com/
Network Technologies & Applications, Inc.	http://www.msn.fullfeed.com/nta/
Network TeleSystems, Inc.	http://www.ntsi.com/
Network-1 Software and Technology, Inc.	http://bb.iu.net/n1/
Networking and Internet Connectivity Consultant	http://www.earthlink.net/free/tedv/webdocs/
NetworkingWizards, Inc.	http://www.umn.edu/nlhome/m072/grigs001/index.html
Networks Incorporated	http://205.138.166.1/networks/
Networks Plus Computers	http://www.sierra.net/ntwkplus/
NetWorth	http://www.networth.com/
NeuroDimension, Inc.	http://www.nd.com/
Neuron Data Elements Environment	http://www.neurondata.com/
New England Business	http://www.ifor.com/
New England Computer Supply	http://emanate.com/necs/
New England Systems	http://www.nes.com/
New Hope Software	http://www.bkptcy.com/newhope/
New Media Think Tank	http://www.webcom.com/~newmedia/
New Perspective	http://www.ccsi.com/n-perspect/
New Software Direct	http://www.cd-rom-online.com/
new stuff inc.	http://www.newstuff.com/
New Technologies, Inc.	http://superhighway.com/
New Technology Computers	http://www.indirect.com/www/newtech/
New Wave Computers	http://www.neosoft.com/~synergy/
New World Graphics and Publishing	http://www.primenet.com/~newwrld/
Newbridge Networks Corporation	http://www.newbridge.com/
Newer Technology	http://www.newertech.com/
Newman Group Computer Services	http://www.dpi.com/Newman/catalog.htm
Newman Group Computer Services Corporation, Inc.	http://www.dpi.com/Newman/newman.htm
NewOrder Media	http://www.nashville.net/~neworder/
News	http://www.ea.com/e3.html
News@Themis Online	http://themis.com/
Newton Factory Direct	http://www.teleport.com/~newton/
Nexial Systems	http://www.nexial.nl/
Nexus srl Firenze Italy	http://www.trident.nettuno.it/~fabio/nexus.html
NH&A	http://www.nha.com/
Nial Systems Limited	http://www.qucis.queensu.ca/home/nsl/info.html
NIC Microsystem, Inc.	http://www.gus.com/emp/nic/nic.html

NICE Technologies	http://www.nicetech.com/
Nightware	http://www.nightware.com/
Nightwish Engineering	http://www.moscow.com/~nitewish/
Niles & Associates, Inc.	http://www.niles.com/
Ninga Software	http://www.freenet.calgary.ab.ca/trade/ninga.html
Nisus Software Inc.	http://www.nisus-soft.com/~nisus/
Nokia	http://www.nokia.com/
NORTEL Entrust	http://www.entrust.com/
NORTH 45 Management Corp.	http://www.globalx.net/n45/n45.html
North American CAD Company	http://nacad.com/
North American Digital	http://biz.rtd.com/nad/index.html
North American Digital	http://biz.rtd.com/nad/index.html
North Beach Labs	http://www.hia.com/hia/nbl/
North Coast Software	http://cbix.unh.edu/ncs.htm
North Communications	http://www.infonorth.com/
North Valley Research	http://nvr.com/
Northstar	http://www.northstar-mn.com/
Norton Lambert	http:www.netusa.com/pcsoft/library/p_289.html
Notes Solution Software	http://www.dct.com/NOTES/
NOVA Concepts Limited	http://www.netins.net/showcase/novacon
Novacor Computer Inc.	http://www.novas.com/
NovaNET	http://www.nn.com/
Novell GroupWare	http://www.novell.com/ServSupp/groupware/
Nowak, Joe	http://www.mcs.net/~nowak/home.html
NSM Services	http://www.idiscover.co.uk/adverts/nsm/nsm.html
NSM Services	http://www.nsm.co.uk/
NTEX datacommunications bv	http://www.ntex.nl/
NTG International	http://www.ntg-campus.com/ntg/
NTT Data Communications Systems - UniSQL	http://unisql.www.nttdata.jp/
NTT Software Corporation	http://www.iijnet.or.jp/NTTSOFT/
Nu-Mega Technologies, Inc.	http://www.numega.com/
Nubody International	http://www.webcom.com/~dml/nubody/nubody.html
Number Nine Visual Technologies	http://www.nine.com/
Numera Software	http://www.numera.com/
NuReality	http://www.nureality.com/
Nutec Corporation	ftp://ftp.netcom.com/pub/ma/marcelo/html/nutec.html
NuTek	http://nutek.sj.scruznet.com/
NutriGenie	http://pages.prodigy.com/CA/nutrigenie/
Nutronic Circuit Company Inc. Printed Circuits	http://www.interactive.net/~nutron/
Nuvo Network Management, Inc.	http://www.nuvo.com/
NW Tech	http://www.eskimo.com/~nwt/index.html
NYnet Computer Store	http://savvy.com/~nynet/comp/comp.html

O

O-M-N-I Software	http://www.cloudnet.com/~jcop/o-m-n-i.html
O2 Technology	http://www.o2tech.fr
Object Agency Inc.	http://www.toa.com/

Object International, Inc.	http://www.oi.com/oi_home.html
Object Technologies	http://www.objectech.com/NEXTSTEP/
Object Technology International Inc. (OTI)	http://www.oti.com/
Object Warehouse	http://www.wwww.com
Objective Edge Inc.	http://www.objectiveEdge.com/
Objective Software	http://www.demon.co.uk/objective/
ObjectSpace, Inc.	http://www.objectspace.com/
ObjectWorks, Inc.	http://www.objectworks.com/
OC Systems	http://ocsystems.com/
Ocean Information Systems, Inc.	http://www.lightside.com/ocean/
Ocean Software	http://odon.com/ocean/
Octave	http://octave.com/octave.html
Octree Corporation	http://www.octree.com/
Odin TeleSystems Inc.	http://www.pic.net/~jari/odin.html
Odyssey Systems, Inc.	http://www.stern.nyu.edu/~mnarayan/
Office Technology	http://www.officetech.com/
Office.IQ	http://www.officeiq.com/
OK! Software, Inc.	http://www.mdn.com/oksoftware/
Okanagan Computer Products Recycling Inc.	http://www.awinc.com/OCPRI/
Okidata	http://www.okidata.com/
Olduvai Corporation	http://www.shadow.net/~olduvai/
Olicom	http://www.olicom.dk/
Olivetti	http://www.olivetti.it/
Olivetti Advanced Technology Center	http://www.atc.olivetti.com/
Olivetti Oy - Finland	http://www.olivetti.fi/
Olivetti Research Ltd Home Page	http://www.cam-orl.co.uk/
Olle Hallin	http://public-www.pi.se/~hit/
Olston-Packard Systems Engineering	http://www.opse.com/
Olympic Computer Technology	http://www.pic.net/olympic/olympic.html
Olympus Software	http://www.mmrcorp.com/corporate/olympus/
Omega Research, Inc.	http://www.gate.net/~omegares/
Omega: Software, accountancy systems (UK)	http://www.knowledge.co.uk/xxx/omega/
Omicron Structured Software (Pty) Ltd.	http://www.onwe.co.za/alon/omicron.htm
Omnes	http://www.omnes.net/
Omni Ventures, Inc.	http://www.discribe.ca/other/omninet.htm
Omnicron Data Systems Home Page	http://www.omnicron.com/omnicron.html
Omniscience	http://www.omniscience.com
Omron Office Automation Products Inc.	http://www.oas.omron.com/oap/oap.html
Omtool, Inc.	http://www.omtool.com/
On Technology	http://www.on.com/
On-Line Services BBS Software Reseller	http://www.ols1.com/
OnDemand Software, Inc.	http://www.ondemand.com/
ONE A DAY Computer Greetings	http://www.automatrix.com/panzl/index.html
One Up Corporation	http://www.1up.com/
One World Distribution	http://www.owd.com/
One World Software	http://www.usa.net/~rduffy/

OnPoint Communications, Inc.	http://www.mwbe.com/
OnPoint Technologies, Inc.	http://www.onpoint.com/onpttech/
OnTime On The Web	http://www.ontime.com/
OnTrac Systems, Inc.	http://www.primenet.com/~ontrac/
ONYX Computers Inc.	http://www.onyxcomputers.com/
ONYX Software Corporation	http://www.onyxcorp.com/
OOP Technologies	http://emporium.turnpike.net/~jlavin/
OpCode Factory	http://www.portal.com/~davidm/
Opcode Systems, Inc.	http://www.opcode.com
Open CAD International Inc.	http://www.opencad.com/
Open Market's University Program	http://www.openmarket.com/omi/nph-univ.cgi
Open Software Foundation	http://www.osf.org:8001/index.html
Open Systems, Inc.	http://www.gmcclel.bossnt.com/osas/
Open Windows Education And Utility Shareware	http://delta.com/openwin.com/openwin.htm
OpenVision Technologies	http://www.ov.com/services/security.html
OPN Systems	http://www.opn.com/
Optibase	http://www.optibase.com
Optical Access International	http://www.oai.com/
Optima Computer Solutions	http://www.optima.com
Optima Computer Solutions	http://www.optima.com/
OPTIMUS Corp.	http://www.optimus.com/~ravaldez
OptionVue Systems Int'l., Inc.	http://www.optionvue.com/
Optivision, Inc.	http://www.optivision.com/
Opus One	http://www.opus1.com/
ORALink Web	http://oradb1.jinr.dubna.su/software/oralink/
Orasis, Inc.	http://www.orasis.com/
Orbitt World Services	http://www.orbitt.com/
OrCAD, Inc.	http://www.orcad.com/
Order Data AB	http://www.algonet.se/~od
ORDERS Plus'95 for Windows	http://www.webcom.com/~bsa/
Orgaplus Software GmbH	http://www.orgaplus.de/
Origin	http://www.riv.nl/origin/
ORIGIN Systems, Inc.	http://www.ea.com/origin.html
Orincon Technologies	http://www.ppgsoft.com/ppgsoft/rippen.html
Orion Instruments, Inc.	http://www.oritools.com/
Ostfeld	http://www.graffiti.it/ostfeld/
Otter Solution	http://www.servtech.com//public/ottersol
Outbound Train	http://www.webcom.com/~outbound/
Outland	http://www.outland.com/
Output Enablers	http://www.io.com/user/oe/
Output Technologies	http://www.tyrell.net/~succeed/
Outsource Direct	http://www.u-net.com/~outsourc/home.htm
OutSource Engineering & Manufacturing	http://www.xmission.com/~outsourc/
Ovation Software Testing, Inc.	http://world.std.com/~ovation/ovation.html
Oxford English Software	http://www.oup.co.uk/oup/elt/software/software.html
Oxford Molecular Group	http://www.oxmol.co.uk/

Oxford Softworks	http://www.demon.co.uk/oxford-soft/
OZ Interactive	http://www.oz.is/OZ/Deps/Interactive/Page1.html

P

P-NET Computing	http://www.kaiwan.com/~pnet/
P.C. Star Computers	http://www.pcstar.com/
P/D/S, Inc. Database	http://vailonline.vailnet.org/
Pac Services, Inc. - CD-Replication, Diskette Duplication	http://www.cyberspace.com/pac/
Pace Computer Learning Center	http://wol.pace.edu/csis/pclc/home.html
Pacific Computers	http://204.174.85.99/default.htm
Pacific Data Management, Inc.	http://www.pdm-inc.com/
Pacific Microelectronics Corporation	http://www.pmcnet.com/~pmc/
Pacific Numerix Corporation	http://www.crl.com/~pacnum/pnc.html
Pacific Rim Network Systems	http://www.alaska.net/~kurtw/pacrimhome.html
Packard Bell	http://www.packardbell.com/
PageWorks	http://www.pageworks.com/
Paladin Computing	http://www.paladin.com/
Palindrome Corporation	http://www.palindrome.com/
Palo Alto Micro Corp.	http://www.inetbiz.com/pam/
Palo Alto Software	http://pasware.com/
Panda Software	http://grafton.dartmouth.edu:8001/panda/
Pangaea CAD Solutions	http://www.niagara.com/~abacus/pangaea/pangaea.html
Pangaea Scientific	http://mulberry.com/~pangaea/
Pangea Creative Media	http://www.magi.com/~brett/multimedia.html
Pangea Systems	http://www.panbio.com
Panther Software Corp	http://www.cadvision.com/panther.html/
Panther Software Corp.'s AppTrack	http://daffy.cadvision.com/Home_Pages/accounts/panther/
PaperFree Systems	http://paperfree.com/edi/index.htm
Pappalardo & Associates, Inc.	http://pai.iquest.net/index.html
Paracel, Inc.	http://www.paracel.com/
Parachute Computer Services	http://www.parachute.com/Clients/Parachute/
Paradigm Genesis	http://www.paragen.com/vr/
Paradigm Systems Corp. Global Information Service	http://www.sf.psca.com/
Paradise Software, Inc.	http://www.paradise.com/
Paragon Computers	http://www.picosof.com/336
Paradon Computer Systems	http://islandnet.com/~paradon/paradon.html
ParaGraph International	http://www.paragraph.com/
Parallel Performance Group	http://www.ppgsoft.com/ppgsoft/loox.html
Parallel Performance Group, Inc.	http://www.ppgsoft.com/ppgsoft/
Parametric Technology Corporation	http://www.ptc.com/
ParcPlace Systems, Inc.	http://www.parcplace.com/
Parian Sales - IBM Aptiva Computers	http://www.bconnex.net/~btracey/
Paritech Systems	http://www.wp.com/paritech/
Parsons Technology	http://www.parsonstech.com/
Parsytec Computer GmbH	http://www.parsytec.de/
Pathtrace Systems	http://mfginfo.com/cadcam/edgecam/pathtrace.htm

Paul Mace Software	http://www.pmace.com/
Paul Newcum & Associates Corp.	http://www.ocm.com/pages/it/paulnew/
Paul S. Adler and Associates	http://www.psadler.com/
PC Catalog	http://www.peed.com/pccatalog.html
PC Coach Training Software	http://www.csn.net/pccoach/
PC Consultants	http://cnwl.igs.net/~pccon/pccon.htm
PC DOCS, Inc.	http://www.pcdocs.com
PC Engines	http://www.best.com/~pdornier/
PC etc	http://www.elron.net/pcetcetera/
PC Heidens	http://www.teleport.com/~pcheiden/
PC Help	http://web.sunbelt.net/~mheath/pchelp1.htm
PC Innovation	http://www.nando.net/xwwwtemp/compad/pcinnov1.html
PC Market	http://www.PCmarket.com/~nms/
PC Physician	http://www.earthlink.net/~pcphysician/
PC Security Limited	http://www.usa.net/pcsl
PC Security Ltd	http://www.usa.net/pcsl/default.html
PC Shareware	http://www.cts.com/~pcs/
PC Source Reference Desk	http://www.inforamp.net/~gfaviere/
PC Systems	http://www.thumbsup.com/
PC Tutoring	http://www.blvl.igs.net/~cunning/
PC's In A Pinch	http://www.syssrc.com/
Pc-Trans	http://kuhub.cc.ukans.edu/~pctrans/
PCI	http://www.pci.on.ca/
PCiTech Computers	http://www.redshift.com/~pcitech1/
PCN Computers	http://www.pcnc.com/
PCs Compleat	http://www.ocm.com/pcscompleat/
Peach System	http://www.korea.com/koenmkpl/cdk.htm
Peachpit Press	http://www.peachpit.com
PeachWeb Plantation	http://plant.peachweb.com/
Peak Computing	http://peak.usa1.com
Pearl Wisdom	http://www.mind.net/pearl/index.html
Peer Protocol	http://www.earthlink.net/~peer/
PeerLogic, Inc.	http://www.peerlogic.com/
Pegasus Software Solutions, Inc.	http://www.iu.net/pegasus/
PelicanWare, Inc.	http://www.teleport.com/~bettes/index.html
Pencom System Administration	http://www.pencom.com/pencom/sa.html
Peninsula Advisors, Inc.	http://www.best.com/~iris/
Penril Datability Networks	http://www.penril.com
PentaGrafx Productions	http://www.cs.mcgill.ca/~desm/
PentaGrafx Productions	http://www.cs.mcgill.ca/~desm/
Pentland Systems Limited	http://www.linnet.co.uk/linnet/pentland/index.html
People-Planner Labor Management Software	http://www.imb.com/
Peregrine Systems, Inc.	http://www.peregrine.com/
Perfection Services, Inc.	http://ivory.lm.com/~psi
Performance Computing Inc.	http://www.teleport.com/~pciwww/
Performance Engineering Corporation	http://www.p-e-c.com/

Performance Software Services	http://www.tach.net/public/tradezone/perform/perform.html
Performance Systems Software, Inc. (PSSI)	http://www.intnet.net/PSSI/
Performance Technology, Inc.	http://www.perftech.com/
Pericom Software	http://www.pericom.co.uk/
Perihelion	http://www.perihelion.co.uk/
Peripheral Pro	http://www.compusult.nf.ca/~infoax/peripher.html
Peripheral Systems Group	http://www.web-view.com/pub/psg/
Peripheral Technology Group	http://www.ptgs.com:3086/
Peripherals Unlimited, Inc.	http://www.peripherals.com/peripherals/
Persoft Inc.	http://town.hall.org/sponsors/persoft.html
Personal Conferencing Workgroup	http://www.gopcwg.org/
Personal Database Applications	http://www.mindspring.com/~pda/
Personal Library Software, Inc.	http://www.pls.com/
Personal TeX, Inc.	http://www.crl.com/~pti/
Personal Training Systems	http://www.ptst.com/
Personal Workstations, Inc.	http://www.pwi.com/
Perspective Visuals, Inc	http://haven.ios.com/~dinosaur/
Peters Toner Cartridge Service	http://www.web-unltd.com/PTCS/ptcswel.htm
Peters-de Laet, Inc.	http://www.pdel.com/
Petroglyph	http://www.best.com/~powers/
PharmaSoft	http://www.pharmasoft.se/
Phase Three Logic, Inc.	http://www.aue.com/capfast.html
Phase3 Software, Inc.	http://www.pacrain.com/~phase3/phase3.html
Pheonix Software Solutions, Inc.	http://www.tcpxray.com/tcpxray/
Phertron	http://www.eunet.be/rent-a-page/phertron/
Philips Media	http://www.media.philips.com/
Phoenix Systems Synectics	http://www.phoenix.ca/
Photodex Corporation	http://www.photodex.com/
Pickering Anomalies and IOTA Asteroid Occultation Section	
	http://www.anomalies.com/
Pie in the Sky Software	http://www.catalog.com/psky/
Pierian Spring Educational Software	http://www.europa.com/pierian/
Pilkington Micro-Electronics	http://www.demon.co.uk/pmel/index.html
Pilot Network Services, Inc.	http://www.pilot.net/
Pilot Systems Inc.	http://www.gmcclel.bossnt.com/pilot/
Pinnacle Programming Services	http://www.pinncomp.com/~ajaz/index.html
Pinnacle Software	http://WWW.CAM.ORG/~pinnacl/
PinPoint Software Corporation	http://www.pinpt.com/
Pixel Express Home	http://www.internex.net/pixel/index.html
pixel Generation, inc.	http://www.pixgen.com/
Pixel Innovations Ltd.	http://web.pixel.co.uk/pixel/
Pixel Pecx	http://www.gayweb.com/206/pixelpec.html
PixelChrome Professional	http://rampages.onramp.net/~pixlchrm
pixelMotion Images, Inc.	http://ba.hypercomp.ns.ca/pix/pix_intro.html
Plaintree Systems	http://www.nstn.ca/plaintree/index.html
Planet AMCI	http://www.webvision.com/amci/

PlanetWatch shareware	http://www.ultranet.com/~guil95/graben/plnwch.html
Plastic Thought, Inc.	http://204.191.254.145/
Platinum Education	http://www.platinum.com/edu.htm
Play Incorporated	http://www.play.com/
PlayLink	http://www.phylon.com
Plexxus Interactive	http://www.cdcanada.com/cdcanada/pi/
Plus&Minus Accounting Software	http://www.talyon.com/
PObox EMail Service	http://www.pobox.org.sg/
Point & Click Software, Inc.	http://www.point-and-click.com/pcsi/
Polygon	http://ppnt-cap.spk.olivetti.com/
Polytel - Programmable Touchpads	http://www.danish.com/polytel/
Pop Rocket, Inc.	http://www.poprocket.com/
Portable Productvity, Inc.	http://www.winnet.net/ppi/
Portables for Hire	http://www.londonmall.co.uk/botm/
Positive Software Company	http://www.pointofsale.com/
Post Software International	http://www.postsw.com/
post.office SMTP Mail Server	http://www.software.com/
PostModern Computing	http://www.pomoco.com/
POW! Distribution Ltd	http://www.pow-dist.co.uk/
Power Computing Corporation	http://www.powercc.com/
Power Convertibles Corporation	http://www.pcc1.com/
Power Design, Inc.	http://www.libertynet.org/~power/
Power Pros, Inc	http://www.gus.com/emp/powerpro/power-1.html
Powercom and One Com	http://www.powercom.com/
PowerOn, Inc.	http://www.iwc.com/poweron/
PowerSoft Innovations: Timesaver Law Office Mngmt.	http://www.pris.bc.ca/pope/PowerSof.htm
PowerTrader	http://deepcove.com/powertrader/
PowerTV, Inc.	http://www.powertv.com/
PowerVar Canada	http://fox.nstn.ca/~powervar/
Praegitzer Industries Web Server	http://www.pii.com/
Praxis International	http://www.praxisint.com/
PRC Inc.	http://www.c3i.wsoc.com/
PRC Inc.	http://www.prc.com/
Pre-Driven Software	http://www.mcs.net/~kevinkj/predrivn.html
Precision Computers Inc.	http://www.teleport.com/~daj/
Precision Digital Images	http://www.precisionimages.com
Precision Microtech Computers	http://www.aisbbs.is.net/pmhome.htm
Precision Software	http://www.charm.net/~ibc/ibc2/precisn.html
Preferred Data	http://www.ramp.com/~cdrom/index.html
Preferred net.Shopper	http://www.preferred.com/shop/index.html
Preferred Solutions Ltd	http://www.maui.net/~russf/ps.html
Premier Computer Source, Inc.	http://www.onramp.net/issb/Directory/ads/premier/
PREP Software	http://www.prepsoft.com/prep/
PrePress Works	http://www.oktasys.fi/prepress/main.htm
Press Releases	http://www.olivetti.com/press.htm
Presslink	http://www.algonet.se/~lysell/

Presto Studios	http://www.prestostudios.com/
Pride Saver	http://www.gayweb.com/201/prdsvr.html
Prime Time Freeware	http://www.cfcl.com/ptf/
Primetime Medical Software, Inc	http://www.scsn.net/~primetim/
Principia Consulting	http://www.cs.colorado.edu/homes/wagner/public_html/
Printer Works	http://www.printerworks.com/index.html
Printerm Data Limited	http://bisinc.com/printerm/
Printers	http://www.starnetinc.com/magtech/home.html
PRISM Communications	http://www.tiac.net/users/cody/index.html
Prism Technologies Limited	http://www.prismtech.co.uk/
PrivaSoft	http://www.megasoft.com/privasoft/
Pro Consultants, Inc.	http://www.homestar.com/procon/
Pro Systems, Inc.	http://www.cybernetics.net/users/prosys/psi.html
Problem Knowledge Couplers	http://www.echonyc.com/~willie/homepkc.html
Process Analysts, Inc.	http://www.pai-colo.com/pai/
Process Plant CAD / CAE Design & Analysis Software	http://www.worldserver.pipex.com/nc/Sidewinder/index.htm
Procom Technology	http://www.procom.com
Procyon Systems	http://www.gate.net/~procyon/
Prode	http://www.prode.milano.it/prode.html
ProDesign Corp.	http://prodesign.com/
Productivity Point International / Technology Point, Inc.	http://www.techpoint.com/training.html
Professional Engineering & Communication Inc. (PEAC)	http://www.peac.com/
Professional Interactive Chinese for Windows	http://www.agoralang.com:2410/venturetech.html
Professional Sound and Music	http://prosound.connectnet.com/
Programmer's Warehouse	http://www.programmer.com/
Progressive Computer Services	http://www.humankind.com/pcs/pcshome.htm
Progressive Computer Services	http://www.wisdom.com/sv/
Progressive Media Arts	http://www.well.com/user/khampton/PMA.htm
Project Visions	http://www.infomatch.com/~chick/projvisn.htm
Promise Technology, Inc.	http://www.promise.com/
Promptus Communications	http://www.promptus.com/promptus/
ProQMS, Software Development	http://www.magicwindows.com/~mwinfo/proqms/
PROSIDE computer corp	http://www.proside.co.jp/
ProSoft Consulting	http://www.escape.com/~prosoft/consult.htm
ProSoft International, Inc.	http://www.webcom.com/~prosoft/
Protel Technology, Inc.	http://www.protel.com/
PSC Asia Pacific	http://www.psc.com.au/
PSC Systems	http://www.psclan.com/
PSI Technologies Corporationes	http://www.psiaustin.com/
PSI-Squared, Ltd.	http://www.inovatec.com/psi
PSi2	http://www.psi2.com
PT Diagnostic Software	http://cybermart.com/paintac/paintac.html
Pulsonic Corporation	http://www.pulsonic.com/
Punch Deck Consulting	http://www.halcyon.com/hawkfish/PunchDeck.html
Punto Soft International cd-rom Italy	http://www.eclipse.it/puntosoft/
PVCS	http://www.intersolv.com/pvcs.html

Q	
Q Group, The	http://www.dfw.net/~tqg/
Q-Data, Incorperated	http://norden1.com/~qdi/qdi.html
QAD Inc.	http://www.qad.com/
Qbik Software	http://nz.com/NZ/Commerce/creative-cgi/special/qbik/
QED Information Sciences, Inc.	http://www.shore.net/~qed/qed1.htm
QED Software Solutions Ltd.	http://www.corpinfohub.com/qed.htm
Qlogic	http://www.qlc.com/
Quadbase	http://www.quadbase.com/quadbase.htm
Quadralay	http://www.quadralay.com/
Quadrus Computer Technologies	http://www.worldlink.ca/Quadrus/
Qualitas, Inc.	http://www.qualitas.com/
Qualitas Trading Company	http://www.holonet.net/qualitas/
Qualitative Solutions & Research Pty/Ltd	http://qsr.latrobe.edu.au/
Quality America Incorporated	http://www.theriver.com/qa-inc/
Quality Checked Software, Ltd.	http://www.teleport.com/~qcs/
Quality HiTec Services	http://www.qhs.com/
Quality Management Services	http://www.wp.com/qms/home.html
Quality Software Management	http://www.utopia.com/companies/qsm/home.html
Quality Software Products	http://www.qsp.co.uk
Quality Systems, Inc.	http://www.aboveall.com/qsi/index.htm
Quanser Consulting	http://netaccess.on.ca/~quanser/
Quantex Microsystems Inc.	http://www.qtx.com/
QuantumWave Interactive	http://www.magic.ca/~qwi/
Quark, Inc.	http://www.quark.com/
Quasarmetrics Ltd.	http://www.cimteg.ists.ca/corp/quasar/quasar.html
Que Computers	http://loonlink.com/que/
Quest Software Inc.	http://quests.com/
Queue Systems, Inc.	http://www.queuesys.com/
QuickMedia	http://www.quickmedia.com
QuickResponse Services	http://www.inetbiz.com/qrsi/
Quicktime VR Service	http://www.kwanza.com/~embleton/service.html
Quinn-Curtis, Inc.	http://205.199.112.21/~quinn/index.html
Qume Corporation	http://www.batnet.com/qume/
Quyen Systems	http://www.level.com/netviz/
QwikShop	http://205.139.129.111/q/qwikshop/default.htm

R	
R & W Techinical Services	http://www.econonet.com/r&w/index.html
R C Systems, Inc.	http://ifu.ifu.net/html/tech/rcs/rcs.html
R R Systems Group	http://www.rrgroup.com/
R&D Networking, Inc.	http://www.premier.net/rdnet.html
R. A. Vess Enterprises	http://www.infi.net/~ravess/index.html
R. Altman and Associates	http://www.altman.com/~rick/
R. Frazier, Inc.	http://www.bnt.com/~rfrazier/
R.I.S Technologies	http://www.ris.fr/

r.u.there?	http://www.personalnet.com/
R2M Software Company	http://www.csn.net/~rmashlan/
RABA Technologies, Inc.	http://www.raba.com/
Racal-Datacom	http://www.racal.com/
Ractek	http://www.digiweb.com/rose/ractek/
RAD Technologies, Inc.	http://www.batnet.com/RAD/
RAD Technologies, Inc.	http://www.rad.com/
Radiance Software International	http://www.radiance.com/~radiance/
Radius	http://www.radious.com/
Rainbow Technologies	http://www.rnbo.com/
Rambus Inc.	http://www.best.com/~rambus/
Ramworks	http://www.ramworks.com/ramworks/
Raosoft, Inc.	http://www.halcyon.com/raosoft/
RapidFire Software, Inc.	http://www.teleport.com/~sven/rapid.html
Raptor Systems, Inc	http://www.raptor.com/
Rational Software Corporation	http://www.rational.com/
Rave Computer Association, Inc.	http://www.rave.net/
Raw Bits Corp.	http://www.rawbits.com/RawBits/
Raxco Inc.	http://www.raxco.com/
Raymond Software, Inc.	http://www.raysoft.com/
RE/COM Group, Inc.	http://www.recom.com/
Ready-Made SoftWare	http://www.mind.net/gallery/
Ready-to-Run Software	http://www.rtr.com/
ReadySoft Incorporated	http://www.tcn.net/~readysoft/
Reale Informatica S.r.l.	http://www.reale.it/
Reality Interactive	http://www.purple.co.uk/purplet/reality/
Reality Online	http://www.moneynet.com/
RealTech Systems Corporation	http://www.realtech.com/realtech/
RealTime Consulting, Inc.	http://www.doit.com/realtime/
Reasoning Systems	http://mosaic.reasoning.com/home.html
REC Communications	http://www.reccom.com/
Red Hat Software	http://www.redhat.com/
RedLeaf Software	http://www.cam.org/~dsavic/
Redwing Computers	http://www.redwing.on.ca/rw-home.html
Reese Web, Inc.	http://www.tampaweb.com/ReeseWeb/
Reflections Software	http://www.acm.org/~cgrosvenor/Reflect.html
Reggio Citta degli Studi	http://www.rcs.re.it/
Reveal	http://www2.pcy.mci.net/marketplace/reveal
Relation Systems, Inc.	http://www.relation.com/
Relational Information Systems, Inc.	http://wl.iglou.com/ris/
Relativity	http://www.liant.com/rel/
Reliable Software Technologies Corporation	http://www.access.digex.net/~rst/
Reliance Consulting, Inc.	http://paradise.net/reliance/
Remedy Corporation	http://www.remedy.com/
Remote Access Security	http://www.cyno.com/cyno/
Removable Disk Drive Subsystems, Raid Systems	http://pmctech.com/

363

Renascence Partners Limited	http://www.rpl.com/index.html
Render-Cam Images	http://www.crl.com/~rci/rci.htm
Reply Corporation	http://www.reply.com/
Research Dynamics	http://www.txdirect.net/resdyn/
Research Machines	http://www.rmplc.co.uk/
Resource Solutions, Inc.	http://www.tiac.net/users/rsi/
Responsive Software	http://www.holonet.net/responsive/
Retix Web	http://www.retix.com/
Reveal Computer Products	http://www2.pcy.mci.net/marketplace/reveal/
Revered Technology, Inc.	http://www.azc.com/client/rti/
Revision Control Engine	http://www.xcc-ka.de/RCE/RCE.html
Revision Labs, Inc.	http://www.teleport.com/~rli/
REXX Reference Summary Handbook	http://www.cfsrexx.com/rrsh-3/welcome.htm
ReZrVoir	http://www.commerce.com/ReZrVoir/RZV_top.html
Rezun Interactive Concepts, Inc.	http://www.kcilink.com/rezun/
Rhino Development Group	http://www1.tecs.com
Richard A. Wells Consulting	http://www.tiac.net/users/raw/
Right to Left Software	http://www.execpc.com/~rtls/
Rightway Computer Training Centers, Inc.	http://www.primenet.com/~rctc/
Rimrock Software	http://www.iea.com/~michaelb/
RingMaster	http://www.accessone.com/ringmaster/
RISCmanagement	http://www.riscman.com/
Ritronics Components Ltd.	http://www.singnet.com.sg/~ritron/memory.htm
Rnet	http://www.edb.com/rnet/index.html
Robert McNeel & Associates	http://www.mcneel.com/
Robert Parlato Consulting	http://pages.prodigy.com/CA/rparlato/HomePage.html
Robinson Solutions, Inc.	http://www.webcom.com/~rsinc/
Robotica Automation Consultants, Inc.	http://www.tiac.net/users/robotica/index.html
Rochester Project	http://www.embark.com/rochproj/
Rocket Lab	http://www.aimnet.com/~blastoff/ROCKET_Lab.html
Rockwell Telecommunications	http://www.nb.rockwell.com
Rockware Europe	http://www.bart.nl/~rockware/
Rockwell Collins Printed Circuits	http://www.rockwell.com/rockwell/bus_units/cca/cpc/
Rocky Mountain Digital Peeks	http://www.csn.net/malls/rmdp/
Rocky Mountain Multimedia	http://www.rockmedia.com/multimedia/
Rocky Mountain Multimedia	http://www.rockmedia.com/multimedia/
Rocky Mountain Systems	http://www.rmsd.com/
Rollins Information Technology Services	http://www.direct.ca/hss/rollins/
Rooney & Associates, LTD	http://www.mirical.com/site/SC/SurplusCity.html
Round Lake Publishing	http://www.starbyte.com/roundlake.html
Royston Development	http://www.routesmart.com/distinct/
RTCC	http://www.maple.net/rtcc/homepage/rtcchome.html
RTS Distributors Limited	http://rtsdist.com/rtsdist/
RTZ Software	ftp://ftp.netcom.com/pub/rt/rtz/www/rtzhomepage.html
Rudberg Computer Management	http://aristotle.algonet.se/~mikaelr/
Running Man Computer Services	http://rampages.onramp.net/~fezziksa/

RVIN Development	http://www.ecenter.com/rvin/main.html
RVIN Development	http://www.ecenter.com/rvin/main.html
Ryan McFarland	http://www.liant.com/rm/

S

S&S International PLC	http://www.sands.com
S.M. Business Solutions Limited	http://www.smsolutions.com/
S.P.C. Microcomputer	http://www.primenet.com/~spc/
SACO	http://www.ufra.net/markt/saco/
SACO Software and Consulting	http://www.ufra.net/markt/saco/
Safari Media (tm)	http://www.safari-media.com/
Safe Software Inc.	http://www.wimsey.com/~infosafe/
SafeSite	http://www.maagnum.com/safesite.html
Sage Solutions, Inc.	http://www.sagesoln.com/
SAIC Wateridge - Computer Security	http://mls.saic.com/
Saiga Systems	http://www.saiga.com/
SalesToolz, Inc.	http://www.primenet.com/~stz/
SAMSoftware Creation, Inc.	http://www.mindspring.com/~drglance/SAMS.html
San Francisco Canyon Compan	http://www.sfcanyon.com/
San Francisco Digital Media Center	http://www.well.com/www/sfdmc/
San Gabriel Custom Fontologists	http://www.tpoint.net/sgcf/
Sanctuary Woods Multimedia	http://www.sanctuary.com/
Sand Dollar Software, Inc.	http://tribeca.ios.com/~sanddllr/
Sanda International Corp.	http://www.versalink.com
Sanders, Christopher B.	http://www.io.com/~csanders/
SAP AG	http://www.sap-ag.de/
Sara Systems	http://www.sara.com/sara-systems/
Saratoga CADD Service	http://www.infovantage.com/scs/
Satori Software	http://www.satorisw.com/satori/
Save On Software	http://www.webstreetmall.com/mall/sos.html
SBE, Inc	http://www.sbei.com/
SBI Computer Distribution	http://www.the-wire.com/SBI/
Scala Computer Television	http://www.scala.com/scala/Welcome.html
Scala Computer Television AS (Norway)	http://scala-gw.anima.no/
Scandia data Computer Exchange	http://www.teleport.com/~peterwdp/
Scandinavian PC Systems, Inc.	http://www.tyrell.net/~spcsinc/
Scandinavian Softline Technology	http://www.softline.fi/
ScanLAN	http://scanlan.com/
Scatliff And Associates	http://www.mbnet.mb.ca/~scatliff/
SCEPTRE	http://www.gus.com/emp/sceptre/sceptre.html
Schaffer Consulting	http://www.schaffer.com/
Schema Research Corp., Database Intelligent Software	http://www.SchemaResearch.com/
Schofield Computer Organization	http://fox.nstn.ca/~rschofie/index.html
Scholastic Central	http://www.scholastic.com/
Science Applications International Corp. Ideas Group	http://baretta.ideas.com/
Science Education Software Inc.	http://www-leland.stanford.edu/~lefig/index.html

Science Software	http://www.rahul.net/resource/regular/products/sci-soft/
SciTech International	http://www.scitechint.com/scitech/
SCS Inc.	http://www.scsinet.com/
SCSI Peripherals / WHOLESALE	http://cybermart.com/scuzzy/index.html
SDI	http://www.demon.co.uk/sdi/
Sea Change Corporation	http://www.netjobs.com/seachange.html
Sea Change Corporation	http://www.seawest.seachange.com/
Seagate	http://www.seagate.com/
Searchlight BBS	http://www.netins.net/showcase/fidonet/slbbs.htm
SeaSpace	http://www.seaspace.com/
Seattle Lab	http://www.seattlelab.com/
Second Nature Software, Inc.	http://www.secondnature.com/
Second Source Used Computers	http://www.magpage.com/ssource/
Sector Zero, Produtos Informaticos Lda	http://www.telepac.pt/softfax/sectorz/szerindx.html
Sector7	http://www.sector7.com/
Secure Computing Corporation	http://www.sctc.com/
Secure Document Systems	http://www.sds4micr.com/
SecurePay	http://www.securepay.com/
SecureWare, Inc.	http://www.secureware.com/
Security Engineering Services, Inc.	http://www.blackmagic.com/ses/ses.html
SEIKO EPSON	http://www.epson.co.jp/
SelfGrow Ltd.	http://www.internet-eireann.ie/SelfGrow/default.htm
Sema Group Konsult AB	http://www.sema.se/
SEMS electronics	http://www.clinet.fi/~seng/index.html
Sequent Computer Systems, Inc.	http://www.sequent.com/public/index.html
Sequential Systems Inc.	http://www.hypermall.com/sequential/
Sequiter Software	http://www.supernet.ab.ca/Mall/Computer/Sequiter/
Serif, Inc.	http://www.serif.com/
Serious Developments	http://www.viper.net/clients/serious/
Servasure Systems, Inc.	http://web.ixl.net:8000/Servasure/
Servicios en Informatica	http://serinf.com/aitool.html
SeXXy Software	gopher://ftp.std.com/11/vendors/sexxy-software
SFA DataComm, Inc.	http://www.sfa.com/
SGI Power Computing	http://www.sgi.com/Products/hardware/Power/index.html
SGO Limited	http://cruzio.com/bus/computers/sgo/sgo.html
Shadow Island Games	http://www.pbm.com/
Shana Corporation	http://www.shana.com/
Shareware For Less	http://www.crl.com/~software/sharewar.htm
Shatz Creations Ltd.	http://www.shatz.co.uk
ShebutQ	http://shebute.com/Home.HTML
Shewey Enterprises Inc.	http://www.slip.net/~shewey/
Shiva	http://www.shiva.com/
Shuss Systems Inc.	http://www.interactive.net/~is/
Shuttle Systems International	http://www.worldlink.ca/~shuttle/
SIB Labs	http://www.dnai.com/~spudde/
Sidea	http://www.sidea.com/

Siemens Nixdorf	http://www.sni.de/public/its/offers/its-13.htm
Sierra On-line	http://www.sierra.com/
Sietec Document Management and Archives	http://www.sietec.de/arc/arc.en
SIG Computer	http://www.wwww.com/sig/
Sight & Sound Software, Inc.	http://www.sight-n-sound.com/~sss/
Sigma Computer Training	http://www.sigma.unb.ca/sigma/sigma.htm
Sigma6	http://www.sigma6.com/s6/
Sikander Associates	http://168.187.100.37/
SiliconSoft	http://he.tdl.com/~silicons/
SilverWare Inc.	http://rampages.onramp.net/~silver/
SimmSaver Technology, Inc.	http://www.dtc.net/vm/simmsaver/top.html
Simon Fraser University Microcomputer Store	http://microstore.ucs.sfu.ca/
SimPhonics, Inc.	http://www.simphonics.com/
Simple Solutions	http://www.locally.com/~simple/
Simple Technology Inc.	http://www.simpletech.com/
Simply Computing	http://aws2.cybernet.ca/egate/simply/simply.html
Simucad	http://www.simucad.com/
Simulation Resources, Inc.	http://www.sri.andrews.edu/
Simulation Technologies Corp.	http://www.winternet.com/~simtech/
SimulTrans, LLC	http://www.simultrans.com/
SINET and ICL Sorbus (Dutch)	http://www.sinet.nl/
SIO Technologies Corp.	http://www.sio.com/
Sirius Business Accounting	http://www.siriusacct.com/sirius/
Sirius Solutions UNIX Store	gopher://sirius1.sirius.ns.ca/
Sistemas de Tecnologfa Avanzada	http://www.sta.sistecol.com/
SITE Computer Services Inc.	http://www.ansa.com/~site/home.html
SITE Computer Services Inc.	http://www.ansa.com/~site/home.html
Skidperfect Software	http://www.shore.net/~chanson/
Skylink Limited, Inc.	http://web.syr.edu/~jslinder/slink.html
Skylonda Group	http://www.skylonda.com/skyhome.html
Sleepless Software	http://www.xmission.com/~nosleep/
SMA Computers,Inc.	http://www.iglou.com/smacomputers/
Small World Software	http://www.smallworld.com/
Smart Books Inc.	http://www.carmelnet.com/SBI/
Smart Micro Computers	http://www.pic.net/uniloc/smart/
SmartShopper Concept	http://www.netaxs.com/people/jhouston/
SmartWorks	ftp://ftp.netcom.com/pub/sm/smartguy/smart.html
SmartWorks	http://www.smartworks.com/catalog/
Smithmicro	http://www.smithmicro.com/
Smoke N' Mirrors, Inc.	http://www.snm.com/
SMRC	http://sweb.srmc.com/srmc/banking.html
SMS	http://www.u-net.com/~compsec/
SMTnet, Inc.	http://www.smtnet.com/
SNA, Inc.	http://www.gate.net/~dransen/SNA.html
SNC International	http://www.sncint.com/sncint/home.html
So Cal Graphics	http://turnpike.net/emporium/S/socal/index.html

Socrates Group, Inc.	http://www.socrates.com/socrates/Index.html
Sofgry Systems	http://www.sofgry.com/Sofgry/
Sofitec S.A.	http://www.sofitec.lu/
Soft-One ClassAct Multimedia	http://www.itsnet.com/classact/index.html
Softbank Corporation	http://www.softbank.co.jp/
SoftCentre Inc.	http://www.eclipse.net/~softcent/
Softdisk Publishing	http://www.softdisk.com/
Softfax	http://www.telepac.pt/softfax/softfax/softindx.html
SoftLinx, Inc. - Enterprise-wide network fax solution	http://www.softlinx.com/
Softmart, Inc.	http://www.softmart.com/
Softool Corporation	http://www.softool.com/
SoftPlan Systems	http://www.softplan.com/websoft
SoftSearch	http://giant.mindlink.net/tia/d_softsearch/
SoftSell Business Systems Inc.	http://www.softsell.com/
SoftSmith Systems Inc.	http://www.inforamp.net/~softsmit/index.htm
Software America, Inc.	http://www.xnet.com/~sai/
Software by Mail	http://www.ozemail.com.au/~swbymail/
Software Clearing House	http://www.sch.com/
Software Construction Co.	http://theyellowpages.com/scc.com/index.htm
Software Consulting Services	http://nscs.fast.net/
Software Design Consultants	http://www.soft-design.com/softinfo/sdc.html
Software Dynamics Consulting	http://www.sdcnet.com/
Software Engineers	http://www.fairfield.com/lwr/
Software ETC	http://www.scott.net/~sw-etc/index.html
Software Express	http://www.he.net/~se/
Software Innovations Incorporated	http://www.innov.com/
Software Magic, Inc.	http://www.rust.net/~lbloom/
Software Net	http://software.net/
Software of the Month Club	http://www.cts.com/browse/somc/theclub.html
Software On-Line	http://www.swol.com/
Software Products International	http://www.cts.com/~spi/
Software Publishers Association	http://www.spa.org/
Software Publishing Corporation	http://www.spco.com/
Software Solutions	http://www1.usa1.com/~softsol/index.htm
Software Solutions Inc.	http://www.gmcclel.bossnt.com/ssi/
Software Spectra	http://www.teleport.com/~sspectra/
Software Tailors	http://www.traveller.com/~rew/tailors.html
Software Technology	http://www.netvoyage.net/~softtech/index.html
Software Testing Laboratories	http://www.stlabs.com/
Software Tools for Artists	http://webcom.com/~stfa/
Software Vend Kiosk	http://www.eskimo.com/~bookie/contents.htm
Software Vendor Systems Center (SVSC)	http://www.svo.com/
Software.com Inc.	http://www.software.com/
Softway Pty. Limited	http://www.softway.com.au/
Softwords Research International Ltd.	http://www.softwords.bc.ca/Softwords.html
Solid Oak Software, Inc.	http://www.rain.org/~solidoak/

Solsource Computers	http://www.solsource.com/
SolTech Systems Corporation	http://www.soltech.com/
SoluTech	http://www.mo.net/solutech/
Solution	http://www.solution.de
Somar Software	http://www.somar.com/
Sonda, S.A.	http://www.sonda.cl/
Sonic Computers	http://www.human.com/sonicc/
Sonoquest Software	http://www.southwind.net/~smiller/
Sony Electronic Publishing	http://www.sepc.sony.com/SEPC/index.html
Sophos Plc	http://www.sophos.com/
Sorrell Enterprises	http://www.maple.net/rtcc/sorrell/index.html
SOUM Corporation	http://www.soum.co.jp/
SourceCraft/Real Software Solutions, Inc.	http://www.rss.com/
South Hills Datacomm	http://www.shillsdata.com/
Southam, Inc.	http://www.southam.com/
Spanlink Communications	http://www.splk.com/
SPARTA, Inc.	http://www.huntsville.sparta.com/
Special Form Software	http://www.specialform.com/sfs/welcome.html
Specialized Business Solutions	http://www.some.com/sbs/
Specialized Technologies	http://gcn.scri.fsu.edu/~alexand/stech.html
Specs(tm) Manufacturing Instructions	http://www.sonic.net/~richw/zip.html
Specter, Inc.	http://www.specter.com/users/janos/specter/
Spectragraphics	http://www.spectra.com/
Spectral Research Technologies	http://www.tenn.com/srt/srt.html
Spectre Technical Services	http://www.sisna.com/tooele/spectre.htm
Spectrum Data Management, Inc.	http://www.infi.net/~spectrum
Spectrum PCUpgrades	http://www.pcupgrades.com/
Spectrum Trading	http://www.spectrum-t.com/
Specular International	http://www.specular.com/
Speech Systems, Inc.	http://www.speechsys.com/
Speedcom	http://www.netindex.com/speed.htm
SpeedSim, Inc.	http://www.speedsim.com/speedsim/
Sports Handicapper	http://www.gate.net/~rutech/
SportsPro Software	http://www.pacnet.ca./spro/
Spotlight Software, Inc.	http://www.dtc.net/vm/spotlight/
Sprague Magnetics	http://www.earthlink.net/~sprague-magnetics/
Springsoft Software On Demand	http://www.springsoft.com
SPRY	http://shopping2000.com/shopping2000/spry/spry.html
SPS Productions	http://www.spsp.com/
SQN Peripherals, Inc.	http://www.waterw.com/~bobt/index.html
SRA - Software Research Associates	http://www.sra.co.jp/
SRA International, Inc.	http://www.sra.com/
SRMC Spider Web	http://sweb.srmc.com/
SRMC's Calendar and Screen Saver Factory.	http://sweb.srmc.com/screen/
SST Inc.	http://www.webcom.com/~sstinc/
Stage Research, Inc.	http://www.usbusiness.com/stage/stage.html

StamiNet Inc.	http://www.staminet.com
Stancom Computing	http://www.iinet.com.au/~cstanley/
Standard Printed Circuits, Inc.	http://www.halcyon.com/rbormann/spc.htm
Star Electronics	http://www.homeless.com/homepages/bryano@gcomm.com.html
Star-Byte Shopping Mall	http://www.starbyte.com/mall.html
Stardock	http://oeonline.com/~stardock/
Stardust Technologies, Inc.	http://www.stardust.com/
Starfish Software	http://www.starfishsoftware.com/
Starks Multimedia Design	http://www.interport.net/~starks/
Starlight Mutlimedia	http://www.drtomorrow.com/drtomorrow/sl.html
Starlight Networks	http://www.starlight.com/
StarMan Group, Multimedia Productions	http://www.indirect.com/www/gstarman/
Starpoint Software	http://sage.cc.purdue.edu/~rpitteng
StarPress Multimedia	http://www.starpress.com/starpress/
Starr Labs	http://www.catalog.com/starrlab/
StarTech Consulting Services Inc.	http://www.apk.net/startech
Starvector Software	http://www.wolfe.net/~svector/sv.htm
Stat Tech	http://www.stattech.com.au/
State of the Art	http://www.gmcclel.bossnt.com/sota/
Station Graphics, Inc.	http://www.pic.net/~station/
STB Systems	http://www.stb.com/
Stealth Computers	http://www.aloha.com/~stealth/
STERIA	http://www.sis.steria.fr/
Sterling Information Group	http://www.sterinfo.com/
Steven M. Christensen and Associates	http://smc.vnet.net/Christensen.html
STG, Inc. - Axiom CASE Tools	http://www.stgcase.com/
Stirling Technologies, Inc.	http://www.stirling.com/
Stollmann ISDN E+V GmbH	http://www.stollmann.de/
Stonehand Inc.	http://www.stonehand.com/
StoneTablet Publishing	http://www.teleport.com/~stack/
StonyBrook Software	http://www.sbrook.com/
Storage Dimensions, Inc.	http://galahad.xstor.com/
Storage Systems Solutions	http://www.ell.com/
Straight Line Medium, Inc.	http://www.infi.net/~slm/
Strata Inc.	http://www.sci.dixie.edu/StrataInc/Home/home.html
Strategic Mapping	http://www.stratmap.com/
Strategic Networks Consulting, Inc.	http://www.snci.com/
Strategic Systems, Inc.	http://www.ssiinc.com/
Stratford Healthcare Management & EDI Software	http://www.stratfordsoftware.com/
Strawberry Tree, Inc.	http://www.strawberrytree.com/
Structured Communications Systems	http://www.structured.com/
Stryder Communications, Inc.	http://www.strydr.com/
STS - Scientific Technical Services	http://www.alaska.net/~lafferty/sts.html
STS Film/Video Production	http://www.xmission.com/~stsfilm/
Studentlitteratur Software	http://www.studli.se/
Studio Audio-SADiE & Octavia Web Site	http://194.72.60.96/www/sadie/

Stylus Innovation, Inc.	http://northshore.shore.net/~stylus/
Subiaco Computer Warehouse	http://www.iinet.com.au/~scw/
Subtle Software	http://world.std.com/~subtle/index.html
Sumeria Product List	http://www.service.com/D3/sumeria/sumeria.html
Summit Software Company	http://www.summsoft.com/
Summit Software Services	http://www.teleport.com/~gregman/summit.shtml
Sun Remarketing, Inc.	http://www.sunrem.com/
Sunbelt Software Distribution	http://www.opennet.com/ntsoftdist/
SunExpress	http://www.sun.com/sunexpress/
Sunnyside Computing, Inc.	http://sunnyside.com/
Sunnyside Software	http://www.adirondack.net/ind/sside.html
Sunquest Information Systems	http://www.sunquest.com/
Sunrise Door Software	http://www.oknet.com/sunrise.html
Super Simple Software	http://www.primenet.com/~glencj/
Superlative Software Solutions	http://www.cat.syr.edu/3Si/
Supra Corporation	http://www.supra.com/
Supra FTP Archive [halcyon.com]	ftp://ftp.halcyon.com/pub/supra/
Supra FTP Server	ftp://ftp.supra.com/
Supro Network Software Inc.	http://www.msen.com/~snsi/
SURE BET	http://www.tiac.net/users/phepp/index.html
SureFind Corp	http://www.surefind.com/
SurfWatch Software	http://www.surfwatch.com/
Sv-Communication Oy	http://www.solutions.fi/svcomm/
SVEC Computer Corporation	http://www.svec.com/
SW International Systems Pte Ltd	http://www.swi.com.sg/
Swan Technologies	http://www.tisco.com/swan/
Swansystems Oy	http://www.inet.tele.fi/classified/swan.html
SWH Technology	http://www.tech.swh.lv/
SWLi, Inc.	http://www.iusa.net/swl/lets.htm
SYEX Express	http://www.syex.com/
Sygma United Inc.	http://www.vir.com/~sygma/index.htm
Symantec	http://www.symantec.com
Symbios Logic	http://www.symbios.com/
Symbol Technologies	http://www.symbol.com/
SymCon Software	http://www.interlog.com/~symcon/
Symplex ISDN Routers with Ethernet Interfaces	http://www.iea.com/~symplex/
Symplex Software Systems, Inc.	http://www.woodtech.com/~kanderson/
Synapse Communications, Inc.	http://www.synapse.com/
Sync Limited UK Multimedia Design	http://www.custard.co.uk/w3service/sync/
Syndesis Corporation	http://www.webmaster.com/syndesis/
Synergetic Micro Systems	http://www.synergetic.com/
Synergetic Resource Corporation	http://www.synernet-indy.com/src/
Synergy Computer Consulting	http://giant.mindlink.net/tia/d_synergy/
Synergy Peephole	http://www.eirenet.net/cork/synergy/
Synergy Technology Systems	http://www.netaxs.com/~jcostom/synergy.html
Syntactica	http://www.syntactica.co.za/

371

Syntax	http://www.syntax.com/
Syspro IMPACT Software	http://www.ni.net/sysprousa.com/
SysTeam Technology Support Division	http://www.systeam.traveller.com/
Systech Data Systems	http://www.sentex.net/~systech/
System Concepts, Inc.	http://www.teleport.com/~drgreen/index.html
System Performance Consultants	http://www.wco.com/~spc/index.html
System Resources Corporation	http://www.srcorp.com/
System/ID Warehouse Catalog	http://www.SystemID.com
Systemcorp	http://www.systemcorp.com/index.html
Systemetrics, Inc.	http://system.com/
Systems Alliance, Inc.	http://www.access.digex.net/~golshan/alliance.html
Systems and Programming Solutions Inc.	http://www.execpc.com/~spsi
Systems Consulting Group	http://www.scg-net.com/
Systems Modeling Corp.	http://www.sm.com
Systems Partners Inc.	http://www.syspart.com/
Systems Resources Consulting, Inc.	http://www.mcs.net/~office/
SYWARE, Inc.	http://www.syware.com/

T

T 'n D Graphics Ltd.	http://www.islandnet.com/~sbaril/
T.E.A.M. Work	http://teamwork.inc.net/
T.H.I.S Computer Solution	http://this.com/
T3plus	http://www.t3plus.com/
T4 Computer Security	http://www.nuance.com/~fcp/
Tabo Software	http://www.planetcom.com/tabo/
TAC Systems	http://www.tacsys.com/
Tachyon Technology	http://www.eskimo.com/~zoey/tachyon/
Tadpole Technology	http://www.tadpole.com/
TAE Plus	http://www.cen.com/tae/
Take 3 Software	http://www.take3soft.com/
Talent Communications, Inc.	http://www.talentcom.com/
Talis	http://www.talis.com/
Tangent Computer Inc.	http://www.tangent.com
Tanisys Technology	http://www.tanisys.com/
Tanner Computer Contracts	http://www.emj.ca/emj/mtanner/tcchome.html
Tantra Computers	http://www.hub.co.uk/intercafe/tantra/tantra_home.html
Tasco Online	http://www.tasco.cl/
Tascomm Engineering	http://www.tascomm.fi/
Tatro Enterprises	http://iquest.com/~btatro/
Taxprep Information Systems	http://www.taxprep.com/
TCP3270 for Windows	http://www.3270.McGill.CA/
TCybernetic Solutions Company	http://www.xmission.com/~cyberman/
TD Technologies, Inc.	http://www.slate.tdtech.com/
Teaching Technology, Inc.	http://www.teachtech.com/~teach
Team America	http://www.vir.com/JAM/team.html
Team Evil	http://www.pt.hk-r.se/~pt94rfe/TeamEvil/TeamEvil.html

Team17 Software Ltd.	http://www.team17.com/
TEAMS: Marketing and Sales Assessment Software	http://mtg-teams.com
TEC Solutions	http://www.tecs.com/tecs
Tech 2000 Pty Ltd	http://www.ozemail.com.au/~tech2000/
Tech Assist, Inc	http://www.gate.net/~wun4all/techass.htm
Tech Knowledge Development Corporation	http://www.icis.on.ca/homepages/tkmbhome/
TECHCO - Global IT Search and Consulting Services	http://www.primenet.com/~techco/
Technetix, Inc.	http://teknetix.com/
Technical Hypermedia	http://www.ttl.fi/abut/
Technical Intelligence	http://www.winternet.com/~techint/
Technical Solutions, Inc.	http://www.entrepreneurs.net/tsol/
TechnoGraphy & Storage Computer in Japan	http://www.storage.com/japan.html
Technologic, Inc.	http://www.tlogic.com/
Technology Associates of Colorado	http://usa.net/tac/
Technology Board of Trade	http://www.tech-board.com/tbot/home.html
Technology Management Center	http://www.webcom.com/~spmi/
Technology Partners	http://homepage.interaccess.com/~tpart/
TechWin	http://www.reconfig.com/techwin/techwin.html
TechWorks	http://www.techwrks.com/
TECnet	http://www.tecnet.org/
Tecnomatix Q.E.I.	http://www.valisys.com
Teknekron Software Systems	http://www.tss.com/
Teknema	http://www.teknema.com/
TeKnowlgy Education Centers	http://www.teknowlogy.com/teknowlogy/
Tekram Technology	http://www.tekram.com/
Tektronix Network Displays Division	http://www.tek.com/Network_Displays/
Telasar Computer Sales	http://www.telalink.net/telasar/index.html
Tele-Images	http://www.saic.com/products/tele-images/
Telecommunications Technology Corp.	http://soho.ios.com/~teltech/
Telemedia Roadhouse	http://www.telemedia.de/
Teletech Systems	http://www.mindspring.com/~fbunn/teletech.html
Telos Corporation - Pangaea	http://www.telos.com/Product/Pangaea/Pangaea.html
teltrust.com	http://www.teltrust.com/
Tempest /	http://www.tempest.dk/
Template Graphics Software, Inc.	http://www.cts.com/~template
TEN - Technology Education Network	http://www.stv.com/stv/
Tenadar Software	http://www.ipp.com/ipp/tenadar/tenadarhomepage.html
TENET Computer Group Inc.	http://www.tenet.com/
Tera Computer Company	http://www.net-serve.com/tera.html
TERMiTE from Pixel Innovations	http://www.pixel.co.uk/pixel/
Terra IncogNETa - Thayer Technologies, Inc.	http://www.vpm.com/tti/index.html
Terra Nova Data Solutions	http://www.teleport.com/~tnds/
Terra Nova Interactive	http://www.terranova.com/~sellers/
Tessera Solutions	http://www.io.org/~vanessa/
Tesseract	ftp://lia.infolink.co.za/pub/tesseract/tsrhome.htm
Tesseract Computer Systems and Software	http://tesseract.bc.ca/tnet/index.html

Tetrad Computer Applications	http://www.tetrad.com/
TGV, Inc Home Page	http://www.tgv.com/
The Cataloger	http://www.hummsoft.com/hummsoft/The_Cataloger.html
The CD-ROM Source	http://www.a1.com/cdrom/cdrom.html
The Computer Spectrum	http://www.mpcs.com/islandc/cspec
The Computersmith	http://www.wp.com/computersmith/
The Deck Designer	http://biz.rtd.com/nad/deck.html
The FIEN Group	http://nt.scbbs.com/tfg/
The Game Factory	http://www.gamefactory.com/
The Imagine Nation Multimedia, Inc.	http://www.usa1.com/nation/register.html
The Information Systems Manager, Inc.	http://www.infosysman.com/
The Internet Factory, Inc.	http://www.aristosoft.com/ifact/inet.htm
The Message Board System	http://www.netins.net/showcase/message/tmb.html
The Moore Company	http://www.europa.com/moore/
The Music Factory	http://pages.prodigy.com/MA/musicfactory/musicfactory.html
The Network Connection, Inc.	http://tnc.www.com/
The Numerical Algorithms Group Ltd	http://www.nag.co.uk:70/
The Plant Software, Inc.	http://www.theplant.com/
The Portland Group, Inc. (PGI)	http://www.pgroup.com/
The Public Access Company	http://uno.tc.net/~brian/paco.html
The Whole Shebang	http://www.shebang.com/
Thermal Solutions	http://www.sauna.com/tsi/
Thinking Pictures	http://www.thinkpix.com/
ThinkNet Inc.	http://www.thinknet.com/
ThinkPad Mobile Computing Center	http://www.wimsey.com/PacificaBlue/thinkpad/
Thinque Systems Corporation - Interactive Shopper	http://www.thinque.com/isis/
Thomas Computer Services	http://www.cquest.com/tcs.html
Thomas-Conrad Corporation	http://www.tci.com/
Thomson Software Products	http://www.thomsoft.com
ThoroVision	http://www.thorovision.com/
Thorware Systems Development	http://www.teleport.com/~thorware/
ThoughtWorks, Inc.	http://www.thoughtworks.com
ThreeToad Multimedia	http://www.halcyon.com/tritoad/
Thrustmaster	http://www.thrustmaster.com
ThunderBYTE	http://www.thunderbyte.com/
Thunderstone Software	gopher://thunder.thunderstone.com/
Thursby Software Systems, Inc.	http://www.thursby.com/
Tierra Software Systems	http://www.cyberspace.com/~tierra/
Tightrope Studios	http://www.tightrope.com/
TimeLess Technologies	http://www.isn.net/~jmacleod/
Times Int'l Computers	http://www.gus.com/emp/times/times.html
Times Mirror Higher Education Group	http://www.tmhe.com
Timeslips Corporation	http://www.timeslips.com/
TimeVision	http://www.timevision.com
TLG Electronics, Inc	http://www.infinet.com/~tlg/
TM Group, The	http://www.tmgroup.com/

Toad Computers	http://www.charm.net/~toad/
Toad Computers Atari Products	http://www.toad.net/atari/
Tools for OrCAD schematic capture	http://www.best.com/~pdornier/orcad.htm
Tools-of-the-Trade	http://www.uleth.ca/~pope
Top Of Mind Help Desk for Windows	http://www.planet.net/molloy/
Topaz-Inform	http://www.topaz.kiev.ua/UMT.html
TopForm	http://eshnav.com/topform/
Toronto Image Works	http://www.magic.ca/tiw/
Torque Systems	http://www.steam.com/Torque/
Toshiba	http://www.tais.com/
ToSoft	http://www.teleport.com/~tosoft/
Total Computer Systems	http://www.getnet.com/~halatos/halatos.html
Total Systems Inc.	http://www.lynqs.com/TSI/
Touch Technologies, Inc.	http://www.ttisms.com/
TouchPoint Interactive	http://www.merlin.com.au/touchpoint
TouchWindow	http://www.touchwindow.com/
Tower Concepts, Inc.	http://www.tower.com/
TOWER Software	http://www.towersoft.com.au/
Tower Technology Corporation	http://www.cs.cf.ac.uk/Tower/TowerHome.html
TRACO Sistemas de Mexico	http://www.spin.com.mx/traco/
Traffic Software	http://www.traffic.is/
TRAN Software Library	http://www.summitmedia.com/tran/index.htm
Trans World Laser Cartridge Recycling	http://www.westdat.com/~bburnett/wdcbp/twt/twt.html
Transarc Corporation	http://www.transarc.com/
Transcription Enterprises	http://www.te-cats.com/
TranSettlements Commerce Networking Services	http://www.transettlements.com.
TransLogic Computer	http://www.eskimo.com/~dakranz/tlc/tlc.html
Travis Computing	http://rampages.onramp.net/~reynolds/travis.html
Trax Softworks, Inc.	http://www.webcom.com/~traxsoft/
Treadwell Group	http://www.treadwell.com/
TRG Inc.	http://www.trglink.com/
Trident Sytems - Touchscreen Solutions	http://tridsys.com/CPG/
TriMetrix, Inc.	http://www.trimetrix.com/trimetrix/
Trinity Data Systems	http://www.trinity.com/
Trinity Software	http://www.hfk.com/webpages/trinity.html
Trinity Systems	http://www.demon.co.uk/trinity/index.html
Triple G Corporation	http://www.tripleg.com.au/
TRITEC Electronic GmbH	http://www.tritec.de/
Triticom	http://www.triticom.com
Tron BV	http://www.publishnet.nl/tron/
Troubador Systems	http://www.troubador.com/
True North Computer Services	http://www.brainlink.com/~north/
TSA Systems	http://www.tsa-sys.com/tsa/
TSP International	http://www.crl.com/~tspintl/
TTi Technologies, Inc.	http://www.hypermart.com/tti/default.htm
Tucker Information Systems	http://www.tyrell.net/~tucker/

Tulsa Chat	http://tonyt.galstar.com/chat.htm
Tumbleweed Software Corp.	http://www.twcorp.com/
Turbo-Doc Medical Records Software	http://www.jayi.com/jayi/turbodoc
Turbosales	http://www.turbosales.com/~turbos/info/index.html
Tuscan Consultants	http://www.limitless.co.uk/tuscan/
TVI Interactive Systems Inc.	http://www.tvinet.com/
TWE Enterprises	http://www.netindex.com/twe.htm
Twelve Hats Multimedia	http://monster.fiber.net/twelvehats/
Two Guys Named Hank	http://www.twohanks.com
Tybrin Corportation	http://www.cp.tybrin.com/
Typhoon Systems Inc.	http://www.magi.com/~gebara/

U

U-Design Type Foundry	http://gs1.com/UTF/UTF.html
U.S. Design Corporation	http://www.usdesign.com/
U.S. Email	http://205.254.224.2/~markg/usemail/
U.S. Micro	http://www.usmicro.com/
Ubi Soft	http://www.ubisoft.com/
UDP, Inc.	http://www.udp.com/
UgaliChat	http://netaccess.on.ca/ugali/chat/index.html
UK HDL Solutions Company	http://www.saros.co.uk/saros/
Ultimate Archive, The	http://www.hooked.net/ralgroup/
Ultra Technology	http://www.dnai.com/~jfox/
UltraData Credit Union Systems	http://www.ultradata.com/
UltraMedia Systems International	http://www.infi.net/~ums/
Ulysses Telemedia Networks	http://www.ulysses.net/
Unforgiven Productions	http://www.xmission.com/~unfo/
UNIBOL	http://www.unibol.com/
Unicom Electric, Inc.	http://www.webstorm.com/unicom/
Unicom Systems Development	http://www.unicom.com/
Unicomp, Inc.	http://www.fortran.com/fortran/unicomp.html
Unicon Conversion Technologies	http://www.cyberpages.com/db/company&1&67
Unified Micro Solution	http://www.unimic.com/
UniForum Professional Training Series	http://www.uniforum.org/
UniLink Software, Inc.	http://www.unilink-inc.com/
UniPress Software - Development Tools	http://www.unipress.com/cat/development.html
Unisoft System	http://unisoft-system.com/net/
Unitec CADKEY DataCAD Dimension Guru	http://www.unitec.com/
United Computer Exchange Corp. (UCE)	http://www.uce.com/
United Computer Group, Inc.	http://www.electriciti.com/~mario/
United Parts Center	http://www.ccnet.com/~winstock/upc.htm
Unitrendix Corporation	http://www.unitrx.com/
Universal CD-ROM	http://www.bigmall.com/
Universal Design	http://www.digifax.com/info
Universal Interactive Systems	http://www.primenet.com/~vladi/
Universal Networks, Inc.	http://www.uninet.com/

Unixpac Pipeline	http://www.unixpac.com.au/
Untangle Incorporated	http://www.io.org/~untangle/unthome.html
Up Front Multimedia	http://north.pacificnet.net/~upfront/
Up Software, Inc.	http://www.dnai.com/~upsoft/
Updata Electronic Catalog	http://www.updata.com/
Upham & Associates	http://www.sonic.net/~supham/
Uptime Computer Solutions, Inc.	http://www.uptime1.com/
US Computer Group	http://www.arcslide.com/c/USCG/USCG.HTM
US Robotics	http://www.usr.com/
Use Image Alchemy over the Web	http://www.handmadesw.com/hsi/web_alchemy.html/
Used Computers, Etc	http://www.xmission.com/~gastown/goldpages/used1.htm
Utility Cost Management, Inc.	http://www.halcyon.com/ucm/
Utopia Technology Partners Inc.	http://www.utosoft.com/~dennis/index.htm
UV&S	http://www.southwind.net/IMS/uv%2bs/catalog1/

V

V-COM Computers	http://www.iceonline.com/v-com/
V.H. Computer Systems	http://www.vhcs.com/
VA Research Inc.	http://www.varesearch.com/
ValCom PCC	http://www.pccval.com/
Validity Corporation	http://www.primenet.com/~valcorp/
Valinor Inc.	http://www.valinor.com/
Value-Ware Software	http://www.awa.com/nct/value/valulead.html
Van Dyke Technologies	http://www.vandyke.com/vandyke/
VanMing Inc.	http://www.eskimo.com/~vanming/
Vanstar Business Application Training	http://www.maui.net/~vanstar/training.html
Vantageware	http://www.vantageware.com/
Vasco Data Security, Inc.	http://www.vdsi.com/
VB Online	http://codd.com/vbonline/
VBxtras	http://www.vbxtras.com/
VCC Computer Catalog	http://www.infinet.com/~venkat/
Vector Technology	http://www.vector.com/
Vedacom Corporation	http://www.sirius.com/~alyon/VEDACOM/
VendorCrypt Secure WWW Software	https://wws.enterprise.net/iw/vcrypt.html
Venture Computer	http://www.venture.co.za/
Verbex Voice Systems	http://www.txdirect.net/verbex/
VeriSign, Inc.	http://www.verisign.com/
Verisoft Corporation	http://www.verisoft.com/
Veritas Software	http://www.veritas.com/
Vermeer Technologies, Inc.	http://www.vermeer.com
VersaFax	http://www.cosi.com/
Versys Corporation	http://www.versys.com/versys/
ViaCrypt	http://www.viacrypt.com/
Vibrant Graphics, Inc.	http://www.vibrant.com/
Vicon Computers	http://www.interactive.net/~vicon/
Vidar Systems Corporation	http://www.access.digex.net/~vidar/

Vidcom	http://www.nas.com/~jcofrin/
Video Images Inc.	http://www.videoimages.com/
Video On Line Mail	http://www.vol.it/UK/EN/MAIL/
Video Production	http://www.aloha.net/~zack/
Videodata Interactive Multimedia	http://snoopy.concom.com/videodata/
VideoServer, Incorporated	http://www.videoserver.com/
Viewpoint DataLabs	http://www.viewpoint.com/
Viewpoint Software Solutions	http://home.eznet.net/~viewpt/
Viewport Systems Inc.	ftp://ftp.netcom.com/pub/vi/viewport/viewport.html
ViewSoft, Inc.	http://www.viewsoft.com/
ViewSonic Corporation	http://www.viewsonic.com/
VIGA Technologies	http://www.viga.com/viga/
Viking Computers - UK	http://www.u-net.com/~vikingc/home.htm
ViON Corporation	http://www.vion.com/
Virage, Inc. Visual Information Retrieval	http://www.virage.com/
Vireo Software	http://world.std.com/~vireo
Virtek International 3D-Ware	http://www.virtek.com/virtek/
Virtual AdVEntures	http://www.virtualadventures.com/
Virtual Communications	http://www.slip.net/~wieneke/
Virtual Consultant	http://www.iquest.net/cw/VC/VC.html
Virtual Entertainment	http://www.cts.com/~vrman/
Virtual Media	http://www.iaw.on.ca/~virtualm/
Virtual Presence	http://www.neosoft.com/~gevans/virtpres.html
Virtual Publishing Company	http://www.accessone.com/~edmitch
Virtuality Entertainment, Inc.	http://www.metronet.com/~friend/virtalty.htm
VirtuREAL Communications	http://www.digimark.net/vr/
Virtus Corporation	http://www.virtus.com/
Visible Decisions Inc.	http://www.io.org/~vizbiz/
Visigenic	http://odbc.visigenic.com/
Vision Achiever	http://os2.iafrica.com/marksman/va.htm
Vision Communications Interactive	http://www.vcom1.com/vision/
Vision Connect GmbH	http://www.v-connect.com/
Vision Interactive Multimedia	http://www.calypso.com/vim/index.html
Vision Training & Technology, Inc.	http://www.vtt.com/
Vision XXI	http://www.hic.net/hicpersonal/d/vxxi2.html
Visionary Designs	http://www.visdesigns.com/
Visionary Solutions	http://www.visionary-solutions.com/
Visioneer	http://www.visioneer.com/
VisionTek	http://www.visiontek.com/
Visix Software Inc.	ttp://www.visix.com/
Visual Basic Online	http://www.vb-online.com/
Visual Frontiers	http://www.vfrontiers.com/~vfrntrs/
Visual Information Development, Inc.	http://erehwon.caltech.edu/vidi/vidi-homepage.html
Visual Numerics, Inc.	http://www.vni.com/
Visual Recall	http://www.xsoft.com/VR1.html
Visual SCCS	http://mirror.wwa.com/mirror/busdir/issl/issl.htm

Visual Solutions	http://www.ultranet.com/~peterd/index.html
Visualogic	http://www.visualogic.com/
VisualTek Solutions, Inc.	http://www.visualtek.com/
ViVi Software	http://www.dsnet.it/vivi/
Vizier Technologies	http://alfred1.u.washington.edu:8080/~neurom/index.html
VMS System Management Tools	http://www.tditx.com/
Voice Recognition Systems	http://iglou.com/vrsky/
Vox-L Inc.'s Home Page	http://www.dataspace.com/vox-l.html
Voyager	http://www.voyagerco.com/interface/gallery.cgi
VREAM	http://www.vream.com/
VSI	http://www.openstep.com/
Vulcan's Forge	http://www.vulcansforge.com/
VYSOR Integration Inc.	http://www.synapse.net/~vysor/welcome.htm

W

W3.COM, Inc.	http://w3.com/
Wachusett Programming Associates	http://www.iii.net/biz/wpa/
Wakebourne plc	http://www.cms.dmu.ac.uk/~gks/wakebourne/
Walker Interactive Systems	http://www.walker.com/
Walker, Richer & Quinn	http://wrq.com
Wall Data, Inc.	http://www.walldata.com/
Wall Street Software	http://www.fastlane.net/homepages/wallst/wallst.html
Wallingford Electronics	http://www.wallingford.com/
Ward Consulting, Inc.	http://www.ward.com/
wARE, Inc.	http://www.ware.com/
Warner Group	http://a092.sysplan.com/
WarnerActive	http://www.warneractive.com/
Warp California, Inc.	http://www.warp.com/
Washington Software Company	http://www.wsa.com/
Watcom	http://www.watcom.com/
Waterstone Consulting	http://www.interaccess.com/users/wtrstone/
Waytec Electronics	http://www.inmind.com/people/waytec/
WCCN Publishing	http://www.netins.net/showcase/wccn/
We Design, Inc.	http://www.we.com/info/we.html
Web Intertainment, Inc.	http://funstuff.com/
Web Page Builder	http://www.stpt.com/shc/wpb/
Webalog, Inc.	http://figment.fastman.com/vweb/html/vidmain.html
WebBase	http://www.expertelligence.com/webbase/
Weber Software and Consulting	http://www.electriciti.com/~wscs/index.html
WebFACTOR	http://www.cdc.net/~wfactor/
WebGenesis	http://www.webgenesis.com/webgenesis/default.html
WebTrack	http://www.webtrack.com/
WeirdStuff Warehouse, Inc.	http://www.weirdstuff.com/
Weitz, Paul	http://www.tiac.net/users/pweitz/
Welcom Software Technology	http://www.wst.com/index.html
Wen Technology Corp.	http://www.iiactive.com/wen/default.htm

West International	http://www.nettime.se/west
Westermann Associates, Inc.	http://mars.superlink.net/user/wwester/index.html
Western International Systems Education	http://imagineer.com/MARKETPLACE/WISE
Westwood Studios	http://www.westwood.com/
WGG	http://www.portal.com/~cbntmkr/utility.html
WH Networks	http://www.whnet.com/wolfgang/
Whirlwind Technologies	http://delta.com/wwtech/homepage.htm
Whirlwind Technologies	http://delta.com/wwtech/homepage.htm
White Pine Software	http://www.wpine.com/
White Pine Software	http://www.wpine.com/
White Pine Software	http://www.wpine.com/
Whittman-Hart IT Consulting	http://www.indy.whrt.com/
Whyte, Darcy	http://infoweb.magi.com/~dwhyte/INDEX.HTML
Wildcat Canyon Software	http://www.wildcat.com/
Williamson Imagineering	http://www.teleport.com/~stevew/index.html
Willow Glen Graphics	http://wgg.com/
Willow Opportunity Center	http://shebute.com/Projects/Willow/Willow.HTML
Willow Peripherals	http://willow.com/peripherals/
Willow Peripherals	http://willow.com/peripherals/
Willows Software	http://www.willows.com/
Wilson WindowWare, Inc.	http://oneworld.wa.com/wilson/pages/
Win/V: The Japanese Language Kit for Windows	http://www.gol.com/winv/winvhome.html
Wind River Systems	http://www.wrs.com/
Windata, Inc.	http://www.digital.com/gnn/bus/windata/index.html
Windows Internet Software	http://community.net/~csamir/pcapps.html
Windward Business Manager	http://awinc.com/windward/
Windward Technologies Inc.	http://www.ultranet.com/biz/windward/
WineBase for Windows	http://www.ozemail.com.au/~kentripp/index.html
WINGate Technologies	http://www.wingate.com
Wingra Technologies	http://www.wingra.com/
WinHealth Systems	http://www.infi.net/winhealth/
WinSell	http://daffy.cadvision.com/com/winsell/homepage.html
Winsor Computing	http://www1.usa1.com/~dwinsor
WinStock	http://www.ccnet.com/~winstock/
WinWeather	http://www.webcom.com/~igs/weather.html
Wiz Zone Computers For Kids Inc.	http://www.wizzone.com/
WizSoft, Inc.	http://www.wizsoft.com/
WK Information Systems Ltd.	http://www.caseware.com
Wolfram Research	http://www.wolfram.com
Woll2Woll Software	http://www.webcom.com/~wol2wol/
Wollongong Group, The	http://www.twg.com/
Woodruff Consulting, Inc. - AMATH Division	http://www.smartpages.com/amath/
Woods Incorporated	http://www.woodsnet.com/
Word Master, Inc.	http://www.wordmaster.com/wm/
Wordlink Inc.	http://www.wordlink.com/
WordPerfect	http://www.wordperfect.com/

WordPro	http://wordpro.com/
Work Group Solutions	http://www.acemail.com/WGS/
WorkFlow Designs, Inc.	http://www.wfdesigns.com/~workflow/
Working Software, Inc.	http://www.webcom.com/~working/
World Mall	http://www.webcom.com/~worldmal/
World Software Library	http://www.softwaremall.com/
World Wide Publishing	http://www.xmission.com/~wwp/
Worlds Inc.	http://www.worlds.net/
Worldwide Componets Network, Inc.	http://www.unisoft.net/wcni.html
WOWNET In Taiwan	http://www.wow.net.tw/
WRQ Web Connection	http://www.wrq.com
WSRCC	http://www.wsrcc.com/
WWW Project Management Forum	http://www.synapse.net/~loday/PMForum/
Wyse Technology	http://www.wyse.co.uk/

X

X Communications Multimedia	http://www.webcom.com/~xcomm/
X Inside Incorporated	http://www.xinside.com/
X'iT Group Creative	http://www.xgroup.com/
x86 computers, Inc.	http://www.abwam.com/x86
Xaos Enterprises	http://www.xaos.net/xaos/
Xcc Software	http://www.xcc-ka.de/
XcelleNet	http://www.xcellenet.com/
Xebec Corp. Online Imaging & Supplies Superstore	http://www.servint.com/Xebec/product-info/toners.html
Xephon	http://www.hiway.co.uk/~xephon/
Xinet	http://www.xinet.com/
XLNT Designs, Inc	http://www.xlnt.com/
XOR Network Engineering, Inc.	http://plaza.xor.com/xor/
Xpert Unix Systems	http://www.xpert.com/
XSI MeDIA	http://www.xsimedia.com/
XSoft	http://www.xerox.com/XSoft/XSoftHome.html
XSoft	http://www.xerox.com/XSoft/XSoftHome.html
Xtel s.r.l.	http://www.xtel.it/
Xtreme	ftp://ftp.netcom.com/pub/ml/mlinksva/html/xtreme.html

Y

Y&Y TeX	http://www.YandY.com/
y.a.c.c. - Yet Another Computer Consultant	http://www.xmission.com/~vir/
Yggdrasil Computing, Inc.	http://www.yggdrasil.com/
Yorick Software Inc.	http://www.msen.com/~yorick/
Young Minds Inc.	http://www.ymi.com/
Your Attache, Inc.	http://www.bedrock.com/mall/attache/home.html

Z

Z Media	http://www.tiac.net/users/zwoods/
Z-Law Software, Inc.	http://mmink.com/mmink/dossiers/zlaw/zlaw.html
Zebra Multimedia Authoring	http://www.quay.co.uk/~zebra/zebrad.htm

Chapter 10

Zendex Corporation	http://www.zendex.com/
Zenith Data Systems	http://www.zds.com/
Zero Surge	http://www.targetus.com/zsurge.htm
Zethcon Corporation	http://www.mcs.com/~tgiesler/zethcon.htm
Zfx, Inc.	ttp://www.tricon.net/Comm/zfx/zfxhome2.html
Zinc Software Inc.	http://www.zinc.com/
Zocalo	http://www.zocalo.com/
Zoo Software	http://sun10.inf.unitn.it/~apeltrin/
Zoom Telephonics	http://www.zoomtel.com/
Zuken-Redac	http://www.redac.co.uk/
Zycad Corporation	http://www.zycad.com/
ZyLAB Europe WEB site	http://www.irt.nl/

Still Don't See What You're Looking For? Try some other sources

AT&T 800 Directory	http://att.net/dir800
Computer and Communication Companies	http://www-atp.llnl.gov/atp/companies.html
CommerceNet	http://www.commerce.net/
Commercial Sites Index	http://www.directory.net/
DCCS Vendors	http://www-dccs.stanford.edu/wst/vendors.html
New Products Archive	http://gopher.metronet.com:70/1h/newprod.html
Portfolio Vendor list	http://www-portfolio.stanford.edu/104132

Magazines

The top PC Magazines are also good sources for the latest information, bugs, and bug fixes. Call these numbers for subscription information or look on your local newsstand for the most recent issues.

PC Computing	800-365-2770
PC Magazine	800-289-0429
PC World	800-234-3498
Windows Magazine	800-284-5384
Windows User	800-627-9860

And Next

We've come to the end of this resource guide, but be aware that the Windows world is constantly changing. New magazines about Windows 95 may come on the market. You may find more up-to-date Web listings. New versions of Windows 95 will be released. Be vigilant, and hang in there. Happy troubleshooting.

382

Index